RATIONAL MYSTICISM

A DEVELOPMENT OF SCIENTIFIC IDEALISM

BY

WILLIAM KINGSLAND

LONDON : GEORGE ALLEN & UNWIN LTD.

RUSKIN HOUSE, 40 MUSEUM STREET, W.C. 1

RATIONAL MYSTICISM

First published in 1924

Printed in Great Britain by
UNWIN BROTHERS, LIMITED, THE GRESHAM PRESS, LONDON AND WOKING

FOREWORD

THERE are two things which we may clearly apprehend in the trend of modern thought. The first of these is the demand for a greater rationality in all matters pertaining to religious belief and experience; and the second is a remarkable and widespread interest in those deeper phenomena of life and consciousness to which, broadly, the terms *occult* and *mystical* are given.

These two facts must be regarded as symptomatic on the outer plane of a very potent and radical change taking place on the inner plane of Man's spiritual nature, where, indeed, really lie the true causes of all that happens on the outer historical plane. There are many other concurrent symptoms of this inner change, and some of these will be dealt with incidentally in the course of this work. The most obvious of them is the Great War, the spiritual import of which is tremendous, but highly mystical in its deeper aspects.

Mysticism is essentially the inner or esoteric side of Religion; and if the demand on the exoteric or outer, on the formal or formulated side, is now so insistent for a *rational* belief, and has certainly overpassed a worn-out theology, it is equally certain that this demand must apply also to the inner or esoteric, which must found on experience and be capable of co-ordination with the general sum-total of our rational knowledge.

Moreover, there is no reason why we should regard Mysticism, in any form in which it has as yet been possible to present it, as having reached finality any more than any other human effort. The mystic as a rule has translated his experiences in terms of a definite religion: even when he has not been himself the definite product of that religion. But in the future, as in the past, new forms of religion will undoubtedly be brought forth. The root principles of Religion and Mysticism are the same for all time, but the form in which those principles are stated must be adapted, even by the greatest teachers, to the age in which their message is delivered; indeed, the teacher himself may be said to be largely the product of the age.

The present age will produce, and is producing, its corresponding type of mystic; not exactly a new type, but one in which the purely religious or devotional element is less in evidence, and a more balanced, critical or *rational* criterion takes its place : *a greater tendency to unite the spiritual and the material modes of our life rather than to place them in opposition and antithesis.*

This will be the keynote of the present work, and in view of this tendency it has seemed to me very desirable that an effort should be made to place mystical experience in general, and modern mysticism in particular, on a more rational basis than has hitherto been the case; to endeavour to find for it a philosophical, and even a scientific, ground which may serve as a corrective to the very *irrational* developments which have been taking place in certain directions, and of which even more is likely to be seen in the immediate future. Such a basis should at the same time enable us to understand in a better relation and proportion the historical forms of Mysticism with which we are already familiar.

The fundamental principles of this basis have already been dealt with in my work on *Scientific Idealism*. In that work I have endeavoured to show how the leading concept of modern physical science—that of an all-pervading Ether, or space-filling Substance—is capable of interpretation in terms of a Monistic and Idealistic Philosophy of a highly spiritual nature; one, indeed, which lends the strongest support to, and gives confirmation of, our deepest intuitions and religious instincts.

The concept of an absolute Substance, or Substance-Principle, gives us a definite substantial basis from which we may not merely deduce the structural facts of the Universe, but may also co-ordinate therewith our metaphysical concepts as to the nature of the conscious Self, both in its finiteness and its absoluteness. At the same time we must remember that this is a *concept*, and therefore subject to all the limitations of the formal conceptual mind. We take it merely as that which is best fitted to give us, in a conceptual form, that fundamental *unity*, an understanding of which is the ultimate aim of both Science and Philosophy ; an understanding, that is to say, of the individual and the particular, simultaneously with a complete co-ordination of the Whole in one indissoluble Unity of a Rational nature. This rational unity or ' Reality ' which Science and Philosophy seek to attain to in a conceptual form, is also the Unity which the mystic seeks to attain to in feeling, or as an actual living reality in his own consciousness.

The higher and deeper aspects of this subject were not fully developed in *Scientific Idealism*. Only one chapter was devoted to " The Higher Religion," and one to " The Ideal Realism." Much remains to be said ; and I hope in the present work to fill in to some extent this insufficiency, as well as to indicate some further developments. I shall hope also incidentally to remove from the term *Mysticism* much of the reproach of irrationality which has so largely attached to it in the past, and to show that true Mysticism must of necessity be rational in the first instance, in the sense that the fundamental principles which give rise to and permeate it are worthy of acceptation, and are clearly anticipated by our highest reasoning powers. But I shall hope to show further that Mysticism discloses a deeper rationality of our whole nature than that which governs our common judgments. I shall hope to show that it is only in those inner depths of our nature to which Mysticism testifies that true rationality is to be found, i.e. a sense of true relation and proportion which is not discoverable in anything which our present ratiocinative faculties can supply, limited as they are by the categories of time, space, and causation. These latter, indeed, are *irrational* elements in our judgments, as being in themselves self-contradictory.

What is commonly regarded as ' reason ' is, in fact, only the specific logic of Necessity : of that necessitous part of our nature which is bound up with ' matter.' But it is the very essence of Mysticism to bring us into touch with the opposite pole of our being ; to enable us to grasp and realise a region of Freedom, a region of Spirit which we intuitively feel to be ours, whilst as yet we are unable to formulate it in terms of the intellect alone, and indeed—as we shall show in due course—cannot in the nature of the case expect to do so.

Thus whilst admitting that in entering this region of Freedom as opposed to Necessity, or of Spirit as opposed to Matter, we have transcended the formal and necessitous logic of the intellect; whilst admitting that pure mystical experience cannot be expressed in terms of the rational concepts of the formal mind : we do not for one moment admit that we have thereby necessarily become irrational in the sense of being opposed to reason. We may have become a-rational or non-rational in so far as abstract conceptual logic is concerned, but only thereby to reach a deeper rationality of our whole nature, a truer appreciation of the relation and proportion existing between the material, the intellectual, and the spiritual.

The rational mind intuitively feels that there must be some link between the higher transcendental region of our nature and the lower necessitous region of time, space, and causation; or in other words, we must think of the Absolute as being absolutely Rational in the sense that it is the resolution of all contradictions and antinomies. Philosophy is the intellectual effort to reach this deeper rationality; but in so far as Philosophy is compelled to employ logic or dialectic it is unable to explicate it, for logic and dialectic pertain wholly to the region of Matter or Necessity. Religion and Art, however, have already touched the region of Spirit or Freedom, the language of which is essentially Symbolism. The unceasing effort of Philosophy to reach this deeper rationality is the acknowledgment of its existence, but we have no words in the English language by which we may distinguish clearly between the higher and the lower reason. We may make a distinction between reason and understanding, as Kant did; [1] but understanding is so commonly used as synonymous with reason, that no real difference exists in our use of the words. We might speak of *pure* reason as being the rationality of our deepest intuitive nature, and as contrasted with formal or conceptual reason as being the operation of the discursive intellect; and, indeed, it is impossible for us to abandon the intuition that the universe in its Wholeness and Completeness must be rational in the deepest and purest sense of the term. But the universe as it exists in our normal consciousness is a duality which the in-

[1] *Vide infra*, p. 164.

tellect obstinately refuses to resolve into a unity; it presents a 'higher' and a 'lower' aspect, an abstract or transcendental region and a concrete or definable one. Pure reason would, therefore, have to be considered as that which belongs to the transcendental region of this apparent duality, whilst the merely rational or understandable would belong to the concrete region; but this would be an inadequate conception of pure reason, since this, when reached, would include the 'lower' as well as the 'higher' as being the rationality of a Wholeness in which all opposites are united and reconciled.

Seeing, then, that these two 'regions' or 'poles' actually exist in our present consciousness, we must at least postulate that there is a rational connection between the two. It is only 'down here' that they appear to be distinct, separate, or opposed; and if such a rational connection is found to be obtained in mystical consciousness, then we must regard Mysticism as being the supremely Rational.

I do not regard as true Mysticism anything which tends to maintain the apparent duality or polarity of our nature, and to keep Spirit and Matter eternally apart: treating Matter as 'illusion' and Spirit as 'reality.' Mysticism is essentially *union*, that is to say *wholeness*; but this can never be attained by a mere ecstatic flight from one pole or extreme to the other. The true mystic, whatever subjective flights he may take, will, I apprehend, bring back with him some message which will enable us to understand more clearly the why and wherefore of our present limitations, and their proper relation and proportion to the super-physical and extra-rational region to which he has penetrated: their proper position and function in the wholeness of our nature. The hall-mark of Mysticism is essentially a completely satisfying *illumination*, in which all the contradictions, dualisms, and antinomies of the formal mind are resolved into an inexpressible sense of harmony and unity; and this as *knowledge* in the deepest and truest sense of the term—" the clearest, the surest of the sure," as Tennyson says in describing his own experience—and not merely as emotion.

But Mysticism has many phases, and no completely comprehensive definition of it is possible. It may frankly be said here, therefore, that what I mean by Rational Mysticism is

Mysticism of the philosophical rather than of the devotional type. This work, therefore, will in a certain sense mediate between a purely intellectual apprehension of the problems involved, that is to say between a method of pure thought, and what we might term pure Mysticism, which lies altogether beyond the forms of our conceptual mind; though for those who regard the matter wholly from the devotional point of view, it may not appear to be necessary to systematise the matter in any way whatsoever by linking it up with Science and Philosophy. For our present purpose, however, something more is necessary than the fact that some favoured individuals here and there have mystical experiences to which certain general characteristics of a religious nature may be assigned. We desire to link up these experiences with our rational concepts as to the nature of ultimate Reality and its connection with the world of Appearance; as also to show that the mystical experience and consciousness lies in the natural line of human evolution. Mystical experiences should energise and illumine our philosophical concepts of Reality with a vitality which no mere metaphysic can supply; and the mystic should take his place as a 'favourable variation' in that great sweep of evolution which is carrying Humanity forward towards a goal as yet only dimly discerned or imagined by the vast majority of the Race, or perhaps even by the most highly gifted seer.

The 'Rational Mysticism' which is here implied will, therefore, found upon a recognition of the principle of the Unity of the Universe: which implies our own unity with the Universe in the wholeness and completeness of our being. What we now arbitrarily divide into 'material' and 'spiritual' is in its ultimate ONE; the material and the spiritual being the modes or aspects of the ONE LIFE which IS the Universe. Whatever enters into our consciousness must be a part of this Rational Wholeness, and the *truth* about it is a knowledge of its proper relations and proportions. Thus I have defined truth as: "*the clear perception of the relation and proportion of things.*"[1]

We may state this in another way by saying that truth is the perception of such a relation and proportion in apparent diversity that this becomes a realised harmonious unity.

[1] *Scientific Idealism*, p. 8.

There must necessarily be degrees of this perception. The final perception of the unity of the whole Universe would be the Absolute Truth, and therefore Absolute Reality, or simply, the Absolute. Such a final perception, however, would not merely transcend anything that we know as thought, but also anything that we know as consciousness. Our perception of Truth or Reality will grow clearer and fuller as we approach to a consciousness of the unitary nature of all that enters into our experience, and will thereby become more and more *rational*. Even the irrational has a rational explanation as a part of the Whole.

We must rationally accept the empirical facts of mystical experience on the same basis as any other facts, but not necessarily the interpretation or explanation of those facts which the mystic himself may formulate; indeed—following the scientific method—we shall be in duty bound in the first instance to check them with our ' rational ' faculty by every means in our power. Many so-called mystical experiences rise no higher than the plane of the formal mind, and can be explained psychologically; but there is no reason why a concept or theory of genuine Mysticism should not be formulated which is quite as ' rational ' or ' scientific ' as many of the concepts or theories of modern psychology. Immediate causes are, however, never wholly adequate to explain anything. If any question is only pushed far enough back, it becomes metaphysical, and ultimately transcendental. We should, however, endeavour to exhaust the more immediate or particular causes before we proceed to the more universal, and if we can explain any phenomenon in terms of the plane to which it belongs, there is seldom any *practical* need to carry the question any further. It is, indeed, only by an accommodation of this nature that we arrive at our common rationality.

That there has been much in the history of Mysticism which in the above sense is irrational, spurious, and mischievous, goes without saying. That there will be much in the future is also certain. Our imperfect human nature enters in and mars the ideal in this as in other things. Much of the reproach which has lain against Mysticism, however, is not so much due to its own sins as to misrepresentations on the part of writers who have been either wholly out of sympathy with the subject, or obviously partisan and prejudiced.

To-day a considerable number of well-known writers are dealing with various aspects of Mysticism from a much more sympathetic point of view, and on a much more rational basis than has hitherto been the case in any standard work. Moreover, there is a rapidly increasing demand for such works, and an intelligent appreciation of them on the part of the general reader.

Though I am profoundly conscious of a lack of many qualifications for dealing with the subject, I think I may at least claim a deep sympathy with it, a freedom from prejudice in favour of any one system rather than another, and a somewhat intimate acquaintance with many forms of the modern movement.

By freedom from prejudice, however, I do not mean freedom from preferences. It will, I think, be tolerably evident all through this work that I have drawn largely upon the Eastern Vedânta philosophy on the one hand, and the theosophy of Jacob Böhme on the other. It will probably be thought by some that I am prejudiced against and opposed to ' Christianity ' ; and if by that term is meant the traditional creeds and dogmas of the Church in their *exoteric* presentation, then I must certainly plead guilty. That traditional ' Christianity ' is a perversion of the real spiritual truth of which it ought to have been a *re*-presentation, is a conclusion which is rapidly gaining ground on every hand. That the Church has no real spiritual hold on our communal life is a fact which the Great War has brought into startling prominence. The world has suffered so much at the hands of the professors and exponents of ' Christianity,' that it is difficult to forgive them ; and in so far as the same spirit is manifested by them to-day in their attitude towards progress in knowledge, and their treatment of those whose only desire is for *truth* : one is compelled to declare oneself to be their implacable foe. This one may and can do without for one moment detracting from the value of the ' simple Christian faith,' which has been, and is to-day, a real inspiration, and the natural and only available spiritual food for so many who can only take their religion on an authority which they have not the natural capacity to examine for themselves, and which they have been taught from childhood it would be a sin to question.

It may also be as well to repeat here what I have said at the commencement of *Scientific Idealism*—that my aim is not to present anything in the way of a formal system which shall be a solution of the various problems which arise in connection with our conscious existence and our present material environment. " By no possibility can the solution of the problem of life and consciousness be placed before any man or woman in mere words or phrases."[1] But my purpose is rather to present a *working hypothesis* which shall not merely cover the known facts of our present nature, but shall also enable us to advance with boldness and certainty into those deeper regions of consciousness and experience which lie beyond the normal perceptions and activities of our physical sense life, and of which we have unmistakable scientific evidence as well as an undeniable intuition. The work is thus pragmatic rather than speculative ; it is not in any way intended as a contribution to the method of pure thought, but aims nevertheless at presenting Idealism as a practical working creed. We may legitimately work on the basis of an hypothesis which in itself is only probable, not absolutely provable. This is, indeed, the scientific method, and we ought to have no hesitation in applying it to our own life, instead of idly giving up the problem.

I would ask my readers, therefore, to bear in mind that I am endeavouring in this work to set forth *principles*, not a system ; and also that where, in the nature of the case, there can be no proof of the *universal* application of a principle recognised as operative in the limited domain of our present conscious existence, we must regard the principle rather as a working hypothesis than as something from which there can be no departure. I am prepared to throw over any one or all of the principles or working hypotheses put forward in this work, so soon as it is shown that an advance has been made beyond them. Those deeper facts of our nature which belong to the province of Mysticism from the very fact that they are inexpressible in terms of matter or of mind, are, when the effort is made to *systematise* them, only too liable to degenerate into creed and dogma ; they become the tools

[1] *Scientific Idealism*, p. vi.

of priestcraft—that parasitical blight of the soul—and the cerements of the spiritual nature of man.

To a certain extent I have shown how the principles which I here endeavour to set forth have been recognised in various Scriptures and by various authors, both ancient and modern. I have endeavoured, however, to keep these quotations within reasonable limits, so as not to overburden the work too much with them. A large volume might easily be filled with them, and I contemplate that they may possibly form the subject-matter of an Anthology at some future date.

If the hypotheses here presented—for which, indeed, I can claim no novelty—appeal to the reader; if they are found to be logically deduced from existing sources of knowledge, and to be no mere *ex parte* statements—well and good. They may possibly appeal to an inner intuition of truth even should they seem to fail in logical deduction; and, indeed, in Mysticism the appeal must be largely to this inner perception. But I ask none, if they be not so inclined, to regard the Universe as I regard it, to look as I look into its mysteries, to feel as I feel the pulse of its Being, or to learn by similar experience the secrets of its Life and its Fate, its Beauty and its Love. There is only one Way, one Truth, and one Life; but these are necessarily apprehended differently by the individual precisely to the extent to which the experience of each individual is *somewhat different* from that of all others. The effort to make every one think or believe alike has been the cause of incalculable evil and cruelty. Truth is both individual and universal; but only when the distinction between ' you ' and ' I ' is lost can truth become universal and identical for each individual.

Meanwhile I look with my own eyes, and hear with my own ears, and understand with my own heart—as you do with yours. Even thus, and thus, have I seen and heard, O my Brother; and what I have seen you may have missed, and what you have heard may have passed me by; and the final Truth is what no man has ever seen or heard.

> "The Most High Seer that is in highest heaven,
> He knows it—or perchance even he knows not."

But of this we may rest assured, that if it were seen and heard it would make our present understanding of little enough account.

Even such, then, must I reckon this work : save that our present seeing and hearing is precisely the one thing which is of most account for each of us.

Our *present* seeing and hearing—yes ; but when we can say that we rightly and clearly see and hear, then each present moment will contain not merely the passing fact but also the *Eternal Fact* ; that full and rounded beauty and perfection of Life which must assuredly lie at the root of all manifestation, and which must be the possession of any consciousness which rises out of our present fragmentary life into unity with the great LIFE that lives and moves in ALL, and which must therefore be *present* in all its fulness at every moment and everywhere.

Such realisation is *Mysticism*. To come to a true and complete knowledge of this : to realise each moment, and as the very heart-beat of life itself, that each moment contains all eternity, and is full-filled with immeasurable Beauty and Perfection—this would be to be a mystic indeed.

And what is all Science, all Philosophy, all Religion, and all Art, but the effort to express and to explicate this eternal Fact ? By this very effort the Eternal Fact is proved to be mystically implicit in every rational mind, and its attainment must be the goal, the final perfection and rationality of the individual in his conscious unity with the Infinite and the Eternal.

CONTENTS

Modern Rationalism—True Rationalism—Philosophy and
Reality—Life, the Reality of the Universe—Philosophy approaching Mysticism—Nature of Mysticism in the past—In
the present—The mystic a pioneer of evolution—Mysticism
and rational inference from present knowledge—Universality
of Life—Intuition and the Ideal—Nature of Art—Mysticism not
originated in the rational faculty—Use of the term 'spiritual'
—The spiritual gradually recognised by the evolving personality—Mysticism may found on existing knowledge—Phases of
evolution—Physical—Mental—Moral and spiritual—Science and
evolution—Indications of an immeasurable development in
the future—The ethical motive—The inner impelling force—
The necessity of knowledge—Evolution the unfolding of an
existing reality—Natural limits of knowledge—Nature has no
arbitrary secrets—Conquest of fear—Faith—Fate—The problem
of Evil—Science, Philosophy, and Religion as three stages of
evolution—The further region of Mysticism—Each stage gives
an added power to the previous one—The province of Science—
Of Philosophy—Of Religion—Religion and Life—Religion an
added quality of life—The historical conflict with Science—
The new order of thought—Mysticism a further advance in
our evolution—The dawn of the mystic faculty—The tendency of
modern Mysticism—Fundamental truth the same in all ages—
Scientific dogmatism and realism—Christianity not new—
Mysticism not visionary and unpractical—Modern Mysticism
less other-worldly—Rational Mysticism will raise the *present* to
a higher power—Mysticism not 'unconsciousness'—Mysticism
and emotion—Böhme's mysticism—The secrets of Nature—
Limitations of expression in art and mysticism—We proceed
to Rational Mysticism through Science, Philosophy, and formal
Religion.

CHAPTER II

CHAPTER III

CHAPTER IV

CHAPTER V

Beings—The Cosmic Christ—The psychic plane—The physical plane—The principle of ' creation '—Inter-relation of planes— Duality of each plane—' Common sense '—Correspondence between Science, Philosophy, and Religion and the various planes.

CHAPTER VI

The unitary nature of Man and God—Western tradition—The great and the small, and our relation to these—We should transcend these physical magnitudes—The Self has bodies on all the planes—The individual expressions of the Self—The potential and the actual in consciousness and in evolution— The nature of real greatness—The nature of the limitations of the individual—Evolution of Humanity as a whole—Relation of Man to the Globe he evolves on—The perfection of the Abso-lute, and the perfection of Man—Relation of Mysticism to Religion—Evolution of Religion—Evolution and esoteric religion —The freedom of the Spirit—Christianity and the Gnôsis—The divine nature of Man.

CHAPTER VII

Difficulty of defining Religion and Mysticism—They both trans-cend intellect—Religion *a spiritual quality of life*—The two aspects of Religion, inner and outer—Christianity and its histori-cal effects—The present renaissance and the ancient Gnôsis— Origen quoted—Religion in the West—Evil of individualism in Religion—Necessity of a cosmic sense in religion—New forms and the survival of the old—Characteristics of religion as a quality of life—Re-orientation of the individual mind—The world and the individual—The world made by Man—Disappear-ance of evil from the world—The unity of the individual and the Race—Religion conquers evil and suffering—The *response* to the religious intuition—The conquest of the lower self by the power of the Higher Self—Limits of the outgoing world-process—The Higher Self as redeemer—Distinction between religion and Mysticism—Religion and worship—Stages in the evolution of the idea of God.

CHAPTER VIII

Mysticism and exoteric religion—Analogy between physical and spiritual evolution—Mysticism the genius of Religion— The two mystical facts—(1) The sense of unity—Mysticism and Occultism—Dawn of the mystic faculty—The three-fold ' Way '—(*a*) Purification—(*b*) Illumination—Cosmic conscious-

ness—Question as to the nature of the Absolute of the mystic—
(c) Union—Plotinus quoted—Ruysbroeck quoted—The principle of Love—Tauler quoted—St. Teresa quoted—The practical results of mysticism—The activity of the classical mystics
—(2) The mystic sense of Love—Love and suffering—"The
Golden Fountain" quoted—The natural law of action and
attainment.

CHAPTER IX

Historical Mysticism and initiation—Mysticism and Occultism
—Gnosticism—The Hierarchy of Initiates—The nature of
Occultism—True knowledge of the Self comprises both Mysti-
cism and Occultism—The path of devotion and the path of
knowledge—Mysticism deals with the Being aspect of Reality,
Occultism with the Becoming aspect—Occultism and Magic—
Böhme's knowledge—Knowledge must be earned—Eliphas
Levi—Louis Claud de Saint-Martin and the ancient Schools of
Initiation—Madame H. P. Blavatsky—Plotinus on the three
methods of attainment—All methods are required for our complete nature—The dangers of Occultism—Its potentiality for
evil prevents the spiritual occultist from disclosing his knowledge—The Christ powers—There are representative beings at
all stages of evolution—The individual fulfils a cosmic function
—The mystic unable to sustain his flight to the Absolute—
St. Augustine quoted—The occultist gradually trains his bodies
or vehicles of consciousness.

CHAPTER X

The necessity of postulating the existence of immaterial
'bodies'—Definition of 'body'—Bodies and Substance—
Definition of 'soul'—The relation of the soul to the body
and the spirit—Definition of 'spirit'—Three sources of information respecting Man and his inner principles or bodies—
(a) The Occult Schools—Man the *measure* of the Universe—
Mind and soul—(b) Seership—Böhme—His "Three Principles"
—Swedenborg—His "Discrete Degrees"—Fabre d'Olivette—
(c) The Greek and other Mystery Traditions—The soul and the
power of 'imagination'—Geometrical diagram to represent
the cosmic and individual relationship of body, soul, and spirit—
The process of creation or emanation—Divine Imagination—
Analogy of dreams—Art 'creations'—Inversion of the physical plane—Consciousness and the external world—The various
planes and the mystical consciousness—Swedenborg and
"altitude" and "latitude"—His "angels"—The nature and

function of Will—Free-will—Destiny—Physical analogy—The Divine Will and the will of the individual—The three keys to the Scriptures—The Buddhist doctrine of the Trikāya—The limitations of our systematised presentations.

CHAPTER XI

The unsatisfying nature of technical metaphysics—The region of Law and the region of Freedom—The interaction of the higher and the lower planes—The sub- and super-conscious—The abstraction of the individual self—The activity of the One Self—The great mystical fact—The Absolute and the relative—Per-sistence and ex-sistence—The self-limitations of the Self for the purpose of experience—The chess analogy—Limitations of physics—The Einstein ' space '—Limitations of metaphysics—Our theory of Substance—The limitations of form—The limitations of the Law and the freedom of the Spirit—The " New Mysticism "—The new psychology—Bergson quoted—Matter and Mind—The nature of the individual—Vale Owen quoted—Our present duty—We make our own happenings—The progress towards Democracy—Experience the only teacher—Value of precepts—E-ducation and in-struction—The individual and the Race—Origin of doctrines and creeds—' Christianity ' and dogma—Religion necessary for a true Democracy—The future Democracy—The necessity of a knowledge of natural law on all planes—Nature of the life hereafter—The law of action—The mystical nature of the ' I '—Spiritual manhood—Rationality and Mysticism—The individual a law unto himself for good or for evil.

CHAPTER XII

The nature of the freedom to be attained—The freedom of knowledge—The freedom of truth—The obscuration of truth by the priesthood—The struggle for freedom—How we are still in bondage—Freedom of the laws of nature—The freedom of the Spirit—Nature of the Self—The rational use of the natural laws of our whole being—The conquest of Matter—The conquest of our lower nature—The development of higher powers—Thomas Trahern quoted—Right thought—The struggle between the higher and the lower—The means of attainment—The strength and the weakness of individual religions—Get back to natural law—The conquest of the body—The conquest of the lower self—The value of a personal Saviour—We only progress through a living experience—The two expressions of the

CHAPTER I

INTRODUCTORY

"Two angels guide
The path of man, both aged and yet young,
As angels are, ripening through endless years.
On one he leans : some call her Memory,
And some, Tradition ; and her voice is sweet,
With deep mysterious accords : the other,
Floating above, holds down a lamp which streams
A light divine and searching on the earth,
Compelling eyes and footsteps. Memory yields,
Yet clings with loving cheek, and shines anew,
Reflecting all the rays of that bright lamp
Our angel Reason holds. We had not walked
But for Tradition ; we walk evermore
To higher paths by brightening Reason's lamp."

GEORGE ELIOT : *Spanish Gypsy*.

CHAPTER I

INTRODUCTORY

BEFORE we can proceed to the more constructive part of our work we must endeavour to clear the ground by means of a few general considerations as to the nature of Rationalism, Religion, and Mysticism.

It has often been claimed for the present age that it is pre-eminently one of enlightenment: by which we are intended to understand that, as compared with previous ages, reason has assumed a supremacy which it has never before obtained.

Whatever of truth or otherwise there may be in such a claim when considered apart from the glamour which our undeniably brilliant scientific discoveries have thrown over the last century, it is at all events certain that anything which solicits the serious attention of the thought and culture of the present day must at least be founded on existing knowledge, or a legitimate inference therefrom, and not on mere authority.

The term *Rationalism* has become principally associated with the modern revolt against the supernaturalism and superstition of authoritative Christian dogma, and the extreme rationalist is commonly a materialist — which is perhaps the most irrational thing that a man can be.

If we ask whether such and such a belief is rational, we make our appeal in the first instance to experience, that is to say to our knowledge of facts; but there is always a tendency to take some facts and ignore others in order to bolster up *a priori* judgments arising from the limitations of our individual knowledge, or from prejudices of religion, class, or heredity. There is also a very considerable tendency to deny facts altogether when they do not fit in with these pre-judgments. The materialist, for example, must necessarily deny any fact which appears to show that consciousness can function independently of a physical vehicle, or can survive the death of the physical body. Perhaps very few of us are rational in the sense that we are wholly free from such pre-judgments. For each individual there is a certain limit which unconsciously influences his outlook upon the world-process, and determines in his mind a sort of rough and ready synthesis of that process. To be truly rational we should be able to accept all facts, those which enter into the experiences of others as well as our own, even though we are not able for the moment to give a *rational* explanation of them in terms of our own knowledge. If we believe in a fundamentally rational whole—and what rational man is there who does not believe this?—every fact must have its proper relation and proportion in that Wholeness, however inexplicable it may appear to be for the present.

Now it belongs specifically to philosophy to co-ordinate our knowledge of facts—and the fact of our knowledge—into this rational Wholeness, which must include *all* that enters into our complex life and consciousness. But in philosophy the adequacy of our reasoning or ratiocinative faculty to deal with the fundamental problem of Life and Consciousness *per se*, with the nature of Reality, or the Absolute, and the relation of the individual or particular thereto, has long been in question, and is to-day finding more explicit treatment at the hands of Bergson and others. This is the philosophical step towards a Rational Mysticism. The *Self* expresses itself in other ways than that of Mind, or ratiocinative processes. The existence of an intuitional faculty, as well as of higher or deeper states of consciousness than that of our normal, is becoming widely acknowledged. The mind cannot transcend itself, for like the body it is only an instrument; but the real Subject, the real Knower, transcends both body and mind. ' Vitalism,' the concept of an active, dynamic, free—one might almost say sportive—*Life* as the great *Reality* of the Universe, is gradually supplanting the idea of the self-sufficiency of matter and force on the one hand, and of an extra-cosmic Deity on the other. Science itself has chased matter into a metaphysical region where it is unable to follow it either experimentally or mathematically. Not matter and force but Life and Consciousness are seen to be the great fundamental fact. Life and Consciousness are not known as matter and force are known, as something external to ourselves. Our knowledge of Life is not even inferred by its interaction with these, but is immediate and direct. Life is not what we possess but what we *are*.

To this fact Mysticism has testified from the remotest ages, and the modern trend of philosophy is now, therefore, seen to be towards the acceptance of Mysticism as a legitimate part of our rational nature. I conceive, indeed, that a Rational Mysticism is actually in the course of making in the flux of modern thought, and that it will presently crystallise out into something which will give the fullest satisfaction to the reason and intellect as well as to our religious, æsthetic, and emotional nature.

The term ' Mysticism ' has hitherto been almost wholly associated in most minds with ultra-religious emotionalism, having no special or acknowledged ground in science or philosophy. That is a mistake which should no longer obtain. Mysticism is essentially religious—indeed there is little to distinguish between Religion and Mysticism when Religion is understood in its truest and deepest sense as the re-union of the soul with its Source, or the supreme revelation to the soul of its unity or at-one-ment with the Infinite and the Eternal. But the present age demands that religion should not be the great exception to our rational knowledge and experience, and Mysticism must come into line with this demand. Science may claim in the first instance the empirical fact of abnormal states of consciousness as legitimate subject for experiment and investigation, and a rational Mysticism may find a basis, though only a preliminary one, in a rational psychology, and from thence pass to philosophy and metaphysic for co-ordination with our existing knowledge in other aspects of life and consciousness. Divorced from such a basis, treated as something separate and apart from the sum of human knowledge and evolution, Mysticism— like so-called Religion itself—is only too prone to degenerate into mere superstition and a disease of the imagination : of which, indeed, we have ample evidence to-day as well as in the past.

We shall endeavour, therefore, to approach our subject through certain scientific and philosophical generalisations : that is to say through what is already valid as knowledge of the laws which govern phenomena and experience, or in general what we term *Natural Law*; and we must show in the first instance that Mysticism is a logical and rational extension of, and in no wise severed from, that knowledge, and the powers and faculties which we have already, through such a long historical process, so laboriously and painfully acquired.

This historical process is known in general as *evolution*, and we must in the first instance glance broadly at the evolution of humanity so that we may adjust our ideas as to the future to what we already know of the past, since it is Mysticism which speaks to us of that future evolution, and the mystic who is the pioneer in a region of experience which later on must become common ground for the whole of humanity.

The fundamental principles of Mysticism, even if not at present as demonstrable as a chemical formula, may claim to be founded on a certain sum-total of human knowledge and experience, and therefore to be at least a rational inference. A rational belief is not necessarily one which is susceptible of direct, or even of indirect, proof. It is sufficient if it commends itself to our mind as a reasonable inference from what we already know, and as such it will be one which we can conceive of as capable of direct demonstration or actual experience under certain circumstances, or given an extension of our present knowledge.

The proposition, for example, that there are inhabitants of the other Planets of our Solar System—not necessarily, however, with physical bodies constituted precisely as ours are—is a perfectly rational one; it is one which the general sum of our knowledge renders extremely probable; indeed, and on a wider basis still, it would appear to be exceedingly irrational to assert that among the millions of worlds which constitute the physical universe, our little speck of matter is the only one on which life exists. Later on, when we have come to a thorough appreciation of the fact that objective or physical matter is no more 'real' than the contents of invisible space, we shall conclude that life must certainly exist in the invisible in immeasurably greater fulness than it exists in the visible: even as physical science is now beginning to realise that the 'energy' of the invisible and impalpable Ether of Space is incomparably greater than anything which appears in physical matter as such.

But we must be prepared for a denial by some, even of these rational propositions. We shall always find some seemingly rational being capable of denying on *a priori* grounds anything which does not appear to fit in with his own special preconceptions. The know-everything-about-something scientific specialist is one of the worst sinners in this respect, and many amusing examples of eating the leek are to be found in the scientific pronouncements of the last century.

There are many things which we intuitively feel to be true and valid, which yet we can by no means prove or even rightly formulate with our consciously acting rational mind. They remain enigmas, and defy analysis, even while at the same time they constitute the very deepest essentials and the strongest motives of any life which rises into an intellectual or spiritual quality. They are not the product of mind, but spiritual forces of which the mind gradually becomes more and more aware and expressive. The man who stifles these deeper intuitions, who turns a deaf ear to the promptings of his own inner nature which perpetually invite him to lift his thoughts and aspirations to the sunlit region of the ideal, misses the very essence and flavour of life.

Take, for example, the whole region of art or æsthetic. Life would be poor indeed without these, but who has ever stated in terms of the formal mind what art or beauty rightly is in the inner springs of our being ? There is an abundance of theory and speculation, more or less ' rational,' but there is no formal proof or demonstration. There is no general agreement even as to what constitutes essentially a ' work of art.' The work appeals to our imagination, to our emotions, to the *spiritual* side of our nature ; but the formal mind, the consciously acting part of our reason, cannot account for this fact, it can only accept it as valid experience. The experience comes to us from a region beyond the mind. In a certain sense it is more rational than anything that the formal mind can constitute ; it is a greater immediacy of knowledge ; it claims the attention of the rational mind with an insistency which tells us that it will be to our infinite loss if we neglect to cultivate it. This will be found to be the case with everything which really counts in life, which really constitutes life itself, which truly appertains to the art of living; and we shall see in due course that Mysticism is the furthest expression of the great art of Life itself.

It would be absurd to suppose that the faculty, the *genius* of art, has evolved out of a mere mechanical facility for representation of natural objects, or in consequence of the improvement of the materials wherewith the artist can express himself. The artist seeks the materials, not the materials the artist. It is art that makes the work, and not the work which constitutes the art. The work is but the sign and symbol of an innate spiritual quality which stands in its own right, which belongs to life itself, and owes nothing to physics or chemistry or mechanics, but is ever bringing these more and more into its service, and may even express itself in the most unpromising materials.

We should, then, be sadly misrepresenting the true nature of Mysticism if we allowed it to be supposed that it has its origin and source in a mere evolution of the rational faculty. It is, on the contrary, the rational faculty which grows towards, and becomes more and more expressive of, all those great inner powers of our life and being which we must broadly term *spiritual*, without, however, attaching to this word any special religious or theological meaning. It appears to be the best word at our command to express all those *idealistic* powers—our appreciation of truth, goodness, and beauty—which are continually striving to find expression in our nature, and which are the very root and essence of everything which gives to life a fuller value and a deeper meaning than that of mere animal existence; as also all that is implied in the term *self-realisation*. The course of evolution shows us a continual yielding up of the claims of our outward life of sense ' reality ' to the pressure of an inwardly experienced ideal which at root is the possibility of including within our own individual centre of consciousness a larger and fuller measure and *quality* of Life itself.

In showing, then, in the first instance, how Mysticism is rational in the sense that it is a legitimate extension of what we already know, we shall only be showing how what is deeper in our nature gradually forces a recognition by the evolving personality. Our evolution is only the fuller expression of what already exists transcendentally and potentially. We have our roots in spirit, not in matter, and the *ideal* is the pledge of an *existing* reality. We may agree, therefore, with Récéjac when he says: " The true field of Mysticism is the Infinite of Reason and Freedom "[1]; and also with Dean Inge: " The mystic is not, as such, a visionary; nor has he any interest in appealing to a faculty ' above reason,' if reason is used in its proper sense, as the logic of the whole personality."[2] Yes; but what is the " whole personality " short of the Absolute Itself ?

The fundamental principles of Mysticism, however, are rational not merely in the above sense, not merely as legitimate deductions from existing knowledge, or as that which the rational mind must accept as a higher authority, but also in that they are susceptible of direct experience by any individual who cares to follow the path which the pioneers have indicated as leading to such experience. But it is not everyone who will care to set out for a newly discovered land, even when the discoverer has brought back the most glowing accounts thereof. To some the region of mystical consciousness may appear to be as unattractive as the North Pole, however certain it may be that there is such a region. This region, moreover, is largely associated in the ' rational ' mind with supernaturalism and superstition, and is therefore *taboo* in academic circles. Some countries are only for the adventurous. First comes the discoverer, then the pioneer, afterwards the flow of civilisation; and often the discoverer, and even the pioneer gets little enough credit for his work. It may even be that in the first instance, and for many centuries, his message and his work are totally discredited, and he himself regarded as a chimerical dreamer, or even worse. The great majority of the human race are still crude realists, and have no appreciation of any relations and proportions other than such as are given by the senses: their ' religious ' beliefs and observances being only such as may minister in some fashion to a vaguely-felt spiritual instinct. This instinct can only be satisfied in the first instance with a grossly realistic or materialistic theology or theogony. So also arises a spurious mysticism, better called *psychism*; this latter,

---

[1] *Essay on the Bases of the Mystic Knowledge*, p. 178.
[2] *Christian Mysticism*, p. 19.

indeed, being much in evidence to-day, masquerading as 'mysticism,' or, alternatively, 'occultism.'

The true mystic, however, testifies to a transcendental region of consciousness in which we come into a much clearer and fuller realisation of the deep source of our life and being than that which either our normal sense experience or abnormal psychical faculties can give to us. The mere psychological fact of a transcendental consciousness we shall find to be abundantly verified by experimental psychology; but the special province and message of the mystic is as much beyond psychology as that of the artist is beyond the mechanical reproduction of the photographic plate. Both the artist and the mystic, however, are dependent upon materials already evolved and fabricated by sense experience in order to body forth that which they contact in the inner region of experience or consciousness. The mystic may speak to the mystic in a more direct or symbolical language than that of dialectic; but the more general appeal must be in the first instance to that which we commonly know as reason, and all the more so in that Mysticism, rightly understood, is not a message from " the back of beyond," but a higher and deeper interpretation of what is already known and visible.

In our preliminary chapters, then, we shall endeavour to see how the fundamental principles of Mysticism found on our existing knowledge, so that we may be able to appreciate on rational grounds the direct message which the genuine mystic brings to us from that deeper region of consciousness into which he penetrates. We must in fact show how science, philosophy, and religion, each in its own appropriate manner, points to the region which the mystic occupies in his own right.

When we consider broadly the history or evolution of humanity as we are able to read it to-day, it discloses as its primary phase a gradual development of physical organism; a biological process; the rise of organic forms out of what we term the inorganic world, and a slowly increasing complexity of structure through plant and animal to man as we at present know him.

In the second phase we have the emergence of that faculty which we call Mind: passing from its earliest manifestation as a mere instinctive knowledge adapted to the more immediate needs of the physical organism, into that higher quality which we apprehend as the rational or ratiocinative mind, and thereby losing much of its instinctual nature, which becomes more or less subconscious.

As a further stage we have the growth and development of a moral and spiritual sense, born of a gradually evolving intuition and perception of a deeper order of things than that of the merely physical and material, and of a certain relationship of the individual to the larger cosmic universe by which we are environed and of which we are a part.

And concerning this cosmic order and our relation thereto, we find within all the historical periods of which we have any records a deep and insatiable desire to know more and ever more of its nature, a restless search and strenuous effort on the part of the foremost of the race, of those whom we rightly regard as our greatest and noblest, to penetrate deeper and still deeper into the hidden secret of the great mystery of Nature and Being which lies without and around us, and the corresponding mystery of our own nature and being which lies within us, and to find the true relation, connection, and unity of the two.

Whence arises this great Quest; what is it which thus stirs and strives within us, ever urging us on to fresh discoveries in science, to wider generalisations in philosophy, to a deeper and purer morality, and greater intensity of religious aspiration and experience?

It has been argued—and will not be re-argued here—that there must certainly be a reality corresponding to this deeply rooted instinct in our nature; that the very fact of its existence is a pledge not merely of its legitimacy, but also of its ultimate realisation. This much, however, may be said here: that the measure of our past evolution, whether individually or as a race, may be regarded as the indication and pledge of an incalculable attainment in the future.

Science presents us with an almost incredible story of our evolution into our present powers and consciousness from some primordial form of protoplasm; and, indeed, were it not that the individual to-day actually commences his organic existence in just some such protoplasmic speck or germ-cell, and recapitulates in a few months the whole evolutionary process, we should be utterly unable to credit the fact.

But in view of this gigantic and marvellous process, what may we not anticipate for the future ? Is there any measure whatsoever of that which we can hope to achieve and become ? May we not legitimately say that the future not merely may but *must* hold for us a reality immeasurably beyond our most daring conceptions, and that whatsoever of knowledge, of perfection, of nobleness, or dignity, or power has been recognised as possible by prophet, or saint, or seer, or mystic, by a Christ or a Buddha, can but dimly adumbrate that future greatness and fulness of life which we may assuredly claim as our destiny and our birthright ? The ideal and the vision of to-day becomes the realisation of to-morrow. That is the plain lesson of the past which science teaches us in the mere biological process without any other considerations, and we may and must lay hold of our future on the same terms as those by which we have achieved our present.

But as regards our continual effort to understand the meaning of this great process, the nature of the cosmic scheme of things and our relation thereto : there lies deep in the innermost of our nature a subtle and ethical motive. It is no mere curiosity which impels us, nor any merely *practical* motive. Deeper than these lies an innate sense of justice and of purpose—which implies also rationality. We desire to justify not merely our own actions as rational beings, but instinctively also we desire to find in the principle of justice some explanation of the great cosmic laws to which we must perforce submit. We are willing to submit to law and order and duty, even to pain and suffering, when we have recognised these as reasonable or rational ; but we are not willing to submit to caprice. In Kant's celebrated formula : " I must because I ought, but why ought I ? "

We see that we must submit to some Power greater than ourselves. The littleness and insignificance of the individual in the cosmic order is only too apparent, and sometimes seems to overwhelm us. Nature apparently recks no more of the individual man than of the individual microbe, or the individual atom ; but we want a reason for it all, otherwise we must be in perpetual revolt. Instinctively we feel that, small as is the individual, *we* are greater than our fate, even whilst we have to submit to it. The cosmic scheme of things is somehow part of us, as well as we being part of it. Our very knowledge and triumph—not over it, but in it and by it—is conditioned by our submission, not by our revolt. We conquer by yielding. Nature always works along the line of least resistance, and supplies us with the key to her own conquest. Some day we shall know and conquer where now we can only submit and seemingly be crushed; and thus we ourselves are immeasurably superior to it all. This is no false pride, but rather the deepest instinct and stimulus of our nature. The man who merely sits down and bows to the " will of God " because he is too indolent or too dull to seek the deep springs of his own being, may possibly appear to be more ' religious ' or ' devout ' than the scientist or the philosopher ; but he who revolts and thereby learns the art of submission, thereby learns his own immeasurable dignity, and the law and justice of his own particular place in the universe, is incalculably beyond the mere hireling of the law. The latter has his eye on a future compensation and reward, the former knows his present place to be also his own dignity and high purpose, let it be ever so lowly as it may in the world's estimation.

The fact, then, of this inner impelling force is one which we can only ignore at peril of individual stagnation and death ; it is one which we must recognise as the mainspring of all effort, of all progress, of all evolution, and of all nobility of character, whether in the individual, the community, or the race. Nature does not allow us to stand still. She compels us to learn by hard and bitter experience. It is not merely our right but also our necessity to know. We cannot increase in any of our powers or faculties of life unless we constantly make the effort to understand ever more and more clearly what we are in the completeness or wholeness of our nature. This knowledge is gained in the first instance by conscious struggle and suffering, and when gained it passes into the subconscious region of the subliminal self, the region of instinct, intuition, and unconsciously exercised faculty. Every function of the body which we now employ so easily and unthinkingly—respiration, assimilation, circulation, repair of tissue, and a thousand other things—has been gained in the first instance by conscious effort and struggle to attain a dimly perceived possibility of further knowledge, quality, or power of life.

So also must it be with our mental and spiritual faculties; with that further expansion of life to which we have not yet attained, but which we clearly recognise as something which we not merely may but also must strive to make our own.

But that to which we thus reach forward is already there —even within ourselves. Evolution means an unfolding of something already potentially existing. Something is first of all in-volved before it can be e-volved. Organic structure could not evolve at all without the pre-existing life, nor could any particular organ, such as the eye for example, evolve unless the *faculty* of sight, the power and desire to see, were there in the first instance. The outer form is only the manifestation and expression of the inner mystic, mysterious *fact* of ceaseless and indestructible life and consciousness.

The fact that we are thus compelled to evolve, apparently by slow and painful stages, is a pledge of the legitimacy of knowledge to the fullest and highest degree to which our instinct can direct us. It is foolishly asserted by some that we are not intended to know certain things, to penetrate certain mysteries of our nature; that, indeed, it is forbidden by the *fiat* of a personal God. Such a plea is a convenient cloak for professional ignorance and indolence. It is absolutely repudiated by what we know of evolution as a natural process. Nature herself compels us to know, whether we are willing or not.

It is quite true, however, that there are certain natural limits to our attainment in any particular period or cycle of evolution. We find limitations enough within ourselves without having any invented for us, but these limitations are perfectly natural, not artificial or arbitrary. They are very largely self-created, but are also racial and hereditary in their nature. In coming into incarnation we must of necessity accept both racial and parental heredity so far as our physical organism is concerned. We may very well doubt whether we can get outside of the great cycle of human evolution, and pass on to some further stage in that great cosmic whole of which our world, or even the Solar System, is but a minute fractional part, until the whole of humanity has reached a certain stage of development, for we belong to the whole cycle, in the future as well as in the past, and humanity is a unitary whole, not a mass of independent individuals.

It is doubtless a fact that there are many things which could be 'revealed' to us which we are not merely unfitted as yet to hear, but even unable to bear. But 'revelation' is as is the natural capacity to receive, and even these very things which are 'hidden' are staring us in the face at every moment. Nature has no arbitrary secrets; she even wooes us to the discovery of her most precious treasures and deepest beauty, and we may assuredly believe that when our present disabilities have really been conquered within ourselves, our present apparent limitations will fall away and disappear as naturally and as inevitably as those limits which we have already overpassed in our great upward cycle of evolution. If we have already passed—or are passing—from the merely animal into the human kingdom, so also we shall assuredly evolve from the human into what we now look up to as the divine.

Nature compels us to know, compels us to evolve, but as individuals we have a certain limit of free choice. To refuse to obey the mandate means stagnation and death; to go forward means a strife and conflict the object of which is not immediately apparent. We are free to make use of the law of inertia, or of the law of momentum, whichsoever we will, and only too often the law of inertia appears the most attractive. But we are between the devil and the deep sea. Presently we find that to draw back is worse than to go forward; nay, when we have once learnt the true law of life, when once the real issue is clearly seen, and the irrational fear of the unknown, the superstitious dread of a supernatural bogy fostered by priestcraft, is fairly conquered, we shall recognise intuitively that we may commit ourselves to the deep sea without the slightest fear, and it will become our natural instinct to swim joyously and triumphantly therein, with ever increasing power and fulness of life. This inner intuition, which so many have already happily evolved, becomes the innate, ineradicable, strong quality of *faith*—by no means to be confounded with that of mere religious belief, or what is commonly called "*the* faith."

Our suffering is the evidence of our free-will. We are not automatons. Seen from a higher point of view it may become clear that we have deliberately chosen much of that 'fate' which, from the limited point of view of the lower personality, is so often apparently not merely inexplicable but also unjust, and so full of suffering and pain. Moreover, much of the conflict and suffering is obviously due to our own wilfulness in not taking to heart the lessons which nature has already taught us, or which our own conscience dictates; to an individual self-seeking which is opposed to the law of human solidarity. This earth might be a very tolerable Paradise, even with our present measure of knowledge.

We should accept the conflict, then, where it is inevitable, as gladly and as joyously as the old Vikings who went into battle as the one thing worth living for. Death has no terror for us, and our wounds are the honourable scars of a victory which is ours even in defeat, the pledge of a nobler and a fuller life not otherwise attainable. The problem of evil lies more in the false premises from which we endeavour to reason, than from the inherent nature of the problem itself. Do not let us refer back to the will of a personal God, or the power of a personal devil, that which merely belongs to our own perverseness.

This continual effort to know more and more of our real nature and environment, and to attain to an ever-increasing fulness of life, expresses itself as the three great categories known as Science, Philosophy, and Religion; and each of these also corresponds broadly to the natural order of evolution: Science representing the physical or organic, Philosophy the mental, and Religion the moral and spiritual stages.

Thus both in our individual evolution and in the evolution of the race as a whole there is a constantly added quality of life, represented broadly by these three stages, and falling under these categories; and it is perhaps necessary to insist here that we cannot regard either of these categories as valid unless it does add something to the fulness of life itself, increasing and enriching its quality, filling us with an ever-growing measure and assurance of its deep and illimitable possibilities, and bringing us into a closer touch with and a fuller realisation of the existence of that " inmost centre " of our being " where truth abides in fulness."

Possibly such a view as this might be termed the higher Pragmatism, and it may certainly be deemed to be that higher optimism which is the natural accompaniment of a deeply rooted faith in a rational universe and a transcendental perfection.

The primitive individual, or the primitive race, is concerned only in the first place with the bare physical facts of existence ; and modern science, in so far as it is merely physical in its scope, may be regarded simply as a somewhat higher degree of this primitive recognition of a material environment and necessity.

But to this is presently added something of a different nature and quality. Man rises from physical necessity to an intellectual need and desire which later on finds expression in that deeper inquiry into the nature of life and consciousness which we term Philosophy. From outward and known physical effects we pass to the search for an inner, subjective, and concealed cause.

This inquiry into the nature of the unknown and subjective side of our life and consciousness is fully recognised as both legitimate and rational. As soon as the discovery is made that things are not what they seem, and that there is some deep and fundamental relation between consciousness as subject and matter as object, the demand is legitimately made for the fullest possible inquiry into and knowledge of this deeper and wider region of our being.

But this is neither a final stage nor is it the highest quality of our life. There is still a third thing which has been coming gradually into existence along with the growth of our physical and mental faculties, a further quality of life which is clearly distinguishable from either of these as dealing with a still higher or deeper region of our nature and experience. It is that inner perception or quality of life which is broadly classified under the term Religion : the dawn of a moral sense, of ideas of duty, sacrifice, virtue, and above all of love.

Religion in so far as it concerns the relation of Man to ' God ' may possibly be said to commence with the conception of a cosmic Power outside and beyond us : a Power to be feared, worshipped, propitiated ; but the religious instinct can hardly be said to have risen into a new or distinct quality of life until the idea of *love* commences to permeate and irradiate it with its purifying and ennobling influence.

Thus in a certain sense we may say that Philosophy is higher than Science, and Religion is higher than Philosophy ;

that each of these expresses not merely an additional quality in our life which the other lacks, but also a quality which is deeper in our nature, and further in our evolution.

If, then, the discovery is made that beyond any of these there lies a still further region of our being not really as yet touched; a still further depth in our consciousness, and a more intense quality of life: it immediately becomes both legitimate and rational that we should seek to experience and attain to it. It is precisely here that the mystic in all ages has been delivering his message. He points to this deeper and higher region of our life and consciousness as one in which we come into still closer realisation and contact with the great Cosmic Life. He points to it as something which he has himself experienced, and he endeavours to convey to us some intimation of its nature, and of the method by which we may attain to it. How little he is able to tell us, and the reason why he is able to tell us so little, we shall presently elucidate.

With regard, however, to these various stages of evolution, we should make a mistake if we supposed that in adding any one stage to another we may leave behind or ignore those qualities which we have already developed. On the contrary, though each stage must give its own special contribution, it must also give an added power and intensity to that which has preceded it; illuminating and enriching the totality with its own peculiar characteristic. Our acquired powers must all go hand in hand in that great Quest which is our own growth, evolution, and self-realisation; they must each and all aid us in our efforts to penetrate and discover the inner secret of our nature: that deep fact of BEING which we clearly perceive not merely as a legitimate subject for intellectual apprehension, but also intuitively feel to be vitally and fatefully connected with our individual life and destiny, as something into which we are inexorably carried by the great cosmic flow of duration, and which surrounds and interpenetrates us at every moment with its pregnant mystery. Whilst each stage may be said to transcend the others, it does so by embracing and merging them in a larger whole, and not by departing therefrom to a separate or detached region of life and consciousness.

Philosophy is subsequent and superior to Science in this respect, that it deals with an aspect of our nature which is not touched by physical methods; that it properly commences the inquiry where science leaves off, in the metaphysical region of mind and consciousness. The province of Science is to garner facts, to observe, to record, to classify and to demonstrate. Science is an exact and demonstrable knowledge of the relation and proportion of things in all regions in which facts can be observed and experimented with. It endeavours to formulate the laws which govern phenomena in the world of manifested physical or material effects, but in doing this it leaves untouched the great problem of our life and consciousness, the real fundamental problem of the relation of consciousness itself to this external world of phenomena, the living vital fact of the existence of a Subject or Knower, and the relation of this *Subject* to the external world as the *Object* which is known or perceived. Philosophy takes the facts which Science brings to light and states them in larger terms: relating them to the deeper metaphysical region of pure thought and consciousness; but we are not independent of scientific knowledge when we have attained to the thought of the philosopher.

What now shall we say of Religion; what is its proper or special province and function? Is it independent of Science and Philosophy; does it occupy a region of its own in which both of these may be left behind and ignored?

This latter is a claim commonly made for it by those who take a narrow and individual view of human life and evolution; such a view, for example, as that which would determine the 'eternal' destiny of the individual by reference to one single life on this earth. It is the view of that dualism or supernaturalism with which the term 'religion' is so commonly associated; and certainly if our 'eternal' state is determined by our conduct or belief in one single incarnation only, we had better turn our whole attention to religion as a preparation for the 'next world,' and leave Science and Philosophy severely alone. With such a narrow view as this, however, we are not here concerned.

From the opposite point of view we find the same extreme mistake. The gradual rise of 'Rationalism' as the result of the comparative freedom of thought brought about by the Reformation, culminating as it did in the brilliant galaxy of intellects of the seventeenth and eighteenth centuries, with the subsequent and even more brilliant scientific discoverers of the nineteenth century, led to a claim being made for the supreme importance of scientific knowledge as the only illuminant which could penetrate the darkness of our ignorance, and give us an assured knowledge of our place in the great cosmic scheme of things.

But those who make this claim are really as limited in their view of human nature as the mere supernaturalist; and their attitude towards religion has been that of confounding its real province and power with its temporary or ecclesiastical forms. In doing this they set on one side one of the most potent factors in the evolution of man.

All history testifies to the fact that Religion is the deepest need, as also the highest expression of Man's nature; it is of supreme importance in its dominating influence on character and action, and it takes the foremost place in the shaping of the destiny of nations and races, as well as of individuals. Even the birth-rate is affected by it.[1]

The inner intuition of religion is not merely instinctive and ineradicable—though here and there it may be temporarily lost by individuals, even of a high order of intellectual attainments—but it naturally increases in power and depth as the individual and the race evolves. The highest type of man is not the man of intellect merely, but one who has added to his life that further moral quality and spiritual force which distinguishes him as one in whom something still more powerful has been brought to birth, and which we characterise in general as belonging specially to the province of religion, though not necessarily in the mere conventional sense of the term as connected with a formal creed, or religous observance.

Science and Philosophy may destroy a superstitious form of Religion, indeed it may almost be said to be indirectly part of their business to do so; but they can no more destroy Religion itself than they can destroy the instinct of love: much less can they supersede it.

Religion might be said to be this same primary instinct of love, transmuted and transformed from its merely individual and selfish form into altruism and a recognition of its operation in that deeper connection of the individual with the universal which is gradually brought to light in an intelligible form by science and philosophy. Or it might be said to be the opera-

[1] Cf. H. Fielding, *The Hearts of Men*, p. 285 ff.

tion of a universal law of love gradually bringing into harmony with itself a slowly evolving organic personality which, in the first instance, considers itself as something separate and individual.

Religion, we repeat, is *a further quality of life*; it is not belief, or creed, or dogma, or ceremonial observance: these being only its temporary, adventitious, or accidental accompaniments: the physical and material forms in which it is forced to express itself in the region of the lower mind and sense perceptions. These forms are purely man-made and man-given, and are generally more of a hindrance than a help to the highest self-realisation, and to that unity and harmony which should result from a recognition of the fundamental law of love. History shows them in general to be the cause of strife not of peace, and our greatest exemplars have always risen above them.

Science and Philosophy, by adding to our knowledge of the relation of the individual to the universal, must inevitably minister to a deeper religious intuition and a higher expression of unity. The scientist and the philosopher, without yielding adherence to any special form of religion, may be more truly religious than priest or pope; and none but the narrowest religionist will fail to recognise the necessary place of science and philosophy in the whole evolution and well-being of humanity. Though the individual himself may not be a scientist or a philosopher, he garners the fruit of these, and without them he could not be what he is in his own individuality and heredity, or in the conditions of his physical, social, or mental environment. No individual can separate himself from the evolution of the race; no individual is an independent unit; his heredity goes back to the earliest beginnings, and the strands of his being are interwoven with the whole web of humanity through all time. That which has passed into his personality, and has become ‘second nature’—the subconscious or subliminal self which governs all our bodily processes—is the accumulated experience of the race, and not of the particular individual; whilst every single thought or action on the part of the individual has its due and corresponding effect on the whole race, and modifies the racial consciousness in its own proper manner and degree.

In man's great quest for truth it is always a deep, and in the first instance perhaps an indefinable intuition, which gives rise to what presently becomes a clearly formulated science or philosophy; and deepest of all in our nature lies the intuition of religion. The ardent search for truth, wheresoever it is found, is in reality the religious instinct; and the scientist or the philosopher who is really inspired with the pure love of truth, is giving to the race his own contribution to this religious instinct just as surely as the professed religious devotee. Scientists are unconscious religionists, even in their materialism, just as they are also unconscious metaphysicians even while they may deride metaphysics. They are in reality seeking just what the religionist or the mystic seeks, the deep source and ground in Reality of their own being, even when the inner instinct which urges them on in this quest does not rise into a conscious religious emotion, or associate itself with the more formal side of religious observance.

Religion, then, is that quality of the soul which prompts it to a passionate search for the source of its existence because of an inner intuition—not always clearly defined, and sometimes even specifically denied by the mere intellect—that there is a source, a depth of our nature and being, from which somehow we are separated in consciousness, or in knowledge, but towards which, nevertheless, we are continually moving, and which contains for us a measure of life incomparably superior to that which we at present realise.

The stronger this intuition becomes, the higher becomes its expression in the individual as morality, duty, sacrifice, virtue, love; and these not as something enforced by law, but as the spontaneous outflow of the soul from its own nature. These are the foundation of all social as well as of all individual well-being; when they decay, when the religious ideal becomes feeble or obscured: the individual, the community, or the nation falls also into decadence and death.

We have, then, to distinguish clearly between Religion itself as an inner quality of the soul, and the historical forms in which this quality has expressed itself from time to time as creed, or dogma, or worship. These, speaking generally, do not mark the growth but the stagnation of religion. As Emerson so pertinently says, " the moment the doctrine of immortality is separately taught, man is already fallen."

Religion itself is independent of all forms. It is the instinctive movement of the soul towards light, life, truth, love. It is as natural and as inevitable as the upward growth of a plant. It implies not merely the inner energising life itself within the seed-germ from which the subsequent product evolves, but also the existence of the source of life and light towards which it expands. The manifestation of this great spiritual Principle in the individual is an added quality of life; it is the growth of the soul by and through the 'material' world; yet above and superior to this as something surpassingly beautiful, even as the beauty of leaf and flower grows up from the darkness and grossness of the soil, transmuted by the alchemy of life from things common and unclean into loveliness and purity.

The historical forms, the terms in which the religious instinct or intuition in man expresses itself from time to time, are necessarily imperfect and mutable. No greater mistake can be made than to suppose that any finality can be arrived at in them any more than in science or philosophy; for nothing that can be stated by the formal mind is more than relatively true. We shall discover presently how and in what way the intuition of the mystic transcends the findings of the formal mind, and therefore approaches more nearly to the final truth, which is not a contrast of truth and error but a unification of all opposites. The final religion is formless and creedless. It is participation in the One Life which is "no respecter of persons."

In the meanwhile that which can satisfy the demands of one age, or of one community, or even of one generation, is not the same as, and does not suffice for, the next. Even that which is considered 'rational' by one generation is apt to be regarded as absurd and false by a later one. In the West the rational element in religion has for centuries been, to a large extent, categorically denied and repudiated. Belief, an unqualified assent to particular doctrines or dogmas, has been placed above reason, and the right of reason to adjudicate in matters of faith has been superseded by priestly authority.

But the clear and pressing demand of the present age is that formulated religion, as presented by its authoritative exponents, should be rational; by which this much at least is meant, that no presentation of it shall come under the

4

reproach of being antagonistic to the known facts of nature and experience.

The historical conflict between science on the one hand, and traditional authoritative Ecclesiasticism on the other, is too well known to be dwelt upon here; but while it may certainly be said that the brilliant scientific discoveries of the nineteenth century have left the final issue of the conflict no longer in doubt—though the distant rumble of the retreating forces may still be heard in Papal Encyclicals and the like—yet it can hardly be held that we have definitely commenced to reap the legitimate fruit of the victory in a nobler and a more rational religion, capable of satisfying in every direction the scientific, intellectual, and social demands of the present age, more strenuous than ever, as it is, in its search for truth. Whilst the field of battle has already been sufficiently cleared, it is only here and there that the real work of reconstruction has begun on the part of recognised authorities, though so much is being done apart from them. The Christian Church, so far as its doctrinal teachings are concerned, is largely a mere rubbish heap of the old traditional forts; yet some at least of the foundation-stones—which, however, are also pre-Christian—remain good, and fit to be rebuilt into the new edifice; and within the Church itself there are not a few who are attempting in some wise to select the materials, if not actually to lay out the ground-plan of the future structure. But the work of these few is sadly hindered by the inertia of tradition and the vested interests which always gather round and tenaciously cling to old-established systems. As Poincaré remarks in his *New Physics*: " Those who have made to themselves a comfortable dwelling-place on the ruins of ancient monuments are often too loth to leave it."

But the real movement, the real work, is outside the Church, amongst those whom the Church by her irrationality has repelled. Amongst these a great spiritual movement is taking place, a natural demand on the part of those who possess a wider and deeper knowledge than the Church has as yet recognised, for a legitimate channel into which their active religious instinct can flow, and in which it can find a free and rational expression.

This demand is something more than the demand for a

re-statement or re-formulation of old beliefs : for a 'new theology,' or even for a re-interpretation of an ancient Scripture supposed to be unique and exclusive. It is a demand for a total abandonment of a method of religion which rests merely on tradition, a religion which is principally concerned with one or more alleged historical facts, now not merely largely in question and doubtful of proof on historical and critical grounds, but also highly improbable in themselves ; especially so since the same ' events ' are found as ' myths ' in earlier religious systems. It is now clearly recognised that any religion worth the name must rest on a much more stable foundation of history than this ; that it must in fact rest on nothing less than the evolution of the whole race, and not on particular events, whether true or otherwise. Individual systems may found on particular events, but individual systems are no longer required by enlightenment and reason ; nothing short of universal principles which are true for all time, and may be experimentally demonstrated at any time, can satisfy the present demand on the part of those who have read the book of nature and of history in a larger light.

The reason, then, for this further demand is not so much because of the actual attack which has been made upon the traditional history and doctrine, and the extremely precarious position which it now holds, as because of a genuine re-formation of men's minds and consciousness. An entirely new order of thought is gradually coming into existence, one which implies a radical change from the old order in more respects than one ; a new outlook upon the world ; a new consciousness of the immanency of the spiritual as both cause and active principle of the material and physical ; not as something which stands apart from the physical, or which is to succeed the physical in order of time, but as something of which the physical is an integral and intelligible part during all time. It is in fact clearly perceived that the laws of nature, the laws and modes of the human soul, and the great structural facts of the Universe are just the same to-day as they ever were, and that man embodies them within himself and does not come to them through any mediator, nor is he ' reconciled ' to any supreme Being through any particular historical event, but through all that great process which is the evolution of the individual and of Humanity as a whole. The ' age of miracles' has not passed—simply because it never existed; or exists as much to-day as ever it did. No alleged miracle can be greater than the 'commonplace' facts of our every-day life and consciousness, before which the true seer and mystic bows in reverent adoration, and does not trouble himself about 'historical events.' "There is nothing under the canopy of heaven greater than the tip of an autumn spikelet," says the old Chinese mystic, Chuang Tzu; and in some such language have the truly enlightened spoken in all ages; stating in the paradoxical language in which alone it can be expressed the great mystical fact that the One Life is present in all its fulness in its very smallest objective manifestations.

It is just this wider and nobler vision of the relation and proportion of things which we believe to be the mainspring of the modern movement; not really a "New Mysticism" in its essence and fundamental principles, but new as to our present age, and especially as regards the limited under-standing of the term 'Mysticism' in its exclusively Christian application which has hitherto been more commonly accepted.

Thus the demand is for actual present and demonstrable knowledge of our spiritual life and powers as well as of our physical nature and environment; for a quality of life pro-ducing visible results, physical, material, and social as well as 'spiritual.' It is not the demand for a religion which shall pilot us as individuals safely to Heaven, but for one which shall enable us to realise in our own persons here and now the divine powers which rightly and rightfully belong to us in our own deeper nature in its oneness with the whole of the Cosmos; one which shall enable us to realise in actual consciousness and quality of life that unity of the individual with Man, and of Man with the Universe, which we have already apprehended in a scientific and intellectual manner.

Such a demand has already touched a quality of religious life, aspiration, and experience which lies beyond any mere formulated religion, and which in all ages has differentiated the true mystic from the mere religionist, the prophet from the priest. Mysticism is essentially religious in its nature, but it is an added quality of religious life which is as distinct from that which the man of only one religion reaches, as is Religion itself from Philosophy or Science within their own proper limitations. It must be placed in a further, and perhaps a final, category as the highest and deepest consciousness which we can as human beings experience of the totality of our nature. It is in fact the natural and legitimate advance into the next stage of our evolution, an advance in which man becomes more than human, a stage in which he definitely awakens to a realisation of his divine nature and powers, and endeavours to enter into possession thereof, here and now.

From what we have already said as to the general trend and process of evolution, it can now be seen that this advance is as natural and inevitable as the step already made from the animal to the human. We claim it on the same terms as the biological process. The great sweep of evolution must inevitably carry us into it, and in this respect, as in the biological process, there will be individuals constituting the favourable ' variations': abnormal developments which will indicate in advance the nature of the further process. The biological process is the result, the concomitant, not the cause, of the inner process, the evolution of the real man. At present the mystic is the exception, the flower of the race; and, as we may see later on, he does not always understand himself. The dawn of the mystic faculty is, in many cases, like the dawn of love in a maiden's heart: an exquisite surprise. It is so wonderful, so fearful, so full of tremulous joy, so real in the immediacy of its knowledge, that no intellectual analysis or justification is asked for. The heart bows in silent submission before the mystery of it; its mingled ecstasy and fear makes of it a sacred and holy thing which it would be sacrilege to analyse or doubt. When to the individual it appears in this regard, it most frequently becomes identified with the particular religion to which the devotee belongs. It also expresses itself in passionate and even erotic language.

But there is a more rational, Mysticism which rises above this stage; a Mysticism which can stand aside from its own emotions as well as from its objective visions or experiences, and which demands a balanced judgment of these in order that proper values may be assigned to them. It is towards this that modern Mysticism tends. There is no reason why we should regard as finally characteristic of Mysticism anything of which we have so far any historical examples, any more than that we should have this regard for anything as yet achieved in Science, Philosophy, or formulated Religion. A new and rational Mysticism must certainly add something to the old, even though the root principles are still the same. The sweep of evolution will always bring forth the new and appropriate type. It is hardly likely that we shall have any more mystics of the type of Angela of Foligno, or St. John of the Cross. But unless we are careful to keep our root principles clearly in mind—those, namely, which have been found valid for all time—the " New Mysticism " may easily be claimed by such as have no right to the title, and Mysticism itself be brought into further discredit.

If, then, we take this high view of the nature of Mysticism, it is imperative that we should guard the term from abuse ; that we should define its province very clearly, and preserve its historical validity by a reference only to those who can legitimately claim to have been mystics in the truest and deepest sense.

It is open to question whether, either in Philosophy or Religion—or even in the still deeper sphere of Mysticism— it is possible to state anything which is fundamentally or substantially new. Old or forgotten truths may reappear like jewels which have lost their setting and lustre, or which have lain in neglect and obscurity owing to the changing fashions of men's thoughts and interests. They do but require to be reset in appropriate form, to shine once again in all their pristine and inherent beauty.

The fundamental truths of man's nature and the great structural facts of the Universe are the same in all ages, and in all historical ages they have obtained the recognition of the wise. It is scarcely possible to find any modern statement of root principles which had not previously been formulated at some period or other of the world's history ; indeed it might almost be said that in proportion as any fundamental statement in Philosophy, in Religion, or even in Science, is new, it is not true. Even Pragmatism, according to some authorities, is not new ; it is to be found in Plato.[1]

In *Scientific Idealism* I have sketched the history of the great scientific dogma of the nineteenth century, that of the indestructibility of matter in its physical atomic form. But

[1] Vide, *Plato's Doctrine of Ideas*, by Professor J. A. Stewart, p. 100.

this dogma has been completely upset and destroyed by the discovery of radio-activity, radium, and of the corpuscle or electron. It was not true, and if our scientists had not been so materialistic, so scornful of the ancient wisdom, so reliant on a crude and unphilosophical realism which had no more imagination than to suppose that there could be an ultimate particle of 'matter' which was only a very much smaller thing than that which we know as matter in bulk, they might at least have paused before making some of the positive statements which have since been proved to be so very wide of the truth, and which now appear so ridiculous. The disintegration and transmutation of the elements was known, theoretically, if not practically, to the Alchemists; whilst the doctrine of an all-pervading Æther, out of which all the lower elements are evolved, belongs to Greek philosophy, and may be traced to much earlier sources.

Our test of truth may even be its very antiquity; not from that mere fact, but because it has thus been proved to have stood the test of time, and now reappears once more. All that is really and essentially true has been recognised and stated over and over again by the best and wisest in all ages, though their teaching is often sadly obscured by the forms in which it has come down to us. It may yet be found and acknowledged that the ancient myths and symbols contain more real knowledge of the structure of the Cosmos than anything which has been disclosed by our modern instruments of research. The origin and meaning of the Zodiac, for example, is still a closed book for our modern savants.

In the more special province of religion we find the same thing. The Christian religion has commonly been regarded as a totally new 'revelation' of truth, yet it is doubtful whether there is a single fundamental truth disclosed in the New Testament which had not been stated long before the Christian era. The real origins of Christianity are obscure in the extreme; but if we are to accept the authority of St. Augustine, Christianity was only a new name for an old religion, for he says: " That which is called the Christian Religion existed among the Ancients, and never did not exist, from the beginning of the human race until Christ came in the flesh, at which time the true religion which already existed began to be called Christianity."[1] That is a conclusion which not a few competent scholars are now reaching. More than that, there are many of these who question altogether the historicity of the Gospels. Many Church dignitaries occupy a half-way position ; they deny the historicity of *some* of the narratives, but accept others. The terms in which the supposed historical Jesus is spoken of by early Christian authorities, as well as the actual events attributed to him, bear a remarkable resemblance to conceptions and myths already current in the ' heathen ' world ; whilst the specific teachings assigned to him, as also those of the great Apostle Paul—who represented the ancient *esoteric* doctrine of a *Cosmic* Christ-Principle or Logos, as opposed to Peter, who represented the historicising element—were truisms in many of the more ancient systems.

As to what has been added to the pure teaching of the New Testament by ecclesiastical authority and priestcraft, and has thereby become known as ' Christianity ' in its historical form : the greater part of it is now discredited and repudiated by the rational thought and criticism of the age. What was new in it was not true, and we may rest assured that if there is anything of which it can be said that it belongs *exclusively* to this, that, or the other religion, then that thing is only a temporary and adventitious excrescence, and has in it no element of permanency or of abiding truth.

In Science we find the same. Modern scientific theories are largely a reversion to ancient teachings : with the added force of experimental evidence and a greater knowledge of detail.

So far as the historical side of our present subject is concerned, we shall have to realise how deeply this is true also of all the essential elements of Mysticism. There is much in the modern revival of so-called Mysticism which we shall have to repudiate as spurious, and in particular it will be necessary to distinguish carefully between Mysticism and all mere psychism, or psychic or ' astral ' experiences, and even between Mysticism and so-called Occultism or Occult Science. Mysticism, again, is not mental healing, much less is it " Christian Science," whatever elements of truth—and they certainly have some—these may have in them.

[1] *Episc. Retract.*, I, xiii, 3.

We must not, however, lose sight of the fact that errors are as liable to reappear as truths ; indeed every revival of what we may broadly term ' good ' would seem to bring with it a proportional recrudescence of ' evil.' There would almost appear to be a general law—operative in this world at all events—whereby ' good ' and ' evil ' are equal and opposite quantities like action and reaction. We shall have occasion, however, to refer to this more fully in a subsequent chapter.

Mysticism has hitherto commonly fallen under the reproach of being visionary and unpractical. " That occupation with the spiritual world which is of the essence of Mysticism inevitably involves a view that at the least lightly esteems the world of sense."[1] This, however, is by no means found to be true as exemplified in the lives of its best exponents. It is the disease of Mysticism rather than its fruit, and we must judge largely of what is true and rational in the modern revival by the extent to which it is able to redeem Mysticism from this reproach. The fact that Mysticism is essentially religious in its nature, that its aims are peculiarly and specially spiritual, does not make it any the less potent for material results, but, indeed, quite the contrary, for it is the spiritual nature and quality in man which determines his material conditions and actions, and not the material which energises the spiritual.

Apart from this, however, we apprehend that it will be found to be one of the features of modern Mysticism that it will contain far less of ' other-worldliness ' than has hitherto perhaps been associated with the term. The modern mystic will not see in the great world-drama something which has somehow gone wrong with God's plans, neither will he see in his fleshly nature something essentially evil and degraded, and to be finally got rid of. He will rather see in the Cosmic Process an unfolding and revelation of the Self to Itself ; of that Eternal Principle which is his own Root Self ; and in his material body he will see an instrument whereby that unfolding is effected : a vehicle of consciousness to be gradually and carefully perfected in harmony with the great cosmic scheme of things of which he is a part.

Since the manifested universe exists in consciousness, we

---

[1] *Encyc. of Religion and Ethics*, vol. ix, p. 114.

must conclude that manifestation—what we know as ' matter,' or the objective counterpart of a subjective self—is a necessity, or attribute, or aspect of that deep Ground of our nature which we speak of as the One, or the Absolute, or the Divine. The great phenomenal world-process is in some way a necessary aspect or integral part of the One Noumenal Subject : that great LIFE, by which, and for which, and as which alone this whole Universe exists. And since this is so, we cannot but regard our own phenomenal, individual, or present embodied life, not merely as a part of that One Life which expresses itself in all this great activity of the Universe, but also as standing in a like phenomenal relationship to our own transcendental Subject or Ego.

Manifestation, phenomena, or appearance, means to our consciousness a limitation and a sequence in *time* and *space*. These are the two fundamental modes by which in our mind or consciousness the universal is particularised or individualised. This particularisation also brings with it opposition, contrast, and apparent separation ; yet, as we have elsewhere pointed out, whilst we only *know* this contrast and opposition, we are at the same time compelled to postulate an underlying unity in which this opposition must necessarily vanish. Our formal mind only grasps an *either-or*, whilst at the same time we clearly intuit an *as-well-as*.

Modern Mysticism, then, must be distinguished by a much clearer apprehension of the *as-well-as*. It will not be an abandonment of the manifested for the unmanifested, of the individual and particular for an abstract unity, but it will be a much clearer apprehension of both of these, the one *as well as* the other, as mutually complementary aspects of the one great Whole. Doubtless by reaching within ourselves to a much fuller and deeper realisation of our true divine nature we shall presently transmute our knowledge of the individual, particular, or phenomenal, into something quite incomprehensible to our present faculties and understanding ; we shall possess phenomenal powers—the true art of creation—which at present are not even recognised in any form, even as ' divine ' powers. But in thus attaining we shall not leave behind us the ' created ' world, as it were in a flight from one part of ourselves to another part vaguely regarded now as something ' higher,' as something contained only in the 'future,' or as something more 'real' than the present contains.

Reality is not one part of the Universe, or of our own nature, as a set-off against another part; it is rather a Wholeness and Completeness. Our true apprehension of Unity must include phenomenon as well as Noumenon, diversity as well as Unity, evil as well as Good. A true and deeper knowledge of ourselves—and there is really no other knowledge—will certainly intensify our present sense of the indissoluble connection and inter-relation of 'spirit' and 'matter,' and will not elevate the one at the expense of the other. They may appear now to be related as image and reflection, but they both *are* in consciousness—" appearances appear"; and perchance we could not know the apprehender without the appearance.

A rational Mysticism, then, will not fly from the definite to the indefinite, but rather will strive not merely to make the indefinite more definite, but also to enrich and ennoble the present definite, to transmute and transform it to a higher power and quality in our consciousness.

> " Nothing's truly seen that's mean:
> Be it sand, an acorn or a bean,
> It must be cloth'd with endless glory
> Before its perfect story
> Can in its Causes and its Ends appear." [1]

In another place Traherne says:

" Suppose a river, or a drop of water, an apple or a sand, an ear of corn or an herb: God knoweth infinite excellences in it more than we: He seeth how it relateth to angels and men; how it proceedeth from the most perfect Lover to the most perfectly Beloved; how it representeth all His attributes; how it conduceth in its place, by the best of means to the best of ends: and for this cause it cannot be beloved too much. God the Author and God the End is to be beloved in it; and it is highly to be esteemed for all their sakes." [2]

Compare with this Eckhart's:

" The meanest thing that one knows in God—for instance if one could understand a flower as it has its being in God—this would be a higher thing than the whole world." [3]

---

[1] Thomas Traherne, *Poems*, p. 84.
[2] *Centuries of Meditations*, ii, 67.
[3] *Mystische Schriften*, p. 137.

Tennyson's "Flower in a crannied nook" also expresses the same mystical thought. That some such transfiguration into "endless glory" can actually take place in our perception of the meanest objects is testified in the following extract from a recently published anonymous and extremely beautiful little mystical work :

"An object of quite ordinary charm seemed, because of that something which now filled me, to expand into prodigious beauty ! The very pavements and houses, mean and hideous as they are, overflowed with some inexplicable glamour. The world was turned into a veritable paradise ! When I thought of it all I was filled with amazement, and still am, for how can we explain such changes in manner of living and seeing ? " [1]

All this may possibly be irrational in a scholastic sense, or in the same sense that all æsthetic perception lies outside of our rational faculty ; but it is surely the highest reason of our whole nature to accept such facts of consciousness as in some degree indicating what might be our normal perception of the objective universe were we rightly to apprehend its nature as expressive of the infinite richness of our own, in our unity with the One Life which lives and moves and has its Being in ALL.

That Mysticism in the past has been largely associated with 'other-worldliness' cannot be denied, but no one who has penetrated beneath the mere historical surface, or who has understood in any degree the limitations of language, its inability to express what lies in consciousness beyond the mere formal mind—no one in fact who has understood in the slightest degree what Mysticism really is as a supreme achievement and quality of life and consciousness—could speak of it as having for its object "the attainment of the intensest form of *unconsciousness*," or of "the dissolution of the soul" as being "an error into which the true mystic inevitably falls." [2] As if, indeed, there could be any *forms* of unconsciousness, or any degrees thereof. Much nearer the mark is the statement of Professor Royce :

"For the mystic, according to the genuinely historical definition of what constitutes speculative Mysticism, to be real means to be in

---

[1] *The Golden Fountain*, p. 31.
[2] *Mysticism in Heathendom and Christendom*, by Dr. E. Lehmann, Professor of Divinity in the University of Berlin, pp. 88, 89.

such wise Immediate that, in the presence of this immediacy, all thought and all ideas, absolutely satisfied, are quenched, so that the finite search ceases, and the Other is no longer another, but is absolutely found." [1]

The manifested universe exists in our consciousness as a great fact, as a part of the Wholeness of our own nature. Our knowledge of it as law, order, succession in time and extension in space, limitation and relativity, constitutes what we know as Science and Philosophy; and this objective or formal knowledge is as necessary for the rational mystic as is the deep inward experience and knowledge attained in higher or deeper states of consciousness—not of "unconsciousness"—of his indissoluble and blissful union and oneness with the great LIFE of All. That One Life brings forth and sustains the whole 'Creation,' and the true mystic will seek to understand rationally and scientifically his connection and powers in the phenomenal as well as in the Noumenal.

One of the principal characteristics of Mysticism is undoubtedly the intense bliss which the mystic experiences in the realisation of his unity with the One Life, and the surrender of his personal will to the 'divine will.' The fact of this soul-satisfying rapture is undeniable, but at the same time it has too often been taken as proof of much with which it has no necessary connection. The rapture of the lover is undeniable, but so also is only too often his blindness to obvious facts. We forgive the lover, however, for the sake of love itself. The modern rational mystic will view these emotional states with a calmer and more balanced mind. He will apply to certain states of consciousness a much wider and deeper knowledge of psychology than has hitherto obtained, and will take account of the known power of suggestion and auto-suggestion. The modern mystic will hardly be satisfied with a bare emotional element, either as proof of a traditional theology, or as sufficing to fill up the measure of his search and effort. Doubtless he will have his hours of exultation, the deepest and fullest satisfaction of his emotional nature, and a sense of the all-sufficing value of his close contact with a divine and universal Love. This will certainly eclipse anything which this world alone can give, but yet it will

[1] Josiah Royce, *The World and the Individual*, Gifford Lectures, First Series, Lecture IV.

not be obtained by abandoning this world, but rather by and through it, by that inner sense which penetrates beneath the mere outward appearance of things and sees the One Divine Life operating in and through all, and which thereby fills each moment, and every point of space, with the fulness of the Whole. He may have his hours of deepest ecstasy, of trance, or of vision, which may be " unconsciousness " so far as the physical senses are concerned, but yet, as Tennyson says of his own experience, " the clearest of the clearest, the surest of the surest, utterly beyond words, the loss of personality (if so it were) seeming no extinction, but the only true life."[1]

The mystic of whom we speak will endeavour, then, to combine wisely the subjective and the objective as necessary and complementary parts of the great Whole. Subjectively he may recognise the validity—the only validity—of states of consciousness, and the internal faculty whereby truth is directly perceived and certainly known. Objectively he will recognise, in the words of Charles Kingsley, that " the great Mysticism is the belief that all symmetrical natural objects are types of some spiritual truth or existence . . . this earth is the next greatest fact to that of God's existence."[2] I think, indeed, the modern mystic may go even further than that, and decline to recognise the one fact as greater than the other.

In all these matters and directions the modern mystic will be a student of such objective mystics and seers as Böhme, or in a lesser degree Swedenbourg, rather than of such purely subjective mystics as Suso or St. Theresa, or even of Ruysbroeck or Eckhart. Böhme undoubtedly possessed, in addition to his subjective spiritual insight, a perception of the relation between the inner hidden nature, the *life* of things, and their outward appearance and properties. Had he had the necessary intellectual training—or possibly had he been permitted to do so—his knowledge, properly formulated, would undoubtedly have put to shame all our boasted modern scientific attainments, utterly inadequate as they are to explain even the origin of physical matter in the Ether of space.

But Böhme teaches clearly that the inner ' spiritual '

---

[1] *Life of Tennyson*, vol. i, p. 320.   [2] *Life*, vol. i, p. 55.

perception is not a mere subjective 'state of consciousness,' but is one which also opens the mind to a clear perception and knowledge of the true value and relation and proportion of the phenomenal world. If we make due allowances for the language he uses as the product of the times in which he lived, and especially for the theological form into which most of his work is thrown, we shall find that his real principles are independent of this language and form, and that he was a true objective as well as a subjective mystic. He distinguishes clearly between " the light of nature," or of the natural mind, and the inner spiritual insight or apprehension of universal principles; but at the same time he teaches that the " light of nature " will only reach its proper attainment by and through the development of the spiritual faculty. Thus in *The Supersensual Life* he says:

" Wherefore seek the Fountain of Light, waiting in the deep Ground of thy Soul for the rising there of the Sun of Righteousness, whereby the Light of Nature in thee, with the Properties thereof, will be made to shine seven Times brighter than ordinary. For it shall receive the Stamp, Image, and Impression of the Supersensual and Supernatural; so that the sensual and rational Life will hence be brought into the most perfect Order and Harmony."

This is plainly a confirmation of Neo-Platonic doctrine, though Böhme knew nothing of philosophical systems. In Plotinus [1] we find the following:

" He, however, who receives that light which is the fountain of truth, beholds as it were more acutely visible objects; but the contrary is not true."

Böhme goes even further, and says:

" Without the light of nature there is no understanding of divine mysteries." [2]

That is the very essence of a rational Mysticism, and is what many besides Böhme and Plotinus have endeavoured to express in such language as they could command: halting enough at times no doubt, and mere confusion and imagination to the matter-of-fact scholar or theologian, but understandable enough to those who have already caught some glimpse of the light which shines beyond our formal systems and materialistic thinking.

[1] *Enn.* V, iii, 8.　　　　　[2] *Epistles*, iv, 13.

Speaking now from personal experience, one may assert confidently that the demand of the present day for a higher and a deeper knowledge will assuredly be adequately met. "Seek and ye shall find" is not a promise, it is a natural law. Nevertheless, it is not mere curiosity which will be satisfied. Not now, any more than in the past, will the deepest secrets of nature become the common property of the age, for the age is not ready for them. Our social conditions, the greed for wealth, the nations in arms, the application of the utmost resources of Science to the invention of more and more destructive weapons : all these forbid that further powers should be placed in the hands of mankind in general.

We do not doubt that there will be many who will speak out of the fulness of their own knowledge ; but their language as in the past will be guarded, will be for the understanding mind and the purified heart—and, after all, the real seekers are still but few.

The deepest secrets of nature, the great structural facts of the Universe, are not matters of physics and chemistry, nor can they ever be demonstrated to the intellect like a proposition of Euclid. They are *living* facts, fatefully connected with the life of each individual, and only to be discovered and demonstrated *within* the individual, by and for himself. They are matters to be experienced rather than demonstrated ; not by an intellectual apprehension of truth merely, but by a living and vital contact therewith. Our highest, and deepest, and most precious experiences, the things which we really *know* because they are part of our being, are precisely those which we cannot demonstrate or prove to others. What, for example, is the mathematical, the physical and chemical, or even the intellectual demonstration, as expressible in language, of that deepest quality of life which we term Love ? We do but waste our words on the air if we speak of this to one who has never experienced the emotion in at least some of its phases.

And even so must it be with the final language of Mysticism. It can only be understood by those who have themselves experienced. For the others—it would be better if they would refrain from criticism, even as it would be better if a man who has no sense of beauty would refrain from posing as an art critic. The artist may not always be a master of technic, but it is the *idea* that is the living thing in him, not the picture. The mystic may not always be a master of language, but it is the truth which he endeavours to express that we should do well to seize ; and learn also to make a proper allowance for the inadequacy of language to express the deepest truths. No one knows better than the greatest master of technic how inadequate are the materials with which he has to work ; no one realises more clearly than the greatest master of language how little language can express of the living truth with which his inmost nature is on fire.

In the subsequent chapters, then, I shall aim at presenting in the first place something of the substance and basis of a Rational Mysticism in what we already know as Science, Philosophy, and Religion ; and in the second place I shall endeavour to set forth the root principles of Mysticism as found in all ages, and apart from the mere historical forms in which these principles have found expression from time to time as the result of the environment of manners, customs, and language into which they have been cast.

Christian Mysticism, as belonging specially to our Western World and age, may perhaps claim a foremost position ; but this form of Mysticism, when stripped of its special Christian terminology and theology, will be found to be in no wise different from the fundamental principles of Mysticism in all ages. What we require, in short, are principles, not forms.

Mysticism being essentially the realisation within the individual of oneness with the Universal or Cosmic Life and Consciousness, I apprehend that as our nature evolves and expands and experiences in a region lying beyond our present limited consciousness, and beyond the grasp of intellect expressible only in formal concepts—or " convenient fictions " as Vaihinger calls them in his *Philosophy of the ' As If '*— there will be a corresponding *rationality* which will give the fullest satisfaction to our sense of the rightness and fitness of things—a satisfaction, indeed, which is very far from being attained by means of our present ratiocinative faculties. It may be that such a rationality, due to the enormously widened range and outlook of the higher or deeper Self, will be such as to make the feeble guesses at truth of our so-called rational mind, the relation and proportion in which we at present view the facts of our life and consciousness, appear altogether distorted and irrational. Our rationality at present is only the rationality of a relation and proportion among external objects, differentiated in time and space, and made *static*. Both intellect and language—as Bergson so well shows—are only adapted to these *artificial* distinctions. The *reality* lies behind and within, in the *dynamic* continuum of Life itself.

Let us proceed, therefore, to work our way up through Science, Philosophy, and formal Religion into the pure free atmosphere of a Mysticism which transcends but does not abandon these, but on the contrary gives to them a validity and a meaning which they must ever lack until they are interpreted in the light of Man's higher divine nature and permanent Centre of Life and Consciousness, which we term the ONE LIFE.

CHAPTER II

PHYSICAL SCIENCE AND MYSTICISM

" I must make a confession, even if it be humiliating. I have never been able to form the slightest conception of those ' forces ' which the Materialists talk about, as if they had samples of them many years in bottle. By the hypothesis, the forces are not matter ; and thus all that is of any particular consequence in the world turns out to be not matter on the Materialist's own showing. Let it not be supposed that I am casting a doubt upon the propriety of the employment of the terms ' atom ' and ' force,' as they stand among the working hypotheses of physical science. As formulæ which can be applied, with perfect precision and great convenience, in the interpretation of nature, their value is incalculable ; but, as real entities, having an objective existence, an indivisible particle which nevertheless occupies space is surely inconceivable ; and with respect to the operation of that atom, where it is not, by the aid of a ' force ' resident in nothingness, I am as little able to imagine it as I fancy anyone else is."

T. H. Huxley : *Science and Morals.*

CHAPTER II

PHYSICAL SCIENCE AND MYSTICISM

THE manner in which physical science contributes to a Monistic Philosophy such as we shall find to be essential to a Rational Mysticism by confirming the fundamental principle of the Unity of the Universe, has been dealt with by me in detail in *Scientific Idealism* ; but it will be as well for the sake of those who have not read that work, as also in order that the present work may be as far as possible complete in itself, to recapitulate here in a brief summary the main facts and their deductions.

Modern physical science has come to the aid of Monistic Philosophy in a most striking manner ; one which not merely supplies us in its very simplest form with the concept of a Unitary Principle at the root of all phenomena, but which affords us also along the whole line of our present inquiry some remarkable analogies and correspondences.

Modern science has now definitely come into line with ancient philosophical teaching by means of its discovery of the close relation which exists between the Ether of Space and what we know as physical matter. As the result of this discovery, modern science now postulates the existence of a space-filling *Substance* in which all that we know as *matter* exists simply as a *mode of motion ;* what we know in general as *force* being also motion of a specific kind in and of this primordial Root Substance. All phenomena, in fact the whole universe of matter and force, both what is perceived by us or lies within the region of our present consciousness, as well as an infinite range of phenomena lying beyond that region, are referred back to this Root Substance, which at present is identified by scientists with the Ether of Space. In *Scientific Idealism*, however, I have shown that the true Root-Substance must necessarily lie beyond the Ether ; but it is sufficient for our present purpose that the Ether stands for a continuous space-filling Substance which completely obliterates the concept of matter as being something discrete and atomic *per se*.

It is true that the existence of the Ether has recently been severely challenged by certain physicists on the ground that it does not enter in any manner into the differential equations of actual mathematical physics, and because all experimental efforts to appreciate it as a material substance having a definite calculable relation to material particles in which mass and velocity can be observed, have so far failed to give any indication of its existence. This *negative* evidence is, however, an extremely dangerous ground for the absolute denial of the existence of the Ether. We need only remind our readers of the very positive assertions which were made last century that the atom of physical matter never had been and never would be resolved into anything else, simply on the basis that all experimental efforts had failed to effect this, and that no observed facts were known which in the least degree showed it to be likely. Since then the atom has been resolved ; and to-morrow the existence of the Ether may, and probably will be, an experimental fact. It is erroneously supposed by many that the Einstein theory of Relativity disposes finally of the necessity for an Ether of Space, but this is a misconception as to the nature and scope of the theory. The theory of Relativity is only concerned directly with the motions of physical bodies, and although it is based on the (assumed) constancy of the velocity of light *in vacuo*, it does not even need to concern itself with any theory of light. Neither theory of light, theory of matter, nor existence of Ether is relevant to the scope of the Einstein theory. Professor Einstein says :

" As a result of the more careful study of electro-magnetic phenomena, we have come to regard action at a distance as a process impossible without the intervention of some intermediary medium. . . . We are constrained to imagine—after the manner of Faraday—that the magnet always calls into being something physically real in the space around it, that something being what we call a ' magnetic field ' . . . With the aid of this conception electro-magnetic phenomena can be theoretically represented much more satisfactorily than without it, and this applies particularly to the transmission of electro-magnetic waves. The effects of gravitation also are regarded in an analogous manner." [1]

[1] A. Einstein, *Relativity*; trans. R. W. Lawson, D.Sc., p. 63.

That is to say, it is only necessary for the purposes of the Relativity theory to consider that in the presence of matter there is a gravitational ' field ' which possesses certain properties, and any relation of this ' field ' to the Ether is quite beyond the scope of the theory. We must further note here that the concept of a four-dimensional space-time which is associated with the Einstein theory has largely relegated to the background in the minds of many physicists the concept and theories of a space-filling Ether ; but it has by no means disposed of the necessity of the concept as a working hypothesis in connection with electro-magnetic theory.

Thus Professor Eddington, speaking of the relation of the Ether to the space-time world or *continuum*, says :

"If a substantial æther analogous to a material ocean exists, it must rigidify, as it were, a definite space ; and whether the observer or whether nature pays any attention to that space or not, a fundamental separation of space and time must be there. Some would cut the knot by denying the æther altogether. We do not consider that desirable, or, so far as we can see, possible ; but we do deny that the æther need have such properties as to separate space and time in the way supposed." [1]

The question is really a side-issue between the physicists who wish to confine themselves strictly to observed facts which can be dealt with mathematically, and those who wish to push their concepts still further and in a more speculative manner. In the main it is the issue as between Relativity and Continuity as *ultimates* in physical concepts ; and it has its corresponding issue in metaphysics as between a Pluralistic and a Monistic universe. Doubtless our empirical experience is wholly on the side of Relativity and Pluralism ; but there is another and a deeper experience which forbids us to take empirical facts, or mere Pragmatism, as our ultimate and final appreciation of Reality. We shall, therefore, take the Ether of Space as conceived by those scientists who believe firmly in its existence, and use the concept as our first stepping-stone to that ultimate Unity and Continuity to which Mysticism is a witness in actual states of consciousness. The concept of a Space-Time " Ether of Events," will serve equally well for those who prefer to think in these terms. Thus Professor Eddington speaks of space-time as, " this undivided fourfold

[1] *Space Time and Gravitation*, p. 39.

order (which) is the same for all observers." [1]   Also, " We believe that there are absolute things in the world—not only matter, but certain characteristics of empty space or Æther.[2] And again, " What we have called the *world* might perhaps have been legitimately called the Æther ; at least it is the universal substance of things which the relativity theory gives us in place of the Æther."[3] We shall, therefore, continue to call this scientific ' substratum ' *Ether*, whilst ·in the further philosophical concept we term it *Primordial Substance.*

Etheric Substance is said to fill " all space " ; by which is meant not merely that it extends outwards to the utmost conceivable limits of space—of which there are none—but also that it fills all space in an inward direction ; in other words it is a *continuous* Substance, without holes or interstices. Euclidean space is here taken as a concrete reality ; the metaphysical question as to the subjective nature of space being conveniently ignored.

This concept is all the more simple and clear—and serves, therefore, the better for our starting-point—because physical science has no need to concern itself with any question as to the existence of life and consciousness in the cosmic nature of this Substance, or with metaphysical questions such as the fundamental one of the relation of Subject and Object, or the nature of Consciousness, as a subjective fact, to the phenomenal world of matter and force as an objective fact. Treating the Ether as a dead mechanical thing, even such a question as to how motion *per se* could arise in, or be an attribute of, this mechanically conceived Root Substance, is too metaphysical for modern science, notwithstanding that the idea of the indestructibility of Motion lies at the root of its favourite doctrine of the Conservation of Energy.

By thus conveniently ignoring all the really fundamental philosophical questions, modern science vastly simplifies the problem, and we may take it in the first place in this simplified form in order to pave the way for the more abstruse questions which we shall presently have to face.

Let us see, then, in the first instance, how modern science has been compelled to abandon the materialism and dualism

---

[1] *Space Time and Gravitation*, p. 36.
[2] *Ibid.*, p. 42.   [3] *Ibid.*, p. 187.

of last century—the dualism of matter and ether—and the dogma of the indestructibility of physical matter *per se*, and has fallen back upon the old philosophical concept of a unitary space-filling Substance as the root and ground of all that appears in the phenomenal world.

The indestructibility of matter, as held so rigidly and dogmatically down to the very end of last century, meant the indestructibility of the physical atom or chemical ' element.' It involved the conception that every chemical substance which was irresolvable into anything else, consisted of ultimate particles or atoms having exactly the same characteristics as those which the substance exhibited in bulk. It was in fact a crude realistic view, based upon the idea that if we could only reduce a substance to small enough parts, we should presently come to finality : to something which refused to be divided any more—in fact to the ultimate *atom*.[1]

But the fact that this ' atom ' must still have extension in space, must still be an object of some bulk, however small, raised a very serious difficulty, for anything which has size can be subdivided—at all events in imagination—*ad infinitum*. A fierce controversy raged round this question of infinite divisibility. The more materialistic physicists, such as Büchner, would have none of it ; for—as Büchner recognised— " to accept infinite divisibility is absurd (for the materialist) and amounts to doubting the very existence of matter."

This difficulty, however, could be conveniently shelved by the physicists as being a purely ' metaphysical ' one, and therefore unworthy of their attention, or at all events as not affecting the actual physical phenomena with which they had to deal. For all intents and purposes the atom existed in chemical combinations as a permanent indivisible unit.

But there was another purely physical difficulty which could not be so conveniently set aside. It was the question as to whether this ultimate particle or atom was hard and rigid, or whether it was elastic in its nature.

Sir Isaac Newton conceived of matter as being composed of : " Solid, massy, hard, impenetrable, immovable particles . . . so very hard as never to wear or break to pieces ; no ordinary power being able to divide what God Himself made one in the first creation."

[1] Gr. *a*, not *temnō*, to cut.

The scientific dogmatists of the nineteenth century never got beyond this view—though there were a few notable exceptions. Atoms were confidently announced to be " the foundation-stones of the material universe, unbroken and unworn. They continue this day as they were created—perfect in number and measure and weight."[1]

This view of the atom was, indeed, absolutely essential to the materialistic atomo-mechanical conception of the universe which then prevailed, and which arose as a reaction against the superstitious supernaturalism which had for so long a time held sway over men's minds as the result of the ecclesiastical authority which had been imposed on the western world for so many centuries.

It will be seen that with both Newton and Clerk Maxwell the idea of matter as a ' created ' article still dominated the situation. Any awkward questions of a metaphysical nature could be conveniently referred to a ' creator '; and though the idea of creation was scorned by the materialists, who held that physical matter was the *fons et origo* of everything —including consciousness itself—yet it may be said that the very general idea about matter which dominated most minds during the whole of last century, and which is perhaps still the popular one, was a crude realism tinged with a theological dogma.

But there remained some awkward physical facts and questions, foremost among which was the one we have already mentioned as to the elasticity or non-elasticity of the atom or ultimate particle. Many physical phenomena demand that the atom should be absolutely elastic, and especially must this be so if the doctrine of the Conservation of Energy is to remain valid. Two hard rigid particles meeting in direct collision would have their motions absolutely destroyed, and thus energy, considered merely as the product of mass and velocity, would also be destroyed. In order that no energy should be lost it would be necessary for each particle to rebound with the same velocity which it possessed on impact; but in order to do this it would have to be absolutely elastic. If elastic, however, it must either be composed of parts which could yield—and therefore presumably it would be divisible— or else some extraordinary physical property would have to

[1] Clerk Maxwell, *British Association*, 1873.

be attributed to it which would make it incompressible and indivisible, and at the same time elastic.

To Lord Kelvin belongs the merit of having endeavoured to overpass these and other difficulties by means of a theory of matter altogether free from the deadening weight of the ultimate particle theory which at that time held dominion with the great majority of scientists, and which is even not yet quite destroyed in the minds of some of the more conservative. As far back as 1867 Lord Kelvin—following up the doctrine of matter advanced by Descartes—put forward his celebrated vortex-atom theory, in which it was postulated that the physical atom consisted of a vortex-ring, or other similar motion in the Substance of the Ether of Space. This theory, however, met with scant approval; it was a long way ahead of its time, and down to the very end of last century physical matter was generally regarded as a thing *per se*, between which and the Ether there was no causal relation.

But with the dawn of the twentieth century a new fact was discovered—a most momentous fact, the importance of which to Science, to Philosophy, and even to Religion, is hardly as yet fully realised.

It was found that the atoms of physical matter are *not* indestructible; that in the case of Radium and a few other substances the atoms are actually and spontaneously breaking up or disintegrating into smaller bodies, to which the name of *corpuscle* or *electron* has been given, and which are only about one hundred-thousandth of the size of the atom itself.

It is now certain that all the so-called elementary substances, or chemical atoms, are built up of varying numbers of these smaller bodies, which are practically atoms of electricity; and that all physical matter is undergoing a process of disintegration, or at least is capable of being disintegrated, though the process is too slow in the case of most of the elements for it to be detected by means of our present physical appliances.

But although the dogma of the indestructibility of matter has thus broken down so far as the chemical atoms are concerned, it might be argued that these smaller bodies, these corpuscles or electrons, may still be minute " solid, massy, hard, impenetrable particles "; and, indeed, this view can hardly be said to have been finally relinquished by our more materialistic scientists. The atomo-mechanical theory of the universe is not yet quite dead in some minds, and the existence of a definite ultimate particle, with the irreducible minimum qualities of mass and extension in space, is still considered to be essential for any but a metaphysical view of matter.

But the theory which now really holds the field is practically the same as that enunciated by Lord Kelvin in 1867. It is the continuous-fluid theory, the theory that physical matter is some form of motion in, or modification of, the Ether of Space. This theory is not merely a far more philosophical one than that of ultimate particles, but it is also supported by some very cogent physical facts, principally the close connection which is now found to exist between physical matter and electricity : the newly discovered corpuscles behaving more like units of electricity than units of physical matter. The electron is an irreducible unit of negative electricity, and the physical atom of matter is now conceived to consist of a central unit of positive electricity round which these negative electrons circulate, as the planets do round our central sun. The atom of matter is a miniature solar system.

According to the new theory, then, the corpuscles or electrons of which the physical atom is composed are some specific kind of motion in this 'fluid' Ether of Space—possibly a vortex-ring, or a 'knot,' or whorl, or 'centre of force'—whilst such manifestations as light, heat, electricity, etc., are other forms or modes of motion ; more specifically, waves or undulations. In fact, not merely all matter, but also all force or energy, is referred to this one universal medium or Substance ; and whereas last century physical science was obliged to regard Matter and Ether as two different things, and to postulate that the phenomenal world was the result of the action and interaction of the three factors, Matter, Ether, and Motion : to-day we have only two factors, Ether and Motion. " We need not regard matter," says Professor Eddington, "as a foreign entity causing a disturbance in the gravitational field ; the disturbance is matter . . . matter is a symptom not a cause."[1]

This immensely simplifies the philosophical problem, though the physical difficulty as to the exact nature of

[1] *Space Time and Gravitation*, p. 190.

the atom still remains, or is, if anything, more complex than ever, for it involves in a concrete form the still deeper question as to the nature of the Ether itself.

At the beginning of last century the Ether was merely a hypothetical medium for the transmission of light; the sole demand made upon it by physicists was that it should 'undulate.' Even here, however, they were not very happy, and there were many obscurities in the so-called undulatory theory of light. The nature of the Ether, even to account for the transmission of light, was found to be not merely a puzzle but also a paradox; the Ether having to be incomparably more 'rigid' or 'dense' than anything that we know as physical matter. With the progress of scientific discovery, the all-importance of the Ether, and the part which it must necessarily play in every possible physical phenomenon, came to be more and more clearly recognised; and with each advance the problem as to its constitution and nature became more and more difficult. The theories which have been elaborated by various scientists are multifarious and mutually destructive; and it appears to be as difficult for the physicist to say what the Ether is, without using paradoxical terms, as it is for the mystic to say what is that deeper region of consciousness which he actually experiences or contacts in his moments of vision or ecstasy. So great is the difficulty, so far beyond the reach of our physical faculties or of physical analogies does the Ether appear to be, that, as already noted, some scientists are frankly giving up the problem, and relegating the Ether to the realm of metaphysical speculation

It is worth while here to note the difficulty which exists equally for the scientist and for the mystic immediately either of these has to deal with a super-physical region of fact or experience. The difficulty lies mainly in our common conventional or physical perception of things, and a language which is only adapted thereto. In order to give a physical explanation of things we must define them in terms of our ordinary sense-perceptions, or we must treat them by mathematical analysis based upon experimental physical phenomena. When we attempt to do this for the Ether, however, we are immediately landed in a paradox, and we have to recognise that any physical analogies which we may employ in order to define it are contradictions of our 'common sense.'

When, for example, we endeavour to transfer to the Ether our fundamental idea of matter as having mass or density, we find that the density of the Ether must be incomparably greater than that of the densest physical matter with which we are acquainted. It is estimated by Sir J. J. Thompson as about " two thousand million times that of lead." And yet to us this ' dense ' substance is impalpable and invisible : in fact utterly inappreciable and non-existent ; and we move freely through it without even a vestige of friction which we can physically detect. Not only so, but the Ether also flows freely through us, through what are to us dense solids, as well as through liquids and gases.

Further, we have nothing in physics corresponding to a continuous medium : a medium that is to say filling all space without interstices, and therefore non-atomic. All our physical dynamics are based on the theory of discrete particles or atoms, having a definite mass, and all our mathematics similarly treat time and space as something consisting of definitely separable ' moments,' though physicists are only just beginning to perceive that their ' point-moments ' and instantaneous ' time-events ' are the merest abstract metaphysical conceptions having no reality in actual experience. They are ' convenient fictions ' only. All physical matter is for practical purposes atomic or molecular in its structure, even though it appears to our senses to be continuous. Although our strongest magnifying powers fail to disclose to us the discontinuity of a piece of ' solid ' matter, the interstices between the atoms and molecules, yet from other considerations physicists are bound to come to the conclusion that " matter is mainly composed of holes " and that these holes are filled with the all-pervading Ether of Space, which streams through them as if our most solid matter consisted of " a bird-cage kind of structure in which the volume of the Ether displaced by the wires when the structure is moved is infinitesimal in comparison with the volume enclosed by them."[1]

This analogy, however, is not a very apt one, since it does not provide us with an adequate mental picture of the structure of a so-called *solid* piece of matter. Not merely is the solidity absolutely deceptive, but so also is the apparent inertness of

[1] Sir J. J. Thompson, *British Association*, 1910.

the individual particles. The real fact is that the apparent motionlessness of so-called *dead* matter is the result of the inconceivably rapid motion of its constituent molecules, atoms, and corpuscles; and all *mass* or *inertia* is due to the same cause. If we would picture to ourselves aright the internal structure of the smallest grain of matter which we can see, even with the aid of a microscope, we should perceive in it a whole universe, comparable in every respect as regards size, space, and motion to the galaxy of worlds which we see when we look outwards into space; for if every individual *corpuscle* could be magnified to the size of our world, it would be found that the intervening spaces would be comparable to the distances between the Sun, Planets, and Stars. " Matter," says Sir Oliver Lodge,[1] "is porous to an extraordinary degree, as porous as a solar system." This refers to matter in bulk, but it is further estimated that even in the atom itself, when we consider the size of its constituents, there is at least 99·99 per cent. of empty space.

Matter, therefore, is not what it seems, the illusion of the senses is complete: not in any metaphysical terms merely, but in sober physical fact; and thus science itself provides the first step out of Realism towards Mysticism, the first essential of which is the realisation that things are *not* what they seem.

But if physical matter is in reality such a thin gossamer-like structure; if the atoms and molecules are as far apart compared with their size as are the stars and planets: what is it that holds them together in a structural form? The component parts of the atom—the corpuscles or electrons or sub-atoms—are moving with enormous velocities within the limits of the atom. When the atom breaks up they are shot out with a velocity approaching that of light—186,000 miles per second. What then is it that holds them together in the first instance, so that the atom itself is a solar system in miniature, and the combination of atoms into molecules is a still larger system, whilst a small piece of so-called solid matter is a whole universe of countless worlds and systems?[2]

The only answer to these questions is once more—the

---

[1] *Fortnightly Review*, January 1920.
[2] A speck of matter barely visible with the highest power microscope has been estimated to contain a million millions of atoms (1,000,000,000,000).

Ether of Space.   It is the Ether which is the ' medium,' the ensouling power, which holds the atoms as well as the Suns and Planets in their proper places and courses.   Our immediate physical concept of this action takes the form of certain ' lines of force ' acting between the component parts of the atom, and between the atoms themselves, to form the more complete system which we call a molecule.   It is also this same Ether which acts between the larger molecules which we call Solar Systems, to form the vast universe of the starry heavens.   Physical science at present pictures these ' lines of force ' as analogous to those which are made visible around the poles of a magnet when we scatter iron filings on a sheet of paper underneath which the magnet is held. They are some form of energy, some form of *motion*, in the *substance* of the Ether.

But if this is so, it is obvious that the real *substantiality* is not our so-called solid matter at all, but the impalpable, invisible, immaterial Ether itself.   Physical matter is but the filmiest, gauziest whiff of vapour in this ' dense ' Ether whose potent grasp supports the structure alike of atoms and of universes.   The real substantiality of, say, a steel chain supporting a hundred tons, is not the physical matter which we see with our eyes, but it is these same ' lines of force ' in the invisible Ether.   What really holds the weight is not our ' solid ' matter, not the merely visible links of the chain, not that which alone we think of as ' real '; but it is the ' lines of force ' stretching from corpuscle to corpuscle, from atom to atom, from molecule to molecule in that mysterious *Substance* which is the ' empty space ' of our physical senses. There is nothing in space to support the World, or the Sun, or the Stars, save that which is *innermost*.

Here, surely, we are meeting with a mysticism of science which matches, and confirms in every way, the mysticism of the intuitive philosopher, and the vision of the seer.   The mystic is essentially one who has perceived clearly that behind all this seeming reality there lies another order of things, a reality which in a certain sense may be said to be not merely more *real* than what now appears, but even exactly the opposite of that which is perceived by the physical senses ; which senses can, in or by themselves, never give to us a perception of more than the shadow of the real Substance.   A continuous medium or space-filling substance is exactly the opposite or antithesis of the discrete particles which we are compelled to regard as physical matter; and the real atom, instead of being the smallest of the small, is the largest of the large, for every so-called atom is nothing less in *substance* than the One Substance—which is the only thing in the Universe which cannot be divided or cut.

Every so-called physical atom becomes so only when considered in a certain limited relation and proportion. If we could see it in its entirety, in *all* its relations and proportions, we should perceive the whole Universe. This is not metaphysics, but plain straightforward physics. Thus Lord Kelvin says : " All the properties of matter are so connected that we can scarcely imagine one *thoroughly explained*, without our seeing its relation to all the others ; without, in fact, having the explanation of all."[1]

Here, then, modern science joins hands with, and shows the way to, the mystic, and is compelled to use the same language of paradox. The real substantiality, that which is more real in the sense of being more permanent, more enduring, more *inner*, is not physical matter, but something which lies quite beyond the reach of our senses. We live and move in it, and are interpenetrated and sustained by it ; no slightest physical phenomenon can take place without its co-operation, it thrills in every atom, it is the very *soul* of everything physical, yet we live and move all unconscious of its existence or of the part which it plays in every thought and act. It is sheer necessity which has driven science back upon this old philosophical concept of a space-filling Ether—or rather *Æther*. Physical things cannot explain themselves.

For the modern scientist this Ether of Space is the last and final word as to the material or substantial basis of the Universe. It is the Root Substance, the *Urstoff*, the *Prima Materia*. It is, in the language of Science as well as of Mysticism, " nothing to the senses yet All in reality."[2]

We may very well question, however, whether the Ether which is immediately responsible for our physical phenomena is in reality the true ultimate Substance : whether in fact

[1] *Popular Lectures*, Nature Series, vol. i, p. 240.
[2] " All mass is mass of the ether, all momentum, momentum of the ether, and all kinetic energy, kinetic energy of the ether."—Sir J. J. Thompson, *Electricity and Matter*, p. 51.

there are not other grades or planes of Substance as far removed in quality from the Ether of Science as that Ether is from physical matter. It is very doubtful whether the modern scientist has made any real advance out of materialistic realism into that of true philosophy. For modern physical science the Ether is still a *dead* Substance—Vogt's " pyknotic theory " notwithstanding.[1]

Modern science is in fact only unconsciously mystical : just as long ago it became unconsciously metaphysical, whilst professing all the time to scorn metaphysics. It is true that the scientist professes to deal only with facts as they arise— though he has not been unknown to reject them on *a priori* grounds. For the present the Ether would seem to be all-sufficient to cover his ground of observed facts, though the multifarious theories which have been invented as to the nature of the Ether amount to a different kind of Ether for each different class of phenomena. There is thus for science difficulty enough in trying to conceive what physical Ether may be, without imagining any further plane of Substance beyond the Ether.

We find Sir Oliver Lodge, in the *Fortnightly Review* for January 1920, denying the existence of more than one Ether as emphatically and as dogmatically as anything that has since been discovered was ever denied by any scientist of last century. The following are his words :

" I hold that there is only one ether so far discovered, or likely to be discovered. . . . Any talk about several ethers, or about an ether attached to the Earth, is nonsense ; and one would think can only be seriously suggested in order to bring into contempt the whole idea of a universal omnipresent continuous medium which welds the discrete particles of matter into an organised cosmos."

Doubtless if the Ether is defined as the ultimate substance of the universe, then there can be only one Ether— but that is begging the whole question.

There may be only one *physical* ether—which is all that the physicists have to deal with—but that this physical ether is the Primordial Substance of the whole Cosmos we shall deny on grounds which will become more apparent as we proceed.

We may point out here, however—with all due deference

[1] Cf. *Scientific Idealism*, p. 188.

to Sir Oliver Lodge and other scientists who hold that the ether is *structural*—that anything that is structural cannot fill *all* space. Structure implies form, and form implies differentiation, distinction; and that which is differentiated from or in a space-filling substance must necessarily be, *qua* form, something different from the pure substance itself, just as physical matter, *qua* matter, differs from the ether from which it is derived, and which it *is* in substance at the next remove. An all-space-filling substance must in fact be indistinguishable from space itself, and is a pure abstraction. Moreover, we must hold philosophically that bodies or forms existing in space are as infinitely divisible in an inner direction as they are extensible in an outer direction.

Meanwhile, we may note that there is no reason why the philosopher should not press his inquiry deeper than the Ether of Science, or why he should accept the Ether—or indeed any kind of 'matter'—as a *dead* substance. He finds much in ancient philosophy as well as in modern experience to teach him that it is not so, and also much to point to the conclusion that there may be several well-defined grades or planes of Substance on which consciousness can function beyond the experimental Ether of physical science, connected principally as this Ether is with the phenomena of light, electricity, and magnetism, and being in fact little removed from physical matter itself, and possibly a very low grade or differentiation of the real Primordial or Root Substance.

In *Scientific Idealism* I have pointed out that we may very well postulate at least four grades or planes of Substance in order to account for the phenomena of our life and consciousness as a whole, and not merely those associated with physics and chemistry. There is one fact, indeed, in physics itself which affords at least a philosophical reason for concluding that the Ether cannot be the ultimate Root Substance. Philosophically we are obliged to postulate that the Root Substance must be 'infinite' or 'absolute' in all its qualities or attributes. As soon as we get differentiation, or discrete modes of the One Substance—such as those special forms of motion, vortical or otherwise, which are supposed to constitute physical matter—we have something which, though all the time never anything else than the One Substance, yet has to be distinguished from it as a time and space phenomenon. It is something *limited*, as distinguished from the 'absolute' Substance itself.

Now there is every reason to believe that the Ether of Science is just as *structural* in its nature as is physical matter, and in the phenomenon of light we have a time and space phenomenon : the transmission of light through the Ether takes a measurable time, even though the velocity is enormous (186,000 miles per second) as compared with any velocities with which we are acquainted in physical objects. In any plane of Substance beyond the Etheric we should have in like manner to conceive that the velocities would be incomparably great as compared with those of etheric phenomena. At every remove, in fact, we get nearer and nearer to infinity or absoluteness—though that 'nearer' must be recognised as merely a form of our mental concept, analogous to the concept of the infinite divisibility of matter or the atom. We can never really reach the Absolute by any mere process of multiplication or addition, yet still, so long as it is not reached, we are always compelled to postulate something further. We are here in fact up against the problem of Space itself—a purely metaphysical problem. Since, however, we are now dealing with concepts, we must say that a differentiated form of Substance exhibiting time and space phenomena cannot be the timeless and spaceless original Substance itself ; it is still only a form or mode of motion which, as such, may conceivably have commenced in time, and may likewise in time come to an end, redissolved into some more cosmic mode of motion, or into the original Substance itself.

Now as regards the transmission of light at a definite and measurable velocity, it has been pointed out by Sir Oliver Lodge that the Ether has here : " given itself away. By transmitting waves at a finite and measurable speed . . . its properties are exhibited as essentially finite—however infinite the extent of it may be." So far then as this particular phenomenon is concerned, as well as in so far that the Ether is conceived of as being structural in its nature, it cannot be Primordial Substance pure and simple. It may turn out to be as atomic as physical matter itself. Once it has been admitted to be structural it can only be the ultimate Substance in precisely the same sense that physical matter, or any other *form* of the Root Substance, *is* that Substance. Let us remember that *size* of atoms has nothing whatever to do with the case. We may reduce atoms to the infinitesimal just as we may extend Solar Systems to the infinite; and if, as Sir Oliver Lodge says, physical matter is "as porous as a Solar System," there is plenty of room, not merely in between the atoms, but within the atoms themselves— each atom being a Solar System—for any number of atomic planes of quite another nature than the Ether, but too fine to be recognisable by any physical means.

Science speaks freely enough about the Ether as filling *all* space, simply because it shirks the little difficulty as to what space itself can be as a mode of consciousness; or as to where or how it can begin or end. It treats it in fact as a definite reality *per se*, which philosophy cannot do. But if science can now speak of the Ether as filling *all* space— that is to say, as being 'infinite' in this respect, it must certainly also recognise that in any quality or attribute whatsoever which we can postulate of it, it must also be 'infinite.' How this applies to the attribute of *motion* which we must necessarily give to it, we shall see more clearly in our next chapter.

In the meantime, however, we may be thankful to scientists for what they are able to give us. We see that we have a clearly defined concept of a space-filling unitary Substance which is all things, and thus we have a scientific concept— or rather we have Science coming into line with an ancient concept—which is in agreement with the philosophical and mystical one of the Unity of the Universe in one Absolute Principle.

Science admits that at least our physical bodies are formed of this Substance; and certainly any 'soul' we may possess, or anything in the way of a dynamical action upon matter by that 'soul;' any 'mind' we may have, not to mention 'spirit,' must equally be a mode of that all-embracing Substance: must owe its qualities and action to the inherent attributes of the Substance itself, and must be some modification, limitation, or mode of motion therein.

Plato wrote: "As our body is part of the body of the universe, thus also our soul is a part of the soul of the universe."

Now although modern science does not deal with ' soul,' yet it is obliged to deal with *motion*, and soul is essentially the inherent *moving* principle, the cause of motion of any organism, or of the universe. The Ether in this sense is certainly the *soul* of physical matter; whatever connection it may have with our larger life and consciousness. Modern science finds that the Ether is the great moving principle, the store-house of every form of physical energy. All physical energy comes to us from the Ether, and returns to the Ether, and matter itself is an etheric phenomenon.

Whatever modes of Substance there may be beyond the Ether we must say exactly the same of them. Each plane will be the ensouling principle of the one immediately below it, the one which has been differentiated or evolved out of it, just as the physical plane has been out of the Ether. The one Primordial Substance, however many removes it may be beyond the Ether, must, when considered in this manner, be the final summation of the series : the source from which all are derived, the eternal *continuum* into which all may be conceivably resolved. From IT all things proceed, to IT all things return, in that cosmic MOTION which is the ceaseless Breath of Eternal BEING. From IT all things proceed, yet they never *are* other than IT, either in outward material form or in inner energising power. " Other than IT there nothing since has been."[1]

" Thou art That," we found to be the final statement of a *Scientific Idealism*.

And what clearer description can we have from modern science of this all-pervading Substance than that which Plotinus gives us? After speaking of our physical world as a world of " sensible magnitudes and masses, each of which has an appropriate place, nor is it possible among these that the same thing should be in many places at once " : he goes on to say :

" But there is another essence opposed to this, which in no respect admits of a separation into parts, since it is without parts, and therefore impartible. It likewise admits of no interval, not even in conception, nor is it indigent of place, nor is generated in a certain being, either according to parts, or according to wholes, because it is as it were at one and the same time carried in all beings as in a vehicle;

[1] *Rig. Veda.*

not in order that it may be established in them, but because other things are neither able nor willing to exist without it." [1]

Some modern scientists are inclined to regard the Ether as having an exceedingly fine-grained, homogeneous structure; the 'grains' probably consisting of some minute form of vortical motion; but, as we have just pointed out, in so far as the Ether is in any respect regarded as being structural in its nature it is just precisely to that extent a departure from, or modification of, the One Substance itself. The structural formation may be regarded as a primitive or first differentiation, but it is clearly not the pure undifferentiated Substance; it is a mode of motion therein or thereof, and as such it might conceivably disappear. What then would be left? No *thing*, but not nothing. The One Substance itself would be left, but there would be no *form* of motion therein; anything that could be considered as objective 'matter' would have totally disappeared. The One Substance would be left, in its pure, eternal, immutable nature; and though all the phenomenal universe had come to an end, that Substance would presumably have within it the *potentiality* of evolving another universe.

If we press our inquiry further, and ask in what that *potentiality* consists, we shall immediately find ourselves floundering in the morass of speculative metaphysics. We may note here, however, that the idea that this One Root Principle or Substance does actually return to this primal undifferentiated state after an incalculable period of evolution and devolution, called a " Day of Brahmâ," is a very ancient concept of Hindu philosophy. The " Day of Brahmâ " is the period during which the objective universe is evolved and runs its appointed course, and it is followed by a " Night of Brahmâ," when all that is objective is again indrawn or dissolved into the One Substance-Principle, and disappears into pure subjectivity. [2]

---

[1] *Enn.*, IV, ii, 1.

[2] It is hardly likely that Shakespeare knew of this ancient philosophical concept when he wrote:

> "The cloud-capp'd towers, the gorgeous palaces,
> The solemn temples, the great globe itself,
> Yea, all which it inherit, shall dissolve
> And, like this insubstantial pageant faded,
> Leave not a rack behind."

But here we are passing into a region of philosophy which lies far beyond the province of modern science—or, for that matter, of modern philosophy. Physically considered, Primordial Substance is for modern science merely a hypothetical 'perfect fluid' in which various forms of motion can arise. It is a mathematical even more than a physical concept. Helmholtz investigated mathematically the properties of vortex-rings in such a hypothetical 'perfect fluid,' and he showed that they would exhibit the phenomena of mass or inertia, and of attraction and repulsion ; but he was unable to show how it would ever be possible to start them, or to break them up if once started.

Physical matter, then, or any 'matter' which may exist for us on any other plane of consciousness—for it is clearly seen in the relation of physical matter to the Ether that it is consciousness alone which determines what forms of motion are 'matter' and what are not—is a phenomenon of motion of Primordial Substance ; but *qua* matter it is not that Substance itself. We may thus say in the language of Mysticism that it both is and is not the One Substance. It is one in *substance* but not in *form*.

So also of the One Substance itself we must say that it both is and is not the objective manifested universe. It is the *Substance* of the universe, but not its *form* or appearance. It is both 'immanent' and 'transcendent.'

From IT all things proceed, and in IT all things exist ; yet these may disappear whilst IT eternally remains. And just as we see that the physical world—differentiated out of the Ether—occupies but an infinitesimally small portion of space : that is to say, that it is only a comparatively negligible portion of the Ether which becomes differentiated into physical matter ; so also we must conceive that even the Ether does not differentiate the whole of Primordial Substance, but that behind or beyond every plane or grade of differentiation—physical, etheric, mental, or spiritual, whatever may be the classification we adopt—there lies the infinite ocean of the One Root Substance-Principle itself, in its pure, eternal, incomprehensible, and immutable nature : the impenetrable GROUND or NOUMENON, the Source and Root, the Life, Energy, Motion, Consciousness, of all that ever was, is, or will be.

To bring our concepts of this Substance-Principle into

line with the third great dogma of modern science, that of Evolution, we must not merely regard physical matter as an evolved product, a time and space phenomenon which, as such, having had a commencement must certainly also have an ending ; but we must also accept in some form or another the ' days ' and ' nights ' of phenomenal existence for the whole universe.   We must at least postulate that portions of the universe will undergo this process of evolution and devolution, or involution, from the Primordial Substance itself through all the grades or planes, however many there may be.   Considered merely physically this will only be an enlargement or extension of Herbert Spencer's celebrated definition of evolution :

"Evolution is an integration of matter and concomitant dissipation of motion ; during which the matter passes from an indefinite, incoherent homogeneity to a definite, coherent heterogeneity ; and during which the retained motion undergoes a parallel transformation."

Spencer, however, had in view here nothing more than physical matter in its atomic state.   Yet he has clearly stated the doctrine of ' days and nights ' in the following passage. We have only to re-read it in the light of a dissolution of matter into the primitive Substance.

" Motion as well as Matter being fixed in quantity, it would seem that the change in the distribution of Matter which Motion effects, coming to a limit in whichever direction it is carried, the indestructible Motion thereupon necessitates a reverse distribution. Apparently, the universally co-existent forces of attraction and repulsion which, as we have seen, necessitate rhythm in all minor changes throughout the Universe, also necessitate rhythm in the totality of its changes —produce now an immeasurable period during which the attracting forces predominating, cause universal concentration, and then an immeasurable period, during which the repulsive forces predominating, cause universal diffusion—alternate eras of evolution and dissolution."[1]

To summarise : we see that physical science in order to explain the phenomena of matter and force, or matter and motion, has now been compelled to fall back upon the old philosophical concept of a single unitary Root Substance or Principle.   The " solid, massy, hard, impenetrable particles, so very hard as never to wear or break to pieces," have had their day, and have been found wanting. So long

[1] *First Principles*, par. 183, p. 536, 4th ed.

as these solid massy particles were considered as independent and isolated units, which might possibly be split
into smaller ones, *ad infinitum*, both science and philosophy
were merely confirming and adding to that multiplicity
of broken images and reflections of the ONE which constitutes in consciousness the outgoing process, or ' fall '
(into matter) ; and from such outgoing no really ' synthetic '
philosophy could ever result. But as soon as it is perceived
that any division or separation of the atom into component
parts leads to something which is more cosmic or universal in
its nature and activities, that in fact it results, paradoxically,
in a larger aggregation : we have not merely a complete
volte-face, but the true turning inwards to the Source and
Root. That which the mystic endeavours to accomplish in
his own life and consciousness thus becomes the recognised
goal of physical science in its effort to explain the phenomenal
world of manifestation.

As philosophers we may welcome this advance which
Science has now made out of the arid region of gross Realism
into Metaphysics, and even into Mysticism ; but as philosophers,
and still more so as mystics, we have some further and more
searching questions to ask about this same ' space-filling '
Substance than those which concern merely the phenomena
of matter and force.

We might very well, for example, ask Science what is this
all space which is so easily, not to say recklessly, postulated
as being completely filled with the Ether ? Can Science tell us
what Space is anyway ; or how we come to be conscious of
spacial extension at all ? If scientists *will* enter the region
of Metaphysics they must be prepared to answer metaphysical
questions, or at all events must recognise the validity of them
as part of their own hypothesis.

" The giving reality to abstractions is the error of Realism. Space
and Time are frequently viewed as separated from all the concrete
experiences of the mind, instead of being generalisations of these in
certain aspects."[1]

The natural tendency of the merely ' rational ' mind is
to think that because its own measuring-rule, marked out in
yards and inches, has been found of service in estimating
certain outward relations and proportions, it is therefore

[1] Bain : *Logic*

adequate to measure the whole content of the universe, and even that which is of an utterly different order and nature, i.e. life and consciousness itself.   Einstein has now shown that in physics time and space are purely relative to the observer, and the term *physical* space is now recognised as something definitely dependent upon the limitations of our sense perceptions of matter.   Mathematically, many different kinds of space are conceivable.   What, then, may not ' space ' be on other planes of consciousness ?

Moreover, there is a little physical problem in this connection which Science has yet to solve.   What becomes of the energy which is radiated out into space from Suns and Stars, and which apparently travels on and on for ever and ever ?   Will Science conduct us to the limits of Space—*pace* Einstein and curved space—either in its outward or its inward extension ?   Or, if admitted that here Science must perforce turn back, baffled and defeated before the problem of infinite extension, will it dare to dogmatise any longer—as it has so often done since the rise of ' Rationalism '—as to the ultimate basis of phenomena ; or to regard itself as the great Initiator into the inmost secrets of Nature, and of our own life and consciousness ?   Will it any longer dare to speak of that Absolute Principle which lies at the Root of all, that Unborn, Eternal, Self-Existent NOUMENON—whether Substance, Being, or God be the proper term for IT: that great LIFE by, and for, and in which this great spacial Universe is spread out—in terms of *dead* matter, or unconscious Substance ?

So far as the real problem of the Universe is concerned—the problem, that is to say, of Life and Consciousness—this space-filling Substance, as at present conceived by Science, is just as barren and arid of any real validity as were the hard massy particles of Newton.   For physical science the Ether is simply a dead substance, and the supposed forms of motion therein are merely mechanically conceived.   Nevertheless, the philosopher may take this bare abstract idea of Substance and Motion, and animate it with the breath of Life until it appears as a living, breathing Potency, the ONE LIFE of the Universe, with whose infinite heights and depths every strand and fibre of our being is marvellously, magically, and mystically interwoven.

But whilst the real problem is thus outside the province of Science, and belongs perhaps not even to the philosopher, but—as we may see more clearly later on—essentially to the mystic and the occultist : we may in the meanwhile be grateful to Science for its enlargement of Truth in the fuller knowledge which it gives to us of the relation and proportion of things in the world of physical phenomena, or external perception. In that region of our life and consciousness, things are related in certain definite ways, and it is the province of Science to discover and classify that relationship.

We may give here one further quotation from Professor Eddington's valuable work on the Einstein theory :

' The physicist's object is always to obtain knowledge which can be applied to the relative and familiar aspect of the world. The absolute world is of so different a nature, that the relative world, with which we are acquainted, seems almost like a dream. But if indeed we are dreaming, our concern is with the baseless fabric of our vision. . . . Physics will continue to explore the relative world, and to employ the terms applicable to relative knowledge, but with a fuller appreciation of its relativity." [1]

Science now offers us as the basis of this phenomenal relationship a unitary space-filling Substance, with ' things ' as particular modes of motion or ' symptoms ' therein. This concept will serve admirably as our starting-point, and we may therefore proceed to exploit it for all it is worth in the interests of the real problem, which is the question as to the nature of our own life and consciousness.

[1] *Space Time and Gravitation*, p. 43.

CHAPTER III

SUBSTANCE AND LIFE

"The unique Substance, viewed as absolute and void of all phenomena, all limitations, and all multiplicity, is the Real. On the other
hand, viewed in His aspect of multiplicity and plurality, under which
He displays Himself when clothed with phenomena, He is the whole
created universe. Therefore the universe is the outward visible
expression of the Real, and the Real is the inner unseen reality of the
universe. The universe before it was evolved to outward view was
identical with the Real; and the Real after this evolution is identical
with the universe."

JĀMĪ.

"Those who do not deduce the creation of the universe and all
things thereof by continual mediations from the First (Being), cannot
do otherwise than construct broken hypotheses, divorced from their
causes: hypotheses which when they are surveyed by a mind with
a clearer and deeper vision of things, do not appear like houses, but
like heaps of rubbish."

SWEDENBORG : *Angelic Wisdom.*

CHAPTER III

SUBSTANCE AND LIFE

IN our last Chapter we have seen how physical science demands for the explanation of the phenomena of the material universe the existence of a space-filling *Substance*, to which is given the name of *Ether*.

But this concept of a universal, primordial or Root Substance is in reality not merely one of the most ancient in all the history of Philosophy, but it continually reappears in one form or another both in Philosophy and in Mysticism. It is the *Mûlaprakriti* or *Âkâsa* of the ancient Vedic Philosophy, the " *Waters* " of Space of the 1st Chapter of Genesis, the *Æther* of the Greeks, the *Universal Solvent* or *Summa Materia* of the Alchemists. In later Philosophy it is the Absolute Principle of Spinoza, and it is a fundamental concept in the Theosophy of Jacob Böhme, who stands incomparably beyond all other Christian mystics both in the nature and the profundity of his seership.

According to Böhme it is the " strong or stern attracting " or desire of the Eternal Ground or Essence of Being which creates for itself the *Substance* in which this " magical imagination " takes form and becomes a " creation." He says :

" Thus we understand herein the Substance of all Substances (*Wesen aller Wesen*) that it is a magic Substance where a Will can create itself into an essential Life, and so pass into a birth, and in the great Mystery awaken a Source . . . and thus also apprehend whence all things, evil and good, exist, viz. from the imagination of the great Mystery, where a wonderful essential Life generateth itself. . . . Now that which is (the *Wesen* or *Ungrund*) draweth magically, viz. its own desiring to a Substance (*Substantz*)."[1]

[1] *Earthly and Heavenly Mystery*, Text V, par. 37, and I, 1.

He says further :

" In this high consideration it is found that all is through and from God Himself, and that it is His own Substance (*Wesen*), which is Himself, and that He hath created it out of Himself." [1]

Also :

" Now the clear Deity needs no coming, for it is in all places beforehand ; it needeth only to manifest itself to or in the place ; and all whatsoever cometh, that is Substance (*Wesen*)." [2]

One might give quotation after quotation to show how this remarkable Seer, the " ignorant " shoemaker of Gorlitz, is in line with the profoundest philosophical thought of all ages.

Seeing, then, that this concept of *Substance* is practically universal, and that it appears and reappears in all ages : there is none which can serve us better as the basis for a working hypothesis, not merely as to the structural facts of the Universe, but also as to the nature of our own life and consciousness, and of that connection of the individual life with the Universal or ONE, the realisation of which in the highest possible degree is the particular province and genius of Mysticism.

That the concept is open to criticism, that it cannot satisfy every requirement of a critical metaphysical analysis, goes without saying ; for this is the common failure of all and every concept of the intellect when pushed to the ultimate. All that we now claim for it is, that it is incomparably the best working hypothesis, the surest ground upon which to formulate and bring down into the region of intellect the mystical intuition of the philosopher as well as the vision of the true seer. We

---

[1] *Three Principles*, Preface, par. xiv.

[2] *Third Apology*, Text IV, Point IV, pars. 27, 28. The German word *Wesen* is sometimes translated Essence, sometimes Substance, and sometimes Being by the translators of Böhme, without any apparent system or reference to the context. Böhme appears to use *Wesen* sometimes in the sense of the essential Being or Ground of Manifestation, but *prior to* Manifestation—in which case it would correspond in this work with what we are calling *Substance-Principle*, before this became in Manifestation Principle *and* Substance, or Subject and Object—and sometimes as meaning a definite Being or Object—more generally what we are here calling *Form*. He does not, in fact, make any consistent use of the word ; but his fundamental notion of Will and Desire acting to bring the *Idea* into substantiality, manifestation, or form, is clear enough. Moreover, this action not merely takes place originally as the *Divine* act of creation, but repeats itself and is operative at every moment in every being, creature, or *Ens*. Thus he says : " Each Ens of the forth-breathed Word hath a free will again to breathe forth out of its own Ens a likeness according to itself."—*Mysterium Magnum*, xii, 24.

are not in this work endeavouring to make any contribution
to metaphysics or the method of pure thought, but our effort
is rather to formulate such a working hypothesis as will enable
the thinker to advance boldly to a practical realisation of the
depths of his own nature without losing his way in a maze
of metaphysical speculation, or being thrown back into
sheer scepticism by the inconsistencies and irrationalities
of dogmatic theology.

It is by the method of hypothesis that all real advance in
knowledge is made : not merely in science but in every
direction in which we reach out to the unknown—which
is infinite compared with the *apparently* known.

Having, then, approached the concept of Unity from the
side of the hypothesis of modern Science as to the existence
of a unitary or absolute *Substance* as the root of Matter and
Energy, we may now further enlarge our ideas as to the nature
of this Substance by linking it up with the facts of Life and
Consciousness.

Primordial Substance considered from the material side
is not Matter itself, but the root or substratum of Matter : it
is that which becomes manifested in consciousness as ' Matter '
when it assumes certain specific forms of motion.

Matter is Substance, but Substance is not Matter. Matter
evolves: that is to say, forms of motion of the One Substance
aggregate together to form a definite *Plane* of Substance; of
which one such Plane is the Ether of Space, whilst another—
a further aggregation or differentiation of the Ether—is what
we are familiar with as physical matter in corpuscles or
electrons, atoms, and molecules. These latter have evolved
gradually out of etheric substance by a process not as yet
clearly comprehended by Science, and they may, therefore,
be conceived of as disintegrating in the course of time into
their original substance, so that the whole physical universe
would then disappear, though the Ether would remain as the
possibility or potentiality of the evolution of a new material
world.

In like manner, however many Planes of Substance we may
conceive of between physical matter and the One Substance
itself, each of these may be considered as evolving from the
substance of the Plane next above it : with a possibility of
returning thereto. There is thus a possibility of all returning

ultimately to the ONE; such an evolution and return constituting the "Days and Nights of Brahmâ" of the Vedânta philosophy which we have referred to in our previous chapter.

If we consider the One Substance itself merely from the physical point of view, it is precisely the opposite of everything that we know as matter and phenomena. It cannot evolve; only the forms of motion therein evolve and change. Conceived of in its own nature it is the changeless, unphenomenal Root of all phenomena; considered actively it is the uncaused Cause of all that we recognise as caused phenomena. Thus it is ever the same as *Being*, and ever changing as *Becoming*.

Now let us clearly understand that *matter*, in the physical sense of the term, must have two characteristics: mass or inertia, and extension in space. We cannot attribute either of these to the One Substance—unless, indeed, we say that it has absolute mass and absolute extension in space. Neither of these, however, has any validity in the physical sense of the terms, for neither can be *measured*. In physical science, whosoever would be saved it is above all things necessary that he should believe in measurement. Science must have some conceivable basis of spacial measurement; it must at least have some conceptual 'point-masses' which do not occupy the same space; but a continuous Substance which fills *all space* has no such basis. Mass must also be measurable— not in terms of space but in terms of *force*, that is to say in terms of physical sensation. Mass does not mean bulk: it means a certain quantity of matter measurable by the amount of force required to move it. Thus two lumps of matter of the same size may have quite different masses. But since we cannot isolate any portion of a space-filling Substance, it possesses for us no mass; or, considered as a whole, it possesses absolute mass. What alone does possess for us mass and extension in space is a certain form, or certain aggregations of forms of motion in and of this space-filling Substance; which forms are appreciable to our physical senses as *matter*; whilst other forms or modes of motion constitute what have generally been termed *forces*, i.e. the immaterial but *not* insubstantial action of light, heat, electricity, magnetism, etc.[1]

---

[1] In this view, however, 'matter' is as *immaterial* as 'force,' and the main characteristic of physical matter, i.e. *mass*, is only a particular example

We see, therefore, that we must disabuse our minds of all physical concepts in relation to the one Root Substance itself, but at the same time we must keep steadily and clearly in view the fact that every *thing* in the Universe *is* that Root Substance ; and more particularly we must realise that *we* are that Root Substance, however much we may limit or however much we may extend what we choose to include in the term ' we.'

Thus we must clearly understand that our present physical body, being compounded of those forms of motion in and of Primordial Substance which constitute physical matter, is still Primordial Substance in essence ; that all the subtle forces which play in and through our physical body are also modes of motion in and of the One Substance ; that any form of subtle body, not physical, which we may possibly or conceivably possess, either now or hereafter, is similarly a form or mode of motion of this Substance ; and that any powers or faculties which we may possess, such as thought, will, emotion, etc., are, in their last analysis, activities of and in this unchangeable Root Substance—unchangeable in itself, changeable in its forms—and, as such, must be, to whatever Plane they may belong, definite substantial forms, whether *vibrations*—a favourite scientific concept—or otherwise.

If this has been clearly grasped and realised, there is no further difficulty in understanding how we may have in the unseen world a body as substantial and ' real ' as our present physical body, and even a copy of that body. The difficulty in realising how such a body can exist in the unseen world is commonly very great for those who cannot think of anything else but physical matter as possessing any *substantiality*, and is an immense obstacle with some ' rationalists ' to any belief in a future life. Science now clears away this difficulty, and—using the language of Mysticism—shows us that the real substantiality lies, not in physical matter, but precisely in that unseen world which is nothing to our physical senses, but *all* in reality. Physical matter is less ' solid ' than the substance of the Ether, so that the thin wraith-like bodies which we commonly ascribe to ' spirits ' should really be ascribed to these same physical bodies which we at present possess,

of energy. This receives confirmation in the fact that the *mass* of a corpuscle has been actually demonstrated to vary with its velocity. Some of the more metaphysical physicists, therefore, are inclined to see in *energy* the fundamental reality of phenomena.—*Vide* Poincaré, *The New Physics*, p. 66.

and which we have been wont to account so substantially 'real.'

Ether is " millions of times denser " than physical matter ; any etheric body, therefore, which we possess must be millions of times denser than our physical bodies, however invisible and impalpable such etheric bodies may be to our physical senses ; the dense Ether itself being absolutely inappreciable to any physical senses or tests.

And why should we not possess such bodies ? Apart from the fact that psychical research clearly points to their existence, is it conceivable that our physical body could materialise at all, or be held together in the marvellous co-ordination of all its parts and functions without some such living substantial matrix or 'soul' ? We shall see this more clearly as we proceed, but meanwhile let us realise that the possibilities of forms of motion in and of Primordial Substance are infinite, and there is not the slightest reason for supposing that they are exhausted by physical matter and force, or even by these *plus* a homogeneous structural Ether.

But the great fact which we have now to consider and take into account is this : *The validity of certain forms of motion in and of Primordial Substance as constituting ' matter,' and the validity of other forms as constituting ' force,' is determined solely by Life and Consciousness.*

In order to understand this let us take first of all such a familiar fact as the consciousness of colours—say red and blue. Scientifically, the difference between red and blue is simply one of rapidity of vibration and length of wave : red light consisting of undulations of the Ether taking place at the rate of 395 million million per second, and having a wave-length of ·0000304 inch, while the undulations of blue light take place at the rate of 697 million million per second, and the wave-length is ·0000172 inch.

Now the blueness or the redness is not in these vibrations, but in our consciousness of them. Why should not the reverse colours be the fact of our consciousness, and the more rapid vibrations be red and the less rapid ones blue ? Or why should these particular modes of motion constitute for us light and colour at all ?

Our consciousness of ' matter ' stands on precisely the same terms ; and if, out of the infinite range of vibrations and other modes of motion taking place at every moment in Primordial Substance, our consciousness can thus discriminate and form for itself an objective world of matter, and light, and colour, and sound, of the *limited* nature which we are scientifically as well as philosophically compelled to ascribe to our material universe : what may not be the further possibilities of Life and Consciousness in its relation to, or action in, the One Substance, on other, deeper, and more substantial or more cosmic planes of existence, or acting in or through other bodies than the physical ?

It is quite conceivable that if Life and Consciousness can thus differentiate *our* objective world out of the infinite potentialities of the One Root Substance, it can also differentiate other worlds quite as 'material,' quite as 'real,' in that Space which to our physical senses is an empty void, though filled with the veriest substantiality of all things. Our final definition of 'matter' must, in fact, be simply *that which is objective to consciousness*, on whatsoever Plane consciousness may be acting ; and the 'matter' of one Plane will be non-existent for the consciousness functioning on another Plane, from the very fact that the 'Plane' is a certain definite and limited mode or order of consciousness.

Such another world, as real and solid and palpable to consciousness as our own, could actually interpenetrate our physical world, and its inhabitants go about their affairs, and move through our space, without our being in the slightest degree aware of their presence ; while our world of matter would be equally non-existent for them ; even though—since the Cosmos is a unity—great events might happen in the one in consequence of what was taking place in the other. Wars and other mundane events are not wholly caused by the happenings on *our* present plane of consciousness.

That such interpenetrating worlds do exist has been one of the commonest teachings of occult science at all times, and their possibility is now supported by all that we know of the constitution of physical matter. We need not, indeed, go beyond the *electrons* of modern science to conceive of the possibility of the existence of these other worlds or planes ; for they could conceivably be constituted of combinations of electrons other than those which go to the making of our present objective 'matter,' or chemical elements.

But deeper even than the fact that it is consciousness alone which assigns to rates of vibrations or other forms of motion the qualities by which we recognise and distinguish them, there is a still further fact to be met by the rationalist who accounts matter so real and independent in its objectivity. Speaking in the ordinary physical sense, no form of motion in a homogeneous fluid, such as the Ether is conceived to be— or as Primordial Substance would be conceived ultimately to be in a physical sense—can be visible at all as an object. If we make vortex-rings in water or in air—both of which are homogeneous to our physical senses—they are not visible until or unless we introduce into them some foreign matter which is visible.　Thus in water we may make a vortex-ring visible with a little colouring matter, and in air by means of smoke.　But this expedient does not apply to what we know as ' matter,' as consisting of, say, an aggregate of vortex-rings in the Ether.　We have no 'foreign matter' to introduce into such rings to make them visible.[1]

When we further consider that the ' we ' who are conscious of an objective world, are ourselves, in all our bodies, in the eye, the brain, the nerve currents, etc., in all our powers and in all our *substance*, this self-same Primordial Substance : we are immediately face to face with the problem of a Root Substance which is both Subject and Object.

What are Life and Consciousness anyway ? Are they something other than inherent attributes of Substance itself; or are they only—as materialists would have us believe— epiphenomena resulting solely in and from complexes of those modes of motion which constitute physical matter ?

With the materialistic position I have dealt fully and completely in *Scientific Idealism*, and there is no need to recapitulate here.[2]　From what has just been said, however, it is easily seen that if those complexes of modes of motion which we call *matter*, and which are our own bodies, can possess the

---

[1] If the reader will perform the following very simple experiment it will greatly help him to realise what is here said about the atom being a form of motion in a homogeneous substance, and about forms of motion in general. Take a moderate-sized cardboard box, and in one end of it cut a round hole the size of a penny.　Now fill the box with smoke, and tap the end opposite to the hole.　A vortex-ring of smoke will immediately issue from the hole, and will travel a considerable distance ; and a candle can thus be extinguished at some distance from the box.

[2] *Vide : Scientific Idealism*, chap. ix. for an analysis of Haeckel's *Riddle of the Universe*.

qualities of life and consciousness with which we are familiar in ourselves, there is no reason in denying on *a priori* grounds that other complexes, on planes of Substance invisible to us, may not have either the same qualities in greater or lesser degree, or other qualities with which we are totally unfamiliar.

But the real question is : how can any such complexes, on any plane of Substance, have life and consciousness at all, if these are not attributes of the One Substance itself ? How can any combination of 'dead' atoms be supposed to be *aware* of other similar combinations, whether such atoms be "hard, massy," etc., or whether they are simply vortex-rings in the Ether ?

One of the greatest of modern scientific problems is the so-called "origin of life." But this term is quite misleading in the use that is made of it ordinarily by scientific writers. Science can no more deal with the origin of life than with the origin of motion, and the problem of each is analogous. What is usually connoted by the term is the origin of living *organisms* on this globe—quite a different matter.

Our own individual knowledge of life and consciousness is immediate and direct, but apart from that knowledge we have no means of recognising their existence save through some material phenomenon, or physical organism; and we say that such an organism is *alive* when we are able to recognise in it some self-initiated motion, as opposed to mechanical or molecular motions imposed from without or by the application of external forces.

That self-initiated movements should become more and more complex as the organism becomes more and more developed stands to reason, as also that other characteristics of life should become more and more apparent ; but what is not reasonable is to suppose that life and consciousness vanish and become extinct at that point where we are no longer able with our microscopes to detect their action. Neither is it 'rational,' if we would know what life and consciousness really are, to endeavour to discover this by hunting them out of sight in their most primitive organisms—primitive only so far as this physical plane of manifestation is concerned.[1]

---

[1] We commonly conceive that motion disappears in 'inert' matter, but the truth is that the very inertness of matter is due to an intenser motion, the atoms and molecules having an intrinsic motion incomparably greater than any that can be imparted to the body as a whole.

Life and Consciousness *manifest* in physical matter just as motion does; but to suppose that they can *originate* in a complex of atoms and molecules is as irrational as to suppose that motion can originate with the formation of those atoms. Motion may be said to be individualised in the atom, and we have already seen that it is certainly limited and restricted when we consider the atom only in its physical constitution and reactions with other atoms. But the motion which is thus individualised and confined within the atom is still part of a larger cosmic whole, part of the electro-magnetic motion of the Ether, if of nothing more. The internal motion of the atom neither originates in the formation of the atom, nor is it disconnected from its source; and the life and consciousness of any combination of atoms stands on precisely the same basis. The more we analyse the atom, the more we break it up into smaller and smaller units, the more does it reveal its connection with a larger cosmic whole, though Science is unable to follow it experimentally beyond its physical manifestation.

So much have scientists been blind to the real nature of the problem, that the wildest conjectures have been made as to how the first germs of life could have been introduced on this Earth. Among other hypotheses it has been supposed that they were conveyed from planetary space by meteors. But this is only pushing the problem one step farther back. Go back if you like to the vast cosmic fiery Nebula out of which our Solar System has evolved, and say if you can how any 'germs' of life—as that term is physically understood—could possibly have existed there.

But now let us see how closely analogous is the problem of Life to that of Motion, and how both must be ultimately traced back to, and resolved in, the One Primordial Substance itself.

If we ask, What is the origin of Motion? we find the problem unthinkable otherwise than by making Motion an attribute of Primordial Substance itself. For consider: we have only three alternatives: (*a*) Motion is inherent in, and is an attribute of Primordial Substance; (*b*) Primordial Substance can originate its own forms of motion: (*c*) There is something in the Universe other than Primordial Substance which can impress motion on or in it.

This third alternative is outside of our Monistic concept

that Primordial Substance is the root and ground of the whole Universe. Besides, it is clearly seen that if motion is impressed upon Primordial Substance by something which has thus to be thought of as separate from and independent of, or, as it were, outside Primordial Substance: that which thus impresses it must itself have the attribute of a power to produce Motion, and we therefore gain nothing by postulating another or further principle.

Our second alternative is not really out of harmony with our first, except in so far as we may feel compelled to accept the scientific doctrine that all motion of a particular kind or form is derived from previous motion of the same or of another kind or form, and therefore that motion in some *form* or other is indestructible and eternal. Such a postulate is necessary for the great scientific doctrine of the Conservation of Energy; but then the conservation of *mass* is also necessary for this doctrine, for motion without mass has no scientifically conceivable energy. The doctrine of the Conservation of Energy, however, is only a generalisation from a few observed phenomena of a limited kind, and the energy radiated into space must be accounted for before it can have anything but a limited physical meaning.

The difficulty of conceiving of Motion *per se* as inherent in Primordial Substance apart from any *forms* is of course insuperable and paradoxical. It has its parallel in the difficulty which the mystic experiences in translating into language his experience of the *formless* world of Life and Consciousness—formless, yet full-filled with the fulness of all things.

Saint-Martin, philosopher and mystic, speaking of "immaterial movement," says : "It may be said with certitude that although it is not possible to conceive of extension without movement, it is nevertheless incontestable that movement may be conceived of without extension, since the principle of movement, whether sensible or intellectual, is outside of extension." [1]

Bergson, also, virtually places "real movement" in a region which has no relation to extension—that is to say in "a qualitative multiplicity, with no likeness to number" (or space).[2] Of pure duration, which is essentially Motion,

[1] *Des Erreurs et de la Vérité*, Ed. 1775, p. 385.
[2] *Time and Free Will*, p. 226.

he says : " Pure duration . . . is not a quantity, and as soon as we try to measure it, we unwittingly replace it by space." [1] Also, " Real movement is rather the transference of a state than of a thing." [2]

But let us see what are the present scientific facts with which we are familiar.

The aggregations of individual forms of motion which constitute physical matter are a limitation of the freer motions of the electrons within a certain space, that of the atom, by reason either of the mutual attraction of the thus limited forms, or of some co-ordinating unit of another nature holding the individual forms in the closed system of the atom ; which closed system we have already had reason to compare to a a miniature solar system.

Now in order to fix our mental picture of the atom, let us conceive for the moment that each component electron is actually a vortex-ring of Ether. What happens when the atom breaks up is this : the constituent electrons or vortex-rings are thrown off into space with a velocity approaching that of light.[3] The motion of these individual units which was previously confined within the limits of the atom has now become a relatively free motion.

We might suppose these vortex-rings to be a primitive or ultimate form of motion in the space-filling Substance ; or we might suppose them to be compounded of still smaller vortex-rings, and that therefore the Ether is not the pure Primordial Substance. If these etheric vortex-rings are compounded of still smaller rings, we should have to conceive that the etheric rings in their turn might disintegrate, and that the free motion of the component rings would be as incomparably greater than the free motion of the etheric rings as these are than the motions of the more compound physical atoms and molecules. As we proceed with this disintegration, the resulting simpler compound would form another *plane* of Substance ; but we should ultimately reach a plane where we should have nothing but a simple vortex-ring, and since at each remove we obtain a free motion of the

---

[1] *Time and Free Will*, p. 106.
[2] *Matter and Memory*, p. 266.
[3] The average velocity of an *a* particle of Radium may be taken as one million miles per minute, whereas an ordinary air particle only travels twelve miles per minute.

individual rings immeasurably greater than that of the individuals of the plane below—treating our physical plane as the plane of the greatest complexity—we shall see that we are compelled to postulate that our ultimate vortex-ring will have a motion so incomparably greater than anything we can apprehend as to be *almost* absolute.

Absolute motion would be such motion that no time whatsoever is occupied in the movement from one point of space to another.[1] Absolute motion is, therefore, the simultaneous presence of a 'body'—our ultimate vortex-rings—at every point of space, and such 'motion' is no motion at all; it is equivalent to absolute rest, to the annihilation of motion and the annihilation of space. Such a concept is physically impossible, for it cannot be *measured*; yet it may be quite possible, even physically, that the movement of one body is transmitted instantaneously to another at any distance. Gravitation, for example, might be such action, for we do not know whether gravitation takes time to act, or whether it is instantaneous.[2] Let us remember that " a body only acts where it is " when we arbitrarily define the *place* of such a body by a limitation of its field of action. Every 'body,' taken in its wholeness, has infinite extension. Every atom of physical matter acts gravitationally throughout all space in accordance with a definite square of the distance law—at least such is the purely physical concept.

[1] It differs here from the 'absolute motion' of science, which is motion having a definite and absolutely and universally invariable time period in space, so as to serve as an 'absolute' standard. The velocity of light in space—or the ether—is at present considered to have this absolute value. Or if it could be proved that the Ether of Space was absolutely stagnant, and we could detect the motion of physical bodies relatively to it—which we cannot—we should have a means of ascertaining 'absolute' motion in the scientific sense of the term, even though the 'stagnant' Ether was only so relatively to our Earth. We are, however, throughout this work, using the term *absolute*, in the philosophical sense of absence of relativity, not in the scientific sense of an invariable relativity.

[2] Such instantaneous transmission would necessitate an *absolutely* dense medium, that is to say it would have to take place in Primordial Substance itself, and not on any 'plane' such as the Ether, which, although "millions of times" denser than physical matter, has still a time factor in its transmission of light and other electro-magnetic waves. Although we must strongly suspect that there is some intimate connection between gravitation and the Ether, no experiment or even conjecture has so far been able to associate the one with the other. Laplace had already in his time concluded from various astronomical observations that if there did exist a time factor in the action of gravity it must be at least 50 million times greater than the velocity of light. We should have to suppose in that case that it took place on a plane of substance as much unlike and 'beyond' the Ether as the Ether is unlike and 'beyond' physical matter.

But the problem of the *origin* of motion is seen from these considerations to be scientifically insoluble, for science cannot conceive of the annihilation of the primitive vortex-rings—if such really exist, if they constitute, for example, a homogeneously structural Ether—nor can it say how such vortex-rings, or any other form it may care to ascribe to the primitive motion-particle, could have originated in a *motionless* and formless 'fluid.' Motion, then, from the scientific point of view, must either have existed eternally in some *form* of motion in and of the One Substance, or there must be some unknown force which can originate forms of motion in that Substance. In either case the *origin* of Motion is quite beyond the reach of scientific knowledge and sense perception.

Now let us see how this bears on the question of Life and Consciousness. Is Primordial Substance dead Substance, or are we compelled to postulate that it possesses that innate power of self-movement which characterises Life, and Life alone ?

Materialists, holding the theory that matter is dead, and that therefore Substance must also be dead, are obliged to postulate that life *originates* in some complex of forms of motion ; but how can it be conceived that any complex can at a certain point suddenly acquire the power of *self-movement* merely as the result of complexity ? If the lesser complexity, if the primitive corpuscles even, have not at least some degree of self-movement, how can any greater complexity give more of this characteristic ?

But if the problem is unthinkable in this direction as regards the characteristic of self-movement, it is still more so as regards that other characteristic of Life, i.e. consciousness. How can any complex of forms of motion possess more consciousness than simpler complexes, unless these simpler complexes possess consciousness in at least some degree ? The real crux is, how can any complex of *dead* forms possess any consciousness whatsoever ? We are using the term consciousness here in the barest sense of awareness. How can any complex of *dead* corpuscles and atoms be conceived of as being *aware* of the existence of other similar complexes ?

But consciousness as we know it in ourselves is something much more than mere awareness. We have already seen that it is able to impose upon two different rates of vibration the qualities of colour ; and, in an extension of this, consciousness involves all that is implied under the term *æsthetics*. Further, there is the moral consciousness. How can any complex of dead atoms be supposed to acquire a moral sense, or at what point of the complex does it arise, and how ? These are questions which Materialism never has answered, and never can answer ; and such clear thinkers as the late Professor Huxley have well perceived that " the honest and rigorous following up of the arguments which lead us to 'materialism,' inevitably carries us beyond it."[1]

What theory, then, can we fall back upon ? Life and Consciousness are unique, with no possible explanation in that which is already postulated to be dead. Like Motion, which cannot be explained by a motionless Substance unless some further moving principle is given, Life and Consciousness cannot be manifested in or through dead matter unless they are postulated to be some other principle than that matter itself. Either all matter down to its very root—that is to say our space-filling or Primordial Substance—is dead, and Life is another and independent Principle ; or Root Substance is itself Life and Consciousness.

We have already seen that in the case of Motion it is not necessary to ascribe this to any Principle beyond Root Substance : and neither is it necessary to postulate such a Principle for Life and Consciousness. Thus, combining the two concepts, we find that Root Substance being *living* Substance, is able to initiate its own motions from within ; that is to say, to generate its own *forms* of motion. The origin of Motion in the Cosmos is in fact precisely that which we find within ourselves as self-moving living beings ; the origin is in the living *Will*. And if we are asked what Will is, we can only reply that it is an attribute of Life ; that we recognise it as one of our own powers as living subjects. Whether or to what extent the Will is ' free ' in our own case is another question. The real fact is that the only principle with which we are acquainted, and which we can possibly conceive of as *originating* motion in an inert or dead substance, is Life itself, with all its attributes of thought, will, emotion, etc.

Later on we may glance at the records of Mysticism as to the action of the living Will whereby the One Substance-Principle

[1] *Hume*, p. 251.

out of its ' absoluteness ' brings forth the manifested Universe ; but it remains now for us to round off our physical concepts and analogies.

We must note, in the first place, that just as we are compelled to ascribe *absolute* motion to Primordial Substance itself in its own nature, so also we must ascribe to it *absolute* Life and Consciousness. Absolute Consciousness is of course Unconsciousness, just as absolute motion is absolute rest ; in other words, both lie beyond the reach of the duality of the formal mind. But without resorting to the concept of absolute motion, we have already seen that a complex of forms of motion such as constitute, for example, physical matter, is a *limitation* of motion. It is neither a physical fact, nor can we conceive, that an aggregation of forms of motion can as such possess more motion than that of which it is aggregated. As a distinct form it must, and in fact does, possess less *manifested* motion ; the otherwise free elements of the complex being now confined within a limited space.

Our experience of life and consciousness is precisely the same. If there is one thing more certain than another about our own life, it is that we are here, in this complex of matter which is our physical body, vastly limited and constrained. Psychical research shows us that when freed from physical sense perceptions, consciousness expands to such a degree that it has been termed ' cosmic.'

If, then, we regard physical matter, and our physical body, as the furthest departure from, or ' lowest ' plane of differentiation of the One Substance, we must conceive that any other bodies or vehicles of Consciousness which we may possess, short of the One Substance itself, must possess the characteristics of Life and Consciousness in ever-increasing degree as they approach nearer and nearer to their Root ; each departure from a ' lower ' plane being a throwing off of limitations and disabilities. Finally we must ascribe to Primordial Substance itself the attributes of Life and Consciousness, not in any *degree*, but in an *absoluteness* of all that we know and find within ourselves as the characteristics of these.

We see, further, that the so-called problem of ' the origin of life ' is quite disposed of. Life does not *originate* in any form or complex of forms any more than motion does. All forms manifest in their own appropriate degree and kind that which is eternally inherent in the One Substance-Principle; and if we must speak of motion as *originating*, that is to say of the origin of *forms* of motion, the only thing that can possibly be conceived of as originating these is Life itself; such Life, in the One Substance-Principle, being eternal and self-existent.

Some chemists have great hopes of synthesising protoplasm —the lowest form of 'living' matter with which we are acquainted—in the laboratory, and even of producing some higher forms of organisms. We should not care to deny altogether on *a priori* grounds the possibility of this, though we must consider it to be highly improbable. But even if accomplished it would prove nothing as to the origin of life.

The case may be stated thus. Granting the possibility of constituting chemically or otherwise the necessary material organism, life might manifest in or through that organism as naturally as magnetic lines of force do in a magnetic substance such as iron. These magnetic lines of force are invisible and impalpable to our physical senses; they reside in the equally impalpable Ether; but, given the appropriate vehicle, they become appreciable in some physical phenomenon. So with Life and Consciousness; they are cosmic and universal, but in order to *manifest* to our physical senses they must necessarily have an appropriate vehicle. Science might possibly discover how to construct such a vehicle in a very low or elementary form; but it is now very generally recognised by biologists that the protoplasm of to-day has a certain evolved or hereditary *psychic* quality, the result of ages of evolution, which could not possibly be given to a mere chemical compound.

Primordial Substance being Living Substance, all matter is living matter in its own degree and kind, and though it may be said of every atom that it is in a certain sense an individual life, just as a microbe is, yet the life which organises it must be considered to be that of some larger Cosmic Life rather than that of some microscopic unit.

Not merely is all 'matter' a manifestion of Life, but all so-called force is the action of living Substance. The magnetic lines of force of the Earth are life currents in a living Body as truly as any of the nerve currents which play through our own bodies, or the thought currents for which our brains act as receivers. Our manipulation of 'natural' forces may appear to be purely mechanical, and in fact is so in our necessary limitations of language. But this does not make the forces themselves mechanical in their origin or sustenance. A microbe would appear to make a merely mechanical use of the circulation of fluids, and of other finer forces also in our own living bodies, and we may do the same in a cosmic body.

No life could exist on our Earth were not the Sun itself a Life; and though Science may not as yet be prepared to accept that our Sun, as we see it, is the physical manifestation of a Cosmic Life (Logos), differentiated and individualised from the One Life, Occultism has taught this for ages. Within the Life of the Sun exist the lesser Lives of the Planets; the ' World Soul ' being no mere poetic fiction. The recognition of the existence and action of such Cosmic differentiations of the One Life is the key not merely to many of the problems of Life and Consciousness, but to the problems of physics also. Matter could not *evolve* into atoms and molecules without a Life to evolve it, any more than protoplasm could evolve into our present bodies.

By correspondence and analogy we thus find that all the ' lower ' forms of life derive from, and are differentiated within, some ' higher ' or more cosmic Life; the whole being summed up and taking place within the One Living Substance which is also the One Life. Outwardly this Life may manifest to us but a very limited aspect of its real nature. Beyond the mere material and physical we lose sight of its phenomenal operation altogether, and are absolutely unable to trace its connection with the universal. But within ourselves we are not thus limited, and it is there alone—if we but *seek* it aright—that we can really apprehend the magnitude, the power and the glory of that eternal LIFE which is our own very *Self*; and which brings forth, sustains, and withdraws all things whatsoever which appear in the Heaven above or in the Earth beneath.

Returning to our physical analogies : Sir J. J. Thompson has pointed out that the physical atom appears to display properties of two kinds. The ordinary physical and chemical properties change with the element with which the atom is combined in any chemical substance ; but other properties are the same for the free or the combined element. This has led to the assumption that the atom consists of a core and an outer shell, and that constant properties are due to the core, and changing properties to the shell. The atom is assumed to consist of a certain mass or core of positive and, possibly, negative particles, but exhibiting a preponderance of positive electricity. This 'core' is surrounded by a shell or by 'satellites' of less rigidly bound, more free negative particles or electrons. The atom is in fact, as already stated, conceived to be a Solar System in miniature. To this we might hazard a further theory, viz. that the constant properties are due to the wider, deeper connection of the atom with its cosmic life, whilst the changing properties are merely that part of its total activity which acts and reacts with other physical units.

We may consider ourselves in like manner. We have a 'core'—the 'divine spark' of the mystics—rooted and grounded in the Cosmic Life and Consciousness, and unchangeable in the changing circumstances and relations of our external individualised life. We have an external life acting and reacting in innumerable combinations with physical nature and with our fellow units. In our case, however, and probably in that of the physical atom also, the 'core' is a larger surrounding body of another texture or plane of Substance, an 'aura'; the physical body being formed *within* this matrix. The body is in the soul, not the soul in the body—even as Plato taught.

If now we ask Science : what, then, *is* this Space-filling Substance—whether the Ether, or something beyond the Ether—which, being the *moving* Principle of the Universe, must be essentially the *Soul* thereof ; or even if we ask : what, then, are the particular forms or modes of motion which constitute physical matter ?—Science cannot reply. This Substance, and all the forms thereof, are *immaterial* in essence, and 'material' only in certain very limited effects. Yet the concept of this Substance must assuredly be eminently 'rational,' for is not Science the most rational thing on Earth ? It is clearly, then, eminently rational to believe in the immaterial and the unextended as the basis of the material and the extended, even in a physical sense. How much more so, then, is this rational in a metaphysical sense. But what we really see quite clearly by this is, that it is eminently rational to be able to *apprehend* a thing without being able to *comprehend* it, much less to prove it. No amount of experience, much less that which comes to us through the senses, can ever prove

8

the universality of any principle, not even that of causation. If this be true in Science, it is equally true in Philosophy and in Mysticism. Science *apprehends* as the root of Matter and Motion an immaterial lifeless *Substance*, but cannot *comprehend* how it could be set in motion—*e pur si muove !*

We may apprehend Primordial Substance as the root and ground of all manifested Life and Consciousness—and we have just as much reason to do so as we have to apprehend it as the root and ground of all motion and matter—without being able to comprehend *how* it is so, or what it may be in its ultimate nature as such. Now, although Science cannot say what Primordial Substance is *per se*, it can say to a certain extent what it is not: all attempts to describe it in physical terms ending in the verdict " not this, not that." Physically it does not possess the quality of mass ; it is inextensible and incompressible, and must also be regarded as frictionless ; indeed, it would not be inconsistent with Science to describe it as the Nothing—for certainly in itself, and apart from its forms of motion it is no-thing. A little touch of imagination added, and it is, even scientifically, the ' Great Abyss,' the ' Eternal Void,' the ' Great Deep,' or the ' Eternal Dark ' of the mystic.

We can rationally apprehend what is here referred to, but we cannot with the intellect, limited as it is by its ' categories,' reach any comprehension of the nature of that which we thus apprehend. Mysticism, however, bears testimony to another faculty by means of which that which is dark for the intellect is illumined and explicated ; and modern philosophy tends to confirm this, and to harmonise the Manifested and the Unmanifest in a Rational Mysticism in which both faculties shall have their due and appropriate sphere of action, and be not wholly unrelated the one to the other.

We find in modern scientific facts and concepts not merely a confirmation of some of the fundamental principles of a Rational Mysticism, such as may be found in all ages, but also the possibility of re-stating those principles in a more intelligible form. Many mystics are well-nigh unintelligible to modern readers owing to the obscurity and unfamiliarity of their language ; yet when their nomenclature and symbolical language is once understood in the light of some fundamental principles they are found to be not merely wonderfully illuminative, but the most apparently diverse systems are seen to be in close and substantial agreement.

We are now in a position to understand clearly that the physical properties of any *thing*, whether it be an atom, a lump of matter, or a living organism, are simply those limited modes of its total activities which are appreciable to our physical senses. The *thingness* of a thing, whether on this physical plane of consciousness, or on any plane more extensive, but short of absoluteness itself, consists simply in a localisation and limitation in a certain specific manner—which we call the 'nature' of the thing—of the thing in itself, which is universal and absolute, and therefore free of all time and space considerations. Let us see how this applies to what we call the 'atom' of matter.

The physical properties of an atom are three in number : (a) it possesses chemical characteristics, that is to say the power of combining in various specific ways with other atoms;[1] (b) it possesses mass, and attracts other atoms in a gravitational manner in proportion to the mass ; (c) it possesses electro-magnetic properties by means of which it acts and reacts with the Ether of Space.

Now the first of these properties differentiates one atom from another, and gives the atom of one chemical substance an individuality differing from that of another chemical substance. Thus oxygen has totally different chemical properties from hydrogen or gold. Oxygen and hydrogen combine together to form water, but neither will act upon gold at all.

To what are these different properties due ? Physicists conceive that they are due to the varying number and arrangement of the electrons which go to make up the atom of the substance. Thus an atom of oxygen is supposed to be made up of many more electrons than an atom of hydrogen, and an atom of gold more than either of these. Also, let it be remembered, these electrons have an intense motion of their own within the limits of the atom, and the external chemical characteristics exhibited by the atom will doubtless be due to the varied combined motions of the individual electrons, or, in other words, to the structure of the atom.

As regards the electrons themselves, when liberated from

[1] With the exception of Group 0 of the Periodic Series, the rare gases of the atmosphere.

the atom they all appear to be alike, no physical difference can be detected. They all behave as definite measurable units of negative electricity.

But now as regards the two other physical properties of matter, (*b*) and (*c*). We must note that these properties are not merely common to every atom or mass of matter, but they have a universal field of action, and are not limited like the chemical properties to action upon some other specific atom.

(*b*) Mass or inertia, and (*or*) gravitation, act from one physical body to another through all space. The Sun attracts the Earth, and the Earth attracts the Sun through a distance of 93 millions of miles. One Planet attracts another, and the existence of Neptune, the outermost member of our System—2,792 millions of miles from the Sun—was inferred, and afterwards discovered, by the gravitational disturbances which it caused in the System. Beyond that again, the nearest ' fixed ' star, *a* in the Constellation of Centaurus,[1] is estimated to be at a distance from us of 24,750,000,000,000 miles ; yet gravity acts between us and that star also. If we go still further into space, to those stars from which light, travelling at the speed of 186,000 miles per second, would take thousands of years to reach us : there also, as between us and those inconceivably distant bodies, gravity must be conceived to act, however infinitesimally.

The important point to observe is, that each atom of matter, having *mass*, contributes its quota to the gravitational field. The attraction between the mass of the Sun and the mass of the Earth is made up of the individual attractions of the masses of the atoms. Also action and reaction of masses are equal and opposite. When I jump up in the air I push the Earth back.

(*c*) The electro-magnetic properties of the atom are also universal, and are known to be intimately connected with the fact of mass. Every vibration of the atom—or perhaps we should rather say, every change of vibration of the atom, such changes taking place by the million million every second —produces a definite electro-magnetic propagation throughout space, so that, as Sir Oliver Lodge has pointed out : " It can be argued for the hydro-dynamic or vortex theory of matter, as well as on the electrical theory, that every atom of matter

[1] Or possibly the " Gilpin " star in Ophiuchus is the nearest.

has a universal though nearly infinitesimal prevalence, and extends everywhere." [1]

Here, then, we have Science proclaiming on purely physical data the mystical fact of the unity of the individual with the universal. There is no such thing as an individual thing, a 'thing in itself' apart from the unity of the whole. It only becomes a *thing* when certain specific modes of its action are recognised under the limitations of time and space to the exclusion of all others. Passed through the refracting prism of Cosmic Mind in the first instance, the universal pure white 'light' is analysed and separated out into individual 'Elements,' and these are still further refracted and individualised by the lower human mind: itself a differentiation of the Cosmic Mind of its own particular system in the Cosmos. Thus arises a world of 'Matter,' which, taken in its totality, is just as much a 'convenient fiction' as are atoms and molecules in their supposed or assumed individual and separate nature—convenient but necessary and inevitable as arising from the fundamental constitution of Mind itself.

We also commonly conceive of a 'thing' as being something separate and individual because we see it in definite outline and shape. But that is only the result of the capacity of our eyes for a certain limited range of vibrations. If we possessed X-ray sight we should see each other as skeletons, and not in our present configuration. As a matter of fact we do actually possess X-ray sight as regards the deeper and larger portion of our individuality, for the outline and surface of our physical body by no means contains or limits the Man : there is a surrounding egg-shaped aura of matter belonging to another plane than the physical—and therefore relatively much more substantial—which we do not see at all with the physical eye. Du Prel, in his *Philosophy of Mysticism*, remarks:

"Were our five senses to be suddenly taken away, and senses of an entirely different kind given to us, though standing on the same spot we should believe ourselves inhabitants of another star." [2]

It is not even necessary to conceive " senses of an entirely different kind." Our present senses of seeing, hearing, etc.— and, indeed, we must always conceive of ourselves as using

[1] *The Ether of Space,* p. 98.
[2] Trans. C. C. Massey, vol. ii, p. 4.

such senses or faculties in some manner or other on whatever *objective* plane of the universe we may be functioning in consciousness—if changed so as to respond to a different order of forms or vibrations of the One Substance, would give us this *other world*, though we never left this Earth, or our present physical body. And what is that " change called death " but precisely this change in our perceptions ? Having lost our gross physical body, our faculties open out on another plane ; but that plane is not necessarily somewhere else in space, and we may enter ' heaven '—or the other place— though we have never left the Earth—as, indeed, we may do without dying, for it is only necessary for us to open our ' inner ' senses to find that these ' places ' are around and within us. To quote Du Prel again :

> " We are not temporarily and spatially divided from that beyond, we are not first transposed there by death, but are already rooted therein, and what divides us therefrom is merely the subjective barrier of the threshold of sensibility. This threshold thus limits consciousness and therewith self-consciousness. Since both are products of evolution, their capacity for further evolution suggests itself at once." [1]

What other properties, beyond the reach of physical investigation, does the atom possess ? What, for example, are its *psychical* characteristics. We have it, even from such a materialist as Haeckel, that it does possess psychic characteristics.[2]

The brain *transmits* thought ; or at all events we may say this in so far as every thought is accompanied by a physical disturbance or action in the brain substance, and the thought is transmitted telepathically from one brain to another. There is every reason to believe that the telepathic action of thought is as universal as the electro-magnetic action of the atom ; but we are too busy with our individual outward affairs to recognise telepathic impacts save in exceptional cases. Thoughts " come into our mind," and we originate very few, if any. With a little wider knowledge we might perhaps trace the bulk of them to some individual or individuals; to the fact that large numbers of our fellows are thinking of that particular subject, and it is " in the air." More important still is the influx which comes to us from beings on another plane of

---

[1] Trans. C. C. Massey, ii, 3.
[2] Cf. *Scientific Idealism*, chap. ix.

existence, but more immediately in touch with our plane. Higher and deeper still we may tap the cosmic currents of thought of Beings of God-like proportions and powers by whom we may be truly 'inspired.' This is the special province of the mystic, and is explicable on a basis as *natural* and 'rational' as the common thoughts of our everyday life. There is nothing more 'supernatural' in the fact of inspiration than in the fact of wireless telegraphy. The brain no more originates thought than the wireless apparatus originates the message it transmits or receives. But the brain, like the wireless apparatus, must be 'tuned' or 'synchronised' to the particular 'periodicity' of the waves in space to which it is intended to respond ; and while our brain is tuned only to the lower and slower vibrations of the practical affairs of our material sense life, it is not able at the same time to receive the higher and finer vibrations of Cosmic Mind.

We shall lay it down as an occult principle—whether accepted by Science or not at the present moment—that every thought in the mind of every individual is as co-extensive with the Universe as is the action of gravity, or the electro-magnetic influence of each atom.

As regards this electro-magnetic action of the atom, we know that it is transmitted through space by the medium of the Ether at the same velocity as light. As regards gravity, we do not know whether it takes time to act or not ; and as regards thought we are in the same case. But we wish here to lay down this principle, based on correspondence and analogy, and following on the concept of Motion with which we have already dealt. Every property or action of the atom which is more *inner*, is also more universal and immediate ; and, seeing that the atom in its ultimate or innermost analysis is, *ex hypothesi*, Primordial Substance itself : its innermost action is absolute, and requires no time for its transmission. Innermost and outermost are, however, only terms of our limited perceptions.

If we are to take our analogies from the action and inter-action of physical matter with the Ether, and seeing that no single motion of any form constituting such matter can take place without action and reaction between it and the etheric plane of Substance immediately 'above' or more 'inner' to it : we must conceive that, however many planes we may constitute between physical matter and the pure Root Substance, there must be a regular series of actions and reactions from plane to plane, which actions and reactions increase in velocity of transmission, until, reaching Primordial Substance itself, they there become absolute. Thus in the One Substance itself we must conceive that all actions ' anywhere ' in the Universe are instantaneously transmitted ' everywhere.' We have here, in fact, a kind of physical concept of the attributes of omnipresence and omniscience usually attributed to a divine Being. We might put the matter in this way : that since we are unable with our conceptual mind to transcend the category of space and realise an *infinite* Wholeness which is present in all its fulness at each *infinitesimal* point of (extended) space, we replace this mystical postulate with the more concrete one of instantaneous transmission, thus *practically* abolishing space whilst yet retaining the concept of extension.

Now, though we should carefully guard against the idea that we can reach absoluteness by any process of multiplication, we cannot conceive otherwise than that such reactions do actually take place from plane to plane, even to the Absolute ; for if we could conceive of a single isolated form, a single ' atom ' which did not so react, or of a plane of Substance which stood by itself and did not interact with the next higher as well as with the next lower : we should have split the universe ; we should have a ' thing in itself ' which had no connection with the One Root Principle. In short, every ' thing ' *is* Primordial Substance, and as such acts instantaneously everywhere. Only on different ' planes ' do *things* act differently in time and space—which planes are at root limitations of Consciousness.

Seeing, then, that the real inner substantiality, mobility, and activity of the atom, and its universal extension, is so largely masked and hidden in our estimation and perception of it as a mere physical thing : what shall we say of its life and consciousness ?

Seeing that in its inmost nature—or rather we should say, in its totality—the atom is nothing less than the One Absolute Substance Itself, it must possess absolute Life and Consciousness ; and if we ascribe to it anything less, anything more circumscribed and limited, it is only because we are ignoring—either through our own limited consciousness, through ignorance, or as a " convenient fiction "—all but a certain limited aspect of its total nature and action.

As it is consciousness which differentiates between red and blue, so also it is consciousness, and consciousness alone, which differentiates between the ' matter ' of our plane and that of another, and raises up such distinctions as inner and outer, the great and the small, the atom and the universe, spirit and matter. Physical matter appears to us to be the *outer*; on another plane of consciousness it may be the inner. But this specific consciousness of a definite ' world,' differentiated or discriminated out of the total content of Substance, must necessarily imply an individual subject or Ego which thus discriminates. The one is the complement of the other; and if this relationship can exist on any one plane —the physical for example—it can equally well exist on any other; or rather, such a limitation—whether considered fundamentally as a limitation of the subject-ego, or as an actual objective reality—can be the *cause* of any number of ' worlds.'

God, if postulated as absolute Consciousness, cannot possibly see the world as we see it. To do so He must limit himself as we are limited—and what else than such a limitation of God *is* Man ?

Since, then, Life and Consciousness are absolute, but are *manifested* in the phenomenal world in a limited manner and form—for so we find them in ourselves, and thereby assume them in other similar forms—we may say, at least as a " convenient fiction," that the conditions and limitations of the phenomenal forms are the conditions and limitations of a corresponding consciousness: that is to say of the in-volved life; e-volution being the return of that in-volved life to the universal.

Physical or phenomenal forms in or by themselves are merely body without a moving principle or soul; they are absolutely meaningless except as referred to a manifesting Life. Just as we may and do consider the atom in a limited manner from a physical point of view, so also we shall commonly consider its innate life and consciousness. But if we think of that life and consciousness as negligible or non-existent because the atom is such a very small thing in our eyes, we shall commit a grave mistake. Have we not already seen that even physically the atom may be considered to have infinite extension ?—and perchance its consciousness is just as infinite, and in reality it is *we* who are small in our feeble imagination of ourselves and of it.

Our greater life, our infinite extension, our oneness with the Universal and the Absolute, has been declared by prophet and seer in all ages, but there have been few to credit it. Man has fallen into matter; the illusion of sense perception is complete; yet to-day not merely the mystic, but Science itself points to our infinite nature, and shows us the way out of our illusion of separateness.

If the mere physical characteristics or activities of the unseen Substance of Space, that is to say, its potencies and potentialities as regards physical phenomena, are such as Science now declares them to be; and if the mere physical characteristics and activities of Life and Consciousness acting in and through our physical bodies are such as we now know them to be : what shall we say of Life and Consciousness not limited by physical conditions, but acting in the greater substantiality of a higher or more inner plane of Substance ?

Science tells us that the amount of energy in every cubic millimetre of etheric space (say the size of a pin head) is sufficient to furnish " a million horse-power working continuously for forty million years," [1] and it is the dream of Science at the present time—doubtless to be realised in due course—to be able to liberate this inter-atomic or etheric energy as a source of power for all our machinery.

If, then, we can succeed in bringing through to the physical plane as physical phenomena these higher potentialities of the unseen world ; that is to say, if we can obtain a control of the deeper and hidden potentialities of Primordial Substance in its objective correlations : why should we not succeed also in bringing through the higher potentialities of Life and Consciousness residing in that Substance ? These exist not merely as potentialities of Substance which it is ours to possess, but as the very essence of our own innermost nature ; as that which is in the deepest and truest sense our very *Self*.

The powers and potentialities of the One Substance— whether that Substance be the Ether, or something infinitely deeper than the Ether—are masked and limited in their

[1] Sir Oliver Lodge, *The Ether of Space*, p. 95.

manifestation as physical matter and phenomena, whether in the atom or in organisms of lesser or greater complexity up to our own present bodies; but the Life thus limited cannot remain in its limitations. Ever and always there is a hunger for the Source, an "*élan vital*," manifesting itself physically in evolution and expansion of powers: the outward form showing ever-increasing development corresponding to the inner expansion and growth of what, for the time being, we must regard as an individual unit of life. It is both individual *and* universal; but for the time being only knows itself as individual. Thus in time shall individual man attain to God-like proportions and powers.

But we do not yet know to the full the powers and potentialities of our present bodies; we are only beginning to realise the extent to which Spirit can use those bodies as an instrument; and when something super-normal does happen: when, the conditions being favourable, that higher power of Life which we call Spirit does manifest in and through our bodies somewhat of its latent nature, we talk of the miraculous, and ascribe it to the supernatural. Many psychic phenomena difficult to explain on normal lines now claim the attention of scientific investigators, and although for such investigators the day is past when such phenomena were denied *a priori*, because they savoured of the supernatural, which Science denied: the idea of their supernatural nature and import still remains in the popular imagination, and messages from so-called 'spirits' are still regarded, even by educated people, as if they necessarily possessed an import and a veracity not accorded to mundane relationships. The arbitrary line of definition between the natural and the supernatural, however, is constantly being pushed farther and farther back by Science. Nature refuses to be placed in a watertight compartment, or to be circumscribed to suit a theological dogma.

We speak of 'natural causes,' but all such causes are *at root* 'supernatural.' They are only 'natural' because we do not trace them to their source, because they all lie within the region of the phenomenal, and are therefore governed by *laws* which we can directly investigate.

The potential or latent powers of Man are as infinite as the One Life itself, even as are the latent powers of every atom; for since the One Substance, which is also the One

Life, is ' space-filling ' and exists equally everywhere, it is, as all true mystics have recognised and stated, present in all its powers at every point of space. " The centre is everywhere, the circumference nowhere." Science now comes to the aid of Mysticism, and enables us to translate this even into the terms of physics.

But that which is *latent* as regards this plane of manifestation is active and *kinetic* elsewhere. All latent or potential energy is in reality kinetic somewhere, and these terms are only convenient fictions expressing a relativity and limitation.

How, then, shall a man bring these latent powers into manifestation in his own body? Assuredly by a process as *natural* as that by which he has attained to his present powers. The physical body can manifest the powers of ' spirit ' very much more than is at present generally recognised ; but if it is to manifest these harmoniously and sanely, the lower nature must be rightly trained and tuned to the higher vibrations, otherwise it will be shattered as inevitably as is the atom by the play of inter-atomic force.

But the physical body is not the Man, nor is the Man limited to action therein. The real substantial body of Man exists on a higher plane of Substance, and is referred to in many different terms in Mysticism. In Christian symbolism, for example, it is the mystic body of the Christ, the new Adam which St. Paul said must be *formed* in us. It is a cosmic body of Root Substance, in or through which the Man is enabled to act on all planes of the Universe, and to enter into the " Divine Fire " without being consumed ; or, as Jacob Böhme taught, it is the real substantiality of Man which " faded " when Adam (Man) fell, so that now we do not even know that we possess it.

"The new man is not only a spirit . . . but a body which subsisteth in the centre of nature, in the fire ; whose body the fire cannot consume." [1]

Material life, then, the life of the individual on the physical plane, whether of atom or of man, is a limitation, a restriction, and a privation. It is the creation by means of this limitation of a multiplicity out of a Unity, each individual in the multiplicity being specialised for a particular function : ministering

[1] Böhme, *Incarnation*, Part I, chap. xiv, pars. 22, 23.

to the Whole, it is true, and still intimately connected with the Whole, but at the same time, and for the time being as an individual, largely or wholly acting as an independent unit in separation from and in ignorance of the essential Unity.

What Mysticism has to say as to the why and wherefore of this limitation, we shall endeavour to elucidate later on; but we may apprehend now that we shall never realise the Unity—that is to say we shall never realise ourselves in all the heights and depths of our true Life—so long as we retain within our consciousness any idea of separateness from anything whatsoever that exists in the Universe; so long as we regard Nature as the not-self; or so long as we arbitrarily separate the natural and the supernatural. The great illusion is the sense of separateness.

And as a fundamental concept, enabling us to realise this Unity intellectually and rationally, there is none better than that of *Substance*, which we are now endeavouring to elucidate —remembering always that it is an intellectual concept, and, as such, subject to the limitations of all concepts, and para-doxical when pushed to an extreme. It has been given age-long credentials by Philosophy, and is now confirmed by physical science itself. It enables us to apprehend that we ourselves are actually one in *Substance*, in whatsoever body we may possess, with that Root Substance-Principle in which, and of which, and by which the Universe in all its heights and depths exists.

We have seen that even physically the unity of Substance is much more than a mere passivity, is much more than as if two or more individual objects were moulded out of the same inert material. The apparent separation and inertness is not real, and every individual atom retains not merely its inner-most and essential nature as the One Substance, but also a never-ceasing activity, action, and reaction with the whole Universe.

Outwardly, in the limitations which our own limited consciousness imposes upon it, the physical atom is only seen and known by certain well-defined characteristics; but even in these we have seen that in two cases physical science may assign to it universal action and extension.

Inwardly, we might with fuller powers of observation and clearer knowledge expand its action until it was indistinguishable from the One Substance itself—this latter being the only real *atom*, or undivided and indivisible Unity.

Whether we take matter, or motion, or life : all physical analogies show us that as we analyse these and trace them back into deeper and still deeper origins, their nature and action does not become diminished and more and more circumscribed, but, on the contrary, expands and expands until it is lost in the absoluteness of the One Substance-Principle.   And as we are, in any and all of our bodies, from the physical considered as the ' lowest ' to the spiritual considered as the ' highest,' *one in substance* with that One Substance-Principle, however separate a thing physical matter may appear to be : it follows, from our theory of Substance as the One Life, that however separate our life and consciousness may appear to be, it is never in reality either separated from or other than the One Life and Consciousness.

We shall not find it strange, then, that there lies within us the possibility, at least at times, of passing out of the limitations by which we ordinarily conceive of ourselves as circumscribed, into a fuller and deeper life and more ' cosmic ' consciousness ; and this not merely in an extended *psychic* faculty—whereby, indeed, many strange and wonderful things are seen and known —but as an unspeakable realisation of the heights and depths and glory and beauty of the One Life itself : free, exultant, eternal.

In this unity of Substance, then, we have a rational explanation of Mysticism ; of the fact, that is to say, that certain of our fellows have been able to reach in a transcendent degree a consciousness of this fact of Unity, and the immeasurable exaltation of life attained thereby.

And if the limitations of our life here are mainly the limitations of ' matter ': the limitations of a material body in which and through which we play our part for the time being on this material plane of the Cosmos—a plane which *qua* plane, and as a whole, must undoubtedly play an essential part in a larger Cosmic Life and Consciousness—we may with the utmost confidence assert that the break-up of, or departure from, these material limitations can and should result in the realisation of a corresponding liberation and freedom of our individual life and consciousness.

We say ' can and should,' because unfortunately there

appears to exist the possibility for the grossly material man—
for the individual consciousness become so dead to spiritual
life as practically to have cut off all possibility of influx from
the higher planes of Life and Consciousness—to fall still
deeper into the illusion of separateness, to clothe himself, on
the disintegration of this physical body, in a still grosser form
of Substance, or 'matter': with a corresponding further
limitation of powers and faculties. Even thus are many
Hells made.

But even so also, measure for measure, and by a perfectly
natural law, the man of pure spiritual aspiration may expand
and exalt his life and consciousness through all the planes of
the Universe, till he touches in consciousness the universality
of the Absolute.

The record of such expansion of life and consciousness by
the still incarnate man is the record of Mysticism—often
tremulous, halting, erroneous, extravagant, ecstatic, and un-
balanced: as merely passing from the one extreme to the
opposite ; but here and there rational, sane, and balanced:
as recognising the individual *as well as* the Universal, and by
no means losing sight of the ONE in the Many, or the Many
in the ONE.

CHAPTER IV

PHILOSOPHY AND MYSTICISM

"But if Man is, as I have just said, only a power in germ which civilization must develop, whence will come to him the principles of this indispensable culture ? I reply that it will be from the two powers to which he finds himself linked and of which he must form a third. These two powers, between which he finds himself placed, are Destiny (the inferior and instinctive part of Universal Nature, called *necessity*) and Providence (the superior and intellectual part of Universal Nature ; the living law emanating from the Divinity, by means of which all things are determined with power to be). Beneath him is Destiny, *nature nécessitée et naturée ;* above him is Providence, *nature libre et naturante*. He is himself, as Kingdom of Man, the mediatory will, the efficient form, placed between these two natures to serve them as a link, a means of communication, and to unite two actions, two movements, which would be incompatible without him.

The three Powers which I have just named—Providence, Man, considered as the Kingdom of Man, and Destiny—constitute the universal ternary. Nothing escapes their action ; all is subject to them in the universe ; all except *God* Himself who, enveloping them in His unfathomable Unity, forms with it the Sacred Tetrad of the Ancients, that immense quaternary, which is All in All and outside of which there is nothing."

FABRE D'OLIVET : *Hermeneutic Interpretation.*

"There is nothing but a controlled and dispassionate Mysticism, one which acknowledges both the objective laws of knowing, and the transcendent nature of the Subject, which can effect that union of Metaphysics and Morals so much desired to-day by the best minds."

RÉCÉJAC : *Bases of the Mystic Knowledge.*

CHAPTER IV

PHILOSOPHY AND MYSTICISM

IN our last chapter we have seen how the scientific concept of a unitary Root-Substance, or Substance-Principle—whereby all individual 'things' may be apprehended as both individual and universal—carries with it the further concept of a Unitary Life and Consciousness—whereby all seemingly individual lives are apprehended as never in reality separate from the One Life or Substance-Principle, but only so in consciousness.

This scientific concept, therefore, constitutes a most valuable contribution to Mysticism, not merely because Mysticism is precisely the realisation in consciousness of this unity of the seemingly individual life with the Universal, but also because—as we shall see more fully later on—it enables us to deal with various states and phases of mystical experience in a connected and rational manner.

We must now turn from Science to Philosophy, and endeavour to show what is the legitimate province of the latter in the great Quest for *Reality*; what are its limitations therein, and how it stands in .relation to the great fact of mystical intuition, vision, and experience.

The concern of physical science with the problem of life and consciousness is, strictly speaking, confined to the study of the physical or physiological characteristics of the organism in or through which these manifest themselves ; and although this science cannot help hazarding some guess as to the nature of life itself as a *force* capable of moving the organism, it has no concern whatsoever, and indeed, in the nature of the case, cannot deal with the question as to the nature of consciousness *per se* ; for, as the late Professor Huxley so clearly pointed out :

" It seems to me pretty plain that there is a third thing in the universe, to wit, consciousness, which, in the hardness of my heart or head, I cannot see to be matter, or force, or any conceivable modification of either, however intimately the manifestation of the phenomena of consciousness may be connected with the phenomena known as matter and force." [1]

Also Bergson tells us that :

"We do not prove and we never shall prove by any reasoning that the psychic fact is fatally determined by the molecular movement. For in a movement we may find the reason of another movement, but not the reason of a conscious state." [2]

To Philosophy, then, belongs this deeper and further inquiry : the question as to the nature of consciousness and its relation to the objective world of matter and force ; or, briefly, as to the relation which subsists between subject and object. More broadly, it belongs essentially to the province of Philosophy to survey the whole range of human experience, taking its facts from Science on the one hand, and from Religion and Mysticism on the other, and endeavouring to weld the apparently isolated and incongruous or irrelevant facts into a rational whole.

We may note here, however, that the new psychology, which studies states of consciousness as such, and apart from physiological conditions, occupies a kind of intermediate place between physical science and pure philosophy or metaphysics.

But it is necessary in the first instance to distinguish very clearly between Philosophy and mere speculative Metaphysic. Philosophy, in so far as it can be systematised, is the effort to reach some ultimate rational explanation of all things : and in this respect, therefore, it is the Science of all Sciences, for Science is at root systematised knowledge. But Philosophy is—as the etymology of the word indicates—a love of wisdom ; and wisdom is by no means synonymous with systematised knowledge. Wisdom is not merely knowledge, but also the application of knowledge to life and conduct. True Philosophy, therefore, must not merely include all that systematised knowledge can supply in every province of human inquiry, but also those elements in human nature which give to man a moral sense, and a mystic intuition : a sense of Truth, Goodness, and Beauty, and an intuition which leads him to seek for a deeper and more permanent and

[1] T. H. Huxley : *Science and Morals.*
[2] *Time and Free Will*, p. 148.

abiding reality than is afforded in his present fragmentary consciousness of himself and of the Universe as a whole.

Science without Philosophy is pure Materialism, and is unproductive of any richer quality of life than that of mere material prosperity—whereby, indeed, history shows us that Man, whether individually or collectively, may more often lose both that which he seeks, and also his own soul, than find it.

Religion, as commonly presented in the West during the Christian era, has attempted to declare itself independent of both Science and Philosophy ; but here again, history shows us that such Religion quickly degenerates into the irrational authority of tradition, dogmatic theology, superstitious credulity, and shameless priestcraft.

But true Philosophy is too often confounded with speculative metaphysic, or with that particular branch of Philosophy which concerns the theory of human knowledge—epistemology. Speculative metaphysic in or by itself is as soulless and arid as Materialism. Nowadays it has largely degenerated into an effort to become more and more technical, so that none but the most highly trained ' metaphysician ' can follow its development. No wonder that those who seek for a living truth should turn aside in disgust from what is thus offered to them by so-called philosophy, and, mistaking the false for the true, should abandon all philosophical inquiry whatsoever.

We may read and analyse and criticise such metaphysical *systems* till the brain is dizzy and the heart sick in its failure to find the certitude it requires ; till, indeed, like Faust we exclaim :

" I have, alas, Philosophy, the Law, and Medicine, and to my sorrow Theology also, with ardent labour studied through and through. Here I stand, poor fool that I am, no *wiser* than I was before."

Or like Omar Khayyám :

> "Myself when young did eagerly frequent
> Doctor and Saint, and heard great argument
>   About it and about : but evermore
> Came out by that same door where in I went."

Study for yourself every system of Philosophy ever launched upon the world, and if you are merely a formal logician with sufficient determination, you will doubtless in due time excogitate a metaphysical system of your own in which the shortcomings of the 'logic' of all previous metaphysicians is successfully exposed, and something more 'rational'—in your own estimation—is substituted. And then ?—Well, then, even if you have really made an advance, a genuine contribution to the method of pure thought, you will only have opened up a further vision of Infinity, and defined more accurately the limitations of the rational mind— unless, indeed, you have not thus happily discovered that the highest 'logic' of life is to *be*, in a manner which demands no explication, no logomachies.

But if you are something more than a formalist, if you have the root of the matter in you, and have opened your mind to an intuition coming from above, or from within, as well as to empirical experience coming from without : Philosophy will yield you a rich harvest, an abundant confirmation of your deepest intuitions. It may not be expressible in words : it will rather be in the nature of *faith*. Out of all the systems advanced you will take a certain distilled essence, distilled by the magic of your own active spiritual nature, and you will find beneath the mere formal thought of each and all a glimpse of the Eternal Fact, the *vision* which the true philosopher has himself seen, and which his system is merely an effort to rationalise in such terms of the formal mind as may be available in the knowledge and dialectic of his age. Possibly you may give your preference to one system rather than to another, as being the one which best expresses your own thought, and most inspires your soul. But whether you do this or remain perfectly eclectic, it will be because you have already within you that to which the appeal is made, and are thus able to recognise the inner meaning and inspiration. That *something* within you which answers to the appeal is not the mere formal mind, but the deeper Self which lies behind, and of which the formal mind is the instrument in exactly the same sense as is the physical body. It is the Self which uses these bodies or vehicles for its own purpose in the outer, practical or empirical life, which is so commonly mistaken in and by itself for the 'reality.' If one thing can be said to be more real than another in a universe which is a unity, it must be the eternal in contradistinction to the temporal, the indefeasible creative Self, rather than the mutable shadow which the Self projects in time and space, and which is no sooner apparently grasped than it has slipped away and become a mere memory, so that life appears to be nothing more than " just one damn thing after another." The *Real* must, in fact, be the ever-present *Now*.

Here, then, we shall touch both the secret and the limitation of Philosophy. The true philosopher is not a mere logician, but also a seer and a mystic. But he is commonly an unconscious seer or mystic, just as the scientist is an unconscious metaphysician. To each belongs the vision of something more than his own special work and the tools which he uses can grasp and shape. To the scientist belong the physical senses, and such instruments as he can devise to increase their range and power. To the metaphysician belongs the mind and the laws of thought ; but what we have to recognise is, that the one is as limited as the other in the tools which he uses ; the final problem, the nature of Reality, is not a matter either of mechanics or of concepts. These latter can only be made or dealt with within the limitations of the formal mind, which has its own ' laws ' ; but these laws are in themselves merely abstractions, just as physical ' laws ' are merely generalisations deduced from the operation of certain limited phenomena. All the so-called laws, both of matter and of mind, are something taken out of a larger Whole, out of a dynamic flux, and made, as it were, static, rigid, individual. There is nothing of *Life* in the laws of matter and force, or in the principles of logic, or in the abstract formulas of mathematics, save what you yourself can supply with your own feeling, imagination, or intuition. It is the artist and the mystic who approach most nearly to the inner nature of the living Reality ; and it is precisely these who depart farthest from everything which savours of forms or formalisms, save only such as are needed for the technic of their work. The more nearly the one or the other approaches to the inner Reality, the more nearly must his work, the expression of his vision, depart from a representation of the concrete, and become purely symbolical.

We have seen the advance in physics from a concept of discrete atoms to that of a continuous medium, of which the atoms are in some way a modification. The more immediate phenomena with which we are acquainted, much less the Universe itself, cannot be explained by discrete atoms And yet the physicist is compelled to confine his language and his practical work to 'atoms,' and to deal mathematically with hypothetical 'point-masses,' or 'point-charges' of no dimensions as if they possessed a substantial reality, whereas they are merely 'convenient fictions.' The metaphysician is similarly compelled to use 'convenient fictions' in his endeavour to express himself in terms of the formal mind? The mischief only arises when the convenient and fictional nature of his representations is not recognised, and the fictions are taken for an ultimate reality. The advance in metaphysics, and also in formulated religion, is analogous to the advance in physics ; and we shall expect to find the same thing in Mysticism also. Fictions are taken in the first instance for realities, until such time as it is discovered that they are totally inadequate to explain the deeper reality which comes into view with our evolutionary progress.

In both science and metaphysics the failure lies in the attempt to render static what is essentially a flux, and to cram into the time and space perceptions of a time and space *making* faculty something which lies beyond this making. The formal mind cannot transcend its own categories, yet we know intuitively that the transcendent exists. Only mystically can that transcendent be reached. The function of the formal mind is in relation to practical life, and consists in individualising or particularising a definite concrete 'world' in terms of time and space out of a dynamic—not a static—Absolute or *Continuum*, to which terms of time and space are not applicable. The mind is the organ or instrument of the SELF, specialised for a particular purpose, and in relation to the *Continuum* it resembles the physical eye in its relation to the Ether of Space ; but the SELF is the *Continuum* Itself, eternal, unborn, the creator of all its organs and instruments and vehicles, the One Reality in and behind all Appearances.

Just as the physical eye limits our perceptions of the 'world,' so does the individual mind. Take any point in space in the room in which you sit—the point, for example, made by a pin-hole in a card which you can then look through—; that point and all adjacent points and every point in the space of the room, is pulsing and throbbing with millions and billions of etheric vibrations per second : not merely with the light waves which cross and recross it from every object in the room, but an infinite number of other vibrations also, which we have no physical senses to appreciate. Out of all this flux the eye selects a certain limited number of vibrations, and behold! we have an appearance of form and colour, a ' world ' of objects.

Yet this ' world ' is plainly only one of a vast number of possible worlds which might be constructed out of the total flux, were our organs of perception differently constituted. You say that you cannot see through the ' solid ' walls of your room; yet you can see through the ' empty space ' of the room, which, however, science tells you is filled with a substance millions of times denser than the solid matter of the walls.

When, therefore, you—the ' self '—only see by means of the physical eye, you are limited by the limitations of structure and function of the eye. But the self which possesses the power of seeing is not identical with the instrument it uses, nor is it limited thereby. There are other means of seeing, even physical things, than that which is employed when the self sees through the physical eye.

So likewise is it with the mind. The formal mind is a larger retina which synthesises into concepts the complex experiences of the self; and in order that we may have a practical, concrete world in common with others, we must not merely have certain experiences in common, but also common concepts and definitions.

Thus our ' world ' is separated out, differentiated, and defined by the ' rational ' or concept-making mind working upon sense impressions, and in our perversity we imagine that the great Universe is no *other* than what is thus ' given ' in our minds. Yet it might be, it is perfectly conceivable, that our state of consciousness and knowledge immediately after death will be such that all our carefully constructed formal systems of philosophy and religion whereby we define—and limit — ' reality,' will tumble like a house of cards; the Universe, or our then ' world,' will be so *other* than what we now apprehend, that our present concepts will have no application. We may find in the annals of psychical research many experiences which are more than a hint that this will be so, in some considerable degree.

But when the formal mind has thus particularised and

defined its world, it persistently refuses to undo it. There is an inertia of mind in this sense as well as of matter. "A cannot be both B and not-B." It cannot be any 'other' than what it is defined as. The centre of the circle is not its circumference ; to say that it both is and is not, is the language of paradox, the language of Mysticism, to be intuitively grasped, but not advanced as 'logic.' Logic must keep to its definitions once they are given, and must move from them to its conclusions as inevitably as a mathematical process.

All the trouble in Metaphysics, then, would appear to be that the logicians, the 'intellectuals,' have attempted to use their instrument—the formal mind—in an illegitimate manner ; they have constantly attempted to measure and define that great *Other*—the ' Absolute,' or the ' Infinite,' or the ' Eternal,' in fact the *Continuum*—with the two-foot rule of the mind, marked off in inches, and quarters, and sixteenths—to any number of merely arbitrary subdivisions which they were capable of inventing. The mind has been used like a machine designed to rule finer and still finer lines on a glass plate : always with a possibility that it may be capable of being improved so as to rule still finer, but with no chance of ever reaching finality, or of working in any other fashion. Metaphysicians endeavouring to define the Absolute, or ' Reality,' are workmen who have not learnt the legitimate use of the tools they handle ; they are trying to use them for other work than that for which they have been designed. When the lines on the glass plate are no longer required, when a ' continuous medium ' replaces the discrete lines, you don't require the tool at all.

But this very trouble has arisen from a deeper intuition of the mind itself that somehow the nature of the Absolute must be such as to include the discrete, the ' lines,' whilst yet transcending them. The problem presses in on all our thinking with an irresistible force which will not be denied to a deeper region of our mind, to what we might almost call a transcendental region of reason ; and so, again and again, the metaphysical philosopher has endeavoured to formulate it : only to have his elaborately constructed system mercilessly upset by some other fellow who presently comes along with a keenly developed critical faculty to point out the inevitable antinomies which must exist in any such system.

What has been accepted of the great philosophers has not been so much their method as some mystic vision of Truth intuitively grasped even though inadequately proved. Thus even Kant did not escape the charge of Mysticism; against which charge Carlyle endeavoured to defend him—having himself an entirely *irrational* idea of Mysticism.[1]

We have the same intuitive faculty exercising itself even in pure Science. The doctrine of the Conservation of Energy, for example, which scientists believe to be universally applicable, is only demonstrable in a very limited manner; yet the scientific mind holds to it most tenaciously as representative of some deep fundamental truth. It is, again, a doctrine of Continuity transcending our common experience of empirical discreteness.

The analogy between the limitations of physicists and those of metaphysicians is very striking. To the physicist pure and simple the Ether is what the elusive ' Other ' is to the metaphysician; he cannot bring it within the empirical region of those elements of number, measure and weight to which he is compelled to limit himself, any more than the metaphysician can deal with that which lies beyond the elements of time, space and causation to which the formal mind is limited. The physicist can neither affirm nor deny anything of the Ether *per se*, and some would even deny its existence altogether; at all events in the Einstein physics there is no part, place, or lot to be found for it. But for the physicist who must needs go beyond the merely empirical to that ' Other ' whose very existence is implied in the fact of the empirical, the Ether is something more than a mere working hypothesis; it stands for a *reality* of which he cannot disabuse his mind. Similarly, the metaphysician pure and simple cannot affirm or deny anything of the Absolute, yet is compelled to accept it in the very nature of those limitations of the Mind to which he is restricted. As has been pointed out by metaphysicians themselves over and over again, the very act of ' determination ' of what anything *is*, is the implication of the ' Other ' which it is not; and the whole of ' Appearance,' taken together, implies a ground in a ' Reality,' of which the Appearance is a Manifestation. The *Self* as thinker, observer, spectator, can never be *objective*; nevertheless, the objective can never

[1] *Vide infra*, p. 163.

be other than the content of the Self ; it can never be absolutely a real and independent ' thing-in-itself.'

Kant, whilst clearly recognising and acknowledging the transcendental ' Other,' rightly placed it beyond the limits of the formal mind. Hegel, whose name is so associated with absolutism, clearly recognised the uselessness of formal logic for the solution of the transcendental problem ; but so inspired was he with the idea that somehow, in some way, the Absolute was ' rational,' that he invented another instrument, his so-called ' dialectic method,' wherewith to accomplish the task. Here again the inspiration is accepted, the method a failure—*pace* the few remaining out-and-out Hegelians. There appears to be a very general consensus of opinion, even among those who reject Hegel's ' method,' that he possessed a rare intuitive insight, and almost an occult power of language, enforcing recognition in spite of intellectual dissidence. He speaks as prophet, not as priest, as hierophant rather than as philosopher. It is his vision, not his ' dialectic,' which prevails. In the inner depths of the self-transcending intellect he has touched a reality which his fire and forcefulness communicates to others in a manner quite distinct from the formal process of his logic, which, like all systematised intuition or mystical vision, fails to grasp and imprison the great ever-illusive ' Other.' Were it not that we mean by Mysticism something much more than this, we should claim him as a typical mystic.

William James, in describing a mystical experience of his own, in which " the opposites of the world, whose contradictoriness and conflict make all our difficulties and troubles, were melted into unity " : speaks thus of Hegel :

"What reader of Hegel can doubt that that sense of a perfected Being with all its otherness soaked up into itself, which dominates his whole philosophy, must have come from the prominence in his consciousness of mystical moods like this, in most persons kept subliminal ? The notion is thoroughly characteristic of the mystical level, and the *Aufgabe* of making it articulate was surely set to Hegel's intellect by mystical feeling."[1]

But to-day the philosophic atmosphere is clearing ; the tools, both physical and metaphysical, are being relegated to their proper use. Physicists have been largely attempting

[1] *Varieties of Religious Experience,* p. 389.

to do the work of metaphysicians, whilst the latter have been trying to do the work of the mystic. The physicists have been unconscious metaphysicians, the metaphysicians unconscious mystics. The reason for this is clearly that within the consciousness of each there lies an intuition of a deeper reality, and the attempt to grasp and formulate it is irresistible : each one endeavouring to do so in the terms of their own particular department of knowledge.

Many physicists to-day, however, have clearly seen their error in this respect, and are in open revolt against the metaphysical tendencies of their confrères. They do not object to legitimate metaphysical speculation, as do purely materialistic scientists ; but they rightly assert that it should be kept distinct from physics proper. In particular, many decline to accept the Ether as anything but a metaphysical speculation.

H. Poincaré, in the preface to his *Électricité et Optique*, says :

" The day will perhaps come when the physicist will cease to be interested in questions unapproachable by positive methods, and will abandon them to the metaphysicians. But that day has not yet come ; man does not so easily resign himself to abandon for ever the heart of things."

More recently Professor Whitehead [1] has published an exhaustive analysis of the position of physical science in this relation, in which he attacks not merely the concept of a physical Ether, but the whole of the traditional concepts of science based on the abstract " convenient fictions " of mathematics, such as unextended " point-masses," and " momentary events " which have no duration, and which are pure abstractions—however ' convenient '—having no reality in actual experience. It is curious to note that he is led to postulate what he virtually calls " an ether of events " rather than to recognise an actual substantial ether ; that is to say, an ether expressing a continuity and overlapping of events in *time* rather than a continuity of substance in *space*. We have already seen Professor Eddington making use of practically the same idea.[2]

[1] *An Enquiry Concerning the Principles of Natural Knowledge*, by A. N. Whitehead, Sc.D., F.R.S. Cambridge University Press, 1919.
[2] Cf. *supra*, p. 71.

We arrive, then, at this view, that neither the physicist nor the metaphysician must abandon their special work and particular concepts, though each may legitimately strive for a comprehension of a deeper reality intuitively felt to lie behind the limitations of their respective methods. But each must refrain from using the wrong tools, and perhaps not be so scornful of others who, working in another department, and with other tools, may arrive at certain results which seem to be altogether foreign to their own conclusions.

Metaphysic is Philosophy without a soul. As such it may have its mechanical and practical function and uses, but it cannot and does not live and survive in men's hearts and minds as true Philosophy should, and as all great Philosophies do, precisely because they carry with them the inspiration of that living fire by which the inner man is quickened and nourished, and which may give, even to a faulty dialectic, an immortal fame. Of all the philosophers whose names are indelibly recorded on the page of history, there is hardly one who does not touch in some manner or other the region of mystic intuition and experience; and it is this, rather than the formal logic, which gives to their work that *inspired* quality essential to a lasting place in the great literatures of the world.

Kant endeavoured to formulate the limitations or boundaries of the 'rational' mind, the nature of those *a priori* judgments which condition and determine our empirical experience; but it is not on account of his formal logic that his contribution to Philosophy has been such an influence. His 'categories' have been somewhat roughly handled by subsequent metaphysicians, yet his main contribution to Philosophy remains valid, and no one recognised more clearly than he himself, that the very limitations carried with them by implication the existence of that which transcends them. Kant, however, did not attempt any reconciliation of the higher with the lower, but rather kept them severely apart, and thereby fell short of a true philosophy.

The truly inspired philosopher is on the same level as the truly inspired artist, musician, or poet. One and all have a perception of the transcendental Fact, the Eternal Vital Reality which is the nature of the Soul itself, and the source of the infinite *expression* of Reason, Beauty, and

Emotion in the Manifested Universe : of which Man himself, viewed from below, is the chief product, and, viewed from above, is the actual Creator.

The artist does not so much seek to explicate the Eternal Fact as to reveal it to our intuition ; he seeks to inspire our soul through beauty of form and colour with a like perception as he himself possesses. The musician also makes a direct appeal to an inner faculty which is susceptible—for an occult reason difficult to explicate—to the influence of sound. The poet makes the same appeal, using for this purpose a language capable of calling up a mental image of the beauty perceived, or an indefinable emotion in the recognition of a beauty that " never was on sea or land." To the philosopher, however, it remains to express the Eternal Fact in terms of our rational faculty, so far as it is capable of expression : appealing thereby through the rational faculty to the deeper intuition. He must endeavour, like the artist, to invent and continually improve a method or *medium* for this purpose ; but, like the artist also, he inevitably finds his materials to be refractory and inadequate. We shall also note that there will as inevitably exist in Philosophy a certain *conventionality* at certain periods, as there does in art, music, or drama.

Mysticism is subject to the same restrictions, and our business is to note what is due to limitation of materials, to limitation of human faculty, or to mere convention, and to separate these from the really essential elements. Only as we are able to do this shall we be free from forms and formulas, but at the same time able to utilise particular forms as occasion may arise.

The profound conviction of all great philosophers may be said to be that there is *some* faculty within us which prompts us to the belief—even where we cannot prove—that at root the Universe is Rational and Intelligible, not merely in the sense that everything which can be or is experienced can also be explained, but above all that it is in some way the expression and the action of an intelligible Principle.

Evolution of human faculty may be regarded as a gradual progress towards that explanation ; but evolution as a *process* seems to be infinite—as, indeed, any progress towards an ' Infinite ' must be. There is, however, a still deeper intuition that somehow this process itself is illusive, and may be transcended, or may at least be regarded from a transcendental point of view, even while experienced. It is the intuition that *process*, experienced only in the category of time considered as a straight line, or one dimensional extension or sequence, is a very incomplete experience of Reality ; that something more *real* may actually be immediately contacted and known ; something which would not evade us, and mock us, and pass away as everything does in this process-show, and which yet somehow this process-show exhibits and reveals, if only we could see it in a larger and wider regard. Somehow the process-show is made out of *Reality* by a limiting process taking place in what we know as consciousness.

Deep within us, glimpsed by philosopher, and more definitely by the mystic, lies the feeling that, if we only knew *how*, we could pass immediately out of this pressure of limitation and nescience into a region of pure reality and assured truth ; not by abandonment of process or ' becoming,' but rather by a true apprehension of its meaning and function.

We do not think that it will be saying too much if we assert that modern Philosophy is moving into a clearer recognition of the legitimacy of such intuitions ; that the change which is taking place means broadly that the methods which have hitherto prevailed are now acknowledged to be inadequate to solve the problems which a deeper knowledge of phenomena on the one hand, and a wider regard for the inner facts of life and consciousness on the other, are yielding us. In this respect, however, philosophy can but go " back to Plato," and the neo-Platonists, or to the still earlier Vedânta.

The history of philosophy shows us clearly that no system of any of the great thinkers has been adequate to sustain the weight of the final superstructure which they have striven to impose upon it. Were it not so, indeed, no further system would be needed : we should have reached finality. The history of philosophy is the history of our failure to solve by intellectual process the nature of the more immediate knowledge which presses in upon us in Life itself. Philosophy—or rather Metaphysic—as the outcome of a mere intellectual process, unsupported by the deeper intuition to which we have already referred, ends in Scepticism and Pessimism ; just as Science, in and by itself, is pure Materialism.

But the deeper region of our nature transcending our mental

operations will not be denied, and it is seldom that the philosopher has stopped short at the limitations of his own formal system, or has been able to express therein the pure Idea of his deeper and mystic insight. Without going back to Plato or the neo-Platonists, what endorsement, we may ask, has logical criticism given to Spinoza's 'Substance,' or Leibnitz's 'Monads'; to Fichte's 'Ego and Non-Ego,' or Hegel's 'Absolute Idea'? Has Schopenhauer—ruthless destroyer of the systems of others—given us anything more logically certain in his universal 'Will and Idea'; or von Hartmann, with all the wealth of his brilliant predecessors to work upon, in his 'Philosophy of the Unconscious'? Must it not be said of each and all of these that they represent something more in Philosophy than the operation of the formal mind; that the philosopher was greater than his system?

Thus we cannot limit the historical value of philosophical inquiry to its merely speculative results, any more than we can limit the value of scientific inquiry to the theories which the scientist forms from time to time to account for known phenomena. There are other elements in man's search for the fundamental and eternal Reality of his life and consciousness than those of either physical or mental processes: elements to which these are subordinate as effect to cause, and which therefore in a certain sense are primary, though we must never forget that cause and effect are in reality only two aspects of one and the same flux—or shall we say *continuity*?

But this very failure of the rational or formal mind which we have now noted, to bring the transcendental Fact into explication, serves to show up in the strongest relief the relation of the mind itself to the transcendental. The Fact lies behind the mind, and is admitted by the mind, by our 'rational' nature, while at the same time it remains inexplicable in terms of mental process.

The great transcendental Fact of an Eternal Self-Existent Principle or Substance, is one which Philosophy acknowledges as an absolute necessity; but as to what that Principle is in its own nature, and in its action as the source and origin of this great Universe of Phenomena, or of what we know within ourselves as life and consciousness: this transcendental knowledge the mind is powerless to grasp by means of those formal

10

concepts which are evolved or derived from our empirical sense experiences. Why is this so; and what are the limitations of the mind as we at present know it?

The answer to this question is now tolerably clear, and involves the acceptance of all that scientific psychology can teach us, as well as a larger and deeper realisation of the powers of the mind. What we have here called the rational or formal mind, may be regarded as largely, if not entirely, a matter of evolution by and through, or co-ordinate with, sense or empirical experience; and if we accept this, while at the same time recognising that the mind can also be influenced from *above*, from the transcendental region as well as from the outwardly empirical, we have a means of reconciling the two extremes of Empiricism and Idealism which have seemed to some to be so diametrically and irreducibly opposed. We are bound to accept all that Science can give us as *fact*; but we are not bound to stop short at orthodox scientific fact, much less at orthodox scientific theory.

Locke's celebrated essay on the Nature of the Human Understanding sought to show that the mind of the newborn babe was a *tabula rasa*, an absolute blank, and the theory was hailed with delight by the ultra-materialists of the day. "The senses," says Locke, "let in particular ideas and furnish the yet empty cabinet." But Locke does not tell us how the cabinet is capable of being furnished at all—or would it not be better if we likened the mind to a sensitised photographic plate? The plate must have certain pre-given requisites, not merely in order to receive impressions at all, but to receive them in the particular *way* in which they are received.

Here Kant comes in with his 'categories,' which are the pre-existing requisites which shape our sense impressions into those formal modes of thought, or concepts, which present 'Reality' to us as so and so. They are the pre-given and necessary condition of the sensitised plate.

We might liken these 'categories' to the definite chemical characteristics and reactions which take place in the silver salts employed in the sensitised photographic film. Given a different chemical element, selenium for example, and the reaction of light is of quite another order and nature. And for aught we know there may be in the Universe—or even in our own Earth sphere—beings who have 'minds' which have quite other 'categories' than those of time, space, and causation which we possess. Why should we limit to some one particular mode the Universal or Cosmic Mind, from which all individual minds must necessarily be derived, even as all the variety of the chemical elements with their innumerable reactions are derived from the etheric substance? Even if there are not various orders or modes of 'mind' in the Universe, there are most certainly various orders of *beings*; that is to say, of individualised *consciousness*; and we have ample evidence in psychical phenomena—let alone the mystical consciousness—that we ourselves can transcend the 'categories' of the lower or formal mind.

It is precisely this which renders so utterly futile, as an attempt to limit and define *Reality*, all that vast cobweb of metaphysical dialectic which has been spun from time to time in the endeavour to reconcile a theologically conceived *personal* God with the actualities of the phenomenal world as it is presented to the mind through the physical *senses*, which, according to Locke, "let in particular ideas." But how can the senses let in *ideas*?

So far as Locke's theory is concerned, it has now been very considerably modified by scientific psychology. The mind is clearly recognised as an evolved product, and as being dependent upon organic structure; but the mind of the infant is not a *tabula rasa*; it has behind it a vast racial heredity. The physical germ-cell transmitted from parent to offspring is, in the scientific imagination, burdened with the whole weight of this enormous heredity, which is in some inexplicable way supposed to be involved in the physical constitution of the cell; and materialists of Haeckel's type would make this psychic heredity within the germ-cell merely a matter of physics and chemistry. There is according to them no life principle: dead atoms and molecules, by the mere chance conditions of environment and temperature, come to arrange themselves in certain ways, and simply transmit their vibrations to their neighbours, with a cumulative effect which presently becomes the brain of man—which is all there is of 'mind.' In this view the brain is, in fact, the 'cabinet' of Locke, or the sensitised plate; but it is an evolved product, and as such is permitted to have certain 'instincts' and other innate psychic characteristics and predispositions. All the same it is, in the view of a materialist, simply a chemically sensitised plate, and nothing more.

This, very briefly, is the one extreme view of the great problem of mind or soul. The other is that of Subjective Idealism : that the external object has no existence independent of the mind ; it is but the thought or idea existing in the mind : all apparent modifications of external objects being modifications of the mind of the thinking subject. The objective world exists in and for and by the individual subject ; it has no independent external reality—it is the 'dream' of the subjective self.

Now in a last analysis, and on the basis of a unitary Substance-Principle which is both Subject and Object, it is evident that we are compelled to fall back upon a form of Subjective Idealism. But we have an ineradicable instinct that so far as the 'I,' the individual thinking subject, is concerned, 'things' exist independently, and that when 'we' lose touch with the objective world of our present consciousness, those 'things' still exist : they exist in the consciousness of other individuals ; and even should the whole of humanity perish and become utterly extinct on this globe, we cannot rid ourselves of the idea that the globe itself would still exist.

But there is in fact no need to run counter in a violent manner to this 'common-sense' view. In so far as the 'I' of whom we speak in this connection is itself an individual thing, other 'things' necessarily exist apart from the content of that limited consciousness.

Our theory of Mind, then, must mediate the two extremes of Realism and Idealism, and must make allowance on the one hand for the existence of a 'real' objective world independent of the *individual* thinking subject, and on the other for the fact that the real ultimate unitary Self creates its own objective universe.

We have a firm conviction that Truth is not to be found in any extreme, but in a mean which includes both extremes. Find the 'least common multiple,' or the 'greatest common measure,' or the 'mean axis,' or the 'centre of gravity,' or the 'moment of inertia'—in short, the centre of balance and poise of any complex of ideas or concepts, and in life itself, and you will not be very far from the truth. All these terms represent a certain unitary relation of parts which, regarded separately, are in opposition one to another. Empirical truth is always a relation and proportion of parts, but root Truth is a wholeness.

We shall, then, in our theory of Mind, place this instrument or vehicle of the Self in a middle position, between—to use our common phraseology—spirit and matter. We must not forget that the real actor, the real knower, is the *Self*; and it is quite evident from the way in which we can direct the operations of our mind, that the mind is merely an instrument by or through which the Self acts, in precisely the same sense that the body is also an instrument for action on the physical plane.

The mind is, as it were, a definite centre in which the Self—which in itself is universal and absolute—can centre itself so as to particularise a ' world.' In order thus to particularise, the Self necessarily limits itself, and these fundamental limitations are the ' categories '—time, space, causation, etc.

Thenceforward all the operations of the Self, considered as mental operations, or ' intellect,' are necessarily limited by these categories; but the Self, now centred in the mind, retains the ' intuition ' of its transcendental nature, and from this intuition spring all those deeper qualities of our life—religion, art, morality, etc.—which are not wholly amenable to intellectual treatment. Hence also the constant but unsuccessful effort of philosophers to explicate Reality in terms of intellect.

We shall deal later on with a theory of Mind or Soul, based upon our fundamental concept of a Unitary Substance-Principle; but we may note here that the Self thus centred as it were in the Mind, and able to look both ways, towards Spirit as well as towards Matter, is extremely liable to lose touch altogether with its transcendental nature, and wholly to ' fall into matter '; and the more so that this ' Fall of Man ' appears to be a particular and definite stage or cycle in the great cosmic process.

There exists in the experience of mystics in all ages definite evidence that the Self can transcend the limits and functions of the mind: even as there exists in the records of psychical research definite evidence that the limitations of the physical faculties can be transcended; though we must carefully guard against identifying this latter transcendence with true Mysticism.

But even without such mystic transcendence the mind is capable of intuitively perceiving, though not of formulating, the elusive 'other,' as well as the present 'reality.' Innumerable quotations might be given, but we will confine ourselves to the two following from Eastern sources.

Gautama Buddha says:

" This world, O Kaccâna, generally proceeds on a duality; on the ' It is ' and the ' It is not.' But, O Kaccâna, whoever perceives in truth and wisdom how things originate in the world, in his eyes there is no ' It is not ' in this world. Whoever, Kaccâna, perceives in truth and wisdom how things pass away in this world, in his eyes there is no ' It is ' in this world. . . . ' Everything is,' this is the one extreme, O Kaccâna; ' Everything is not,' this is the other extreme. The perfect one, O Kaccâna, remaining far from both these extremes proclaims the truth in the middle." [1]

An old Chinese mystic, Chuang Tzu, says:

" And inasmuch as the subjective is also the objective, and the objective also subjective, and as the contraries under each are indistinguishably blended, does it not become impossible for us to say whether subjective and objective really exist at all ? When subjective and objective are both without their correlates, that is the very axis of Tao. And when that axis passes through the centre at which all the Infinities converge, positive and negative alike blend into an infinite One." [2]

If, then, we find that our Sages could thus recognise and formulate, albeit in paradoxical language, the possibility of reconciling what the merely formal mind regards as extremes : it is still what we call 'mind' which is capable of perceiving this truth. It is the mind which works intuitively as well as rationally and empirically. The mind is, in fact, dual in its nature and functions; it can turn its attention to, and receive from, a transcendental region, as well as from the outer world of sense.

Let us understand, then, in the first instance, that what we at present know as mind—and in particular our everyday, working or practical mind—is moulded by, because it acts and reacts with, our sense perceptions and empirical

---

[1] Oldenberg : *Buddha*, trans. W. Hoey, M.A., p. 249.
[2] *Musings of a Chinese Mystic*, p. 45 (Wisdom of the East Series).

experiences. We work in our everyday life by means of our inherited racial mind, and we fit our empirical experiences into its innate categories—the prepared 'cabinet'—from our childhood up. It would be much better for some of us if our minds were actually a *tabula rasa* in many respects as regards this racial inherited mind. Later on in life, when we have fully apprehended the necessity of negating the experiences of the senses, and of turning our mind in the other direction, towards the transcendental region, our hardest work is to undo and counteract the false suggestions coming to us from the external world which the mind is so inherently prone to accept as 'reality.'

We must recognise, then, that what we commonly call the mind, the psycho-physiological function, is dominated by empirical experience and racial heredity: that is to say that the formal 'concepts' which the mind constructs as to the nature of the external world, are determined by these experiences, or at least evolve *pari passu* with them ; or, as Bergson puts the matter : " Intellectuality and materiality have been constituted, in detail, by reciprocal adaptation " ; and, " Both are derived from a wider and higher form of existence. It is there that we must replace them, in order to see them issue forth." [1] But we shall also have to recognise that the mind is open to the transcendental region, this " higher form of existence," and not merely may, but does, receive impressions therefrom which are radically different from our formal concepts as product of our empirical sense experience, and are even, so far as we can formulate them, precisely the opposite of all that we are able to formulate 'down here.' This is Bergson's " Intuitionism " : closely allied to what we understand as Rational Mysticism.

We have already seen how every true philosopher thus receives his inspiration ; but what is already true in Philosophy is still further in evidence in Mysticism. The mystic is one who *par excellence* has opened his mind to the reception of transcendental truth. Some mystics have sought to do this by wholly closing the mind to the outer world ; but here again we shall pronounce for a mean, and not for an extreme. The true mystic, the rational mystic, is one who can recognise and harmonise both worlds, and make a Wholeness of them,

[1] *Creative Evolution*, p. 197.

not a separation ; and whilst some of the deepest mystic experiences may be, and indeed must be, in the words of Plotinus, "the flight of the Alone to the Alone," we may perhaps venture to suggest that the soul of man can only truly lose itself in the ONE when thereby it finds itself in all its fulness in the Many. "Foregoing self, the Universe grows ' I.' " [1]

We shall, then, accept to the full all that science can demonstrate as to the evolution of mind, and its interaction with and relation to physical nature. Nothing is more natural than that evolution—that is to say, *manifestation*—of mind should accompany evolution of physical organism. When we are told by materialistic scientists that, "we have this stupendous mass of (scientific) evidence converging along a dozen lines to the conclusion that the mind-force is continuous throughout the animal kingdom, and is rigidly and absolutely bound up, so far as every particle of scientific evidence goes, with the nerve structure, and is, at the lower end, continuous with the ordinary force of the universe " [2]—when we are told this as conclusive for the theory that the mind does not exist apart from physical organism : we are fully prepared to accept the " stupendous mass of evidence," but not the *naïveté* of the conclusion. For it is quietly assumed that the nature of the " ordinary force of the universe " is absolutely well known : that it is, in fact, nothing but the mechanical energy of dead physical and chemical atoms and molecules. " The peculiar phenomena of consciousness," says Haeckel, " must be reduced to the phenomena of physics and chemistry." [3] Thus the materialist simply begs the root question : What is the " ordinary force " of the universe ?

We find Haeckel, notwithstanding the above pronouncement, postulating a certain grade of substance which he denominates " sensitive and thinking." He even speaks of " the all-embracing energy of *thought*," thereby apparently making thought the " ordinary force " of the universe. He presents to us, indeed, in a most striking manner the hopelessness of the attempt to intrude physics into the domain of metaphysics and the problems of life and consciousness.

---

[1] *Light of Asia.*
[2] McCabe: *Haeckel's Critics Answered*, p. 57.
[3] Vide, *Scientific Idealism*, p. 180.

We have already seen that we cannot carry our purely physical concepts back to a continuous Substance. We cannot even carry them back to the next remove, i.e. to the Ether of Space ; still, the concepts are quite valid so far as they will legitimately go, and we have every right to use them for all they are worth, so long as we do not allow them to harden into materialistic dogmas, or unconsciously permit them to close up other avenues of knowledge, and our own intuitional faculty. The concept of individual forms of motion existing in one Unitary Substance is, in itself, and apart from the question as to the ultimate nature of the Substance *per se*, a very simple one, and in all respects analogous to the philosophical or metaphysical one of individual forms, modes, centres of consciousness, or 'monads.' It helps us to reconcile the essentially *discrete* nature of phenomena and mind with the essentially *continuous* or interpenetrative nature of life and consciousness *per se*.

The old physical doctrine of individual, discrete, ultimate, indivisible atoms or particles, each of which was a ' thing in itself,' has now given way to the more philosophical concept of a continuity of Substance; and—as Sir Oliver Lodge so aptly puts it—" We cannot go back to mere impact of hard bodies after having allowed ourselves a continuous medium." But if it is true in physics that we cannot go back to mere discrete discontinuous particles, it is equally true that in metaphysics we cannot go back to discrete individual Egos or ' Souls,' after having perceived the fulness and beauty of a ' continuous substance,' as the One Life, the One Self, of the Universe. The old idea of separate individual souls corresponds in every way to the old physical doctrine of discrete atoms ; it is simply the result of a crude realism, such as even now can take the " ordinary force " of the universe to be nothing more than what our physical senses can appreciate as mechanical energy. But the old theological doctrine is giving way to a restatement of the still older philosophical doctrine of psychical and spiritual continuity ; of a Supreme SELF which includes all individual selves in its " all-embracing energy " ; of a sub-conscious or sub-liminal —or rather supra-liminal—Self, whose depth and continuity with the supra-conscious Universe is infinite as that Universe itself.

This metaphysical concept follows naturally from the physical one as soon as we have recognised that the One Substance is both Subject and Object, and that no individual or particular manifestation of it can be other than the ONE itself, seen, known, or manifested partially, imperfectly, or in a limited manner.

When, therefore, the materialist tells us that Mind is one with the " ordinary force of the universe," we are quite ready to assent, for we recognise that Motion—which is the activity or ' ordinary force ' of the most ' ordinary ' thing— is the activity of the One Substance, which activity—as we shall presently show—cannot be other than that of Life and Consciousness *per se.*

Modern Philosophy, like modern Science and modern Mysticism, is moving forward into new-old concepts ; into a recognition of certain fundamental principles which we may find quite as clearly stated in the oldest philosophies as they are ever likely to be stated to-day. The only difference is that to-day Science is supported by a wealth of detail and experimental evidence which we do not find in the older systems.

Dialectical method may be said to have resulted to-day in the re-discovery of the limitations of the formal mind ; but— and this is the main point—when we turn our attention from the immediate aim of Metaphysics as an effort to formulate completely the problem of Life and Consciousness within the limitations of mental process or logic, to a wider view of Philo- sophy as an attempt to deal with our *whole* nature : we see that the very failure implies a progress in the sense of a continually increasing conviction of the reality and importance of that very thing, or region, which eludes the operation of the formal mind : the existence of a transcendental region of life and experience intuitively or immediately contacted and known, but which persistently escapes all our efforts to impose upon it the limitations characteristic of the individual mind and consciousness.

In other words, the problem of Life is not the same as the problem of Mind. Life itself is immeasurably more than thought or psychic activity. The mind is only the instru- ment of Life, and thought only one of its functions ; and whatever is known only by the formal mind is limited by the

' categories ' in just the same sense that what is perceived by the eye is limited by the structure of the eye. Life is continuous, but the formal mind is discrete—or perhaps we might say the *maker* of the discrete.

We have noted a revolt on the part of some physicists against the too metaphysical speculations of their confrères, and we may now note that a similar kind of revolt in modern philosophy against methods which are too speculative to be of any practical value is to be found in what is known as *Pragmatism*; and to round off what we have already said as to the inadequacy of formal logic in any attempt to storm the Absolute, we may give the following quotation from a well-known work by the late Professor William James, whose name is so closely associated with the cult of Pragmatism:

" For my own part, I have finally found myself compelled to *give up the logic*, fairly, squarely, and irrevocably. It has an imperishable use in human life, but that use is not to make us theoretically acquainted with the essential nature of reality. Reality, life, experience, concreteness, immediacy, use what word you will, exceeds our logic, overflows and surrounds it. If you like to employ words eulogistically . . . you may say that reality obeys a higher logic, or enjoys a higher rationality. But I think that even eulogistic words should be used rather to distinguish than to commingle meanings, so I prefer bluntly to call reality if not irrational then at least non-rational in its constitution—and by reality here I mean reality where things *happen*, all temporal reality without exception." [1]

Professor James goes on to say that what has led him to this definite renunciation of formal logic in connection with the problem of reality has been the influence of the modern apostle of " Intuitionism," Professor Henri Bergson:

" I have now to confess that I should not now be emancipated, not now subordinate logic with so very light a heart, or throw it out of the deeper regions of philosophy to take its rightful and respectable place in the world of simple human practice, if I had not been influenced by a comparatively young and very original French writer, Professor Henri Bergson. If I had not read Bergson, I should probably still be blackening endless pages of paper privately, in the hope of making ends meet that were never meant to meet, and trying to discover some mode of conceiving the behaviour of reality which should leave no discrepancy between it and the accepted laws of the logic of identity." [2]

We may note, however, that this is only a return to a principle recognised and expressed in many ways at different

[1] *A Pluralistic Universe*, p. 212.   [2] *Ibid.*, p. 214.

periods and by various teachers. What Professor James here says of the practical function of the intellect is paralleled, for example, in the following passage from Plotinus:

" For this (pure intellect) is not a practical intellect, as looking to that which pertains to external action, and which in consequence of not abiding in itself, is a certain knowledge of externals. There is, however, no necessity if intellect is practic, that it should know itself; but this is the province of that intellect which is not engaged in practical affairs." [1]

The whole teaching of neo-Platonism embodies precisely this distinction between the lower reason or intellect which knows things, or ' reality,' only as an appearance, and the higher intellect, or " intelligible nature," in which " the objects of its perceptions are not external to itself." [2] In other words, this is a direct and immediate knowledge in which the knower and the thing known are one.

"One kind of intelligence is the intellectual perception of another thing, but another is the perception of a thing by itself, or when a thing perceives itself; the latter of which flies in a greater degree from duplicity, or doubleness in intellection. But the former wishes also to avoid this diversity, but is less able to accomplish this wish. [3] For it has indeed with itself that which it sees, but it is different from itself. That, however, which intellectually perceives itself, is not separated essentially from the object of its perception, but being co-existent with it sees itself. Both, therefore, become one being. Hence it perceives in a greater degree because it possesses that which it perceives. It is also primarily intellective, because that which perceives intellectually ought to be both one and two." [4]

In this higher intellectual perception we may see clearly the higher function of the mind which Professor Henri Bergson is now endeavouring to grasp and set forth, and for which our only available word appears to be *intuition*. Bergson is only trying to deduce and express it in more modern terms, and in the light of our scientific knowledge.

As regards the incapacity of the mind to grasp the problem of Absoluteness, we may, passing farther back, note that it was taught by Gautama Buddha. It is thus voiced by Sir Edwin Arnold in his beautiful poem " The Light of Asia."

[1] *Enn.*, V, iii, 6.   [2] *Ibid.*, V, xi, 5.
[3] This is exactly Professor James's difficulty which we have just quoted.
[4] *Enn.*, V, vi, 1.

"OM, AMITAYA! measure not with words
  Th' Immeasurable; nor sink the string of thought
Into the Fathomless. Who asks doth err,
  Who answers, errs. Say nought!"

We might also quote once more from our old Chinese mystic, Chuang Tzu:

"For man's intellect, however keen, face to face with the countless evolution of things, their death and birth, their squareness and roundness—can never reach the root. There creation is, and there it has ever been." [1]

One might give innumerable quotations from various sources in support of this fundamental fact as to the nature of the intellect or mind in its twofold aspects of higher and lower—the lower being what we commonly know as mind in its logical functions, whilst the higher is its function in intuition and mysticism: or, using the term *soul* instead of *mind*, we may say with Eckhart, "The soul is created in a place between Time and Eternity: with its highest powers it touches Eternity, with its lower Time." [2]

What is surely needed to-day, when God is so familiarly spoken about in the pulpit, is a very clear recognition of this principle; and indeed we think that very many are repelled from the sermonising in our churches and chapels precisely because they have recognised that the preachers are talking about something of which in reality they know nothing.

"The things which are in part can be apprehended, known, and expressed; but the Perfect cannot be apprehended, known, or expressed by any creature as creature. Therefore we do not give a name to the Perfect, for it is none of these. The creature as creature cannot know or apprehend it, name nor conceive it." [3]

"Now mark! God is nameless, for no one can know or say anything of him. Anent which a heathen philosopher observes that what we know or predicate about the First Cause is what we ourselves are rather than what the First Cause is." [4]

"To understand God is difficult, to speak [of Him] impossible. . . . I have it in my mind, O Tat, I have it in my mind, that what cannot be spoken of, is God." [5]

"Incomprehensible is that supreme Soul (Atman), unlimited, unborn, not to be reasoned about, unthinkable." [6]

[1] *Musings of a Chinese Mystic*, p. 61 (Wisdom of the East Series).
[2] Sermons xxiii.   [3] *Theologia Germanica*.
[4] *Eckhart*.   [5] Hermes.
[6] Maitri Upanishad, vi, 18.

We shall investigate later on the method by which this *Absolute*, unreachable by the intellect, is brought down thereto by the method of hypostasis. When the method is lost sight of, and the hypostasis is taken for the reality, and is hardened into a dogma: then begins the strife and war of creeds and sects. The doctrine of the Logos is the principal hypostasis with which we commence to relate the unrelatable Absolute to the universe of our perceptions and conceptions. Concerning this concept Max Müller has some very interesting matter in his work on *Theosophy or Psychological Religion*, and he tells us that " The *Logos*, the Word, as the thought of God, as the whole body of divine or eternal ideas, which Plato had prophesied, which Aristotle had criticised in vain, which the neo-Platonists re-established, is a truth that forms, or ought to form, the foundation of all philosophy." Yes, of philosophy, the effort of the *mind* to reach to the Absolute ; but Mysticism must and does transcend these hypostases.

If now, as we have seen, modern philosophy is prepared to meet Mysticism somewhat more than half-way, by acknowledging not merely the existence of a transcendental region of life and consciousness which the formal intellect cannot reach, but even the existence of a higher faculty or function of the mind, an intuitional faculty by which the real flow and pulse of Life itself is more immediately contacted and made one with ourselves : it behoves Mysticism also to make the effort to meet the philosopher half-way, and not to place itself in a region totally isolated from the practical interests of the life in which we are immersed, or to give the impression that its roots lie in a shadowy region of incoherent vision altogether isolated from or unconnected with those aspects of reality with which Science and Philosophy can deal in a logical manner.

We shall perhaps have to understand Mysticism in a somewhat different regard from that in which it has hitherto stood, though its fundamental principles must remain the same. It cannot, however, stand still, any more than Science, Philosophy, or Religion. Man evolves mystically as well as intellectually and physically. But Mysticism, no more than any of the other categories of man's evolution, can afford to isolate itself from the sum of our knowledge, much less to rest on mere authority. It must take its place as a legitimate part of the wholeness of our nature, and constitute a higher rationality : not in the sense of a higher 'dialectic method,' but because of a greater intimacy and immediacy with the things of our common life ; this more intimate and sympathetic contact with our great communal life being the result of its deeper contact with the One Life in and through which all that can possibly 'appear'—or, as Professor James says, " happen "—must exist.

"Mysticism," says Tuckwell,[1] " genuine mysticism, is no bare, ecstatic, religious emotion stripped of rationality—if, indeed, there could be such a thing ; nor does it, strictly speaking, transcend reason. Rather it is, let us repeat once more, a sublime, rational immediacy, in which the elements of thought and feeling, after having diverged and been distinguished in our reflective, self-conscious mind, meet and harmoniously blend once more."

We may summarise what we have advanced in our present chapter in the following quotation from Deussen's *Elements of Metaphysics*.[2]

" We have shown how the viewing of things from without, whether by the subjective method of Kant or the objective method of empirical science, leads finally to an inscrutable entity (the thing-in-itself, affection, force), which is for ever unattainable by way of external experience. For wherever we may turn to grasp the thing-in-itself—there stand ever between it and ourselves, as a darkening medium, the innate forms of our intellect, showing us how it appears in time, space and causality, but not what it is in itself. All things in the world are accessible to me only from without—with one exception. This exception is my own self (*âtman*), which I am able to comprehend *firstly*, like everything else, from without, and *secondly*, unlike anything else, from within. . . . My ego, as object of inner experience, is free from space and causality, and there remains only the form of time in which expanded inner experience is reflected in the intellect. Thus time is the only barrier which hinders me from knowing by the inner view, what I am as thing-in-itself."

If Bergson's *quasi*-mystical, *quasi*-metaphysical effort to show that, " time, conceived under the form of a homogeneous medium, is some spurious concept, due to the trespassing of the idea of space upon the field of pure consciousness," [3] and his further effort to show that, " We do not *think* real time

[1] J. H. Tuckwell : *Religion and Reality*, p. 311.
[2] Paul Deussen : *The Elements of Metaphysics*, pars. 146, 147.
[3] *Time and Free Will*, p. 98.

(i.e. duration) but we *live* it, because life transcends intellect,"[1] can stand the test of 'time' in the progress of philosophical thought : then we shall have made a very considerable advance indeed towards a purely intellectual apprehension of that inner region of the self which has hitherto appeared to be absolutely cut off from the intellect, and to have been left to the 'irrational' vagaries of the mystic.

We might even claim, therefore, that to-day some of our metaphysicians have climbed to a height from whence the promised land is seen afar off. But it is only the mystic who, by the self-realising method of mysticism, can enter that fair land, " flowing with milk and honey,"[2] where all doubts are resolved, all opposites and contradictions of the intellect swallowed up in one harmonious Unity; all Truth, Beauty, and Love *known* as the very nature and being of the timeless, deathless *Self*.

[1] *Creative Evolution*, p. 49.
[2] Symbols of spiritual food and nourishment—*ambiosia*.

CHAPTER V

THE ABSOLUTE AND ITS MANIFESTATIONS

"Though the Absolute cannot in any manner or degree be known, in the strict sense of knowing, yet we find that its positive existence is a necessary datum of consciousness; that so long as consciousness continues, we cannot for an instant rid it of this datum; and that thus the belief which this datum constitutes, has a higher warrant than any other whatever. This conclusion which objective science illustrates, and subjective science shows to be unavoidable . . . is also the conclusion which reconciles Religion with Science."

HERBERT SPENCER: *First Principles*.

"Now this cannot be expressed or described, nor brought to the understanding by the tongue of man; for God hath no beginning. But I will set it down so as if he had a beginning, that it might be understood what is the first Principle, whereby the difference between the first and the second Principles may be understood, and what God or spirit is. Indeed, there is no difference in God, only when it is inquired from whence evil and good proceed, it is to be known, what is the first and original fountain of anger, and also of love, since they both proceed from one and the same original, out of one mother, and are one thing. Thus we must speak after a creaturely manner, as if it took a beginning, that it might be brought to be understood."

JACOB BÖHME: *The Three Principles of the Divine Essence*.

CHAPTER V

THE ABSOLUTE AND ITS MANIFESTATIONS

WE have seen very clearly that in all cases in which we bring our formal conceptual intellect to bear upon the problems of life and consciousness, there is an apparently irreducible duality which the mind cannot overpass by any logical or dialectic method ; but we have also seen that alike in Science, Philosophy, and Religion there is the continual effort to resolve this duality, and that it is seemingly the mind itself which intuitively reaches out towards a fundamental Unity.

In the expression of this intuition, the religionist, the philosopher, and even the scientist, may use a language of paradox or of symbolism which is practically akin to that which the mystic employs ; and we can hardly deny the qualification of *mystical* to many writers who lay no claim to have realised a transcendental Reality in actual consciousness in any manner corresponding to that which is claimed by those who have been historically recognised as genuine mystics. Among our modern writers, Emerson and Walt Whitman stand pre-eminently for this intuitional mysticism ; and even Carlyle, though he had no understanding of and little enough of sympathy with mystics in general,[1] not merely uses the language of Mysticism in all his best and most intuitional work, but specifically acknowledges the difference between an intuitive ' Reason ' and an intellectual ' Understanding.' He has strong sympathies with Kant, whom he endeavours to defend against the charge of mysticism. A short quotation from what he says in this respect will not be out of place here.

[1] " Even in mystics, of an honest and deep feeling heart, there may be much to reverence, and of the rest more to pity than to mock."—*Miscellanies*, Art. " State of German Literature."

" We state what to ourselves has long appeared the grand characteristic of Kant's philosophy, when we mention his distinction, seldom perhaps expressed so broadly, but uniformly implied, between Understanding and Reason (*Verstand* and *Vernuft*). . . . Reason, the Kantists say, is of a higher nature than Understanding ; it works by more subtle methods, on higher objects, and requires a far finer culture for its development, indeed in many men it is never developed at all : but its results are no less certain, nay, rather they are much more so ; for Reason discerns Truth itself, the absolutely and primitively *True* ; while Understanding discerns only *relations*, and cannot decide without *if*. . . . Not by logic and argument does it work ; yet surely and clearly may it be taught to work : and its domain lies in that higher region whither logic and argument cannot reach ; in that holier region, where Poetry and Virtue and Divinity abide, in whose presence Understanding wavers and recoils, dazzled into utter darkness by that ' sea of light,' at once the fountain and the termination of all true knowledge." [1]

This is most excellent Mysticism in our appreciation of the term as a Rationality transcending Intellect ; and it agrees with Harnack's definition of Mysticism as " Rationalism applied to a sphere above reason " ; or, as Dean Inge would have it, " Reason applied to a sphere above Rationalism." [2] The very language is traditionally mystical. Compare it with the following words in which Dionysius refers to this same transcendental cognition.

" A darkness that shines brighter than light, that invisibly and intangibly illuminates with splendours of inconceivable beauty the soul that sees not." [3]

We find no reference to Dionysius in Carlyle's works, and little enough even of the German mystics ; and Carlyle would surely turn in his grave if we were to attribute to him any Mysticism, even of a philosophical nature.

' Reason,' then, is that faculty which sees things in their wholeness and completeness ; ' Understanding ' or Intellect is the faculty which sees them in separation and discreteness ; nay, it is the very essence of Mind functioning as Intellect to *produce* this separateness and discreteness ; to distinguish between subject and object ; to dramatise *Ideas* in time and space by creating temporal and spacial limitations and objective relationships. Have not all our great philosophers seen

---

[1] *Miscellanies*, Art. " State of German Literature."
[2] W. R. Inge : *Christian Mysticism*, p. 21.
[3] Dionysius : *De Mystica Theologia*, i, 1.

that pure Reason, pure *Reality*, transcends Time, Space, and Form ?

Let us quote again from our *mystic*, Thomas Carlyle.

" Pierce through the time-element, glance into the Eternal. Believe what thou findest written in the sanctuaries of Man's Soul, even as all thinkers in all ages, have devoutly read it there : that Time and Space are not God, but creations of God ; that with God as it is a universal HERE, so it is an everlasting NOW." [1]

Our immediate task at this point is to present a theory or working hypothesis of the origin of this Time-and-Space making faculty which we call *Mind* ; in the first instance as a " creation of God," that is to say, in its Cosmic aspect in relation to the Absolute ; and, secondly, in its application to the individual mind or self, and as a key to the power which we possess of transcending understanding or intellect : not merely by intuition, but in an actual unitary consciousness.

The Absolute is for the formal intellect a bare abstract concept devoid of any attributes or relationships, and we are sinning against the logical findings of the intellect when we speak of the Absolute as having any *relation* to Cosmic Mind, or to Manifestation. The metaphysical Absolute is as empty of any qualities as is pure abstract Space without Matter to occupy it. Nothing can be affirmed of it. It is not even Being, nor is it Non-Being. It is not the Conscious any more than the Unconscious. " The *rational* Absolute," says Récéjac, " is nothing but the extreme point where we arbitrarily suspend causality, continuous and successive magnitude, nothing but an artifice to arrest the indefinite progression of our ideas." [2]

We might illustrate this arbitrary jump from continuous and successive magnitudes in the following manner :

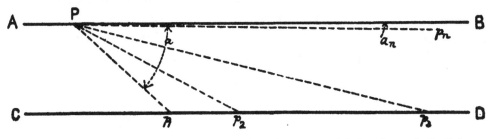

Let AB, CD, be two parallel lines, which, by definition, can be extended to infinity without meeting. Consider any

[1] *Sartor Resartus*, Book III, chap. viii.
[2] *Essay on the Bases of the Mystic Knowledge*, p. 38.

point P on the line AB to be sending out rays in the direction CD. We find that these rays touch CD at particular points p_1, p_2, p_3, etc. ; and we also find that the smaller the angle a, the farther does the point p travel along the line CD in the direction of D. If we take an extremely small angle a_n, the line P — p_n must be extended *almost* to infinity—according to our common idea of *almost*—but still, not having as yet coincided with AB, it must conceptually meet the line CD *somewhere*. But however much we may diminish the angle a_n it will always be capable of being conceptually subdivided ; in other words, we can never say that at the next decrement the point p_n will suddenly cease to be on the line CD and will be transposed to the line AB, or infinity.

We have to make the same arbitrary jump when we conceive of the Absolute in the mode of a space-filling Substance. We have arbitrarily brought it down into ' space '—into one of the categories of the mind. Let us be quite clear that this concept of a space-filling Substance, which we are here taking as our working hypothesis, can only *mediate* between our intellectual and scientific apprehension of the *manifested* universe, and that deeper region of our life and consciousness which is the province of the intuitive philosopher and of the mystic, and which can never by any possibility be expressed in terms of the conceptual mind, limited by the categories of time and space.

But despite this intellectual nescience and negation, the mind still turns to the Absolute as the Root, the Causeless-Cause, the Fulness and Perfection of all things, even though this latter concept appears to imply an Absolute in which all things are already and eternally ' given.' A revolt against this apparently *static* Absolute has led some thinkers to the other extreme of an Absolute postulated as being eternally in the making, or a Reality in the *flux* of things, or even a Pluralistic Universe. Thus Bergson, the modern prophet of the " Philosophy of Change," says :

" The flux of time is the reality itself, and the things which we study are the things which flow . . . by following the new conception to the end, we should come to see in time a progressive growth of the absolute, and in the evolution of things a continual invention of forms ever new." [1]

_____
[1] *Creative Evolution*, pp. 363, 364.

He tells us again that, " The universe is not made, but is being made continually. It is growing, perhaps indefinitely, by the addition of new worlds." [1]

He finds " reality itself " in Time, hypostasised as *duration* ; and duration, he tells us, in a not very happy metaphor, " is the continuous progress of the past which gnaws into the future and which swells as it advances." [2]

But we naturally ask here : what is there in the future to " gnaw into " if it has no content ? Moreover, how can the universe *grow* or *swell* by the addition of new worlds unless the *substance* is already there or ' given ' out of which these new worlds are formed ? Bergson apparently means us to accept this physically, but whether physically or metaphysically, some substance must necessarily be ' given ' in the first instance.

Closely examined, an Absolute in the making involves just as many metaphysical difficulties and contradictions as a so-called static Absolute. It must be so, for the one concept *by itself* is just as much due to the disabilities of the formal intellect as is the other, and must necessarily come to an *impasse*.

Bergson gives us an able and brilliant contribution to our knowledge of the practical function and limitations of the mind, intellect, or ' understanding ' in its association with matter, and advocates a new (?) method in philosophy, that of commencing with " the intuition of immediacy," and proceeding therefrom to analysis and concept. Thus he says :

" These fleeting intuitions, which light up their object only at distant intervals, philosophy ought to seize, first to sustain them, then to expand them and so unite them together. . . . Thus is revealed the unity of the spiritual life. We recognise it only when we place ourselves in intuition in order to go from intuition to the intellect, for from the intellect we shall never pass to intuition." [3]

And again :

" Let us then concentrate attention on that which we have that is at the same time the most removed from externality and the least penetrated with intellectuality. Let us seek, in the depths of our experience, the point where we feel ourselves most intimately within our own life. It is into pure duration that we then plunge back, a duration in which the past, always moving on, is swelling unceasingly with a present that is absolutely new." [4]

[1] *Creative Evolution*, p. 255. [2] *Ibid.*, p. 5.
[3] *Ibid.*, p. 282. [4] *Ibid.*, p. 210.

This is the main thesis of Bergson's philosophy, and he appears thereby to have galvanised the dry bones of Metaphysic into a temporary semblance of life. The method may be accepted—though it is not new—and even the result *so far as it goes* : for how can we doubt that the more we " concentrate attention on that which we have that is at the same time the most removed from externality and the least penetrated with intellectuality," the nearer we shall get to fundamental Reality ? This has been the great method of Mysticism and mystical philosophy from the very earliest records which we possess. " Concentration, or Yoga," says Patanjali in his *Yoga Aphorisms*, " is the hindering of the modifications of the thinking principle " : that is to say, those constant changes by which the mind moves and is diffused over a multiplicity of subjects and objects. It is only in proportion as the mind goes out to this multiplicity and externality that the fundamental Unity is lost to sight, and we appear to depart from Reality. We can never really depart from Reality. We are immersed in It ; we live and move and have our being in It. There is nothing in the whole Universe which is not truly and absolutely *real*. But it has to be perceived in all its relations and proportions before this absolute reality is perceived ; and meanwhile, we perceive only *aspects* of Reality, and foolishly call one aspect more real than another. They are only more or less real in the sense that we perceive more or less of their fundamental nature and unity, and the ' less ' is their externality perceived through the medium of the formal intellect and physical senses.

Unreality is merely a term for the ignorance which isolates, separates, divides, and antagonises.

We may see by this that Bergson has, in his own manner, arrived at an intuition that the great World Process, the great push of evolutionary Life, the great *élan vital*, becomes more and more real the more we grasp *duration* in its wholeness and completeness as what we *live*, not what we think. " We do not *think* real time," he says, " but we *live* it, because life transcends intellect." [1]

But this process of *becoming* is only one half of our life ; only one half of the ONE LIFE. Moreover, as we shall hope to show presently, it is precisely the half which is *made* by

Creative Evolution, p. 49.

intellect, and is transcended when intellect is transcended. Bergson never really transcends intellect ; his philosophy is still psychological only, not spiritual in the deepest sense of the term. Other philosophers, and more particularly certain mystics, have already obtained an infinitely deeper vision of " life complete," or " the unity of the spiritual life," than that partial view which presents it only as a process of becoming. They have seen it as Being as well as Becoming, as transcendent as well as immanent.

For the intellect, Being appears to imply that all is already 'given,' whilst Becoming appears to imply that it is ever in the making. But it seems to us strange that Bergson, recognising as he does so clearly that it is the limitations of the intellect which raise these alternatives and antinomies, should deliberately choose one of these as sufficient in itself to give us the whole content of Reality.

But even when we have said this, we have still to note certain passages in his writings in which this partial view of Reality appears to be, for the moment at least, transcended. It is curious to note, indeed, how even the most confirmed materialist, pragmatist, or pluralist, slips at times most unconsciously into the wider *mystical* view. This has been noted more particularly in *Scientific Idealism*, in the chapter dealing with the materialism of Haeckel, by an analysis of his *Riddle of the Universe*. It crops up over and over again in William James's writings, and we may now note Bergson saying :

" Every human work in which there is invention, every voluntary act in which there is freedom, every movement of an organism that manifests spontaneity, brings something new into the world. True, these are only creations of form. How could they be anything else ? We are not the vital current itself ; we are this current already loaded with matter, that is, with congealed parts of its own substance which it carries along its course." [1]

" Something new into the world," yes ; into the world of *manifestation*, the world of *form*. But what is this " own substance " which " congeals " as matter, if it be not the one eternal Substance-Principle to which nothing can ever be added, for which we are contending, and which must at least contain the *potentiality* of any and every *form* that can possibly arise in the world of becoming or manifestation ? If it is the

[1] *Creative Evolution*, p. 252.

potentiality of form in the manifested universe, we may even go so far as to say that it must exist in some *form* in the unmanifested unitary Substance of the universe ; but it is not a time and space form, and, therefore, for the intellect, it is formless.

One more quotation, and we shall find ourselves actually employing the language of mystical paradox :

" We can thus conceive of succession without distinction, and think of it as a mutual penetration, an interconnection and organisation of elements, each one of which represents the whole, and cannot be distinguished or isolated from it except by abstract thought. Such is the account of duration which would be given by a being who was ever the same and ever changing, and who had no idea of space." [1]

Yes, ever the same as *Being*, and ever changing as *Becoming* ; or shall we say, ever the same as *Substance* and ever changing as *Form* ?   The as-well-as is here recognised instead of the either-or, and we must needs state that the Absolute is *both* of the two intellectual opposites.   Or, better still, recognising that our intellectual either-or terms cannot be applicable to both aspects of the ONE, we may state it as Ruysbroeck does : " God, according to the Persons, is Everlasting Activity, but according to the Essence and Its perpetual stillness, He is Eternal Repose." [2] Persons, Form, Process, Becoming : these stand for the " ever changing " of Bergson.   Essence, Substance, Absoluteness, Being : these stand for his " ever the same."   But what a long way we have here travelled from a ' duration ' which is continually " swelling " by the addition of something which it does not contain in its own inherent nature, and which is non-existent outside of it until absorbed by it.

Bergson's *duration* is the present which includes the whole past, but for which the future is absolutely non-existent until somehow it becomes an *increment* of the flux.   We would ask Bergson, however, whether he has never *felt* when he has been able to seize his " fleeting intuitions "—when he is " most removed from externality and the least penetrated with intellectuality "—that somehow or other we *overtake* the future event, that it is certainly *there* already ?   We do not get rid of time—even if we can be said to get rid of space—

[1] *Time and Free Will*, p. 101.
[2] *The Seven Degrees of Love*, chap. xiv.

when we merely hypostasise the past into a ' duration '; nor so long as we have still past *and* future; or even if we say a *present* which is not the fleeting moment, but the *whole past,* always " gnawing " or " swelling." We are here still in the region of intellect. The absolute *Present* includes the future as well as the past, but it is just this which evades the intellect, though it is a fact in the ' intuition ' of many. Moreover, pre-vision is also a fact, as well established as any other psychical phenomenon. There appears to be, so to speak, a fourth dimension of time: a dimension at right angles, as it were, to that flux which we commonly think of as a line extension, not as a solid, but which, if apprehended, would make ' events ' into a ' solid ' which would include the future as well as the past. Bergson's *duration* may, it is true, be said to be a solid, but it excludes the future: it is a solid which is always " swelling." Or shall we say that this requisite *fourth* is something which is neither time nor space; that here again it is the intellect which differentiates time and space out of a *something* which the intellect cannot, in virtue of its specific function, grasp as a whole, as a ' thing in itself '? Are not time and space, in fact, one of the *dualities* of the mind? This *something* which is neither time nor space has already entered into metaphysical speculation, and even into mathematical physics, as a homogeneous *space-time.* We should regard it not as being made in successive layers of past, present and future, nor as a here and a there, but as something out of which these are produced when it is sectioned, as it were: artificially cut across by the intellect; something, in fact, which is a *continuum,* a kind of *substance* of events, an " ether of events," as Professor Whitehead comes very near to calling it.

" The continuity of nature is to be found in events, the atomic properties of nature reside in objects. The continuous ether is the whole complex of events; and the atoms and molecules are scientific objects, which are entities of essentially different type to the events forming the ether." [1]

Mathematical science also appears to be approaching this concept of a future which is already *there*—a concept which is now receiving very substantial support in the annals of

[1] A. N. Whitehead, F.R.S.: *An Enquiry Concerning the Principles of Natural Knowledge*, Part II, Art. 15, 8.

psychical research. When we endeavour, however, to bring the idea down into the region of intellect, we are immediately confronted with a *static* Absolute, and an apparent fatalism.

Perhaps the following passage from *The Secret Doctrine* of H. P. Blavatsky states the matter as well as it is possible to state it.

"Time is only an illusion produced by the succession of our states of consciousness as we travel through Eternal Duration, and it does not exist where no consciousness exists in which the illusion can be produced. . . . The present is only a mathematical line which divides that part of Eternal Duration, which we call the Future, from that part which we call the Past. . . . The sensation we have of the actuality of the division of Time known as the Present, comes from the blurring of that momentary glimpse, or succession of glimpses, of things that our senses give us, as those things pass from the region of ideals, which we call the Future, to the region of memories that we name the Past. . . . The real person or thing does not consist solely of what is seen at any particular moment, but is composed of the sum of all its various and changing conditions from its appearance in material form to its disappearance from earth. It is these ' sumtotals ' that exist from eternity in the ' Future,' and pass by degrees through matter, to exist for eternity in the ' Past.' No one could say that a bar of metal dropped into the sea came into existence as it left the air, and ceased to exist as it entered the water, and that the bar itself consisted only of that cross-section thereof which at any given moment coincided with the mathematical plane that separates, and, at the same time, joins, the atmosphere and the ocean. Even so of persons and things, which, dropping out of the ' to be ' into the ' has been,' out of the Future into the Past—present momentarily to our senses a cross-section, as it were, of their total selves, as they pass through Time and Space (as Matter) on their way from one Eternity to another : and these two Eternities constitute that Duration in which alone anything has true existence, were our senses but able to cognise it there." [1]

Let us turn to a mystical work for a much better presentation of this Absolute Principle than Bergson has as yet been able to give us, whatever he may succeed in doing in the future.

In that gem of mediæval Christian Mysticism, the *Theologia Germanica*, we find the unknown writer saying :

"That which is perfect is a Being, who hath comprehended and included all things in Himself and His own Substance, and without whom, and beside whom, there is no true Substance, and in whom all things have their Substance. For He is the Substance of all things, and is in Himself unchangeable and immoveable, and changeth and

[1] H. P. Blavatsky : *The Secret Doctrine*, vol. i, p. 69.

moveth all things else. . . . But the perfect cannot be apprehended, known, or expressed by any creature as creature. Therefore we do not give a name to the Perfect, for it is none of these. The creature as creature cannot know nor apprehend it, name nor conceive it." [1]

But it is further explained that this Absolute Perfect may be known when the " creature-nature," that is to say the lower self, the " I and myself," are transcended ; or, as Bergson now puts it, when we are " most removed from externality and least penetrated with intellectuality." It is only the creature *as creature*, that is to say in his intellectual sense of separateness, who is ignorant of the Absolute Perfect. When the " creature-nature " is overcome or overpassed, and the false sense of separateness of the " I and myself " transcended —not metaphysically merely, but with an added quality of *mystical* consciousness which is the supreme goal of Religion— the clear realisation of the Absolute Perfect is obtained. All great teachers have taught this in some form or another, and Bergson appears to be now re-stating it, but only so far as mind and matter are concerned : only metaphysically, and not in any manner as yet in relation to the moral and religious aspects of the question.

When the Absolute is considered as ' God,' or ' God ' as the Absolute, theology is necessarily up against the same antinomies, with the added difficulty as to the *personality* of God. We cannot assign to the Absolute in its own nature any attributes or personality, for attributes imply their opposite, and personality implies otherness or relativity. We might possibly say, as Bradley suggests, that it is *supra-personal*,[2] but that is the greatest concession which could be made to the theologians. It is on this account that the distinction has been made by many mystical Christian writers between ' God ' and the ' Godhead ' ; the former being considered personal—usually in the three Persons of the Trinity— whilst the latter is the inexpressible Absolute which cannot be an *object* of either knowledge or worship. Thus the Godhead is the ' Divine Dark,' the ' Abyss,' the ' Formless ' of some of the Christian mystics ; but only because it is these for the intellect, not for the mystical consciousness. Thus Eckhart says :

[1] *Theologia Germanica*, chap. i.
[2] *Appearance and Reality*, chap. xxvii, p. 533.

" All that is in the Godhead is one.   Therefore can we say nothing.
It is above all names, above all nature.   The essence of all creatures
is eternally a divine life in Deity.   God works.   So doeth not the
Godhead.   Therein are they distinguished—in working and not working.   The end of all things is the hidden darkness of the eternal Godhead, unknown and never to be known." [1]

Mysticism is not an attempt to explain the Absolute, but
to experience It.   It is in fact the very attempt which
Bergson now urges on philosophers as if it were some new
method.

Mr. Bradley, in his well-known work *Appearance and
Reality*, endeavours to show that every category of the formal
mind or intellect, every merely empirical fact of our experience, is self-contradictory, and can only find a truly *rational*
solution in a unitary Absolute which, in itself, must necessarily be completely harmonious and free from all self-contra-
diction.   " Ultimate Reality," he says, " is such that it does
not contradict itself . . . and it is proved absolute by the fact
that, either in endeavouring to deny it, or even in attempting
to doubt it, we tacitly assume its validity." [2]   And again :
" The universe is one in this sense, that its differences exist
harmoniously within one whole, beyond which there is
nothing." [3]

But abstract logical thought, as such, he shows, cannot
reach this Unity without perishing, for this function of the
mind is wholly discrete, relative and discursive : it is an
either-or, and cannot deal with Reality as being at one and
the same time a Unity and a Multiplicity.   " When thought
begins to be more than relational, it ceases to be mere thinking." [4]   And yet he contends not merely that it is the highest
reason to postulate this unitary Absolute, but that we can
and do actually know something about it intellectually and
empirically, simply because all our experience falls within
and qualifies the Absolute.   If we do not and cannot in the
very nature of thought know by means of thought what the
Absolute *is*, we at least can and do know partially what it
does ; and this knowledge of what it does cannot be discrepant
with what it *is*.   If, then, we could suppose the duality inherent in thought to be transcended, thought would cease to be

[1] Quoted by Vaughan: *Hours with the Mystics*, vol. i., p. 189.
[2] Second ed., p. 136.   [3] *Ibid.*, p. 144.   [4] *Ibid.*, p. 171.

thought and would become something else ; but in doing this it would become, paradoxically, something more rational than thought itself. " When each fact and end has forgone its claim, as such, to be ultimate or reasonable, then reason and harmony in the highest sense has begun to appear." [1]

That this is precisely what happens in the mystical consciousness is our main thesis throughout this present work, and we may note in Mr. Bradley's volume a most valuable contribution on the part of a pure metaphysician to the fact of this supreme rationality transcending the categories of the formal conceptual mind. That this supra-rational Absolute is also the One Unitary Self may also be deduced from Mr. Bradley's work.

But the intellect must continually endeavour to find a method of bridging this seeming gulf between the Absolute and its Cosmic Manifestations as the individual and the particular : between the Infinite ONE and the Infinite Many ; a gulf created by the intellect itself, and not acknowledged by ' pure reason.'

If, as indeed is certain, the concept of the Absolute is as old as the oldest philosophy in the world, and has been stated as clearly in the *Vedânta* as it has ever been stated since : it is equally certain that we shall find traces, however far we may go back, of a method of bridging the gulf. This method has been known ever since the days of Greek philosophy as that of *hypostasis* ; and it consists in giving an individual or distinct existence to certain *aspects* of the Unitary Whole, and—more particularly in Religion—the ascribing of personality to these aspects considered as separate existences or Beings. It is not a logical method, but a kind of metaphysical *tour de force*. There is no mystery or difficulty about it when it is clearly recognised that the method itself is merely a device to bring that which is beyond the formal concepts of the intellect, and beyond manifestation, into the form of a concept whereby it may be related to the manifested Universe, and to our own individual nature. Moreover, we must not forget—what we have already shown—that the Absolute itself is not arrived at logically, it is not arrived at by any inductive method proceeding from particulars to universals, and therefore we have as much right to come back from the

[1] *Appearance and Reality*, p. 429.

Absolute to particulars by an arbitrary process as we had in the first instance to proceed from particulars to the Absolute.

The method of hypostasis only becomes a source of difficulty and a ' mystery ' when its true nature is lost sight of, and certain hypostases are put forward as objects of superstitious worship and dogmatic belief, as is the case in most exoteric religions. It is not so, however, in its purely philosophical aspects. But whilst saying this of the *method* of hypostasis, we must not overlook the fact that there may be, and probably is, a profoundly ' mystical ' fact underlying the philosophical necessity. We must, indeed, conceive that concrete number in the manifested universe must necessarily spring from some definite principle in the transcendental region of our consciousness—a principle which *translates* itself into concrete number in the lower region of the formal mind.

We need not be afraid of making use of this device of hypostasis; it is a time-honoured method, and, indeed, we can neither understand our immediate problem of the relation of the Absolute to Its manifestations, or of the Cosmic Self to the individual self, nor even the various aspects which Religion and Mysticism have assumed from time to time, without its aid.

Let us apply it then, in the first instance, to our abstract Substance-Principle. How or in what manner are we to conceive of the World of Manifestation as arising in or emanating from a bare abstract *Substance*, ' filling all space '— though as yet no space exists—and containing no forms or ' modes of motion,' though It contains the potentiality of all possible forms which can ever arise in an infinity of manifestations, and is the ONE LIFE which originates and perpetually energises these forms so long as they exist in the manifested Cosmos ; or, shall we say, in a conscious *Subject* which objectivises as a manifested Cosmos in time and space the contents of Its own subjectivity ?

Strictly speaking, the Absolute in its unmanifested state is not a *Subject* any more than an *Object* ; Subject and Object are united in It as something which is utterly beyond our comprehension, and which appears to our intellect to be a mere blank negation. But as soon as we commence a thinking process at all in this relation, our first instinct would be to postulate the Absolute before manifestation as being a bare subjectivity, seeing that no objectivity exists.

In that bare subjectivity, objectivity arises " in the beginning." The ' beginning ' is the commencement of the evolution of any particular Cosmos—that is to say of a time-space phenomenon. The Absolute as Noumenon is eternal ; the Cosmos as Phenomenon is temporal ; as it had a beginning, so also it will have an ending.

We are not compelled to postulate that our own particular Cosmos is the only one in the totality of the Universe. We are not compelled to postulate that the Absolute ever exists in a bare subjectivity without a corresponding manifestation. We are only compelled to postulate the temporality of any *particular* phenomenon, whether it be an atom or a universe. There may be an infinity of Universes coming into and going out of existence perpetually, and each of these may have its own special time-space relationships, which may be quite different from ours. The ' doctrine of relativity,' in its philosophical aspects, may possibly find here a final resting-place. It is certain that, in its basis in physics, it will not remain where it is, seeing that we have merely negative evidence as to the non-existence of the Ether. It will as inevitably be compelled to abandon its present ground in the light of further discovery, as was the doctrine or dogma of the indestructibility of the physical atom of matter which was so tenaciously held during the last century.

When we speak, therefore, of *the* Cosmos, it must be understood that we refer only to the Cosmos with which we as conscious human beings are concerned ; but, *mutatis mutandis*, we may conceive of the same principles as operating in the birth of any Cosmos, or of any portion of a Cosmos.

In postulating that objectivity arises out of pure subjectivity, we have already stated the first principle of Subjective Idealism. Objectivity in its origin arises in and for and by the power of the One Absolute Subject, which thereby objectivises Its own content. Of the nature of this process we can form no conception until we have understood the exercise of the like creative power within ourselves as individual subjects. It is very unlikely that any mere psychology as a science will give us this understanding. It is one of the deepest mysteries of our nature—a secret carefully guarded, yet unconsciously exercised by all. In its cosmic aspect it has been conceived to be an exercise of a Will, a Desire, or of that power of the Mind which we term Imagination. It has been conceived that it was a necessary process for the ' Unconscious ' in order that It might attain to clear Self-consciousness, or Self-realisation ; in order that It might reveal Itself to Itself.

These speculations cannot be regarded as having any value if disconnected from processes which are operative *now* ; unless, in fact, they throw some light upon what takes place in all the operations of life and consciousness. Some of the mystics have endeavoured to enunciate this principle. With Böhme, for example, Will, Desire, and Imagination were not merely the originals of the World Process, but they are the great creative potencies producing substance and form in every operation of Nature. The following quotation puts this matter very clearly :

" We acknowledge that the will of the Abyss hath brought itself into a longing (*Lust*)[1] and imagination of itself, whence Nature and the creature have their original, which now also out of the partibleness of the exhaled will hath its own will and imagination to form and image itself according to its longing (*Lust*) and desire (*Begierde*)[2]. As we see such changing in Nature, how Nature imageth itself into so many kinds and properties, and how those properties do every one desire their like again." [3]

What Man, the ' Creature,' has created in this manner in the present material world of our lower consciousness, is only too appallingly evident. Will, Desire, Imagination, the three most potent forces in the Universe, all applied by the individual for individual and selfish ends, for his " own self-will," have wrought out a world such as we now see, in which the Great War is only a very partial revelation and result of the deep-rooted depravity of Humanity ; the result of Man's original ' fall,' which we may conceive to have taken place by the operation of the same outgoing principle, and now exhibiting a duality of good and evil. Of this, however, we shall have more to say hereafter.

Given, then, on the one hand a pure unconditioned Absolute,

---

[1] The German word *Lust* must here be taken in its primary meaning of pleasurable desire, joy, delight.

[2] *Begierde*—eager desire.   [3] *Baptism*, chap. i, par, 17.

and on the other hand an empirically known objective universe of *forms*, which have only a temporary existence as *objects*: there must have been "in the beginning" a creative act producing Form; though not in the first instance those multifarious physical forms which we cognise on this 'lower' plane of manifestation. We must, in fact, guard against the notion that this preliminary creative act has any correspondence to any act in time and space which we can intellectually define. It is not a *first* act in a sequence of events, but a *sustained* act; the act that is the Cosmos during the whole of its manifested existence. To draw a very rough mechanical analogy, in a machine which is continually in motion, the motive power, whatever it may be, must be continuously generated and operative.

We have, then, at the commencement of manifestation, the production of *Form* as a mode of motion in a Substance-Principle previously postulated to be formless and motionless— with the motionless motion of absolute motion. In the very conception of this production of Form we have already separated, hypostasised, or brought into distinct existence, three aspects which were primarily *in abscondito*, or void of any relation to each other. These three aspects are Motion, Substance, and Form. Absolute motion becomes the definite limited motion of a Form, though not necessarily as yet in time and space. But in so far as that definite motion is conceived of as *originated*, to that extent also we must conceive of it as an *act* on the part of the Absolute. Substance, hitherto indistinguishable from bare abstract Space, now becomes that which is acted upon and made to assume a form of motion. Form arises as a definite mode of motion, as a distinct 'thing'—the product of the action and the substance acted upon.

Stated in another manner we might say that we have in the first instance separated the One Absolute Substance-Principle into a duality of Principle-Subject and Substance-Object; and in the second instance we have created a Trinity of (1) an Actor—the Absolute Subject; (2) that which is acted upon—Primordial Substance; and (3) Form—this latter being the result of the interaction of the first two. The Actor is the ever-concealed Causeless-Cause, the eternal *active* nature, or *Life*, of Substance itself. But this Substance now becomes a passive principle which is acted upon; it becomes the 'Mother' of all Forms in the Cosmos.

These three hypostases have very commonly been represented in terms of human procreation, in which case they become Father, Mother, and Son. When considered in this manner, the 'birth' of the Cosmos or the 'Son' is an 'immaculate conception.' Substance-Principle becomes Father-Mother, but Substance as 'Mother' brings forth Form, or the 'Son,' in an immaculate manner, for Father-Mother is the ONE containing within itself both the male and the female creative potencies. The 'Father' is the active principle, but remains *in abscondito,* or returns as it were to the 'Abyss,' the 'Divine Dark'; or rather never issues therefrom, but remains the Ever-Concealed, the transcendental Deity or 'Godhead': as also the transcendental Subject, the eternal inscrutable "I am that I am."

These hypostases are the origin and root of all the cosmogonical myths and doctrinal Trinities which are to be found in so many and various records in all ages, and in which the terms of human procreation are usually employed to *symbolise* the original process of creation or emanation. The original and pure form of the concept has been sadly distorted in the Christian dogma; the cosmic idea of an immaculate conception having been transferred to Mary as the *physical* mother of Jesus of Nazareth, not of the Cosmic Christ, or Logos, whilst the origin and cosmic function of the Holy Ghost is obscure in the extreme; this individual hypostasis, in its early history, being sometimes spoken of as male and sometimes as female. The Holy Ghost would seem at the best to correspond with the Gnôstic *Sophia,* or Wisdom—in some systems the Substance aspect of the Divine Unity.

It will not be out of place here to give a quotation from one of the early Christian theologians. The following passage is from Tertullian:

" All are One, inasmuch as all are of One; by unity, that is, of substance; and yet notwithstanding there is guarded the mystery of the divine appointment, which distributes the Unity into a Trinity, ranging in their order the Three, Father, Son, and Holy Ghost; three, that is, not in essence but in degree, not in substance but in form, not in power but in manifestation, but of one substance and of one essence and of one power, forasmuch as there is one God, from whom these degrees and forms and manifestations are set down under the name of Father, Son, and Holy Ghost." [1]

What we have to note here is, that these hypostases are "set down under the name of" many other terms in pre-Christian systems. When we have grasped the principle and the necessity which gives rise to it, we shall not attach any specially authoritative value to any one system in particular, but we shall see in each the natural product of the environment in which it arose. It is only by detaching ourselves from specialised forms that we can ever reach that ultimate Reality which, though the Father-Mother of all Forms, is Itself the one Formless Truth.

We have already postulated that the production of Form in Primordial Substance is the simultaneous production of a subjective consciousness and an objective 'thing.' The first Form produced, or the collectivity of Forms, then, is not merely the production of the primordial Form or Forms of an objective Cosmos—or the first 'Plane' of the differentiation of Substance—but is a *Being*. We have here stepped from that which is beyond Being—shall we call it *Be-ness*? —to that of which we may now affirm both Being and Consciousness.

What, then, is the nature of that Being, that Supreme Spirit, or Self, or 'God,' who now *is* the particular individualised Cosmos in its very highest aspect; and who, in a certain sense, may be said to *become* subsequently all that that Cosmos becomes in time and space as a process of evolution or a great World Drama?

Here again we may summon to our aid the very oldest philosophical thought. It is that of an outbreathed or outspoken *Word*. Spirit is from *spiro*, to breathe; Brahmâ is associated in the Vedânta with breath and speech; whilst in the Greek philosophical concept of the *Logos* we reach not merely an extreme refinement of the concept, but one which was adopted by the early Christian theologians and applied to the presumed historical character Jesus of Nazareth, who was supposed to have been a special and unique incarnation of the Logos Himself; the divine 'Son.' [2]

[1] Adv. Prax. 27. Quoted by Sanday: *Christologies Ancient and Modern*, p. 25.
[2] For an extremely interesting exposition of the meaning, origin, and use of the term *Logos*, and its adoption by dogmatic Christianity, the reader

The term *Logos* means, primarily, *Word*; but it means not merely Word as embodied in sound, but also as embodied in thought; it implies a Trinity of Motion or Breath, Thought or Idea, and Word or Form.

Considered as the outbreathed or outspoken *Word* of the ever-concealed Absolute, the Logos may be taken as the potency of Sound producing Form in Primordial Substance. There is an occult potency in sound as a form producer, not merely on the physical plane but also on the higher planes of Substance, with which as yet we are little acquainted or entirely ignorant; but we find traces of a belief in this potency existing from the most ancient forms of religious worship down to the present day, though there is no recognition of it in our modern Church services.

The Logos, then, as the outspoken *Word* of the ever concealed Absolute, is the "first-born Son of the Father." He is the embodiment of the 'Thought' or 'Idea' of the Cosmos as it exists in the 'Mind' of the Godhead; and as such He *is* the Cosmos in its Wholeness and Completeness: not as a time-process, nor as extended in three-dimensional space, or even in space-time, but in that—to the intellect—incomprehensible and inexpressible Unitary Perfection which may sometimes be reached and comprehended in a transcendental mystical consciousness. Thus Jacob Böhme, speaking of this mystery, says:

" Here again we need an angel's tongue; for the mind ever asketh *How* and *Where?* For when the deep is spoken of, which is without comprehension and number (or measure), the mind always understandeth some corporeal thing. But when I speak of the virgin of the wisdom of God, I mean not a thing that is (confined or circumscribed) in a place; as also when I speak of the Number Three; but I mean the *whole deep* of the Deity without end and number (or measure)." [1]

The subjective *selfness* of the Logos is that of the Absolute: as, indeed, it is in the ultimate of every individual *self*, whether of a God or an atom; but we can hardly conceive of what we might perhaps venture to call the actual consciousness of the Logos, nor of His self-consciousness,

may be referred to Max Müller: *Theosophy or Psychological Religion*; and also to Hatch, Hibbert Lectures, 1888: *The Influence of Greek Ideas and Usages upon the Christian Church.*
[1] *The Threefold Life of Man*, chap. v, pars. 55, 56.

as being distinguishable from that of the Absolute Itself, for "in Him dwelleth all the fulness of the Godhead bodily," or in a manifested form.

In so far as the Logos contains the Cosmos in his own Being, and *is* the Cosmos in its Wholeness and Completeness, He constitutes the 'highest' or spiritual plane of the Cosmos: a plane which, in the real understanding of it as a plane of consciousness, is not something which is either 'higher' or 'lower,' or more 'inner' or more 'outer' than that of physical matter, but is that unitary consciousness to which the mystic may sometimes attain, but which he finds it impossible to explicate in terms of intellect. In this respect the mystic is the 'favourable variation' which indicates the future line of evolution for humanity; for assuredly the "full-grown man" will ultimately attain to "the measure of the stature of the fulness of Christ," the Logos.

There is no more difficulty in understanding the principle and intellectual necessity of the concept of the Logos than there is in the case of the Trinity; but there is the whole depth and mystery of our own nature to be comprehended before we can attain in our own proper life and completed consciousness the full understanding of that which these intellectual concepts so feebly and inadequately express.

We need not stay here to speculate as to whether there are, in the unfathomable depths of the Absolute, an infinity of Logoi, or only one Logos; whether all possible Universes exist eternally as one immutable unchangeable *Idea* in the Divine Mind, or whether even the idea of 'Ideation' must be conceived of as transcended in the supreme absoluteness of the ONE. Many speculations as to the nature of the Logos were rife when the original Greek idea was being appropriated and applied, first of all by Philo to the Mosaic Scriptures, and subsequently by Christian theologians to the traditional life of Jesus, and to the evolution of a Christology. These speculations gave rise to the most bitter strife and dissensions. They are of interest to us as disclosing the various forms which the concept has assumed, or may assume, when viewed in the light of certain *a priori* assumptions; but they one and all stand on the same level so far as *authority* is concerned. It does not matter in the least to us whether or not Clement of Alexandria had "fallen a victim to the unfortunate negative method which he calls 'analysis' " [1]; or whether, when he states that "the Son is the Consciousness; the Father only sees the world as reflected in the Son," he is stating a " bold and perhaps dangerous doctrine " [2]; or whether Origen is " sounder " than Clement when he " attributes self-consciousness and reason to God, who therefore does not require the Second Person in order to come to Himself." [3]

We may leave such speculations to those who consider that *belief* in such matters is all-important, and that such belief must rest upon authority and not on reason. What we must recognise and keep steadily in view is the fact that when we endeavour to represent these transcendental matters as *processes*, we are just as much compelled to make use of, and we are just as much limited by, the empirical or formal conceptual mind or intellect as is Life itself when it endeavours to express itself in physical matter. We are compelled to anthropomorphise. We are doing so as certainly when we speak of God as the 'Father,' and the Logos as the 'Son,' as when the Jews conceived of Jehovah as having and exhibiting in his actions every characteristic of a 'fallen' human nature.

It is no part of our present work to give a detailed scheme of Cosmogony; indeed, we have not the necessary data to construct such a scheme unless we fall back upon traditional sources or mystical vision, such, for example, as that of Swedenborg or Jacob Böhme. Deeply interesting and suggestive as are many of these systems, we are not here relying upon any of them for our premises and conclusions, though we must acknowledge our indebtedness to them not merely for the inspiration which they afford, but also for the possibility of forming a much wider generalisation from our existing scientific knowledge than would otherwise have been the case. There are a very large number of traditional cosmogonies, some of them, as for example that of the Kabalah, or of the Gnostics, being extremely elaborate. More recently we have had a modified and more or less synthesised presentation of these ancient cosmogonies put forward in modern Theosophy.

We may, however, note here the continual recurrence in most of these cosmogonies of the number seven. In some

[1] W. R. Inge: *Christian Mysticism*, p. 87.
[2] *Ibid.*, p. 87.   [3] *Ibid.*, p. 90.

way or other this number appears to be a governing number in our present Cosmos. It is found in the actual physical phenomena of light and sound, whilst Crookes, Mendeleëff, and others have shown that it also applies to the evolution of the chemical elements.

Many systems of cosmogony postulate seven planes of the manifested Cosmos, or seven modifications of Primordial Substance, with corresponding planes of consciousness—our physical plane being the 'lowest.' We have not sufficient scientific data, however, to construct these seven planes, but I have pointed out in *Scientific Idealism* (p. 233 ff.) that we require at least four planes of Substance to account for the whole of our nature; these four planes being—from 'below' upwards, or more inwardly—the physical, the etheric (psychic or 'astral'), the mental, and the spiritual.

These planes may be considered in two aspects: (*a*) as differentiations of Primordial Substance, and (*b*) as planes of consciousness. When we consider them as differentiations of Primordial Substance, each 'lower' plane appears to be formed out of the substance of the next 'higher' or more 'interior' plane by a limitation of motion—the forms or 'matter' of the lower plane being in some manner aggregated out of the finer forms of the next 'higher' plane. This at all events is the relationship which appears between physical matter and etheric substance, and we may carry the concept, *mutatis mutandis*, to the still higher or more interior planes.

We must not forget, however, that no plane is really distinct or independent, and that outer and inner are only relationships of our present consciousness. No single movement of physical matter, whether atomic or molecular movement, nor any movement of matter in bulk, can take place without a corresponding disturbance of the Ether; and it appears to be an inevitable conclusion, when we consider the fundamental unity of the Universe, that such disturbance must have its equivalent on all and every plane.[1]

The apparent separation of one plane from another, and the limitations which physical objects have in our consciousness, are in fact illusions which the scientific intellect can conceptually transcend, though we are not able to transcend them normally in actual consciousness. When we use the

[1] Vide, *Scientific Idealism*, p. 241.

term *illusion* in this sense, we may say that the material world of our normal consciousness is not the illusion of an unreality, but of reality seen in a limited and incomplete manner, and only an illusion when taken in a realistic sense as a reality *per se*.

When we consider these planes as planes of consciousness, we have again an apparent discreteness or independence. Normally, we conceive that we are only conscious on the physical plane : that is to say, we are only conscious of an *objective* world on that plane. Subjectively, however, we are conscious of our thoughts or ideas, which we must postulate to be ' things ' on their own plane just as truly as the vibrations on the etheric plane which convey to our physical eye the picture of external objects are *things* on their own plane. We must also postulate that our *whole self* exists and is conscious on all and every plane, for the *whole self* cannot stop short of the One Universal Self. Modern psychology now recognises the fragmentary nature of our normal consciousness, and the existence of a sub-liminal consciousness, if not of a supra-liminal region. Each of these must exist on its own appropriate ' plane.' We shall have to consider more in detail in a subsequent chapter the question of the relation of our subjective to our objective consciousness on the various planes of the Cosmos ; but we must first of all, and as the conclusion of this chapter, consider what is the relation of the Logos to these Cosmic Planes, whatever may be their number or character.

Can we intellectually form any concept of that relationship other than as a time-process ? On the other hand, can we conceive that the consciousness of the Logos, or the manner in which the Logos knows the Cosmos, is in any way like our own intellectual apprehension of it, or is in any way a *process* ?

We have postulated that in the consciousness of the Logos the Cosmos exists in its Wholeness and Completeness—not merely as it stands from moment to moment, but in its completeness as a process from beginning to end. But this is an intuitional or mystical postulate, and not an intellectual concept. When we come down to the latter we have to deal with time and space relationships, and must consider the Cosmos as a process having a past, present, and future.

We conceive, then, that the plane of the Logos, as constituting the *first* differentiation of Substance, and also as constituting the 'highest' plane of Consciousness in the Cosmos, is the *Spiritual Plane*; and the *Forms* on that plane are what we are compelled to call pure *Idea* of all that, on lower planes, manifests in time and space as an unfolding or evolutionary process. We might possibly take these *Forms* as equivalent to the 'Ideas' of Plato. They are eternal Prototypes or Paradigms.

We have now to conceive of the lower planes as evolving successively; they are a further emanation from, or creative act on the part of, the Logos, who now becomes the *creative* God or Demiurgos of the evolutionary time-process, which can only be said really to commence in the consciousness of any being when this further emanation commences.

In the creation or emanation of the next lower plane, then, the Logos limits Himself; for each descending plane is a limitation both in respect of Form and of Consciousness. But it is only *other* than the One Substance and the One Consciousness when the limitation is considered as a separate thing apart from its indissoluble inner connection and oneness with the Spiritual Plane of Being from which it emanates.

Now the plane of the Logos, the Spiritual Plane, being the plane of pure non-spatial Mind or Idea, we shall not be far wrong if we postulate that the next lower plane, which we have termed the Mental Plane, is the plane of Mind Forms: though not yet of the formal limited intellect which we know as *mind* in our present limited consciousness, for this latter is born from below rather than from above. It is, however, the plane where we may say that time and space are 'born,' for it is the function of the Mind on this plane to create concrete 'things' out of abstract Ideas—the Ideas which exist eternally on the higher plane of the Logos. This plane, however, we must still consider to be cosmic in its nature, not individual: that is to say, the *Forms* are cosmic, and will be interpenetrative rather than located as in our present conceptual space. It is the plane of Cosmic Mind, or Cosmic Man, and the Forms may still be conceived of as archetypal or paradigmatic. In a certain sense it is the cosmic *Soul*, energised and overshadowed by the *Spirit* of the higher plane of the Logos. It thus stands, as Eckhart says of the human soul, " between Time and Eternity: with its highest powers it touches

Eternity " (the spiritual plane beyond Time), " with its lower, Time " (the lower planes which are the creation of Mind under the categories of Time, Space, and Causation). Thus the individual soul has its correspondence with the Cosmic Soul.

The animal soul belongs to the psychic plane, overshadowed by mind as its ' spiritual ' principle. The soul of the individual man only evolves slowly from the psychic to the mental plane, and at the present time we find a very great preponderance of the merely animal soul in a large proportion of Humanity, whilst every one experiences in his own person more or less of the atavism of the animal stage through which the Race has passed, and is passing ; the tendency to revert to type rather than to press forward towards the intuitively felt ideal. And it is because the human soul stands thus " between Time and Eternity," because it is born out of Eternity (the Spiritual Plane) into Time (the Mental Plane) as being itself the embodiment of the Time-Process which commences on the Mental Plane ; and because it is now on its return journey back to its source, that it exhibits a dual nature—half spiritual, half animal—and has the terrible responsibility of choice between the higher and the lower. " Choose well ; your choice is brief, and yet endless."— (Goethe.)

And so, in the doctrine of the Buddha, we are told :

> " Within yourselves deliverance must be sought ;
>   Each man his prison makes.
>   Higher than Indra's ye may lift your lot,
>   And sink it lower than the worm or gnat."

The complement of this teaching is, that this ' deliverance ' can only be accomplished in proportion as the carnal (animal) mind and will are given up and subordinated to the higher ' divine ' will : that is to say, in proportion as this higher will, the will and power radiating from the spiritual plane, is voluntarily invoked and utilised for the conquest of the lower nature. This is the invocation of the Christ principle *within* ; and the whole process falls into line with Man's natural evolution, whether we look at it cosmically or individually, and is quite independent of any arbitrary theological dogmas as to the necessity of a certain *belief*. These dogmas, however, in their turn may be seen to contain the essence of the matter, but misapplied and distorted.

Let us pause for a moment before dealing with the next two lower planes, to consider in what light we might regard the *Forms* on the two highest planes.

In so far as we may conceive of there being a differentiation of Substance on the plane of the Logos, and remembering that every differentiation of Substance is not merely to be considered as an individual Object, but also as an individual Subject : we can only conceive of these differentiations on the plane of the Logos as constituting individual creative Potencies, Beings, " Planetary Spirits," or Gods ; but we must remember that we can only thus individualise or hypostasise them because we can more or less readily distinguish differentiated or individual qualities in the operation of Nature on the lower planes of manifestation.

These creative Beings or Gods appear under different forms and names, and in different numbers in different Cosmogonies, but are more often seven in number ; as for example the seven *Rishis* of the Puranas, the seven lower *Sephiroth* of the Kabalah—the three higher constituting the Trinity—and the " seven Spirits of God " of the Revelation of St. John, which reappear in Böhme's teachings as the " seven Fountain Spirits."

We shall not here ascribe any specific number to them, but shall merely postulate that there are on the plane of the Logos great creative Potencies having distinctive functions as the formative and energising *Life* of the Cosmos in its evolutionary aspects ; and we may leave the student to enumerate them according to any system for which he may have a preference. They may, for example, be identified with the *Ideas* of Plato, with the *Logoi* of the Stoics, with the *Æons* of the Gnostics, or the *Hierarchies* of Dionysius ; or, going back to a still earlier source, with the *Prajâpatis* of the Vedânta philosophy.

It is only when we consider the Cosmos in an evolutionary manner that we conceive of the process as one which proceeds from Unity to Multiplicity ; each plane in the descending series exhibiting a greater multiplicity or differentiation, and each *Form*, considered as a Unity on the higher plane, exhibiting its multiplicity—or its potency as a creator of multiplicity—on the lower plane, which thus, in a certain sense, appears to be more remote from its source in the ONE.

We have thus the same principle working throughout,

in the ' lowest ' as in the ' highest,' or " as above so below."
On the higher plane, a collective Life constituting a unitary
Consciousness, or a comparatively simple number of creative
Potencies or Beings or ' Monads ' ; on the lower plane, a
multiplicity of Monads or *lives*, which are subjectively indi-
vidual consciousnesses, and objectively individual ' things.'

Considering now the activity of thought on the Mental
Plane, and remembering that we are not yet dealing with our
own individual activities, but are considering these planes in
their Cosmic relations and functions, we must conceive that
the Mental Plane constitutes *Cosmic Mind* or Cosmic Man.
This Mind is the creator of the lower Cosmic Planes as a process
or becoming—as a great time-and-space drama.   The great
Potencies, the ' Gods ' of the higher spiritual plane, here
' become ' or differentiate into a host of lesser creative forces :
into cosmic ' thoughts ' which presently become ' things,' or
' Nature.'   But thoughts are living things, living potencies
on their own plane, both in Nature and in Man ; and they
only ' become ' things on the lower plane in the same sense
that the great Creative Potencies on the higher Plane *become*
the lower planes of manifestation, yet remain unmoved on
their own plane.   They are immanent in all the phenomena
of the lower planes, but *remain* transcendent on their own
plane.

If Man, Humanity as a whole, could only realise His origin
and source, and the fact that in spite of His ' fall ' and His
present nescience He still *remains* in that source, He would
very quickly transform this world of His false imagination of
separateness into that ' Kingdom of Heaven ' which appears
to be such a far-off vision, yet even now stands in our midst,
could we but open our inner eye to perceive it.   And what,
indeed, is the Christian ' Faith,' in its origin and inception,
but the revelation of this oneness of the ' Son ' with the
' Father,' and the oneness of Humanity in the ' Son,' the
Logos.   This teaching of the relation of the *Cosmic* Christ to
Man has, however, been wholly lost in the materialistic dogmas
of the Christian Church ; in which dogmas certain supposed
historical events—for the most part derived from earlier pre-
Christian myths—are made the sole basis of Man's ' salvation '
or regeneration.

It is because we *remain* in our root and source, although

we have also gone out from it, that mystic attainment is possible. The mystic can never do other than find the Kingdom of Heaven, and God, and all the Hosts of Heaven, and the Starry Firmament, and the whole Universe within *himself*. He penetrates the heights and depths of his own being, even to that source where he still *remains*, and from which neither he nor any smallest created thing can ever really be separated. This aspect of the subject, however, we shall develop more fully in a subsequent chapter.

The Mental Plane is not merely the plane of Cosmic creative Mind or Thought, it is also the plane of Nature's memory, where everything that has ever happened in thought, word or deed, is indelibly recorded, and may be recovered by the individual. The fact that " things have souls " is one which modern psychology is beginning to recognise more and more clearly. Its most familiar phenomenon is that of psycho-metry. In this respect the ' soul ' is the sub-conscious or sub-liminal Self of Nature, corresponding in the Cosmos to what is now so well recognised by psychology as part of our own individual nature ; indeed, we must remember all through these attempts to systematise the Cosmos, that Man can have nothing in his individual nature which has not its corre-spondence in the Cosmos, and is not derived therefrom, and sustained thereby.

When we come down from the Mental Plane to the Etheric or Psychic, and to the Physical, we are dealing with the two planes of which we have a more immediate sensory experience. It is true that the Etheric Plane is one of which we have as yet a very inadequate knowledge, and that knowledge merely in connection with a few limited physical phenomena, and not at all as yet in any demonstrable manner with our psychic activities. There are a large number of psychic phenomena, however, which appear clearly to necessitate the existence of an intermediate plane between the physical and the mental. The more general name for that plane in its association with these phenomena is *astral*. This is a term, however, which is not likely to be used by science in the immediate future. Moreover, we can hardly use the term *etheric* in this connection, since the Ether of science is too much of a physical thing. it is not really the next plane, considered either as substance or as consciousness ; it is a higher state of the substance of the physical plane, a state beyond the solid, liquid, and gaseous of which we are objectively conscious ; and science will shortly discover that it is not continuous and space-filling.   In future, therefore, in dealing with the Cosmic Planes from the point of view of consciousness rather than of substance, we may employ the term *psychic* for the plane intermediate between the plane of our true mental consciousness and activities, and our physical objective plane ; for it is to this plane that we shall refer all those phenomena which are at the present time broadly classified as psychic.[1]

The Psychic Plane we must conceive of as being in substance a modification or differentiation of the substance of the Mental Plane, whilst the Forms, the *Lives* thereon, or therein, are the immediate creative potencies, or " Nature Spirits " responsible for the building of all physical forms, including physical matter in its atomic and molecular construction.

Physical matter is not *dead*, for it is never anything else than the One Living Substance ; and all *forms* of that Substance, whether Gods or atoms, are *lives*.

On the Etheric or Psychic Plane are to be found the elemental forms or lives which build minerals, crystals, plants, flowers ; and also those which constitute the *animal soul*, not yet evolved to self-consciousness on the higher Mental Plane. On this Psychic Plane also exists that subtle ' double,' matrix, or *eidolon*, familiar in certain psychic phenomena, and without which our physical bodies could not be held together and co-ordinated in all their functions.   It is within that subtle etheric or ' astral ' body, on the psychic plane of consciousness, that we function immediately after death, and from whence all so-called spiritualistic phenomena proceed—very few of these having any really *spiritual* characteristics at all. There is a very general consensus of evidence that a further plane is subsequently attained, from which no ' spiritualistic ' phenomena, so-called, can be obtained.   This would be more truly the ' spiritual ' plane, or the real ' heaven world,' though we shall have for certain reasons to locate this on the mental plane, which still falls short of the true spiritual plane of the Logos.

[1] For further information on this subject the reader may be referred to the present author's work entitled *The Physics of the Secret Doctrine*.

The physical plane needs no further explanation here; but we may consider it broadly in its relation to the 'higher' planes, as also a certain analogous relationship between the whole of the Cosmic planes in the following manner.

Postulating in the first instance that manifestation implies a duality of subject and object, we have the whole Cosmos divided into a subjective half and an objective half. The subjective half is the plane of the Logos, or rather the plane of the Trinity, of which the Logos is the personal representative. We next consider that the objective half is a reflection in time and space of the subjective half, and it will, therefore, be itself a Trinity : that is to say, the three lower planes—the mental, the etheric, and the physical—will constitute the objective half of the Cosmos.[1]

Now we have seen that the primal creation is a Trinity of Motion, Substance, and Form, but that these three only become differentiated or distinct when we postulate that 'creation' as taking place. The One Substance has no distinct existence until we consider it in its active aspect as the producer of Form. We might say that when that takes place, Substance-Principle becomes Principle *and* Substance—a distinction without a difference. Thus we may say, as Jacob Böhme does, that the creative *Spirit* " brings Itself into a substantiality," and within that substantiality It creates Form. The substantiality arises when the creative act of Will or Imagination takes place—and it is always taking place—and the third factor is the Form, the *Object*, or the Cosmos which arises within that Substantiality.

Now consider the higher Trinity as a Unity again repeating this creative act in the wholeness of the Cosmos, and not as if the mental, etheric, and physical planes were successive emanations the one from the other. The process of this second creation will be, *mutatis mutandis*, the same as that of the original creation. The *subjectivity*, or active creative potency, the first Triad in its totality, becomes in the second Triad creative or Cosmic Mind, the 'Father.' This subjectivity or 'Spirit' " brings Itself into substantiality," or becomes the 'Mother,' as the Etheric Plane; and out of that substantiality produces those Forms, or the 'Son,' which are

[1] See Diagram, p. 337, *infra*.

13

the physical forms of our objective consciousness, including our own physical bodies. At the root of the whole process is the mysterious power of the SELF to objectivise Its own content.

" I am the Ego which is seated in the hearts of all beings ; I am the beginning, the middle, and the end of all existing things," says Krishna, the Logos, in *Bhagavad-Gita*.[1] Also : " I established this whole universe with a single portion of myself, and remain separate." [2]

Let us take again the single physical analogy which is available to us in the relation which we recognise as existing between the etheric and the physical planes. It is but a single portion, a very minute portion indeed, of the etheric *substance* that becomes physical matter, whilst the etheric plane as a plane " remains separate." But though it thus remains separate, it responds throughout its whole unitary nature to the slightest movement of physical matter ; it is separate only when viewed from the lower physical consciousness. The movement of a single atom moves the whole Universe.

May we not carry this analogy back to the Absolute Itself ? It is only when viewed from the standpoint of the lower separative mind that the Absolute appears to be remote, disconnected, transcendental, unmoved ; and thereby the whole secret and process of Mysticism is, and has been from time immemorial, the getting rid of the " sense of separateness."

It remains only to note, in respect of the aspect which these planes present to our consciousness, that each plane will have a higher and a lower aspect : the latter being that which is most prominent in our consciousness as the characteristic of the plane, whilst the former is very considerably modified by the influence of the next higher plane. Thus the physical plane presents to us its main characteristic as being that of matter in a palpable, tangible form, or as having solidity, mass or inertia, and apparent indestructibility. But it shades off from solid to liquid, and from liquid to gas, and from gas to radiant matter ; the latter, in the form of the *electron*, commencing to exhibit the electro-magnetic characteristics of the Ether. Our *ideas* or normal consciousness, our ' common

---

[1] Chap. x, 20.   [2] *Ibid.*, x, 42.

sense' of the physical plane, is wholly derived from its lower palpable and visible characteristics; and these make of the great bulk of mankind at their present stage of evolution mere 'realists' of the grossest and most material kind.

"Common sense," says Maeterlinck, "makes an admirable, and necessary, background for the mind; but unless it be watched by a lofty disquiet, ever ready to remind it, when occasion demands, of the infinity of its ignorance, it dwindles into the mere routine of the baser side of our intellect." [1]

The two aspects of the psychic plane present this same lower or "baser side," and a higher one overshadowed by the intellectual qualities of the mental plane: these same *intellectual* qualities, however—as we have already abundantly demonstrated—being only in their turn the *lower* aspects of Mind, the higher aspects being abstract philosophical thought and spiritual intuition. To the psychic plane in its lower aspect we assign the animal 'soul': the animal intelligence or instinct, not yet risen—so far as we can tell—to a definite ratiocinative process, and also all merely animal passions and desires. It is to this plane also that we assign what is commonly referred to in psychology as the sub-liminal or sub-conscious self in its main characteristics, as being what F. W. H. Myers calls the vast "lumber-room" of the self. In what are usually referred to as psychic phenomena in general—although the bulk of these phenomena must be referred to this lower aspect of the psychic plane—there are many which touch the higher regions, and might even be assigned to the lower mental plane.

The characteristics of the lower aspect of the mental plane are those which are understood by our common and conventional use of the term *reason* as a process of co-ordination of our common sensory experiences; and it is—as with the other planes—by this lower aspect that we mainly judge of the characteristics of the plane. But we have already seen, and we shall see still further, that Mind in its higher aspects approaches so nearly to a true spiritual quality, that we are accustomed to locate the self or ego, the human *soul* in its eternal nature, in this higher region.

[1] *The Life of the Bee*, chap. vii, section 99.

The spiritual plane is too far removed from our cognisance or experience—save in the deepest mystical consciousness—for us to venture upon any generalisation as to its 'higher' or 'lower' aspects; but we might say that in the 'higher' it unites with the Absolute, whilst in the 'lower' it is the personality of the Logos.

The above is but an outline of a systematised Cosmogony, which will be found to be mainly in accordance with many and various systems dating back to the remotest antiquity. It may be used to some extent as the key to the facts of our outer empirical experience, as well as to those inner and deeper and less clearly charted regions to which the mystic penetrates. The student may elaborate this outline from whatever source he may deem most reliable, most inspired, or most authoritative; but he needs to bear in mind continually, that *any* such system is but an artificial chart with more or less empirical lines of longitude and latitude connecting, but also separating and dividing, the two great poles of Being and Becoming which the intellect places in contrast and opposition, but which are essentially a Unity and a Wholeness.

We shall deal more in detail with this chart in Chapter X.

We may note here, in passing, the correspondence between the categories of human experience known as Science, Philosophy, and Religion respectively—the latter including Mysticism—and the 'Planes' which we have taken as our chart of the universe. Science operates on the 'lower' planes of the physical and the etheric, the planes of 'matter and force' considered quite apart from consciousness; though the etheric plane considered as a *psychic* plane is now beginning to engage more than a mere fragmentary attention. Philosophy operates on the mental plane, in the region of the formal conceptual and categorical mind. Religion, and more specifically Mysticism, reaches the spiritual plane of the Logos, and is concerned primarily with the transcendental and the eternal.

The fundamental Reality of the transcendental plane must not merely be essentially *other* than the empirical knowledge of the intellect, linked up as it is with our sense impressions, but is certainly—in the fulness, completeness, power, and bliss which it discloses to the mystic as the reality of his own nature

—far beyond our most daring speculations. With the mind we see at the most but as in a glass darkly the reflection of the eternal beauty and perfection of the Divine Life from which we have proceeded, yet have never left ; to which we return ; yet shall never reach until we have realised that we stand in IT eternally.

CHAPTER VI

COSMIC MAN

" I have gone the whole round of creation : I saw and I spoke ;
I, a work of God's hand for that purpose, received in my brain
And pronounced on the rest of His handiwork—returned Him again
His creation's approval or censure : I spoke as I saw :
I report, as a man may of God's work—all's love, yet all's law.
Now I lay down the judgeship He lent me. Each faculty tasked
To perceive Him has gained an abyss, where a dewdrop was asked.
Have I knowledge ? confounded it shrivels at Wisdom laid bare.
Have I forethought ? how purblind, how blank, to the Infinite care !
Do I task any faculty highest, to image success ?
I but open my eyes—and perfection, no more and no less,
In the kind I imagined, full-fronts me, and God is seen God
In the star, in the stone, in the flesh, in the soul and the clod."

BROWNING : Saul.

" I died from the mineral and became a plant ;
I died from the plant and re-appeared in an animal ;
I died from the animal and became a man ;
Wherefore then should I fear ? When did I grow less by dying ?
Next time I shall die from the man
That I may grow the wings of angels.
From the angel, too, must I seek advance ;
' *All things shall perish save His Face.*'
Once more shall I wing my way above the angels ;
I shall become that which entereth not the imagination.
Then let me become naught, naught ; for the harp-string
Crieth unto me ' Verily unto Him do we return ! ' "

JALĀLŪ'D-DĪN RŪMĪ.

CHAPTER VI

COSMIC MAN

CAN we by any possibility, by any of our most daring conceptions, assign to Man in his unitary nature a position and function in the Cosmos, or a relation to the Absolute, or to ' God,' which shall in any degree whatsoever approach that in which he stands in the *reality* of his being and existence? All our deepest intuitions forbid that we should accept that which we *appear* to be, our present limitations, as the *reality* of our nature.

Western tradition sets forth that Man was made in the image and likeness of God ; but in the exoteric form of that tradition it has never been realised what is implied thereby. It is only in the esoteric Christian doctrine or Gnôsis, and in the case of a few Christian mystics, that we find any apprehension of the unitary and complementary nature of God and Man— a truth which had been reached ages previously in Eastern tradition, and summarised in the formula, " That art Thou."

Western exoteric tradition, wedded to the literal narrative of Scripture, has riveted its attention on the ' fall ' of Man, and has never asked what Man *is* as a unitary Cosmic Being— has never, indeed, taken Man in any unitary sense at all, but has only dealt with Humanity as a succession of individuals, who come into the world from nowhere, and who may or may not be ' saved ' by means of a special " favoured-nation " clause when they go out of it again.

If for any it be too high a doctrine that even the individual may claim his oneness with the Absolute ; that he never is anything less either in past, present or future, however much *qua* individual he may apparently be separated from his fellows or from Nature, or from spiritual attainment, or limited or dwarfed by the infinities of time and space : then we must necessarily leave that individual to work out his salvation by the light of some less daring, less cosmic conception which may be more in line with the limitations of his intuition, his capacity for abstract thought, or his inherited prejudices.

Such a concept of the divine nature of Man must, indeed, necessarily appear, relatively to Western religious tradition and dogma, to be very much more than too greatly daring. It calls up all sorts of theological bogies, not the least of which is the dreaded spectre of Pantheism, than which nothing is better calculated to send a cold shiver down the adiathermic spine of orthodoxy. Let such, therefore, who cannot face with equanimity the larger view of Man's unity with the Cosmos and the Absolute, remain fixed to their "impregnable rock" of exoteric tradition. There is much safety in such a position, albeit only the safety of the shell-encrusted limpet. Nay, is it not even their high destiny and privilege to be such, in a universe where even limpets, seen in their wholeness, are no more and no less than are humans or gods ? Yet let them not think that they will remain limpets for all eternity, however long their desire to remain such will hold them to that state of consciousness. In the course of incalculable ages, even the limpet will be evolved out of all recognition. Still less should they deceive themselves into thinking that the Universe is, or ought to be, all rock and limpet ; that in the great ocean of Life in which they are immersed there can be no salvation for any free-swimming creature. Sufficient unto each at each and every moment is the part and lot for which he feels himself fitted ; the Great Law will itself carry him on to a larger and fuller life just in proportion as he willingly and gladly co-operates at each step and at each moment by whatsoever his hand or his brain findeth to do.

> " Here is all fulness,
>   Ye brave, to reward you ;
>   Choose well ; your choice is
>   Brief, and yet endless."—GOETHE.

For those who have reached—whether by intuition or otherwise we need not here inquire—a larger view, even that " highest summit of human thought " which the transcendental doctrine presents, and who can, therefore, appreciate a deductive method which makes this its starting-point, we may now advance a few considerations which will place the present facts of Man's evolutionary nature in their broadest light, and will link them up with the concepts of Cosmic Evolution which were stated in our last Chapter, and more particularly with the concept of the Logos.

In doing this let us take leave once and for all of our conventional ideas of great and small, and realise what Emerson has so well expressed in the lines :

" There is no great and no small
To the Soul that maketh all ;
And where it cometh all things are,
And it cometh everywhere."

We shall find that it is our conventional but unreal perception and conception of time and space which is the greatest barrier in the way of a true realisation of the nature of the Self. Is the individual so very small in comparison with the globe on which he lives, that if we do but go a few thousand feet up, our fellow creatures appear to be mere microbes crawling on its surface ? Is our span of life so short that if we take a geological age to be only the equivalent of a single day in the whole history of the Globe, the individual lives merely for a fraction of a second ? Is the Globe itself a mere corpuscle in that larger unit which we call the Solar System ; and the Solar System in its turn a mere atom in the infinitude of worlds and systems which the starry heavens reveal ? Well then, let us look at the reverse picture, at the immeasurable greatness of the individual even when estimated by these common but merely relative standards of time and space.

The most notable achievement of Science during the last twenty years has been to penetrate the hitherto arcane region of the internal structure of the atom of physical matter. This atom is so small in our estimation of the terms small and great, that we are told by Sir J. J. Thompson that if some one had started counting out one atom per second a hundred million years ago, he would not yet have gathered a sufficient number to be detected chemically. Or we may say that it takes about a trillion to make a perceptible speck of matter. From the Newtonian conception of this atom as a " solid, massy, hard, impenetrable particle," which was held almost to the close of last century, physical science has progressed in about twenty years to a concept which sees in it a Solar System in miniature.

It is conceived of as consisting of a central nuclear body corresponding to the Sun, very minute compared with the whole size of the atom, but to which the greatest part of the *mass* of the atom is due.   Surrounding this central nucleus are numerous rings or shells of the smaller units now known as *electrons*, which correspond to the Planets—the linear dimensions of these being only about one-hundred-thousandth of the atom itself. If we take the whole Solar System as far as the orbit of Neptune to represent an atom in the Cosmos, the linear dimension of the Earth is only about one three-hundred and fifty-thousandth that of the atom; so that the correspondence is a very close one.   The whole atomic system is in a state of intense activity, and the energy confined within its limits is enormous.

Even in his physical body and proportions, then, the individual man, built up of atoms and molecules and cells, is an inconceivable Cosmos of infinite magnitude.   If he is infinitely small in one direction, he is infinitely great in the other.

What is the real meaning of these infinite and infinitesimal physical magnitudes—magnitudes which, as it were, cancel each other out in plus and minus ?   The self, the subject, the ego, stands ever at the centre, and is the zero-point from which all these infinities radiate.   The Self is the unit, the unique number *one* : capable of a process—a world-process—of infinite multiplication and of infinite subdivision, but in which the multiplication may equally be regarded as an infinite subdivision, or the subdivision as an infinite multiplication. Shall we, then, abase ourselves before the infinitely great, or exalt ourselves over the infinitely small, as these are apprehended as process in time and space ?   If we are wise we shall do neither, for they are our own creations.   The very fact of their infinitude in either direction, paradoxically deprives them of any validity in abstract thought or transcendental Reality. The consciousness, the subject, the Self which truly apprehends them has already transcended them, and knows itself to be of another order and nature.   They are a *how* and not a *what.* Objectively they are manifestations, expressions, appearances, and, more particularly, *limitations* of an infinite, eternal, unborn, self-subsisting LIFE, which is Subject as well as Object, the knower as well as the thing known ; and which, knowing Itself as such, knows Itself to be superior to, as well as active in these Appearances. They should have no power to spell-bind us in their mere *physical* proportions. The infinitely great is just as much a limitation as the infinitely small. Why should *magnitudes* of any kind move us to degrees of emotion, or wonderment, or awe, or fear? Is there any more cause for these in the immensity of the starry heavens than in the commonest material object which we daily and momentarily contact? The cause for silent adoration lies not in the outward appearance or size of the object, but in the thought of the Root or Ground of its being; the One Eternal Infinite Power by and through and in which the humblest flower, or blade of grass, or " tip of Autumn spikelet " exists, and is brought into manifestation equally with the universe of Suns and Stars. We are deluded by mere *appearance* if we go no deeper than the outward fact; nor shall we ever apprehend *truth* until we have freed ourselves from this illusion of magnitude.

The wonderment does not lie in the degree of the fact, but in the fact itself—the great fact that the Universe is not a mechanism but a LIFE, and that we *are* that LIFE. The real cause of all emotion—whether it be the exquisite dawn of love in youth or maiden, or the intense fervour of creative genius, the ideal of the poet, the artist, or the philosopher, or whether it be the religious fervour of the saint, or the rapt ecstasy of the mystic—lies in the fact that it is the revelation of the Self to the self, the great discovery by the individual self of the potentiality of its own infinite nature. Perchance we find here, as some have thought, the *cause* of all this manifested drama in time and space. " To taste of reality and illusion, the great Self becomes twofold." [1]

The discovery is made by the individual self *first* as a *rapport* with something which appears to be a separate entity, an *object* of desire, of love; but afterwards it becomes a *union* in which the distinction of subject and object is lost; and in that union is found the supremest freedom, the supremest love, and thereby also the supremest bliss.

The movement of Suns and Planets and Star Systems is no greater fact than the movement of my little finger. Millions of microcosmic systems come into and go out of existence with each breath that I draw. THAT which I am, and THAT

[1] *Maitri Upanishad*, 7, 11. Deusen's trans.

which the starry heavens reveal in their own manner and degree, are one and the same LIFE. Do you think that it is any greater thing for ' God ' to act in the infinite Cosmos than it is for you to act in your own body ? The chemist wishing to demonstrate the properties of a substance, does not need many tons for his purpose : a few grains are all that he requires. Is there any greater wonder, when we consider the fact itself, in the explosion of a hundred tons of gunpowder than there is in the explosion of a single grain ? The fact of being able to know, to see, to feel, to think, to love, is the great mystical fact, in no wise altered by any degree of it, though the degree may and does serve commonly, and in the first instance, to bring the fact more vividly into realisation for the individual self. When rightly and philosophically appreciated, the in- finities lose for us their artificial extensive values ; they dis- close to us our own illimitable nature, and we enter into that revelation with an exultant faith in an infinite Perfection, and the unspeakable joy of a realised Freedom.

" Verily, he who has seen, heard, comprehended, and known the Self, by him is this entire universe known." [1]

There is still a further reason why we should not allow these physical magnitudes to limit our concepts as to the real nature of our being. It is because they *are* simply physical magnitudes ; because they belong only to that furthest plane of differentiation and apparent separation which we term physical matter, or physical consciousness, and have no validity in the deeper strata of our being, or in what we more generally speak of as the ' higher ' planes of consciousness. They are almost wholly non-existent on the psychic plane, and practically entirely absent on the mental plane. This is a matter of actual experience and evidence in connection with psychical research, and is as verifiable as any other scientific fact ; though it must be remembered that many scientific facts, even of a physical nature, are unverifiable by the individual without special qualifications and long and arduous training. But in the light of our fundamental principle of the Cosmic nature of the Self, and the unity of the individual self with the Cosmic Self, it is not difficult to accept the evidence of psychical research, and the further evidence of certain mystics, that when freed from the limitations of the physical

---

[1] *Brihad-āranyaka Upanishad*, 2.4. 5b. Deusen's trans.

senses, time and space are largely or entirely transcended, and their magnitudes disappear. When thus freed, we say that the self—the individual self—is acting on the psychic plane or the mental plane, as the case may be; though it may be doubted whether psychical research is as yet cognisant of any phenomena deeper than the psychic plane. What it is important to realise is, that the self does actually possess an appropriate body or vehicle for, and exists on, each and all of the planes, however many there may be; they are part of our cosmic wholeness, and we have our life and action on these planes *now*, and not merely when we part from our physical body at death. Were it not so we could have no existence, no life, or functions, or thought, or consciousness on this 'lower' or physical plane, any more than the physical atom could exist, or have mass, or inertia, or energy, apart from its etheric nature and existence, its unity with the one Substance. To pass in consciousness from the limitations of the physical plane to the comparative freedom of the psychic plane, and from thence to the still greater freedom of the mental plane, and so to whatsoever higher or deeper plane there may be, is merely to fall back upon our own cosmic nature, the depths of our own being; upon a 'self' which at each step becomes less and less individual and separate, and more and more cosmic in its unitary nature; until, in the supreme mystical experience and ecstasy, we 'become' that which we always *are*—the One Absolute Self.

Neither Subject nor Object is primary. That which is both Subject and Object we call the Absolute, and its primary *aspects*—which in the conceptual mind are a duality —we designate Principle and Substance: Principle being the universal omnipresent potentiality of every individual subject, whilst Substance is the potentiality of all and every individual object or form which, under the category of *time*, appears first of all non-spatially as Idea or Logos, and subsequently as the manifested universe of Matter extended in space. Every single object, we have already seen, *is* the One Substance, and therefore contains the infinite potentiality of form which that Substance contains in its infinite nature. But the infinite potentiality for form which Substance contains is, in its other aspect, the infinite potentiality for Idea: which potentiality we arbitrarily separate as belonging to Subject in distinction from Object. Every individual object, then, is not merely in its real nature infinite Object, but also infinite Subject ; for the two are one. But it does not manifest this absoluteness, for if it did so there would be no universe of infinite variety. Its very nature and function *qua* individual is to manifest in part only, and so to create a universe in which separation, extension, and process, is law and necessity.

This is somewhat quaintly expressed by the author of the *Theologia Germanica* as follows :

" All this resteth in God as a substance but not as a working, so long as there is no creature. And out of this expressing and revealing of Himself to Himself, ariseth the distinction of Persons. . . . And without the creature, this would lie in His own Self as a Substance or well-spring, but would not be manifested or wrought out in deeds. Now God will have it to be exercised and clothed in a form, for it is there only to be wrought out and exercised. What else is it for ? Shall it lie idle ? What, then, would it profit ? As good were it that it had never been ; nay, better, for what is of no use existeth in vain, and that is abhorred by God and Nature. However, God will have it wrought out, and this cannot come to pass (which it ought to do) without the creature. Nay, if there ought not to be, and were not this and that—works, and a world full of real things, and the like— what were God Himself, and what had He to do, and whose God would He be ? " [1]

It is clearly seen that individualisation—the coming into existence of the ' creature '—takes place by a process of limitation which is more or less in the nature of an illusion ; and this we may assign for the sake of clearness to the *subjective* nature of the individual object, be it atom, man, or god. We have further located this limiting process in what we know as Mind : in Cosmic Mind in the first instance, creating certain Cosmic differentiations which subjectively are great Cosmic Beings, creative Potencies, or Gods ; and objectively, or substantially, are Planes of Substance and Cosmic Bodies. On each Plane a repetition of this process takes place, down to the smallest atom, so that the same law, the same principle of unity in diversity, applies to each part as well as to the Whole.

It is not merely true that individualisation is necessarily limitation, and also that without that limitation there could be no universe of infinite variety, or of any variety at all ; but it is equally true from another point of view that the individual

---

[1] *Theologia Germanica,* chap. xxxi.

must, to a very large extent, be dependent upon this limitation of consciousness for the proper performance of his individual function in the Whole. The individual is inhibited by Nature from any further degree of consciousness or knowledge than such as is immediately required for his place and function in the economy of the Whole. The immediate function of the individual—whether individual atom or individual man—is *action* in a certain definite manner. For that purpose it, or he, is shut out from all immediate consciousness of any environment other than that in which and upon which he is to act and react ; it is that, and that only, which forms his 'world.' From this point of view we may regard organism as being not so much in the nature of an aid to consciousness, as an instrument for the limitation thereof. Who is there with any *faith* who does not expect an immeasurably enhanced consciousness and knowledge when free from the limitations of the physical body ? Such an enhanced consciousness, indeed, when the physical senses are inhibited, is already a well-recognised fact in psychology.

But the individual is not absolutely and entirely shut out from the whole content of Infinity with which, as an environment, he acts and reacts, and which, as a *reality*, is the infinite content of his own Self. If he were absolutely shut out, there could never be any consciousness of a *beyond*, of anything in any way transcending immediate environment. Always and ever there is an irradiation of the so-called actual from a transcendental region, the region of the ideal ; this being the more or less consciously felt influence of the infinite *Potential* of the Absolute ; and to it is due the great push of evolution. The tiniest atom feels it ; for the atom *is* the infinite Potential as well as the limited actual. And if now it is only given to the atom, or to any lesser or greater individual as we reckon small and great, to be thus limited and restricted, it is also given to it to feel and to hear in a manner which must always be *mystical*—as being inexplicable in the categories of the actual and empirical to which the individual for the time being belongs—the silent, invisible, yet irresistible call and attraction of the Infinite Potential, which, in that very attraction, confers upon the individual the power to respond to It, and to expand even to Its own infinite and immeasurable richness and fulness of Life.

14

Let us clearly realise that the potential must be as existent as that which we call the actual; it is only potential and unmanifested in so far that it exists beyond the plane of our present perceptions, our present action and function. Potential energy is just as much a reality and an activity as kinetic energy; it exists somewhere and is active somewhere. In the case of physical energy we may at least relegate it to the etheric plane.[1] If I do or become a certain thing, it is because I possess the capacity for doing or becoming that thing; that is to say, the capacity to do or become it is part of my nature, part of myself. It is just as much in existence, just as much a reality before the actual doing or becoming, as it is in the present action, or after the action.

The human germ-cell, a mere speck about the one-hundred-and-twentieth part of an inch in diameter, contains the potentiality of evolving into the completely organised human being; and biologists would fain discover in the structure of that cell —or rather in the structure of the nucleus of that cell—the cause of heredity as well as of variation.[2] There is certainly plenty of room in that minute cell for unlimited variations of structure; for it is itself a mighty cosmos of the microcosmic solar systems which we call atoms. We may, in fact, readily admit that individual variations of structure, corresponding to that which subsequently evolves therefrom, do exist; but that the *causes* of heredity or variation lie in the structure, we must deny on the same terms that we must deny that the cause of any physical structure lies in the structure itself, at any period whatsoever of its existence. Always and ever we have to seek deeper and still deeper for causes; and there is no term until we have reached the Absolute. Whether it be the formation of an atom or of a human germ-cell, the whole potentiality of the Absolute goes to its making, and is latent— another convenient fiction—therein. It is merely convention or convenience which necessitates that we should stop short at any more proximate cause. We may say that the human germ-cell becomes a full-grown man of a definite type and not any other animal, because of a certain definite structure of the germ-cell; but physical organism *qua* organism is—in so far as it can *manifest* anything—merely the capacity to respond more or less definitely to certain cosmic forces. These forces

[1] Cf. *Scientific Idealism*, p. 79.   [2] *Ibid.*, p. 266.

are everywhere ; at every point of space exists the whole living potentiality of the Absolute ; but the atom, or the man, or the god, will only manifest so much of it as, in his form-limitation *qua* atom, man, or god he can respond to. And if materialists and empiricists would have us think that consciousness is merely response to external stimuli or environment : we shall ask them, Where does external stimulus or environment begin or end ? Every plane acts and reacts with every other plane ; the very principle of the unity of Nature—and Nature cannot now, in the light of our scientific knowledge, be restricted to the physical plane—makes all Nature our environment.

When Sir J. J. Thompson states that " all mass is mass of the ether, all momentum, momentum of the ether, all kinetic energy, kinetic energy of the ether," [1] he is not merely stating a physical fact, but also unconsciously enunciating the great fundamental principle that all phenomena whatsoever are only special cases of the activity of Root Substance, however many planes there may be beyond the etheric.

Even now, in our physical bodies, we possess powers of conscious response to cosmic forces which do not act through our ordinary sense organs. We possess inner senses which we utterly neglect, and the existence of which many are foolish enough to deny *a priori* when evidenced by others, because forsooth they have no experience of them in their own limited nature. Psychical research shows us that both the past and the future may become objectively present in our consciousness ; and that it is as possible to see an object on the other side of the world as it is to see one in our own immediate vicinity.

If we *must* talk in terms of time and space, of great and small, of existence and becoming : let us at least recognise that the true nature of a thing, its true *greatness*, is only discoverable in its inner nature and relations, not in its outer size, function, or form ; for the outer measure and relationship of the thing is always dwarfed by something greater, and still greater again, until, in relation to infinity, a Solar System becomes as infinitely small as an atom. But when we consider the inner nature and relations of a thing, the thing itself, however small it may be, expands to infinity, and itself becomes the Infinite. It is then found to be the one infinite Substance, with the

[1] *Electricity and Matter*, p. 51.

potentiality of all that ever was, is, or will be—that potentiality being infinitely more *real* than the fragmentary portion which we are pleased to call the actual *present*. The Cosmos is not great because of its outer expansion in diversity, but because of its inner compaction in Unity ; or shall we say that it is great in both aspects when we view these as complementary modes of the ONE LIFE ; the outer being but a reflection of the inner in opposite terms ; the infinite object corresponding to the infinite subject, the infinite multiplicity to the infinite Unity.

There is just as much room for ' me,' on the potential side, in an atom as in a germ-cell ; and, indeed, we have heard of a ' permanent atom ' as the starting-point of the physical development of the individual. Weismann would have us believe in the continuity of the germ-plasm—the germinal cell of one individual being derived in a direct line of ancestral descent from germ-cell to germ-cell. Whatever of truth or otherwise there may be in this theory, what we wish to enforce here is, that so far as size is concerned it does not matter whether the continuity is preserved in a single atom or in a single biaphore containing billions of atoms ; the one is just as capable of becoming a human being as the other, for it has behind it the whole potentiality of the Absolute, but is nevertheless determined as to its immediate development by local conditions and limitations. Thus although I am in the totality of my being never anything less than the Absolute, I am limited as an individual manifestation both by the organism in or through which I am manifesting—be it atom, germ-cell, or full-grown body—and also by a local environment which belongs to some larger or more cosmic unit constituting the *nature* of the species to which I belong, or the plane of Substance out of which my body or vehicle is formed. Whilst I am thus limited by organism, I limit myself also in consciousness ; I think of myself as individual and separate, and what I think, that I empirically am. Yet even while I am thus affirming myself to be individual atom, or man, or god, I am at the same time negating my affirmation. The very affirmation of a limitation or individualisation is the negation of that limitation by implication of a larger something which is affirmed as being that of, or from, or in which the limitation takes place, and to which it bears a relation. The One Self is necessarily negation as well as affirmation. The Self in action continually affirms, ' I am this, and this, and this.'   But ever there is the eternal negation, ' I am not this, and this, and this—" neti, neti "—for I am also its opposite, and I am always more than any individual thing, and still more, and infinitely more, and there is nothing that can contain and limit me.'   Thus in the *Bhagavad-Gita* we find Krishna (the Logos) saying :

" I am the Ego which is seated in the hearts of all beings ; I am the beginning, the middle, and the end of all existing things. . . . I am, O Arjuna, the seed of all existing things, and there is not anything, whether animate or inanimate, which is without me.   My divine manifestations, O harasser of thy foes, are without end." [1]

We may now clearly apprehend that in the world of action of our present consciousness, in which the fundamental principle is duality, opposition, affirmation, negation : there exists not merely the duality of subject and object, or self and not-self, but also a duality in each constituent of this fundamental duality ; for in the object or not-self we have the duality of substance and form, or matter, which, *qua* matter, apparently possesses a nature of its own ; and we have in the subject the duality of the One Self and the individual self ; the latter thinking itself a separate entity or ego, and in fact always acting as such in the immediate field of its activity or environment.

It is convenient to refer to these two aspects of the One Self as the higher or cosmic, and the lower or individual self ; or simply to distinguish the one as the *Self* and the other as the self.   The distinction is as arbitrary and empirical as that between atom and substance ; but then all distinctions of language are such : they necessarily express an either-or in a universe in which the law of *action* is differentiation and opposition.   The function of the lower or individual self is to be to the higher or Cosmic Self what the atom, or the cell, or the organ is to the larger unit or body of which it is a part. The law is always multiplicity within unity.   But if the atom, or the cell, or the organ were in actual consciousness anything *more* than that which they are in their individual nature, how could or would they effectively fulfil their limited function ? The *more* exists as a latent potentiality ; and in Man it becomes more or less clearly recognised and defined as the hope of attainment of an ideal and infinite perfection.   How, indeed,

[1] Chap. x, 20, 39, 40.

can we conceive it to be otherwise than that that which has gone out from the ONE—or *appears* to have done so—should return thereto ? Such a *return* is not merely the root of all religion, but it is what we actually recognise in the world-process as we at present know it, or what is commonly called evolution : which is at root an expansion of life and consciousness acting in or through more and more highly organised physical forms.

But that such an expansion should take place at all, there must have been a previous limitation or involution—an in-volution of life or spirit, an e-volution of matter or form—and we have already outlined our conception of the Cosmic Process as a whole as being such an evolution of matter and form followed by a devolution of these and a return to Spirit or Unity. In minor cycles within the great universal cycle we may find both of these movements in operation. Worlds and systems evolve and devolve in, and out of, the One Substance.

In all these fundamental distinctions of Substance and Matter, Self and Not-self, God and Man, Higher Self and lower self : we may recognise that the relation and function is the same in each and every case. What the Absolute or ' God ' is to Cosmic Man, so is the Higher Self to the lower self ; and it is only as we discover, realise, and solve that great mystery within our individual selves, that we can do so also for the Cosmos as a whole. For in very fact what we call the Cosmos as a whole—as if it were something outside of and immeasurably greater than ourselves—is entirely and wholly within the illimitable limits of our own being and consciousness.

When we look at the evolution of Man, or Humanity as a whole, on this Globe, we find that the distinguishing feature of that evolution within the periods of which we have any knowledge, is the gradual attainment of the power to recognise the cosmic nature of the Self as well as the individual nature of the self. This power rises from feeble beginnings, as religious aspiration, or philosophical intuition, to a higher degree, if not yet to its fullest fruition, in Mysticism.[1] We attribute

[1] In Mr. Edward Carpenter's work, *Pagan and Christian Creeds : their Origin and Meaning*, three stages of this evolution are distinguished as (1) Simple Consciousness, (2) Self Consciousness, and (3) Universal Consciousness. This latter is the *mystical* consciousness which has not yet dawned for the great majority of the race.

this power in the first instance to the evolution of what we call Mind. That there should be a concomitant evolution of organic structure in the brain, the instrument of mind, is not merely to be expected, but is the only condition under which any such development of mind could manifest itself on the physical plane. There must be the corresponding organ, or basis of manifestation, on whatsoever plane the Self is acting. In other words, the Self must have a *body* in order to *manifest* on any plane whatsoever. But the Self which possesses the potentiality of that manifestation is no more attributable to the body or vehicle than the potentiality of mass, momentum, or kinetic energy in the atom is attributable to the structure of the atom. The structure of the atom will admit of just so much manifestation of that cosmic potentiality—attributed as we have seen to the nature of the ether—as will admit of its being an atom of a specific kind, and no more ; and the same principle holds good whether the individual be an atom, a cell, a plant, an animal, a man, or a god.

If the physical evolution of a man dates from a germ-cell —or perchance even earlier, from a single atom—it is equally certain that we must trace back the physical evolution of the Race to the earliest appearance of any form of organised life on this Globe, and even to the mineral kingdom itself. Behind the glowing mass of nebulous matter constituting this Globe in the early stages of its existence, lay the potentiality of evolving the vegetable, the animal, and the human kingdoms, up to Man as we at present know him physically. In each and every case this potentiality only lay *in* matter in the sense that matter only manifests in varying degrees and with varying characteristics that which exists in the potentiality of *Substance* on higher or more cosmic planes ; whilst behind the potentiality of Substance, as the root or noumenon of matter or object, lies the eternal potentiality of Consciousness or Subject as the inseparable correlative therewith.

Even if we are to think of the evolutionary process as Bergson would have us think of it, as a continual creation of something absolutely new in virtue of the ever-presence of the whole potentiality of the past : that *whole* ever growing or " swelling " in some occult manner by feeding on itself : shall we not still have to postulate that it has already had an Infinity in which to swell, and that therefore its content or potentiality must be infinite ?   The infinite fulness and richness of this potentiality is, therefore, the same, whether we regard it in this light, or whether we regard it in the light of an Absolute which needs no such process in order to become what IT eternally IS.   In any case the potentiality does not lie in matter as such, but in the Cosmos as a whole : that is to say in *Substance*, not in its phenomenal forms.

Looking at cosmic evolution as a whole, or looking merely at the evolution of this Globe where cosmic principles are repeated—as indeed they are in the evolution of any single atom—we may now ask ourselves more definitely : What position does Man collectively—Humanity in its totality of past, present and future—occupy in relation to the whole process ?   The position which we assign to him in succession to the mineral, the vegetable, and the animal kingdoms is a purely arbitrary one.   We say that the human germ-cell is *human* from the very earliest stages to which we can trace it.   We know that the stages of its development are a recapitulation of the larger cosmic stages of the evolution of living forms on this Globe.   May we not then enlarge our concept of Man as a cosmic being at least to this extent, that what the individual germ-cell is to the individual man, so is the cosmic germ-cell—that is to say the primordial form and stages of evolution of this Globe—to Cosmic Man ?   This Planet is a Man-bearing Planet ;   it cannot be considered in this connection otherwise than as the field of evolution of Man. But our fundamental principles forbid us to conceive of any such field of evolution otherwise than as an integral part of the constitution of Man, the evolving entity itself ;   for subject and object are inseparable.   That which cuts us off from an appreciation of this unitary nature of Man and his environment, is simply our lack of knowledge and understanding of the action and interaction of the deeper and more universal planes, on which Man exists in a more unitary manner than on the physical plane.   The whole evolution of this Globe is indissolubly connected with the evolution of Cosmic Man on a plane of consciousness which at present we term the physical ; and however far back we may go in the embryo history of the Globe, we are dealing with a corresponding history of the physical evolution of Man.

There is every reason to believe—whether by analogy, or

by the authority of the ancient traditions embodied in the Scriptures of various Religions—that there are other orders of Beings in the Cosmos besides Man ; and each of these will have their appropriate field of evolution. We shall thereby assign to the Sun and Planets an appropriate Cosmic Life which, in its individual aspect as Sun or Planet, will be a Being of which the physical body or Globe is the expression on the physical plane. There is no single physical unit without a *soul*; for every physical thing exists on all the planes of the universe. The 'World-Soul' is MAN ; and in and through MAN the whole evolution of this Globe takes place.

But we must carry the principle of Unity in diversity still further. This Earth is only one of a number of Worlds or Globes all dependent upon the Sun for their life and energy. The Solar System is in itself a Cosmic Unit, and as such must have a unitary LIFE. It might be convenient to call that Life a Logos. The principle of correspondence and analogy must serve us here in the great as in the small. Individual man is the Logos for his own body, that body being macrocosmic relatively to the individual. Cosmic Man is the Logos for his own Globe. The Solar Logos stands in the same relation to the whole of His System ; and however much further afield we may go into the Cosmos, we must consider that each smaller unit is comprised within some larger one, until we have reached—though we never can reach it in this manner—the one Supreme Logos of the whole Manifested Universe.

Let us not forget that this *extension* is our intellectual apprehension of the matter. By intuition we realise that in a certain sense it is pure illusion, and that of that Supreme Logos—and even of the 'lesser' ones ; aye, even of Man himself—it must be said :

> " Where it cometh all things are,
> And it cometh everywhere."

In the Consciousness of the Supreme Logos, Man, together with all other Cosmic Beings, must constitute a Unity which not merely as a whole, but also in each of its parts, must stand in its complete perfection of purpose and function, the complete fulfilment of the Eternal *Idea*.

If, then, we ask why Man appears to us to have 'fallen,' why Humanity now appears to be such an imperfect, weak, necessitous, erring, ignorant, suffering being ? : the reply will be, in the first place, that we do not see Man in his Wholeness ; and in the second place that this ' fall ' was necessary in order that he might fulfil his cosmic function.

We only see a minute fragment of Man, either in what he is historically—that is to say as an evolving unitary being—or in what he is eternally in his spiritual wholeness and perfection, " made in the image of God."

Historically, we only know of Man during the very limited period of a few thousand years. Scientifically, we must assign to him millions of years during which he has existed and will continue to exist on this Globe. In the vast evolutionary time-process of our Earth, Man appears to us superficially to be a mere succession of individuals, with no particular function in the economy of Nature or of the cosmic process as a whole. In the course of incalculable ages he has evolved physically from the lowest forms of Protozoa. Each individual man evolves thus to-day ; repeating in the short space of nine months the whole evolutionary history of the Race from that point. We may go still further back to physical matter itself, in which we do not as yet scientifically recognise any form of life, though it must necessarily be as *potential* in the atom as in the protozoa. In the course of incalculable ages still to come, Man may, and doubtless will, evolve a physical body which will be as unlike his present body as the body of a horse to-day is unlike the five-toed animal somewhat resembling a small fox from which we can trace his direct descent. Among other things it is highly probable that before Man has finished his evolution on this Globe, the physical separation of the sexes will have vanished. These are matters, however, which cannot be decided from any scientific knowledge which we at present possess ; whilst the information which is given in certain occult schools would be out of place here. I have, however, shown in *Scientific Idealism* [1] that Man is the parent stem of the great Tree of Life on this Globe—the animals having evolved from Man, and not Man from the animals. The present animals are collateral descendants from the intermediate types or species which, in this definitely directed evolution, formed the direct line or parent stem of Man's genealogical tree. Present physical man has evolved through the animal Kingdom, as

[1] Chap. xiii.

also through the still earlier vegetable and mineral; so that in *physical* history these Kingdoms come first. Every individual man, in his pre-natal development in the womb, evolves through these lower Kingdoms; but yet we call the embryo *human*, even its very earliest stages, when it is recapitulating the evolution of the *animal* Kingdom.

If we could see Man in his wholeness on the more inner planes of the Cosmos, we should find a still closer connection between him and the material world in which he functions; we should in fact see Man as the creator of his own world. If we see and know Man now only in such a fragmentary manner on the horizontally extended line of the evolutionary time-process, it is equally certain that we see and know even less of him on the vertical line of his direct connection with the Absolute; that is to say, in his existence and functions on the deeper and more universal and unitary planes of the Cosmos

Consider well that even physically we see but a fragmentary part of any individual man, and—save in exceptional cases hardly as yet credited—nothing at all of his actual existence on the higher planes of Substance or Consciousness. How much the more is it true that we see and know but an infinitesimal part of Cosmic Man in his whole nature, extending through every plane up to the Supreme Logos. If we could see and know the whole of any individual man, we should see and know Cosmic Man; and if we saw and knew Cosmic Man, we should see and know the Logos; and to see and know the Logos, the ' Son,' is to see and know the ' Father,' the Absolute. This is only carrying to its logical conclusion in the connection between Life and Matter, or Subject and Object, what Science has already recognised for Matter only; for Lord Kelvin tells us that:

" All the properties of matter are so connected that we can scarcely imagine one *thoroughly explained*, without our seeing its relation to all the others; without, in fact, having the explanation of all." [1]

If, then, we could know Man in his wholeness and completeness; if we could know him " in spirit and in truth " : should we not have to recognise that in spite of the nescience, the imperfection, the ' evil ' of that fragmentary part of him which is all that is immediately present in our consciousness, his

[1] *Popular Lectures and Addresses*, Art. " Constitution of Matter."

wholeness and completeness constitutes a divine perfection
of Truth, Goodness, and Beauty of inconceivable richness and
infinite fulness ?

This question admits of no other than an affirmative answer
from those who take it as a primary and fundamental postulate that the Absolute, or God, is in Itself or Himself such an
Absolute and Infinite Perfection, and at the same time is ' All
and in All.'

The syllogism may be stated thus :

God is Absolute Perfection.
God is the Universe in its Wholeness and Unity.
Therefore the Universe in its Wholeness is Absolute Perfection.

We can only deny this by denying or qualifying either the
major or the minor premise. It is possible to postulate an
imperfect Absolute, an Absolute ' in the making.' But this
is a spurious Absolute which never emerges from the time-
process. It is a counsel of despair of the formal mind. It has
never been the mystic's Absolute, nor that of any great
Religion. We shall cease to believe at the peril of our sanity
in an eternal divine Perfection at the root and source of all
things. All that is deepest and strongest in us leads us to
believe in such a Perfection. But the perfection of the whole
implies the perfection of the part. It implies the perfection
of the Logos as the *Idea* of the manifested Cosmos ; and it implies the perfection of Man *now* in *his* wholeness and completeness, however imperfect the fragmentary parts may appear
to be. In a perfect Whole every part must be perfect. The
measure and standard of the perfection of a part is the proper
fulfilling or exercise of its function in the whole ; and dare we
affirm, with our fragmentary and imperfect knowledge of
Man, that he does not fulfil that function ? Even the Devil
must be conceived of as perfect in his part and function in the
Cosmos. We call many things in Nature vile ; but are they vile
to the One Life which lives and moves in them just as much
as in us ? Our empirical consciousness tells us that Man is
sinful and imperfect ; but our intuition, and even our logical
faculty, tells us that whether as the ' creation ' of a perfect
God, as being the image and likeness of such a God ; or whether
in another aspect Man can claim to be, in the wholeness of his
nature, nothing short of the Absolute itself : He must necessarily

be as perfect as the God who ' creates ' him, or as the Absolute which he *is*. Thus, quite apart from Mysticism, we find that this conclusion may be arrived at philosophically. Professor Royce arrives at this conclusion as the result of a close and rationalistic analysis of the meaning of the concept *Being*. He says :

" All finite life is a struggle with evil. Yet from the final point of view the Whole is good. The Temporal Order contains at no one moment anything that can satisfy. Yet the Eternal Order is perfect. We have all sinned, and come short of the glory of God. Yet in just our life, viewed in its entirety, the glory of God is completely manifest. These hard sayings are the deepest expressions of the essence of true religion. They are also the most inevitable outcome of philosophy. . . . In the bare assertion of just these truths, that appear to our ordinary consciousness a stumbling-block and foolishness, the wisest of humanity, in India, in Greece, and in the history of Christian thought, are agreed." [1]

The reconciliation of an empirical sense of evil with the intuition of an absolute Good is only a part of the general problem of the intellect in its inability to reach the ' thing in itself.' We have to make our choice between empiricism or materialism as giving us a true perception of things in their *reality*, and the idealism or intuition which looks to a transcendental perfection only partially discovered or manifested in external things of our present consciousness. We have already made our choice ; and, indeed, we see most clearly that the evolutionary process is itself one in which empiricism is continually being jettisoned, and the ideal brought into the region of the real.

Professor Edward Caird has a very illuminative view of this question in a passage in his work on *The Evolution of Religion*.[2]

" The thought of a God who *externally* dominates over the course of nature and history is a compromise which cannot permanently be maintained. In the long run, a religion based on such a conception must advance to the idea of a spiritual principle which is immanent in the object as it is in the subject, or else it must carry the opposition of the subject to the object to the point at which the latter is contemplated as purely evil or negative. That which is outside of God

---

[1] *The World and the Individual*, vol. ii, p. 379.
[2] Vol. ii, p. 63. 1893 ed.

is necessarily that which is opposed to Him, and that which is opposed to the divine must be evil, so far as it can be regarded as having any positive existence at all. We may illustrate this process of thought by the development of the Kantian philosophy as it is shown on the one side in the pessimism of Schopenhauer, and, on the other side, in the optimism of Schelling and Hegel. The former is the necessary result, if Kant's first tendency to oppose reason to sense, and consequently the subject to the object, be insisted on, and carried out to its consequences. This opposition forces Kant himself to conceive the realisation of the moral idea as a *Progressus ad infinitum*; but even infinite time is not enough for the impossible task of uniting the moral with the natural, the sensuous desires with the law of reason. Hence it was open to Schopenhauer to argue that they could not be united at all. On the other hand, if we admit the postulate of Kant, that the moral idea *must* be realised, and if we go on with him to recognise, as he recognises in the *Critique of Judgment* and the *Essay on the Idea of Universal History*, that in a sense it is realised already, or is progressively realising itself in nature and history, then we must advance beyond Kant in a different direction. We must reduce the opposition between sense and reason, or between consciousness and self-consciousness to a *relative* opposition, which exists in order that it may be transcended. In other words, we must adopt something like the evolutionary optimism of Hegel."

Cosmic Man exists on all the planes of the Cosmos, and in an appropriate manner fulfils his function thereon. If Man appears to be individual and fragmentary on the physical plane, he must appear to be less so on the psychic plane, and still less so on the mental plane, whilst on the spiritual plane we can only postulate that he exists in his eternal perfection as the unitary Man, "made in the image of God."

Shall that image be less perfect, less complete than that which it manifests? Even if it manifests in part only, that part must necessarily be perfect as part of a perfect Whole. That part or image exists as the Logos; and if spiritual Man has fallen, then has the Logos Himself fallen. Doubtless there is a sense in which Man has fallen, and a corresponding sense also in which the Logos has fallen; but in the latter case we do not call it a 'fall,' we call it 'the mystery of the Incarnation.' We cannot resolve that mystery with the intellect any more than we can resolve the mystery of apparent individualism and separation in a fundamental Unity, or an apparent evil in a fundamental or absolute Good. We say that these are appearances not Reality, and we strive ever to apprehend the Reality underlying the appearance. But this much at least we can apprehend, that in each and every case where we say, in the conventional language of the formal mind, that the Unity *becomes* a multiplicity, or *appears* in separation and opposition : the fundamental Unity is in no wise thereby in any sense divided ; it still *remains* in all its absoluteness. The Ether does not cease to be Ether, *qua* Ether, when it differentiates into physical matter ; and moreover it is only the minutest portion of the whole Ether which thus differentiates. Cosmic Mind does not cease to be Cosmic Mind, as such, when a portion of it differentiates into individual minds ; nor can we conceive in any manner that it is thereby, so to speak, emptied of its content. The spiritual plane is not emptied to make the lower planes, nor is spiritual Man emptied that Man may exist on the lower planes. All these are *appearances* ; and we can take our choice as to whether we will continue to view the Universe in this fragmentary manner, or whether we will make the unitary Reality our permanent and all-embracing standpoint.

How can anyone have a due appreciation either of his own nature or of the nature of ' God ' when he views Man only in the limited and fragmentary manner of the individual ; and can even imagine that the relation of God to Man is mostly connected with the ' salvation ' of a comparatively few individual selves or fragments which are necessarily impermanent, which are *appearance* only, and which can never be ' saved ' until they have themselves determined to be ' lost ' in the eternal reality of the ONE ?

" Then the man says : ' Behold ! I, poor fool that I was, imagined that it was I, but behold ! it is, and was, of a truth, God ! ' " [1]

Man has come out or ' fallen ' from his spiritual estate, yet he remains there in his divine perfection. His fall is his mission and function in the Cosmos ; and the Cosmos is a manifestation of an eternally existing divine perfection. There can be no final perfectibility in an infinite time-process regarded as always adding something more to an imperfection. The only sense in which the time-process can be regarded as leading to a final perfection is in the attainment of a fulness of consciousness of an already existing perfection from which the individual is

[1] *Theologia Germanica,* chap. v.

temporarily shut out in order that he may fulfil his necessary function in the Cosmos. Thus the individual can only attain to perfection by knowing what he *is* in his oneness with the Perfect. Imperfection is in limitation of consciousness, not in the fulness of the Eternal Reality. And may we not say that long before we reach that fulness of realisation we shall have assuredly discovered that for every pang we have suffered in this so-called evil world, there is compensation a million-fold ; that "our light affliction *which is but for a moment* worketh for us a far more exceeding and eternal weight of glory"? We attain to perfection and are 'saved' only by attaining to "the full-grown man, unto the measure of the stature of the fulness of Christ," the Logos, the Cosmic Man, who has 'fallen' or 'incarnated,' has been crucified on the Cross of Matter, yet remains as the perfect manifestation of the ever-concealed Causeless-Cause.

But we cannot attain to this *fulness* as the result of any outward growth ; it is the opening up of our inner conscious-ness ; an expansion inwards in that 'direction' in which every individualised 'thing' becomes more and more universal. All 'sin,' all 'evil' thus resolves itself into a cherished sense of egoity or separateness ; and the more a man seeks to preserve that sense of egoity the more he is lost to the realisation of the illimitable fulness and perfection of his eternal and immortal nature. That perfection stands in its wholeness and complete-ness in the consciousness of the Logos, the Cosmic God-Man— even as a process the end being complete from the beginning— and it does not appear to be beyond the power of the individual to reach some such unitary consciousness even now, whilst still in a physical body. The attainment of this unitary consciousness is Mysticism ; or perhaps we should rather say, that in so far as there is a mystic 'Way' to be travelled before the realisation is actually attained, Mysticism is the effort to attain. The mystic may be at various stages of the Way, but we shall still call him a mystic, because the goal is clearly realised as attainable ; because he has set out to climb to the very summit of the Mount of Transfiguration, whilst others merely walk vainly round and round the base.

Mysticism is the fruition of religion, but it is also a distinct departure from it as religion is commonly understood and practised. Mysticism may be said to commence as soon as the individual commences to perceive his unitive nature, to perceive his indissoluble oneness with that Divine Life which is all things. Mysticism cannot obtain in any system of religion which places God and Man in eternal separation as creator and creature, or in which God is eternally transcendental; in short it cannot obtain in any supernatural or dualistic religion without exhibiting a distinct departure therefrom. Dualism and supernaturalism belong to the earlier stages of religion wherein the religious instinct rises no higher than the formal mind, and where, consequently, religious beliefs are more or less grossly materialistic and anthropomorphic. Mysticism must necessarily transcend this, for it commences when the individual is able to escape from the necessitous nature of the formal mind into the higher region of spiritual freedom. This freedom may be a deep and profound *faith*, a *Pistis*, before it becomes a definite attainment, a *Gnôsis*. Thus before Mysticism comes religion as commonly understood at the present time: the 'faith' expressed in a definite belief or creed, and the observance of prescribed ceremonies. This is *exoteric* religion: religion as known historically. It bears the same relation to true spiritual Religion or *quality of life* that the historical evolutionary process of Man does to his true and eternal spiritual nature. It rises from low forms of Fetish worship to gorgeous Ritual performed in stately Temples. At first with fear and trembling, and, later on, in strange Images made with hands, the individual seeks to draw nigh to *That* which in reality he carries in his own inner nature; *That* which is closer and nearer than any external thing. For long and seemingly interminable ages, the individual and the Race retain this false sense of separateness, and man is a pilgrim and a wanderer in the very midst of a *Reality*, ever present, here and now, and of infinite fulness, richness, and bliss. Viewed as a time-process, the great sweep of Cosmic evolution inevitably carries Man forward to the full realisation of his true nature in its oneness with the Absolute; but so long as the sense of separation exists, this progress must take the form of a more or less refined, though always anthropomorphic, concept of a personal Deity, with appropriate forms of propitiatory or laudatory worship; and a necessitous professional class inevitably arises to minister to the demand

Exoteric religion is always formal, limited, and thereby exclusive. It finds no truth, no safety outside of its own particular concepts, and these concepts are always more or less crudely realistic, are products of the formal mind, so that spiritual things are thereby conceived of only in terms of time and space.

Esoteric religion and Mysticism, on the other hand, rise into the true region of Spirit, the region of freedom; and we may make this further distinction between these and exoteric religion, that the latter belongs to the region of necessity or law, the others to the region where the soul realises its infinite and inalienable freedom. Life for the individual is necessitous or free just in proportion as it identifies itself on the one hand with form, or on the other hand with principle. Principle, Spirit, can take endless forms and be in nowise bound or limited by any. Life itself, whilst taking on innumerable forms, is essentially free. It is never limited or defined by the form; it is always something more than ' correspondence with environment ': though this may be, in a certain sense, the intellectual measure of it, and therefore satisfactory to Science—which is itself necessitous. And since life thus perpetually escapes from and transcends the region of necessity, the region of matter and intellect: shall we not thereby recognise what we intuitively feel in our inmost being, that Life belongs to another order of things than the necessitous; that it is essentially free, and that Freedom exists as the opposite pole of Necessity as certainly as Subject stands opposed to Object.

Subject, or Spirit, is Freedom; Object, or Matter, or Form, is Necessity; but only Necessity when taken as a reality in itself, and as if it were not the veriest outcome and revelation of pure Freedom.

Many attempts have been made by great teachers to raise Religion into this region of Freedom; but the great mass of Humanity is still too materialistic, too much under the sway of the empirical ' reality ' of the senses and the formal mind, to be able to appreciate the true inner nature of Religion in its spiritual freedom and spontaneity. Some 1,900 years ago the effort is reputed to have been made by one of the great spiritual teachers of the world; but nothing is sadder in the whole history of Religion than the failure to appreciate the pure spirituality of the Gospel of Freedom as contained in the New Testament. No religion has ever held souls in bondage to the extent that so-called Christianity has done; no so-called religion has ever resulted in such appalling crimes.

That the reputed life and teachings of Jesus, as also of the great Apostle Paul, are profoundly mystical, and intimately connected with the ancient and pre-existing Gnôsis, is a fact which research and scholarship is bringing more and more to light. We might even accord to the Christian Scriptures a foremost place in the presentation of that Gnôsis; but there is much work to be done, and probably many other ancient documents to be discovered, before their real value in this respect can become generally recognised. In the meanwhile, as St. Augustine tells us : " The Narratives of the Doctrine are its cloak. The simple look only at the garment, that is upon the narrative of the Doctrine; more they know not. The instructed, however, see not merely the cloak, but what the cloak covers."

What was known as Gnôsticism in Hellenistic times was a survival in a more or less corrupt form of pre-Christian Mysticism. It goes back to Plato and Aristotle and Heraclitus in Greece, whilst its Eastern sources in Egypt and the Far East have still to be traced.[1]

" Recent investigations," says the Rev. F. Lamplugh in the interesting introduction to his English translation of *The Gnôsis of the Light* (Codex Brucianus), "have challenged the traditional outlook and the traditional conclusions and the traditional ' facts.' With some to-day, and with many more to-morrow, the burning question is, or will be—not how did a peculiarly silly and licentious heresy rise within the Church—but how did the Church rise out of the great Gnôstic Movement, and how did the dynamic ideas of the Gnôsis become crystallised into Dogmas ? "

Christian Mysticism will be found to approximate more and more closely to Gnôsticism the more we discover about the latter. At present we have only fragmentary records of it, and these are mostly derived from its ' Christian ' opponents, who did all they could to misrepresent and ridicule it. " Each opponent, with the dialectical skill which was common at the

[1] Cf. Mead: *Fragments of a Faith Forgotten.*

time, selected, paraphrased, distorted, and recombined the points which seemed to him to be weakest." [1]

Those who dragged Christianity, or rather the Gnôsis, down from its pure spirituality into a system of materialised dogmas, were naturally bitter foes of a Mysticism which they could not understand, and which appeared to throw discredit upon their own authority as exponents of the relation of God to Man. It is even so to-day; but to-day they have not the power to bind consciences and to stifle knowledge. And so to-day it is the Gnôsis which is reappearing and the theologian who suffers discredit.

The fundamental teaching of the Gnôsis is *the Divine Nature of Man*. At intervals throughout the Dark Ages of ecclesiastical bigotry and dogmatism, has appeared here and there some bright star of mystical knowledge and vision, to proclaim this great truth. God and Man, Man and God: complementary aspects of the One Absolute Immutable Divine Perfection, from which the individual—when he has reached a certain stage of his evolution—is only separated by his own wilful denial, which further experience will correct; for that supreme bliss of union to which here and there a few individual mystics have attained, is the pledge of the potentiality of the real nature of every man coming into this world.

Great as is the mystery for the intellect of the Absolute and the Relative, of Reality and Appearance, of God and Man, of the Word made Flesh, of the Higher and the Lower Self, of Good and Evil—all these being synonyms for the same illimitable and eternal Fact—there is that within us which claims this mystery, this Fact, as the very essence and reason and substance of our being. However small or low or mean or outcast we may appear to be in our individual aspect in the world of Appearances, we have behind or within us, as it were, the other pole of our being; the infinite potentiality of the transcendent and inconceivable richness, and fulness, and glory, and ineffable bliss of the eternal and immeasurable Perfection of the ONE LIFE in Its Absoluteness.

And towards that Perfection all individual things, from atom to man, from man to god, do and must inevitably and

---

[1] Hatch: *The Influence of Greek Ideas and Usages upon the Christian Church*, p. 9.

irresistibly move ; sowing and reaping as they go ; here sorrow and pain and Dead Sea Fruit ; there a measure of joy and gladness, and the ambrosial grain of the Eternal Wheat Fields ; drinking now of the bitter waters of Marah, and anon of that Spring of Living Water from which if a man drink he shall assuredly thirst no more.

CHAPTER VII

CHARACTERISTICS OF RELIGION

" By religion I do not mean the church-creed which a man professes, the articles of faith which he will sign and, in words or otherwise, assert ; not this wholly, in many cases not this at all. We see men of all kinds of professed creeds attain to almost all degrees of worth or worthlessness under each or any of them. This is not what I call religion, this profession and assertion ; which is often only a profession and assertion from the outworks of the man, from the mere argumentative region of him, if even so deep as that. But the thing a man does practically believe (and this is often *without* asserting it even to himself, much less to others) ; the thing a man does practically lay to heart, and know for certain, concerning his vital relations to this mysterious Universe, and his duty and destiny there, that is in all cases the primary thing for him, and creatively determines all the rest. That is his *religion* ; or, it may be, his mere scepticism and *no-religion* : the manner it is in which he feels himself to be spiritually related to the Unseen World or No-World."

THOMAS CARLYLE: *On Heroes.*

" When we have broken our god of tradition, and ceased from our god of rhetoric, then may God fire the heart with his presence."

EMERSON : *The Over Soul.*

CHAPTER VII

CHARACTERISTICS OF RELIGION

RELIGION has many phases, and Mysticism has many phases, hence it is extremely difficult to give a comprehensive definition of either. No such definition has ever been given : no definition, that is to say, to which some exception cannot be taken.[1] It is still more difficult to say specifically what it is that differentiates the one from the other, unless we systematise the whole range of our experience in a more or less artificial manner. Some such system as that which we have given in our previous chapter on the Absolute and its Manifestations must necessarily form the basis of any religious philosophy, and will enable us to formulate certain definite concepts as to the nature of Religion and the further province of Mysticism which—if their limitations as concepts are continually kept in mind—will be of the greatest possible assistance to us in so far as it is necessary to think clearly about these matters.

Neither Religion nor Mysticism is *primarily* a matter of intellect at all. We must bear in mind that all our philosophy, metaphysics, and theology, all our formulated thought, is the effort to interpret experience in terms of intellect. The primary thing is experience, and Religion and Mysticism are no exceptions in this respect ; they are inner experiences, inner conditions of the subject-ego, states of feeling and emotion which produce definite results in the outer action of the individual and in his attitude towards the world of his environment ; and whilst the intellect may endeavour to find a reason for this, and theology may dogmatise about it, this can only be done as an effort which is secondary to a state of feeling or consciousness which transcends intellect both

[1] For numerous definitions of Mysticism, cf. W. R. Inge, *Christian Mysticism*, Appendix A.

in its reality and its authority. The authority, indeed, results from its deeper reality, using the term reality in the sense of *immediacy* of empirical experience. Professor Royce insists that the mystic is the greatest empiricist, and the most practical of all empiricists in his effort to obtain pure experience. " I should maintain," he says, " that the mystics are the only thorough-going empiricists in the history of philosophy."[1]

There are many individuals who must certainly be considered to be truly religious in a primary sense, but who have no formulated belief at all, or who, having a wide knowledge of various forms of religious belief—that is to say of the *intellectual* endeavours to express the great fundamental fact of Religion itself—have not found it necessary to give in their adherence to any one in particular : indeed, it is this latter and wider knowledge of the terms in which Religion has expressed itself at various times and seasons, and under varying conditions of man's knowledge and evolution, that we must consider to be the safeguard against irrational belief and superstition, with all their attendant evils. " He who knows one religion knows none."

It is very easy to use the term Religion as if every one knew exactly what is meant by it, but as a matter of fact it has not the same meaning for the devotee of one religion that it has for another, and it has not meant the same thing at various periods of the world's history. Moreover, in its primary nature Religion is not merely a different thing from what it is in its secondary aspects, but, paradoxically, the two are in opposition to one another : Religion in the secondary sense of the term having been historically one of the most fruitful causes of all that is the opposite of Religion in its primary nature.

If we really go to the root of the matter we cannot define Religion *primarily* otherwise than as *a spiritual quality of life.* The truly religious man is the man who manifests this spiritual quality in his life—let the form of his religious belief be what it may. If there is one thing that we expect Religion to do for the individual, it is to produce in him a quality of life in which rightness or righteousness, virtue, truth, charity or love, are the predominating factors. We

---

[1] *The World and the Individual,* vol. i, p. 81. Cf. also 80, 83, 285.

shall bar out here all question of beliefs, forms, doctrines, dogmas, or ceremonies, for these are only Religion in the *secondary* sense ; yet it is in this secondary sense that the term Religion is commonly understood, and it is in this sense that Religion is known historically, and is studied in its inception and developments. But Religion is primarily an instinct or intuition, the deepest and most potent that man possesses, for it is the instinct of his own deeper nature in its unity with the Cosmos ; and it has behind it all that that unity implies of infinite potentiality. It is of the heart, not of the head. No man was ever converted to any religion by logical argument. If the arguments for any particular belief were valid as logic, every ' rational ' man would be compelled to accept them ; yet nothing is more apparent than that the arguments, the ' proofs ' of any particular religion which may be considered to be absolutely valid by the devotee of that religion, are utterly inadequate for the devotee of another religion which possesses equally satisfying ' proofs ' of its own divine authority. Or take one religion only. All Christians appeal to the Bible for their ' proofs ' ; yet the differences among Christian sects are not merely notorious, but have been and are the cause of incalculable evil. We must go deep into the causes of the varieties of spiritual *instincts* which individuals and communities and races possess, before we can account for the differences in religious beliefs : differences so great that one religion may possess a personal God who superintends the minutest affairs in the life of each individual, whilst another has no personal God at all, but only immutable spiritual law.

The fact is that in religion ' proof ' does not mean the same thing that it does in the ordinary affairs of life. In Religion it means appeal to inner feeling or instinct. If a man feels the need of a heavenly Father to superintend his affairs, and ' send ' him good fortune, or possibly affliction : his God will be even such ; if he does not, then no argument for the existence of such a God can ever convince him. If we were to grant the historical truth of every deed and word attributed in the Gospels to Jesus Christ—which we are very far from doing—which of all Christian sects should we accept as having the true interpretation of the facts ? Shall we necessarily accept any ? The Jew does not accept them, neither does the Brahmin or the Buddhist.   There is no logical proof of any formulated religion, for logical proof must be valid for *all* men.   We cannot here argue from effect to cause, for the cause lies deeper than intellect.   A man is not religious because of the beliefs, but he believes because of his religious nature.   A truly religious Christian would have made an equally good Buddhist had such been his religious heredity. Whatever touches the heart is beautiful to the intellect as well as to the eye, but the beauty is in the ideal which the thing represents to the individual, and not in the thing itself. We can only argue from effect to cause in religion in the primary sense, for the man is religious or not in the instinctive hidden source of his character and actions.   Where these do not agree with his creed, he may profess the creed but ignore it in practice.   The greater part of the Sermon on the Mount is universally ignored by professing Christians.[1]

If we ask the question as to whether the World as a whole is to-day more religious in the primary sense than it ever was before, the answer is perhaps problematical ; but what we do see very clearly in history, and in our own present communities is, that Religion *as a quality of life* becomes more and more obscured, inoperative, perverse, the more Religion is referred to or identified with a formulated belief, or is based upon an outer instead of an inner sanction ; upon a supposed divine revelation or authority, historically and supernaturally given, rather than upon the spiritual nature of Man himself : upon what we may call the *natural* laws of his spiritual nature ; operative here and now and for all time, and plainly visible in their outer effects in individuals and communities.

Religion in the primary sense never grows old or decays ; it is, indeed, the hope that springs eternal in the human soul. But Religion in the secondary sense is a thing of time and form ; and however great or impregnable it may appear to be in its own time and place, it presently goes the way of all other temporal and formal things.

The representatives of Religion in the secondary sense

---

[1] " The ethics of the Sermon on the Mount, which the earliest Christian communities endeavoured to carry into practice, have been transmuted by the slow alchemy of history into the ethics of Roman law.   The basis of Christian society is not Christian, but Roman and Stoical " (Hatch: *Influence of Greek Ideas and Usages upon the Christian Church*, p. 169).

have been known now for many ages as Scribes and Pharisees. They exist to-day, and must exist so long as outer observance, ceremonies, forms, formulas, and dogmas are taken as the *substance* of Religion. For many long centuries that which has passed for Religion in the Western World has been under the dominance of these formalists. They have not merely been in bitter opposition to any change in their stereotyped creed, but also to the advance of scientific knowledge, and to any form of intellectual freedom which appeared to depart from their own dogmatic theology. They have also been the perpetrators of unspeakable cruelty and evil of every description. The same spirit abides in them to-day, and manifests itself in the same works wherever the opportunity serves, though their actual political and temporal power is now happily so far destroyed that they cannot proceed to torture and murder. And still they say, "If we had been in the days of our fathers, we should not have been partakers with them in the blood of the prophets."

We are not hereby saying that that 'faith' which is professed as the religion—in the secondary sense—of some 564 millions of the inhabitants of the World at the present time, has not been of the highest value to millions of individuals in their spiritual life and evolution, or that it is not so to-day. So long as the traditional beliefs and doctrines of Christianity do actually suffice to produce, or are concurrent with, that right or righteous quality of life which is Religion in the primary sense, we should welcome them, however narrow, palpably erroneous, or even repellant they may be in some respects. Even the crude beliefs and methods of the Salvation Army or the Revivalist are welcome for the reformation they often effect in the lives of thousands who would not otherwise be touched in their inner nature; nor will anyone quarrel with the 'simple faith,' the "sincere milk of the word" which has been the nourishment of so many "spiritual babes" in the past, and which must continue to be so for many a generation yet to come. It is only when the accredited leaders and teachers have *nothing else to offer* to those who have passed beyond this stage, that the mischief begins, and so-called religion falls into disrepute and decay.

Can any of us by any possibility conceive of the difference it would have made—shall we say merely during the Christian era—if it had been universally recognised that Religion is *a quality of life*, and not a profession of belief; that a man is ' saved ' by what he is, not by what he believes; that formulated creeds and all religious observances and ceremonies are necessary and useful only in proportion as they are aids in producing and stimulating this religious quality of life; and that what may be appropriate in this respect for one individual, or for one community, or for one age, may be utterly unsuitable for another? The recognition of this principle is now, happily, becoming very widespread outside of the Christian Church; and to a certain extent within it also. It makes no difference to a man's ' salvation ' whether he is a Brahmin or a Buddhist, a Mohammedan or a Christian, or whether he professes no formulated religion at all as a matter of belief. It would seem to be hardly necessary to state this to-day to any rational man, were it not for the fact that so soon as any question of religion so-called comes in, many men, perhaps the great majority, who are rational and logical in all other matters, abandon this rationality in the strangest and most perverse manner; their attitude in this relation being, that if the facts are against them, so much the worse for the facts. As a rule, however, they do not know and do not want to know any facts which would be liable to upset their cherished beliefs. Probably they are wise in their generation.

We have no hope of any change of heart in this respect on the part of our modern Scribes and Pharisees; they are as stiff-necked as those of any generation. And though it has been written in unmistakable letters of blood and fire for nigh on two thousand years, that their creeds and shibboleths can never be for the healing of the nations; and though as the direct result of the failure of ecclesiastical Christianity to exhibit the true primary nature of Religion, the ' Christian ' nations have just been engaged in the greatest and most diabolical war that was ever waged for the kingdoms of this world; we see no more change of heart on the part of Christianity in certain of its established hierarchies than we do on the part of the German nation. Both would do the same things over again if they had but the power.

But outside of the Church, a great spiritual renaissance is taking place, which, on its outward and formal side, is a return to certain wider and deeper views of Man in his relation to a transcendent Reality which are found to have been taught long before the Christian era; which are implied in the Christian Scriptures in allegory and symbol; and which, St. Augustine tells us, "never did not exist," and only "began to be called Christianity when Christ came in the flesh."

There is pretty strong evidence to show that some of the early Church Fathers and theologians who helped to establish Christianity on its dogmatic basis, knew better than they formulated. Some of them were true initiates in the esoteric Gnôsis to which Christianity owes so much, and which lies at the root of all the great spiritual teaching that Man has ever received. This Gnôsis has been re-stated and confirmed by mystics and mystical philosophers in all ages, and has always been available for those who have had eyes to see and ears to hear.

Origen states definitely that the initiate who possesses the real Gnôsis or Wisdom does not need the historical events of the Gospels, which are only particular instances on the physical plane of spiritual principles which are in eternal operation.[1] He also teaches the pre-existence of the soul, and that spiritual law of cause and effect which had been taught for ages by Eastern Philosophy, and known as the law of *Karma*. Thus he says:

"The present inequalities of circumstance and character are thus not wholly explicable within the sphere of the present life. But this world is not the only world. Every soul has existed from the beginning; it has therefore passed through some worlds already, and will pass through others before it reaches the final consummation. It comes into this world strengthened by the victories or weakened by the defeats of its previous life. Its place in this world as a vessel appointed to honour or to dishonour is determined by its previous merits or demerits. Its work in this world determines its place in the world which is to follow this."[2]

This is a very near approximation to the old Vedânta doctrine of Reincarnation and Karma.

Some of the old Christian theologians and philosophers knew the necessities and the limitations of the forms into which the intellect is compelled to materialise spiritual

---

[1] Cf. W. R. Inge: *Christian Mysticism*, p. 89.
[2] *De princip.*, 3. 1. 20.

realities. They knew that these realities could only be presented in myth and symbol ; and they knew also that the masses could only be taught in a limited and exoteric manner ; and, indeed, this principle of an inner and an outer doctrine is clearly part of the method attributed both to Jesus in the Gospels and to Paul in the Epistles. But the recognition of this principle was gradually lost as the Church became more and more a worldly organisation and a political power ; and so it resulted that it was not merely more and more impossible to present the inner doctrine, but this doctrine itself appeared to be more and more opposed to the outer or popular form, and thus in time it became the great heresy, whilst those who might have shed the light of the knowledge of truth over the resulting ' dark ages ' were persecuted and burnt at the stake. For this great and damnable sin of a Church fallen under the blighting influence of a political necessity from which it has never recovered, the Christian World has had to pay a terrible and bitter price ; whilst the Church itself, powerless to prevent the recent great war, has fallen into nescience and discredit with the world at large. The new wine is being put into new bottles.

Religion in the West, ever since theologians took it upon themselves to formulate their ' plan of salvation,' and to graft an anthropomorphised metaphysic on to the pure inner spiritual truths of the Scriptures, has become narrowed down to a mere matter of personal salvation—and the Devil takes the hindmost. To-day the Roman Catholic Church teaches that there is no salvation outside of its own special ordinances. The Anglican Church has the Athanasian Creed which damns for all eternity those who do not believe in the metaphysical doctrine of the Trinity. Other sects have more or less specialised ideas as to what it is necessary to *believe* in order to be ' saved.'

No doubt there is a sense in which the individual is saved, and a sense in which he is lost ; but it is certainly not in the commonly accepted sense that Mr. Smith and Mrs. Brown are to be Smith and Brown for all eternity : taken up into glory—if they go that way—with all their own special family relations. Yet how very natural all this is, seeing that Smith and Brown are—Smith and Brown. If we go to Burmah we find that the Burmese Smith-Brown has no very clear idea as to what happens to him after death ; but he utterly disbelieves that he will meet there with those to whom he has been attached on Earth, for these are only earthly and personal attachments. But he '*knows*'—in the same sense that the Christian '*knows*' that what he believes is true—that until he has freed himself from the very last trace of earthly desire, desire for sentient life, he will be reincarnated over and over again ; and it is the commonest thing for children to remember their past incarnations, and to give details of them which are verifiable.[1] This question, however, as to what is permanent and what is temporal in the individual, will receive more specific treatment later on. We may merely remark here, that all *mystical* teachers have taught that it is only in proportion as the *self*—the lower personal self— is lost, that the real Self can be found.

When a religion falls into individualism, when it promises individual and exclusive salvation to its devotees, and is itself thereby individualistic as regards other religions : it cannot fail to result in evil ; for individualism, self-seeking, self-interest, is at the root of all evil, whether it be in nations, communities, or individuals. Religion cannot really be understood, even in what it accomplishes for the individual, unless we consider it in a unitary manner, unless we consider it in connection with the whole vast evolution of Man on this Earth. We must not merely consider this as a time-process, but we must also take into account the cosmic nature of Man in his existence on, and connection and interaction with, co-existing Planes of the Cosmos, before we can really appreciate the nature of Religion at its root and source, or justly assign to particular forms or phases their causes and functions.

History shows us broadly that all formulated religions are always degraded and materialistic, or elevated and spiritual, just in proportion as their devotees have a narrower or a wider conception of Man's relation to the Cosmos : the conception of Deity always being enhanced concurrently with Man's appreciation of his own inner cosmic nature. The cosmic nature of Man, and his essential divine nature, is to be found all through the Scriptures ; it is there plainly to be read, but it was too high a doctrine for the under-

---

[1] Cf. H. Fielding Hall : *The Soul of a Nation.*

standing of those who had the ultimate making of the creeds
and dogmas with which so-called Christianity has been historically associated ; and it is still too high a doctrine for
all save a very few of our modern theologians ; these few
being in consequence barely tolerated by the great majority.
The doctrine belongs rather to Mysticism than to theology.
It may, in fact, be said that the great defect of Christianity
as a formulated religion has always been its lack of a cosmic
sense. It has always been not merely geocentric, but also
very markedly provincial, or even parochial. The cosmic
sense was not lacking in certain of the early Christian
philosophers ; they derived it from their Greek training and
environment, where it was abundantly in evidence. They
could not have accepted Christianity in its derivation from
the Gnôsis without it. It reappears to some extent in some
of the later Christian mystics, but it could not survive in
the exoteric religion of the masses which finally determined,
and still determines, the general level of Christian doctrine.
It is this level which makes, rather than is made by, the
professional representatives of religion, who thus follow the
law of supply and demand as surely as cotton goods or any
other commodity.

Forms of religion, like everything else in this world of forms,
change and decay. They " have their day and cease to be "
as " knowledge grows from more to more." New religions,
so-called, spring up and overlap the decay of the old forms
and formulas. New teachers arise, new hierophants, and the
new wine must be put into new bottles. Yet the old forms
may and must persist for many an age. They do so in virtue
of their acquired momentum and vested interests, as well
as from the fact that each does actually, for the time
being, express a fundamental fact in human experience.
Gautama Buddha was a reformer of Brahmanism and the
laws of Manu ; yet Brahmanism still holds sway over some
210 million souls. Notwithstanding Christianity as a reformation of the Jewish Religion and the law of Moses, Judaism
is still the religion of some 12 million followers of the Mosaic
tradition.

The inertia of concrete formulated concepts, and even of
abstract ideas, more especially when they have attained to
the rank of *dogmas*, is due to the fact that they assume a

practical character, and act and react on our life in precisely the same manner as if they were actual definite objects of experience. They are, so to speak, the solid objective vision of the mind ; and in innumerable cases of psychical experience we find them assuming a definite objective vision for the physical eye also, and even producing physical lesions, as in the case of the stigmata of St. Francis. Visions of ' God ' are of common occurrence ; visions of the Virgin even more so. Blake represents God pictorially as a tremendously powerful Old Man : as for example in the drawing entitled " Space," where He is represented as stooping down to measure out Space with a pair of compasses. Now Blake drew his ' dead ' characters, Prophets, Apostles, etc., ' from the life ' ; they were objectively visible to him, and we can hardly doubt but that his mental concept of God was that of a Being as solid and real as He is pictorially represented to be, and which anything may come to be in actual vision if the mental image is strong enough. Blake, indeed, specifically tells us that, " God doth a human form display to those who dwell in realms of day." But whether strong enough or not for actual vision, *ideas* are things which have all the characteristics of solidity and inertia which we commonly attribute only to physical and material things ; and like physical things they have a corresponding persistence in consciousness.

Beneath all the changing forms and modes of Religion lies the great fact of Man's spiritual nature, carrying with it not merely a *moral* implication which is absent from Science and Philosophy, but also producing a certain *quality of life* which neither of these in or by themselves can supply.

But in so far as a formulated religion, apart from this quality of life, is the effort to state the relationship between the individual—or between Man collectively in his lower, material, and evolutionary life—and a transcendental spiritual *Reality* : that Reality cannot be other than the Reality which Philosophy recognises as lying behind the *Appearances* of the phenomenal world. If, however, Philosophy, as we have already seen, cannot reach or explicate that Reality, or state its relationship to the individual and the particular in terms of the formal conceptual mind, what possibility is there of formulated Religion being able to do so. In other words, what possibility is there in this respect of a *theology* which can overpass the province of philosophy ?

We must frankly admit that there is none. In so far as theology is a *science*, its efforts to explicate the nature of God and the soul stands in precisely the same limited and necessitous condition as science and philosophy in general; and it is just as liable, and even more so, to mistake ' convenient fictions ' for realities. But theology—we are not speaking now of progressive theology—realising these limitations, endeavours to sustain its precarious existence by importing into its method an authoritative divine revelation; and it is very largely this which differentiates theology from philosophy. Theology is fundamentally associated with dogma; and to the extent to which it becomes a system or a science, it is not so as proceeding from objective facts to certain and demonstrable conclusions which must necessarily appeal to the common rationality of mankind, but merely as finding reasons or arguments for ' facts ' supposed to be divinely revealed. The theological ' arguments ' for the existence of a personal God of the Jehovah type have sufficed for centuries to satisfy those who already believed in such a God; but they utterly fail to convince those who have no such belief; and they fail simply because they have no real scientific or philosophical validity. To-day they are more discredited than ever: not because men disbelieve in God, but because they have ceased to believe in the particular kind of God which theology has endeavoured to foist upon them for so many centuries, and which could only prevail where a wider and deeper knowledge was unreached or suppressed.

Theology can only claim to be a science in so far as it may be systematised belief; and we are already beginning to make some progress in a Science of Religions: meaning thereby a systematised knowledge and comparative study of all and every form of religious belief. As we do this, and only as we do this, we are able to understand more and more clearly what are the essentials and what are the accidents of Religion; and thereby we shall not merely free ourselves from the dogmatism of theology, but we shall also evolve a wider, deeper, and nobler philosophy of Religion, based upon the common elements which Religion possesses for all men, and one which will be free to adapt itself continuously to the progress of knowledge in all and every department of the great search for Truth. We shall thereby find in every advance which is made by Science and Philosophy, in their own particular fields of activity, a continual and progressive confirmation of, and addition to, a wholly *rational* expression of the spiritual facts and experiences of Man's nature to which Religion in its own right primarily testifies.

We have now to ask ourselves more specifically what this quality of life is, whilst in our next chapter we shall endeavour to understand how or in what manner Mysticism can be considered as differentiating itself from Religion in the more ordinary phases of the latter.

Let us consider here for a moment our Cosmic Chart. We have postulated that Man exists on all Planes of the Cosmos, but so far as our present personal consciousness is concerned, and in so far as we consider ourselves to be conditioned by the great evolutionary Time-Process, the ' higher ' planes come into operation or manifestation in Man successively, from ' below ' upwards : first the physical, then the etheric or psychic, then the mental, and finally the spiritual ; and this is not merely in harmony with all the facts of science, but is the most ancient doctrine of religious philosophy and mysticism.

In so far as Religion is primarily the awakening in Man of a spiritual consciousness, or quality of life, it is essentially a re-becoming, a re-union in consciousness with that source in the Eternal from which—from the point of view of the individual—Man has gone out into time and space, but from which, as we have already clearly apprehended, he has never in reality departed. Man, as his spiritual nature evolves, can only *manifest* that which already exists in the Eternal. What, then, may we postulate to be the characteristics of the Spiritual Plane of the Cosmos as manifested in the individual when he attains to this supreme quality of life, or stage of his evolution ?

In all ages men have deified and worshipped some reputed super-man, or God-man : a Krishna, a Buddha, or a Christ. These represent more or less traditionally what each individual man may become in virtue of his own inherent spiritual nature ; though the doctrines which have accumulated round the original traditions have not always stopped at this simple explanation. We cannot doubt, however, notwithstanding the purely mythical character of most of the so-called 'history' of these World-Saviours, that there do exist in the scale of evolution those who are as much beyond the average man as the latter is beyond the amœba; nor should we consider it to be irrational to suppose that from time to time some one or other of these might incarnate for a special mission to humanity. We conceive, indeed, that there is no break in the scale of evolution, from the lowest to the highest. Each stage has its living representatives; and the man who has " overcome the world " stands no longer in need of re-incarnation, but passes on to higher or more cosmic activities. We must turn to Eastern religious philosophy if we want any teaching regarding the stages which lead up to this final perfection and emancipation, for Christianity does not recognise the evolutionary progress of the soul through the Race, and accords to the individual only one life on Earth.

Let us inquire, however, what it is that religion in general accomplishes for the average individual who comes under its influence. We must of course distinguish here between the merely formal religionist, the average church-goer, and the man who is really touched and moved by this spiritual quality of life, and in whom it effects a radical change of nature: the man who is " born again," or " twice born." This new birth may be sudden: a sudden uprush from the subliminal self, or it may be gradual, or it may be innate in the man from the time of his physical birth: being the fruit of many previous well-spent lives. A man may in fact have more or less of *genius* for religion; genius being an innate knowledge *acquired* through the past experiences of the individual ego. The change which religion effects in a man's life is, of course, most striking in the case of sudden conversion; but in whatever manner it may come, its characteristics are unmistakable.

Of these characteristics we note in the first place, and fundamentally, a distinct orientation, or re-orientation, of all the elements of a man's life. It is the more or less complete turning round of the will, desire, and imagination of the individual in the opposite direction to that which is taken by the 'man of the world'; so that now the man, instead of going 'outwards' towards individualism, self-seeking, the acquirement of wealth, or happiness in ‘the things of this world,’ turns towards an objective or ideal, which has this fundamental characteristic in each and every case—though it does not take the same *form* in each and every individual, nor in various religions—that it aims at the ultimate liberation of the individual from the evil of ‘this world’; from sin, suffering, and death.

Although this must be considered to be the first and foremost characteristic of any experience which can in any way be interpreted as being *religious* in its nature: simply because Religion is at root the instinctive turning of the individual to the source from whence he has gone out in apparent separation: it goes without saying that it will be found in very varying degrees of development in the individual at various periods of his evolution; and hence in very varying degrees in individual communities, and at various periods of the world's history. Dimly and unconsciously at first, and mainly as the result of suffering, the individual begins to realise that in fixing his hopes and desires on the things of this world he is travelling in the wrong direction, whilst the dawning sense of morality, of an ideal of Goodness, Truth, and Beauty, leads him to look to ‘another world’ for the realisation of that which appears to be impossible of attainment in the present one.

Some writers endeavour to do for Religion what biologists do for life: they endeavour to find its *origin* in the most primitive forms. The method is radically wrong in each case. We can neither find the origin of life, nor its quality, in outer appearances and forms which, as such, manifest only the barest beginnings of the infinite potencies of Life Itself. It is only as we find quality added to quality in Man's individual nature that we begin to appreciate the infinite fulness and richness and beauty of that One Life which the individual only manifests in greater or lesser degree. Each added quality of Life as it becomes manifested in Man—whether individually or collectively—has its vague and nebulous dawning; its peculiar and special characteristic at first only faintly tinges the individual life, and very gradually becomes a distinct and clearly recognisable quality. Thus we have ‘low’ forms of intellect as well as low forms of Religion in the first instance. Broadly speaking, indeed, that spiritual quality of life which is Religion is still in a very undeveloped stage in Humanity as a whole. The vast depravity of human nature which the recent war has disclosed is proof enough of that. War itself would be an impossibility if Man had really evolved in any degree his spiritual nature. In truth the world has many religions, but very little Religion ; much religion in the secondary sense, but little enough in the primary sense. The present is the cycle of Man's mental rather than of his spiritual evolution.

Broadly speaking, individuals aggregate into communities, tribes, nations, and races by reason of a mutual attraction of like to like, this attraction being fundamentally what the individuals are in their *inner* nature. Having been born thus into a certain community or nation, the individual most commonly, and on the average, simply accommodates himself to his environment ; his thoughts, habits, politics, religion, are those of his parents, or of the social circle in which he has been brought up ; and he acquires *class* habits and prejudices more or less ' upper ' or ' lower,' more or less respectable or criminal. And we who judge almost entirely by what the outward man is, praise or condemn accordingly ; almost always forgetting that the greatest sinner not merely has in him the potentiality of the saint, and that that potentiality may be very near indeed to the surface, so that at any time it may break through and appear as ' conversion ' —of which there are thousands of modern instances—but we also forget that the man has the same spiritual source and nature as ourselves, and that even such as he is outwardly, we might have been—and perhaps have been in previous lives—but for our more fortunate present outward circumstances. What sense, indeed, is there in condemning a man for that which you yourself may have been at any time in the course of your evolution, or may yet be for aught you know ? Besides, in *reality*, is not his act even now your act, seeing that there is but one Self ? It is often more of a ' misfortune ' than otherwise that a man is a criminal : a misfortune of heredity as well as of environment ; whilst our present intensely individualistic state of society and of international politics is entirely adverse and opposed to all that is calculated to give the average individual a ' fortunate ' environment for the free development of his spiritual nature.

It is thus that the religious man in general, and the extreme religious devotee in particular, finds himself up against the ' world,' and considers it necessary in some cases to isolate himself entirely, to take vows of chastity and poverty, to become an ascetic and a recluse, or to seek refuge in a religious community where his own particular method of spiritual life is recognised and finds support from a common interest and practice. This is doubtless wise in many cases; but although religion is primarily a separation in heart and desire from the world as at present constituted in its outer state and activities, it is not necessarily an outward separation, and a man may be *in* the world, and may even acquire a goodly share of material prosperity by honest labour and trade, and yet not be *of* the world. The man who seeks *first* " the kingdom of God " may find in this world, even as at present constituted, that " all these things are added unto him." Yet still the saying is true: " How hardly shall a rich man enter into the Kingdom of Heaven."

The world is in fact a very complex place, and the forces and motives which determine the actions of individuals are extremely various, subtle, and difficult to trace in individual cases, though they may one and all be assigned to certain broad principles. Now the broadest of all these principles is that Man, as we know him, has gone *out* from his unitary Source into differentiation, individualism, and egoity; he has ' fallen ' from his primordial state as a spiritual being; he has fallen into Matter, and has created for himself, by a false imagination or consciousness, this complex world of *Appearances*, which, nevertheless, he is now—at the stage which he has reached in that great return process which we call evolution—able to recognise as an Appearance, behind or transcendental to which lies the *Reality* of his nature and of the Universe.

The World of Man's present consciousness was not made *for* Man, it was made *by* Man—at least such is the *esoteric doctrine*—and the individual is indissolubly connected with Humanity in its Cosmic Nature in all the past, present, and future of the great World-Process.[1] We can only speak of forsaking the world in so far as the term ' world ' stands for the outgoing process, and the individualistic and egoistic

---

[1] See quotation from Walt Whitman, p. 322 *infra*.

desires which give rise to the evil which is concomitant therewith.

The question as to the necessity or otherwise of Man's ' fall ' does not enter in here. It is the way of return with which we are concerned. We have simply to recognise that Religion is the expression of the desire for this return, and is, therefore, a departure from and a renunciation of all that the world holds to be desirable in so far as that desirability is associated with the things of time and appearance in the outgoing process, and not with the return to the eternal Reality.

But as a matter of fact, the world, as being that environment which Man makes for himself—both Cosmic Man and individual man—as being the outer reflection, the objectivised content of his own inner nature and consciousness : is being re-made continually ; so that when Man collectively has really become spiritual in his desire-nature, the ' kingdoms of this world ' will also have become the spiritual habitation of Man. The possibility of this is apparent to us without any dogmatic teachings as to a ' Judgment Day ' ; or even without any theories as to a ' fall.' Does anyone doubt but that if the whole of humanity had really acquired that spiritual quality of life which is true Religion : what we call evil would have largely or entirely vanished from the world ? Moral evil would of course have disappeared entirely ; it would be impossible for one individual to do other than seek the welfare of his fellows as he would his own. He would not merely do no injury to others, but all anger, hatred, malice, jealousy, and pride would have been replaced by an active love and helpful sympathy. Concomitant with the disappearance of moral evil, bodily ailments and disease would also disappear. It is not yet realised how much of these is due to the evil passions of the mind. But, looking at this merely in its physical aspect, we should see that all those unhealthy physical conditions under which such a large bulk of our population live would not be tolerated for one moment. We should see to it that the physical conditions under which each individual lived were absolutely natural and therefore healthy. Further, hereditary disease would disappear ; the parents would have no ' sins ' to transmit to their offspring, and there would be no hereditary tendencies to physical depravity.

But we may look deeper than mere physical causes in this matter. Such a spiritual regeneration as we are here indicating, such a re-orientation of the whole of Humanity towards that 'higher' plane where Truth, Goodness, and Beauty exist in their fulness of perfection, would bring into operation spiritual, mental, and psychic causes or forces which would react upon, and give us a control over, our physical bodies in a manner hardly as yet realised even by those who practise 'mental healing,' 'new thought,' 'Christian Science,' or other forms of *quasi*-religious experience by which this fact is beginning to be apprehended.

There remains what we call 'natural' causes of evil: noxious animals and natural forces such as lightning, cyclones, earthquakes, etc. These might be, and probably would be, entirely neutralised by a much wider and deeper scientific knowledge; and here again we may enunciate the principle that if Man were only rightly aspected *spiritually*, he would not merely obtain a control of natural forces which at present is denied to him, and which, indeed, he has not as yet even imagined to be possible, but Nature herself would meet him more than half-way, and his own transformation would effect a corresponding transformation of the whole of that 'Nature' which at present he regards as external to and detached from his being.

Religion in the primary sense as a quality of life is in fact the only *practical* way to abolish evil, physical as well as moral; but it is obvious that this cannot be accomplished until every individual has reached a certain stage of evolution, has attained to that spiritual quality of life which is the cessation of evil because it is the negation of the cause of evil, the reversal of the outgoing process whereby good and evil become separately operative principles, and whereby Man is cut off in consciousness from the true source of his life and from illimitable freedom.

Nothing can be clearer in the Science of Religions, in the utterances of all great teachers, in the exemplification of their lives, or in the records of religious experience at all times, than the fact that whatever we may regard as the cause of Man's present condition, the great *practical* fact lies in the necessity for this re-orientation of the will and desire involving a departure from individualism. The necessity is perceived in a social manner even before the religious basis of it is recognised ; and Socialism is a more or less imperfect attempt to put it into practice. But Socialism must inevitably fail so long as the individual is at heart individualistic and egoistic. Socialism, right in principle, begins at the wrong end, or at best is only half the process—the latter half, not the beginning and the root of the matter. The essential preliminary is the reformation, the 'change of heart' of the individual.

The method by which religion effects the regeneration of the individual, the particular objective form of his belief, and even what he expects to attain thereby, may vary in many respects : so widely, indeed, that one formulated religion may even appear to embody a radically different principle from another, and will inevitably be deemed to be 'false' by that other. But at root the principle, and what is attained thereby, is the same in each and every case ; and it is to this fundamental principle that a true Science of Religions—which thereby should also become a rational theology—should lead us. Pure religion is of the heart, not of the head. Its source is in the spiritual region transcending intellect : the region which is also its goal. Like the central Sun in the physical world, the spiritual centre of Man's life and consciousness exercises a continual, even if unrecognised, attraction. Man must turn towards this Centre inevitably as soon as his centrifugal outgoing impulse is exhausted, or checked by a natural law to which we shall presently refer.

The attraction of this centripetal spiritual force, the nature of which is Love, has been beautifully expressed by Mr. Edmond Holmes in the following lines :

" What though with will rebellious I thwart thy omnipotent will,
Through purgatorial æons thy spirit will draw me still ;—
Draw me through shame and sorrow and pain and death and decay ;
Draw me from Hell to Heaven, draw me from night to day ;
Draw me from self's abysses to the self-less azure above ;
Draw me to thee, Life's Fountain, with patient passionate love." [1]

But in the world as at present constituted : a world which as a whole has certainly not re-oriented itself ; a world in which evil and sin and suffering largely predominate : the individual in whom religion has become a real power will be largely concerned in the first instance to free himself from

[1] *Sonnets and Poems,* " The Creed of my Heart."

this evil and suffering; and in the second place he will be more or less actively moved to effect the conversion of others to that form of belief to which he attaches his own religious feelings and emotions. It is perhaps only natural that the characteristic which religion mostly assumes for the average individual at his present stage of evolution is the desire to escape from the evil of this world: if not actually during life in the world, then at least in the world to come. Religion is here still individualistic. Individual salvation, individual bliss in an individualistic community of 'saints' all having the same 'religion,' is the ideal cherished by most religious people; of whom it must be said in this respect, that although they may be genuinely religious in the primary sense of the term, they have not yet transcended the limitations of individualism. They pray, "Thy will be done *on earth* as it is in heaven"; but very few have any hope of this being done save by a supernatural cataclysm, a 'Judgment Day'; and so far as they are individually concerned, they hope to enter 'heaven' at death, and thereby to have done with this sinful world for ever and ever. There are at the present time certain 'Christians' in daily and hourly expectation of the visible appearance of Jesus Christ "in the air," in clouds of glory, to take his Elect bodily up into Heaven, so that "millions now living will never die."[1]

But there is also to-day a broader, deeper, and nobler apprehension of spiritual truth and of the real facts of Man's spiritual nature, linked up with the undeniable scientific facts of his evolution. In this wider view, regeneration is not a matter for the individual only, but for the whole unitary Race: for Man is fundamentally one as well as many. The individual is an integral part of the Race, he cannot separate himself from the Race. The attainment by the individual of 'salvation' merely as an escape from evil and suffering is a form of spiritual selfishness. Here, and now, and on this Earth, and as a whole, Man must effect his salvation; and the individual who is thinking primarily of his own escape has much yet to learn. John Wesley, on seeing a convict in chains, is reported to have said, "There but for the grace of God goes John Wesley." But Walt Whitman says: "I do

[1] Cf. *The New Europe*, and other works by Sydney Watson.

not need to ask the sick man how he feels, I am the sick man." The sin of another is our sin when we have truly identified ourselves with Humanity, and with the mystical Christ who " bears the sin of the world."

The study of Oriental religions has done much to quicken in the Western World a sense of the unitary nature of Man, for in those religions there has always been room for the fullest and deepest philosophical concepts. We have been too long habituated to the narrow individualistic dogmas of orthodox Christianity. All this vast evolution of Man does not take place in order that a comparatively few individuals subsequent to the year I, A.D.—or at the literal " second coming " of Christ—may be ' saved.' The indissoluble connection of the individual with the evolution of the Race as a whole is principally associated with the Eastern doctrines of reincarnation and Karma, which, however, are outside of our special consideration at this point.

If, then, we ask what it is that religion actually does accomplish practically for the average individual, independently of any particular form which it may assume as belief or ' faith ': we shall find that, broadly speaking, the main fact is that it brings into operation within him a certain power or force which is usually felt to be, or is credited with being, an outside and supernatural power which enables him to rise superior to the evil conditions which he finds in the world around him, even when these conditions are causing him the greatest suffering and pain. It gives an *exaltation* over suffering which is something much more than a mere stoical endurance. In extreme cases, suffering is deliberately sought and self-inflicted, and even turns to a perverse kind of pleasure. Take for example the following, related of Marguerite Marie, the founder of the Order of the Sacred Heart, as a typical case of which many other examples could be given:

" Her love of pain and suffering was insatiable. . . . She said that she could cheerfully live till the day of Judgment, provided she might always have matter of suffering for God ; but that to live a single day without suffering would be intolerable. . . . ' Nothing but pain,' she continually said in her letters, ' makes my life supportable.' " [1]

[1] Bougaud : *Histoire de la bienheureuse Marguerite Marie*, Paris 1894, pp. 265, 171: Quoted by James : *Varieties of Religious Experience*, p. 310.

The extreme of suffering in ascetic practices is not the product of any one religion; it is the product of intense religious devotion and fervour independent of the accidental form of doctrine or belief with which it is associated. It is the result of an intense realisation of the necessity of conquering the lower nature, as being the cause of evil, and of the separation of the individual from the spiritual reality of his life and consciousness. What we have mainly to note here, however, is merely the fact that in greater or lesser degree the individual does acquire a conquest over the lower self, and the evil in the world around him, which only genuine religion as a re-orientation of the personality is able to effect.

We shall find, moreover, that in each and every case where this genuine re-orientation has taken place, there is a definite experience of a *something* which responds in the individual to his efforts to reach out or adjust himself to the new objective. This *something* will usually be ascribed to some supernatural power or personal divine Being : for most religions have some concept of such a Being as the object of devotion and worship, whose favour can be sought and obtained by appropriate means. We shall inquire more definitely in a subsequent chapter as to the nature of this response ; but to whatever source it may be ascribed, the main fact is that there *is* a felt response, and the individual does acquire new power, whether it be to suffer and endure as an ascetic or a martyr, or whether it be to overcome ' sin ' within himself, or whether it be merely by his ' new thought ' —which is practically a re-orientation of a religious nature— to effect the cure of specific disease, or to attain to a general state of ' health, wealth, and happiness.'

We might also note that the general or characteristic attitude of the individual towards this influx of power must be that of a passive yielding up of the will of the lower personal self ; a giving up of all direct effort and strife with evil in order to allow this higher power to accomplish what the individual in the strength of his lower nature could not possibly effect. How *could* the lower nature accomplish it ? The very nature of the ' lower ' is to go out into differentiation and individualism in the opposite direction to that which the man now seeks. It is that part of the man which has its existence and function on the mental, psychic, and physical planes in their *outgoing* aspects, and it cannot do otherwise than war against that which seeks to turn it from what appears to it to be its immediate and essential good. It is characteristic of all the individualism and self-seeking which is at the root of evil, that at its inception, and for a long time, until suffering has corrected it, this self-seeking appears to be the most desirable thing. When the operation of the cosmic law in the outgoing process is the production of individualism, anything which opposes this must necessarily appear thereby to be undesirable and evil; and hereby the relative nature of evil may be more clearly apprehended. We must in fact postulate in accordance with our cosmic plan of the Universe, that since individualism, duality, separation, commences with the emanation of the lower planes—that is to say, when concrete mind, or the Mental Plane comes into existence—it is at this point, and in this very fact, that good and evil arise. Neither the one nor the other is knowable in the Absolute, nor even on the Plane of the Logos. We naturally regard the Spiritual Plane as wholly 'good,' but only so as in contrast with the 'evil' which we experience in separation from it. Where evil is unknown, good is also unknown. Both are terms arising from the duality of the separative mind. Thus in the allegory of *Genesis* we have the forbidden fruit represented as the fruit of the tree of the knowledge of good and evil.

But as there is a limit to the outgoing process, so also there is a limit to the contingent evil. At some point, at some limit, the cycle must change from downwards to upwards. There are two ways in which we might regard the inevitableness of that change; possibly each of these may be true in certain respects. We may in the first place conceive that the times and limits of the great cosmic cycles are definitely fixed beforehand. We may say that 'in the beginning' the limits were already fixed; and, indeed, since we have postulated that in the consciousness of the Logos the whole world-process is seen as a Whole from 'beginning to end,' the limits and the 'times' are inevitable. But between time as we apprehend it, and 'real time'—or shall we call it with Bergson 'duration'?—as it appears in a consciousness which transcends 'unreal' or empirical time, there is a subtle difference which can only be intuitionally grasped; and though it may be inevitable that in so many definite millions of solar years "the Sun will grow cold, and the Stars grow old, and the Books of the Judgment Day unfold," yet in *duration* that time may possibly be lengthened or shortened. The performance of a musical composition may be accelerated or retarded at the will of the performer, both as regards clock-time and what we may call emotional time: that is to say the time which it may appear to occupy in the consciousness of the performer; but within the limits of the composition itself there are a fixed number of notes and bars and phrases, however fast or however slow the performance may be.

In the second place we may conceive that there is a kind of natural-law-limit to the outgoing process, analogous to what physicists discover in the relation of velocity to inertia in the electron. The electron cannot overpass the velocity of light, because at that velocity its mass or inertia would become infinite. Now it may be that in physical nature, or in the physical plane—*metaphysically considered* in its relation to consciousness—and in the 'evil' associated therewith, we have a *natural* limit of the outgoing process: a process which cannot overpass the differentiation, inertness, and 'deadness' of physical matter, and all that is associated therewith in the consciousness of the Ego. Metaphysically considered, matter may be taken as the extreme limit of our consciousness of the not-self.

Some systems of religio-philosophy have regarded matter as wholly evil in itself; and this agrees with our own conclusions in at least this respect: that since evil—or the contrast between good and evil—arises through an apparent, though not a real, individualisation and separation from the Unitary Reality: that which is apparently the most separated might well be regarded, from an external point of view, as being wholly evil. Good and evil thus separated appear to have a kind of quantitative equality like action and reaction.

Meanwhile we can at least see this much about evil in its effects as suffering: that it is by and through suffering that the individual is checked in any evil course, though that check is not always apparent in any one particular incarnation of that individual. Even in the highest form of mental suffering in which no 'moral' evil is involved—the loss, for example, of one who is deeply and passionately loved—we have to note that this results from a form of individualism which must ultimately be transcended. It is not, however, to be transcended in a cold isolation of the individual, an egotistic withdrawal from all attachments, but in such an expansion of love for all that there is no possibility of its becoming individual and exclusive in any selfish sense. Many a good Christian has considered that God has 'taken' the loved one for the express purpose that thoughts and desires should be turned more earnestly towards spiritual things ; and has thus caught a glimpse—albeit a distorted one—of this deeper law as enunciated in the Gospel.[1]

The active principle which effects in man that 'change of heart,' that re-orientation which is the root and substance of Religion, can only be something which is itself in its own nature unaffected by the outgoing will and desire; something which is in itself 'sinless,' as being unaffected by the will to individual sentient life. In other words, it must be something which belongs to and acts from the Spiritual Plane, the Plane of the Logos. It is what we here call the Higher Self, the "Light that lighteth every man coming into the world." In exoteric Christianity it is revealed in one individual historical man, who is therefore postulated to be sinless; though there are incidents in the Gospels—as for example the destruction of the property of other people : the Gadarene swine—which, if taken *literally,* are not usually considered in this light when done by ordinary individuals.[2] In esoteric Christianity and in Mysticism, the active principle is the indwelling Divine Nature *in* which the greatest sinner as well as the greatest saint lives and moves and has his being ; for that principle is the life and being of the one as well as of the other, and it is only in appearance and function that the sinner can seem to be more separate than the saint.

To sum up : Religion takes its place in the line of human evolution, in the first place as a consciousness, more or less well defined, of a relation between the individual and some Cosmic Power ; and in the second place as a reversal of an

[1] Matt. x, 37.
[2] It is the beauty of the *esoteric* doctrine that these stumbling-blocks of literal interpretation are entirely removed, and the inner *spiritual* meaning is brought to light.

outgoing process by which the individual has become separated in consciousness from the source of his being or existence in that Power: this reversal, or re-orientation, resulting in the manifestation of *a quality of life* distinguished as *spiritual* in its nature.

But Religion as commonly understood never reaches the full realisation of a return to unity with Deity or the Absolute; it is only when it rises into Mysticism that that realisation is attained. Mysticism is a more or less definite realisation of that which in ordinary Religion is merely a dimly discerned far-off possibility, because the region of the formal mind has not yet been transcended. We might distinguish further between the two by saying, that Mysticism seeks to interpret the manifested and the temporal in terms of the Unmanifested and the Eternal, whereas Religion reverses this, and seeks to explicate the Absolute or ' God ' in terms of the empirical consciousness. In Religion there is still a *relation*; the consciousness is of duality, and the lower and the higher selves are still in apparent separation. In Mysticism, on the other hand, there is *identity*: or rather the lower rises into the higher and is lost therein. Translating this in terms of our Cosmic Chart we shall say, that in religion the individual is still centred in, or operative on, the Mental Plane, but with his aspiration, will, and desire, directed towards the next higher or truly Spiritual Plane, the Plane of Unity. The religionist is still dealing with his ' soul,' and he is seeking to ' save ' it. The mystic, on the other hand, rises above the concept of a separate soul, or of salvation, for he enters in consciousness that Plane where all souls interpenetrate, and all sense of a separate egoity is lost.

These distinctions, however, must necessarily be more or less artificial. The religionist often sees afar off the Promised Land which the Mystic actually enters—at times. Religion must necessarily be largely tinged with Mysticism even before the real mystic evolves; indeed the whole of Religion is in a sense *mystical*, though it is not Mysticism. It may perhaps be said broadly to be the first stage of that threefold division of the mystic ' Way ' which is so commonly distinguished by mystics, and with which we shall deal in our next chapter.

And because Religion has not yet risen to the plane of Unity but is still a *relation*, one of its principal elements is worship ;

and this worship must necessarily assume a great variety of individual forms according to the intelligence of the worshipper. We find, however, the true relationship of these forms to the Supreme Reality stated in the simplest language in the *Bhagavad-Gita*, where Krishna—speaking as the Logos —says :

> " Those who through diversities of desires are deprived of spiritual wisdom adopt particular rites subordinated to their own natures and worship other Gods. In whatever form a devotee desires with faith to worship, it is I alone who inspire him with constancy therein, and depending on that faith he seeks the propitiation of that God, obtaining the object of his wishes as is ordained by me alone." [1]

It is inevitable that God should, in the first place, be depicted in terms of human personality, passion and emotion ; and that such concepts should vary with the stage of development of the individual or the Race. If you abstract human passions and emotions, what is left for humanity to understand or represent to itself in Divinity ? There is nothing that a man can understand of God but what the man is himself. " Nothing is known of God : He is pure Unity : and what we know of Him, that we ourselves must be." [2] The abstraction of a metaphysical Absolute, however, or of a " pure Unity," is utterly inadequate for an exoteric Religion. It is only in Mysticism, or the highest form of religio-philosophy, that it can obtain. Primitive man ascribes personality to the great Forces of Nature ; being in this respect, indeed, instinctively much nearer to the truth than later developments of the intellect. The lightning, the thunder, the earthquake : these are manifestations of his great and powerful Gods ; to be feared, propitiated, and worshipped. Later on, Nature in general becomes personified : the woods and the rocks, the rivers, the seas, and the mountains have their special Gods and Goddesses ; and Pan and Faun and Dryad are born. These Gods and Nature Spirits, however, make no demand on morality ; they only require respect, and propitiation, and sacrificial worship.

In the next stage, Monotheism appears ; but the supreme God is still characteristically human ; He hates as well as loves, He is jealous and revengeful as well as merciful ; and

[1] Chap. vii, 20, 21, 22.
[2] Angelus Silesius : *Spiritual Maxims.*

at this point—the point where morality begins to intrude into the question—although He is the supreme and only God, another Personality has to be discovered to account for evil, and the Devil makes his appearance ; or else the world is divided between two Personalities, such as Ormuzd and Ahriman : the process of abstraction of human qualities has begun.

The next stage results in speculative theology. All the evil is now abstracted, and God is postulated to be supreme good as well as supreme wisdom and power ; but personality remains. Theology must necessarily cling to personality ; to abstract that would be to leave nothing whatever which the intellect could grasp. Theology vainly endeavours to say what God *is* ; but, as Professor Caird has pointed out : " Under the conditions of human thought, it is impossible to determine what anything *is*, except by the negative process of distinguishing it from other things, i.e. by saying what it *is not*."[1] The final stage is reached by philosophical thought and mystical experience—so far as these can be *stated*. In philosophy we have the Absolute, which is *Reality* ; in Mysticism, the Divine Dark, which is the Infinite Light ; and in each case the so-called negative method is alone applicable. God is not this, that, or the other ; not because these have a positive existence apart from him, but because He—or IT— is both these and also the opposite of these ; being in very truth the ONE and the ALL.

So many theologians, as for example Dean Inge,[2] have failed to see that this ' negative method ' carries with it the implication of a higher affirmative. That its influence in practical mysticism as the so-called *via negativa* can be and has been subjected to abuse, goes without saying ; but even Dean Inge is in the end constrained to say, " I do not think that the negative road is a pure error."[3]

And so, paradoxically, this is not the negation of anthropomorphism but the completion thereof ; for, having been negated and rejected in its lower forms, it reappears in a higher and unitive manner. Having abstracted from our concepts of Deity all that is purely human as man knows himself in his lower separative nature, there is for the

---

[1] *The Evolution of Religion*, vol. i, p. 147. 1893 ed.
[2] Cf. *Christian Mysticism*, p. 110 ff.   [3] *Ibid.*, p. 115.

'rational' mind seemingly nothing left but an abyss of nothingness and darkness from which the 'natural' man shrinks in dismay. But when *this* rationality is transcended, when the individual has stripped *himself* of the seemingly individual and concrete: lo! just in proportion as he does so, there dawns in his inner consciousness the day-spring of the Eternal Light of the true *Self ;* that infinite Light which is also ineffable Bliss and Love.

For as the darkness is in *Himself,* so also is the Light ; and in the knowledge of the *One Life* " the darkness and the light are (shall be) both alike *to thee."*

CHAPTER VIII

CHARACTERISTICS OF MYSTICISM

" Mysticism does not stand beside the other phenomena of Nature unconnected with them, but forms the last communication between all phenomena. So far from it being an obsolete view, much rather obsolete are those, though modern, conceptions in which it has no place. So far is mysticism from belonging only to a surmounted past, that much rather will it first attain its full significance in the future. As well the Kantian ' Critique of Reason,' as the physiological theory of sense-perception, and Darwinism, point convergently to a view of the world into which mysticism will be organically fitted."

Du Prel: *Philosophy of Mysticism.*

' You never enjoy the world aright, till the sea itself floweth in your veins, till you are clothed with the heavens, and crowned with the stars : and perceive yourself to be the sole heir of the whole world, and more than so, because men are in it who are every one sole heirs as well as you. . . . Till your spirit filleth the whole world, and the stars are your jewels ; till you are as familiar with the ways of God in all Ages as with your walk and table ; till you are intimately acquainted with that shady nothing out of which the world was made ; till you love all men so as to desire their happiness, with a thirst equal to the zeal of your own ; till you delight in God for being good to all : you never enjoy the world."

Thomas Traherne: *Centuries of Meditation.*

CHAPTER VIII

CHARACTERISTICS OF MYSTICISM

WE have already noted that Mysticism may be distinguished or differentiated broadly from Religion as commonly understood, in that it is on the one hand the inner or *esoteric* aspect of religious doctrine, symbol, and tradition, and on the other a much higher consciousness of spiritual realities—more specifically a sense of *union*—than is reached by the normal religious faculty.

Further, Mysticism seeks to interpret the facts of our normal life, consciousness, and experience in terms of spiritual Realities of a transcendental nature; whereas *exoteric* Religion invariably drags down the spiritual into the material, both conceptually and in practice, being unable to transcend our common empirical experience and the categories of the formal mind or intellect.

The point of view of the mystic being transcendental as regards the formal mind, or discursive intellect, it is only with great difficulty that mystical intuition, experience, and consciousness can be related to or expressed in terms of our common empirical experience or normal consciousness; whereas *exoteric* Religion, being mainly realistic, finds no difficulty or anomaly in formulating its spiritual world, or ' kingdom of heaven,' mainly in the same terms as those which obtain in relation to our present understanding.

While we must recognise that even *exoteric* Religion results from an intuition of spiritual realities, yet in so far as it is the expression of that intuition in beliefs, doctrines, and dogmas, these are, so to speak, only a deposited sediment of these higher intuitions. We have already noted, however, that in so far as we may broadly divide the mystic ' Way ' into three stages, we may take Religion in general as being the first stage of this 'Way'; only it must be Religion as the expression of *a quality of life*, and not merely as a conventional expression of a formal belief. But in so far as the individual still has a form of belief from which he cannot depart without giving up his 'religion,' he is still in the first stage only; his 'world' is still only in the deposited sediment of those elements of thought in which the philosopher and the mystic find a freedom from which he is debarred. We might, indeed, trace a very broad analogy here between the spiritual evolution of the individual and the physical evolution of the race. There is reason to believe that the lowest forms of physical life on this globe in what is recognised as the animal kingdom—which we have already seen to be embryo Man—commenced in the ooze and slime, the sediment at the bottom of tropical oceans. In the second stage we have fishes, free-swimming creatures in the great ocean : corresponding here to philosophical thought, and constituting in its highest aspect the second stage of Mysticism. In the third stage, Man emerges from the water, first of all as an amphibious creature, capable of breathing the free air of the upper region, and finally as one altogether free from the limitations of the two lower planes of life through which he has passed—the 'earth' of the physical plane, and the 'water' of the psychic plane. The 'air' which he now breathes is that of pure spiritual life. But there is still a higher region, that of 'fire'; but this is an extreme mystic achievement, perhaps not as yet really touched by any classical mystic who has recorded his experiences, or if touched, too transcendental even to be mentioned.[1]

Mysticism is the *genius* of Religion. It stands to formal Religion as creative genius in art does to mere imitative realism. But how shall the uninitiated, the man who has never seen or felt that which the genius represents, understand or appreciate the real work of art or the message of the mystic ? These must necessarily be to him as unintelligible as pure mathematics to the man in the street. " *Quel diable de jargon entends-je ici ?* " says Robert N. Vaughan—quoting Molière—as a heading to one of the chapters of his super-

[1] Is it altogether unrelated to this phase of his evolution that man is now obtaining the physical means to traverse the vast expanse of the air ? Is it altogether unthinkable that he may in due course obtain the means to traverse still higher regions ?

cilious work, *Hours with the Mystics*.[1] Truly if it was that to him—and the whole work shows that it was little more than that—what can the mystic say but, Amen ? The mystic speaks to and for a certain perception, a certain capacity to understand and appreciate which is as distinct from the common realism of so-called Religion as is the perception of the genius from that of the man who only recognises in music a certain ' tune,' or in a painting or a statue a more or less correct representation of a material object. At the same time we must consider that neither the artist nor the mystic has any right to label as art or as mysticism that which is merely unintelligible. We cannot emphasise too strongly that in the one case as in the other there must be a real application of the *Idea* to our life in general; that is to say it must serve to raise and ennoble the life which we live here and now, by infusing into it a quality not otherwise obtainable.

If we take Mysticism to be the realisation by the individual subject, in actual conscious experience, of the wholeness and perfection of his life in its unity with the Universal Subject, usually termed the Absolute or God : we must still recognise that there must be degrees of this illumination, and that Religion necessarily constitutes the starting-point, the first stage. From thence onward there will be of necessity a mystical element in our life and consciousness, even though we may be very far from experiencing or even recognising that which the mystic has very definitely before him as the goal of his efforts.

Mysticism, like Religion itself, has faint and feeble beginnings, many phases of experience, and many degrees of attainment. It begins in intuition, it rises into more or less infrequent, more or less clear, states of realisation, illumination, and knowledge ; but it is doubtful whether its full fruition has as yet been realised by any of the mystics who are commonly regarded as classical examples ; and it could not be expressed or understood even had it been so realised.

Whatever may be our fundamental principles or concepts of the nature of the Universe as a whole—whether they are purely scientific, or even materialistic, or whether they are

[1] Vol. i, p. 6o.

purely philosophical or metaphysical, or whether they are dogmatically theological—there are two outstanding characteristics of mystical experience which must be treated as empirical facts, and which can be brought within the sphere of our general fund of knowledge, however transcendental the mystic state of consciousness in itself may be.

(1) The first of these facts is the invariable sense of unity or wholeness which accompanies the mystic experience. It affords a very strong support and argument for that intuitive philosophical sense of unity which finds its expression in various concepts of a monistic character. When we have once clearly realised—whether by intellect or by intuition we need not here stay to inquire—that there is nothing whatsoever in the Universe that is really separate, individual or discrete; that every 'thing,' if we could see it and know it in its wholeness and completeness, would expand to infinity and become the Absolute All; that every 'atom' is balanced against the whole Universe, and acts and reacts at every moment with the Whole, and that therefore the Whole is present at every moment, in every thing, however minute it may be: we have taken a very long step towards an understanding of the true nature of Mysticism; for Mysticism is essentially *a unitary consciousness* transcending the duality and separation which is established by the formal mind or intellect.

Speaking of this characteristic, William James says, in a most eloquent passage :

" This overcoming of all the usual barriers between the individual and the Absolute is the great mystic achievement. In mystic states we both become one with the Absolute and we become aware of our oneness. This is the everlasting and triumphant mystical tradition, hardly altered by differences of clime or creed. In Hinduism, in Neoplatonism, in Sufism, in Christian mysticism, in Whitmanism, we find the same recurring note, so that there is about mystical utterances an eternal unanimity which ought to make a critic stop and think, and which brings it about that the mystical classics have, as has been said, neither birthday nor native land. Perpetually telling of the unity of man with God, their speech antidates languages, and they do not grow old." [1]

[1] *Varieties of Religious Experiences*, p. 419.

Récéjac has pointed out that the mystic Absolute takes possession of the whole soul, and is thereby in contradistinction with the rational Absolute which always withdraws to the heights of the mind as we seek to approach and grasp it with the intellect.[1]

We have found that Religion is primarily an added quality of life which leads the individual to re-orient himself in his relation to the transcendental Reality. Religion—the religious faculty—follows in the natural line of evolution of Humanity, as a spiritual quality of life in succession to that quality which the Race acquires by the evolution of mind or intellect ; **that is to say**, the power of co-ordinated or ratiocinative thought and self-consciousness which follows the animal instinct stage. Where, then, shall we look for indications as to the nature of our further advance beyond a religion which does not rise above the formal mind, if it be not to Mysticism ? Mysticism is an expansion of consciousness as much superior to mind or intellect as this is superior to the dulness of the animal consciousness. Mystics, however, of any pronounced type are still few and far between, though a touch of mystical consciousness, a faint foreshadowing of the faculty, is common enough.

Considering evolution as an advance from within *outwards*—or, in other words, as the *manifestation* outwardly, and in stages, of an inner impulsive *Life*—we cannot fail to recognise that any evolutionary advance of the individual, or of Humanity as a whole, to a higher stage in the *inner* nature, must produce a corresponding advance or modification in every vehicle of consciousness on the planes lower or more ' outer ' than that in which the advance is first made ; and this advance will make its appearance latest of all on the lowest or physical plane. We have no means of knowing scientifically what modifications of structure take place on the psychic plane of substance, before the animal kingdom evolves into the human by the addition of mentality ; much less do we know anything in respect of the previous stages. But we do know what physical modifications have followed this advance : the principal one being the development of brain structure. We may have reason to conclude that there is a definite change in the substance of all the bodies

[1] Cf. *The Bases of the Mystic Knowledge*, p. 126.

or vehicles of the mystic; even in the physical atoms and molecules. This question, however, belongs to Occultism rather than to Mysticism; to knowledge of the structural facts of the Universe, not to mere states of consciousness. The term Mysticism as commonly understood does not include this knowledge; the mystic hitherto has been but little concerned with the structural facts of the universe, or even of his own body.

Before we can say definitely that the advance has been made on the outer plane from any one stage to another, we have a gradual dawning as it were of the higher faculty or quality of life; the coming faculty tinges with its special characteristic the substance of the lower planes, that substance out of which our bodies or vehicles on those planes must necessarily be formed; and, in favourable circumstances, individuals will be forthcoming who will foreshadow the advance which sooner or later must be made by the whole Race. Now we have been forced to the conclusion that in so far as that spiritual quality of life, of which Religion is the outcome, is concerned, Humanity is still very far from having attained to it in any degree. There could be no War had Humanity so attained; and there are innumerable things in our so-called civilisation which could not possibly exist if a really spiritual quality of life existed in the community as a whole. We are compelled to say, therefore, that at the present stage of Man's evolution he is merely *overshadowed* by the powers and potencies of his higher or spiritual nature. The spiritual quality of Life is not yet sufficiently established in the substance of his mental vehicle, or what we commonly designate as Mind or Soul; and, not being established there, it not merely fails to effect the corresponding change or modification of the lower vehicles, the physical and the psychical—since it is mind, thought, which is the immediate agent in determining the condition of these—but these latter, by virtue of their intrinsic inertia, are in opposition to the advance; they are obstacles which have to be fought and overcome before attainment can be reached by the lower self, or manifestation accomplished by the Higher Self.

But if Humanity, Man, is still so unregenerate in his mental substance and vehicles, if he is still largely on the outgoing cycle, so that the great majority of individuals in the world are still " carnally minded " as to desire, and materially minded as to intellect : we cannot expect that the still further stage, the really spiritual consciousness which Mysticism adumbrates, will be anything but a very sporadic and exceptional phenomenon ; nor can we expect that the ' common sense '—in the literal meaning as that which is common to all—the common ' rationality ' of the intellect— which is merely the reaction of the mind with the outward objective world of physical sensation—shall be able to express in any terms whatsoever the nature of that higher spiritual unity which is plainly the opposite of the individuality and discreteness to which the mind of Man as a whole is directed, and in which he finds his ' world ' and sphere of action.

But if at the present time the mind of Humanity has not yet evolved sufficiently to be expressive of the transcendental fact, as well as of the ' lower ' fact ; if the *rational* Absolute is still for the mind an insoluble paradox : there is no reason for us to suppose that it will always be so. What, indeed, is the meaning of all this philosophical effort to reach the Absolute by mental process, but the instinctive urge of *faculty* which must always precede development of organism, whereby the faculty presently becomes operative in greater or lesser degree in the organism ; as for example the faculty of sight presently evolves the more or less perfect physical organ of sight. Has there been no such effort as Man evolved from perception to apperception, from animal consciousness to self-consciousness ? And what is the effort now—the effort of all the world's philosophers, and sages, and seers, and mystics—but the effort to rise from self-consciousness to the still further stage of Self-Consciousness : the effort of *Cosmic Man*, not of the individual merely ? It is in Cosmic Man, or the substance of the Mind of Cosmic Man, that this evolution primarily takes place ; the results on the lower plane and in the individual will follow inevitably and in due course.

When we regard the matter from the lower point of view of the individual, it appears in the light of an *attainment* ; it becomes a process and a progress by the individual in certain more or less well-marked stages ; and in so far as it is necessary to distinguish these stages on the mystic 'Way,' we cannot do better than to adopt in the first instance the threefold division which appears in some form or another in almost all the classical literature of Mysticism. Some such division is undoubtedly useful in many respects, though each stage necessarily shades off and is illumined by the higher one before the latter becomes definitely recognisable. In some cases, however, there is some specific event which serves to mark the change from one state or stage to another, and we shall presently note one or two instances of this. The three-fold division is, in fact, by no means an arbitrary one. It corresponds with the cosmic facts of our nature, and will be clearly understood by reference to the cosmic chart we are making use of in this work. Nevertheless, in so far as there is a growth from one stage to another, the stages are only distinguishable in the same way that we can distinguish the ideals and activities of childhood, manhood and old age; though at the same time, in each of these, it may be possible to distinguish some event as marking the change, or at all events the realisation of the change. Thus sudden conversion often marks the commencement of the first or religious stage; some definite illumination of the whole mind and consciousness may mark the commencement of the second stage; and some transcendental or ecstatic vision or experience the introduction to the third.

Various names have been given to these stages, but it will be most advisable to distinguish them broadly by the quality of the attainment which definitely belongs to each stage.

(1) We have seen that Religion is essentially a re-orientation of the thought, will, and desire of the individual towards the Source of his being, and its development is essentially a *purification* of the individual from all the " beggarly elements " (Gal. iv, 9) to which hitherto he has directed his desires, and has been in bondage. The first stage, therefore, we shall recognise and name as being the stage of *Purification*.

Purification or Purgation is the name usually given to it by most Christian mystics. The aspiration here is not necessarily for union; indeed, as we have already seen, and as expressed by *exoteric* religion, ' God ' is still commonly regarded in this stage as an *object* of adoration and worship, and the distinction is still made between Creator and creature, self and not-self. The purification which takes place at this stage, therefore, must be a double one : in the first place a moral purification of the lower self, taking the form of freedom from attachments to the things of sense, from evil passions and desires, and, above all, the purgation of the self-will of the individual self : that clinging to individuality, to egoity, which is the most difficult thing of all to eliminate, since it has behind it the whole accumulated force and activity of the previous outgoing existence of the individual. In the second place this purgation will be an intellectual purification from, or a rising out of, those formal concepts which are the " deposited sediment of intuition," so that intuition itself may have free play.

We find, then, that this first stage belongs broadly to our normal life and consciousness on the physical and psychic planes, when that life has definitely assumed a religious character. It consists of a gradual sublimation of the elements of these planes, so that they become in time proper and fitting vehicles for the indwelling and manifestation of the higher life and consciousness pertaining to the cosmic plane of Mind, illumined by the still higher and more universal realities of the truly spiritual Life of the Cosmos. These latter cannot act in and through the lower vehicles, the psychic and physical bodies, unless these have been sufficiently purified or sublimated by the thought and will of the individual, constantly directed and aspiring towards the larger life.

(2) In the second stage we must consider that Purification has largely been effected, and the resultant characteristic we may term—again following our classical examples—*Illumination*. It is sometimes also called Enlightenment, and sometimes Contemplation, but the latter term is the method rather than the attainment of this stage. We might say broadly that this is the stage which we must assign to the greatest number of our mystics, both classical and modern. We may take its principal characteristics to be as follows :

(a) In the first place there may be a definite philosophical appreciation and understanding of the great fact of the unitary nature of the individual with the Cosmos. There is a definite mental attitude in which the One is seen in the

Many, and the Many in the One. This is the philosophical Mysticism which finds its clearest and deepest exposition in the Adwaita Vedânta philosophy of Sankarâchârya, and in the Neoplatonic philosophy of Plotinus. The whole philosophy of the Upanishads is summed up in the fundamental principle that the individual soul and the Universal Soul, Brahman, or Atman, are indissolubly *one*. Knowledge does not *effect* this union, it only discloses it by dissolving as it were the mists of illusion brought about by the desire for individual sentient life, whereby *Reality* is hidden from our sight. Thus the mystic ' Way ' here—as later in Christian Mysticism, and fundamentally in all Mysticism—is the conquest of the lower personal self, the overcoming of the desire for individual existence, of the power of the " I and me," and even of the desire for individual ' attainment.'

In Plotinus we find the same fundamental philosophy. " The One," he says, " is present everywhere, and absent only from those unable to perceive it."

(*b*) In the second place, and as another phase of this stage, there may be a definite foretaste of the unitary consciousness which is the distinctive mark of the third stage. This fore- taste has sometimes been called ' Cosmic Consciousness,' but it can only be this in a relative sense, for it falls very far short of the unitary consciousness which is reached in the third stage. It is not necessarily of a distinctive religious nature. As a modern example of it we might instance Tennyson's experience, to which we have already referred (p. 62). Dr. Bucke, in his classical work *Cosmic Consciousness*, gives innumerable examples of a similar nature, some of which are, whilst others are not, of a religious character. One of the best-known examples of this phase, in its religious and emotional or devotional aspect, is that of Brother Lawrence as described in his *Practice of the Presence of God*.

As an example of a somewhat different phase of this stage we might mention a modern mystic, " Æ," whose profoundly interesting book *The Candle of Vision*, and also his poems, are known to many students of Mysticism, who will recognise therein much which relates to the stage we are now dealing with. We shall place Blake in the same category, as also Swedenborg.

The question as to which of the more classical of the

devotional Christian mystics should be assigned to this stage, and which should be considered as having attained to the third degree in their furthest and most exalted experience of the unitive state, is not an easy one to determine, and in any case must depend upon a more or less arbitrary point of view. At the most, those of them who may possibly have had the supreme mystical experience of a transcendental union with the Absolute, have only had this very intermittently and sporadically. We are inclined to take the general view that none of them have really touched the absolute Absolute, but only a relative Absolute—if we may use such a term—an Absolute, that is to say, which is absolute only to Cosmic Man in his present stage of evolution, but is not the true or universal Absolute. It is difficult to give specific reasons for such a view without a very voluminous exposition which would be quite out of place here. We shall endeavour to throw some further light upon the question in a subsequent chapter. Briefly, however, we might now say that from the point of view which we have taken in our chapter on the Absolute and its Manifestations, it is not possible for the individual to transcend the Consciousness of Cosmic Man, that is to say of the Logos ; and that even that Consciousness, transcendental, ineffable, and absolute as it is, so far as it is related to and includes the whole of Man's Cosmos, we must, nevertheless, consider to fall short of Absoluteness. In so far as the Logos only represents a particular Cosmos as a manifestation of the absolute Absolute, His consciousness falls short of absolute Absoluteness. Thus a Vedântin would say that the Logos only sees the Absolute, or Parabrahm, through the veil of Cosmic Substance, or Mûlaprakriti.[1] We might even say that for our present Humanity the Absolute is the Solar Logos only, and not the Logos of the larger Cosmos. Dean Inge appears to have appreciated this from his own special point of view when he says :

" There is no trace whatever in St. Paul of any aspiration to rise above Christ to the contemplation of the Absolute—to treat him as only a step in the ladder. This is an error of false Mysticism ; the true mystic follows St. Paul in choosing as his ultimate goal the fulness of Christ, and not the emptiness of the undifferentiated Godhead." [2]

[1] Cf. T. Subba Row : *Discourses on the Bhagavat-Gita*, p. 10.
[2] *Christian Mysticism*, p. 70.

We might, however, question " the emptiness of the Godhead," for it is only ' empty ' by reason of the necessity which lies in the intellect of using the ' negative ' method to express its transcendental fulness. Many mystics, especially those of the ultra-devotional and erotic type, have deceived themselves in respect of the Absolute or ' God ' with whom they have supposed themselves to be in ecstatic union. Some have discovered their mistake at a certain stage, when a higher stage has been revealed ; but this is not often the case. Thus Jacopone da Todi considered that he had reached the unitive state, and uses the most rapturous and emotional language in reference to it, but acknowledges afterwards that he had not reached the true unitive consciousness.[1] Baron von Hügel remarks upon the same experience in the case of Catherine of Genoa.[2] The same mistake may possibly apply to the highest consciousness that any mystic has as yet been able to attain. There may be a still further or deeper ' Absolute.'

(3) The third stage of the mystic ' Way ' is that of *Union*. It has sometimes been characterised as that of ecstasy, but it is not advisable to use this latter term, for there are many lower forms of ecstasy which are by no means representative of the unitive state, and may, indeed, be merely psychological or even pathological. It is quite true that the unitive state must be one of ecstasy : using the term both in its emotional and pathological significance. The subject is wrapt away into total unconsciousness of both bodily and mental activities, and enters into a state of unspeakable bliss ; but the real criterion of the genuineness of this state is that which is brought back from it, that which it effects in the life of the individual, and not the psycho-pathological state itself, nor its mere emotional content.

Seeing that every mystic testifies in some way or other to the fact of this supreme vital union with *That* which, under whatever symbol or concept it may be presented, is experienced as the very Root and Source and Essence of the individual life or ' soul ' : it is extremely difficult to make any selection of examples unless it is desired to present some particular phase of this experience, or rather some particular type of

[1] Cf. Underhill, *Jacopone da Todi*, p. 244 *seq.*, and *Laude*, xci, p. 475.
[2] F. von Hügel : *The Mystical Element of Religion*, vol. i. p. 235.

the numerous aspects under which it has been presented in the recorded experience of the classical mystics. We have already noted that we cannot assign to this stage such visionaries as Blake or Swedenborg, and we should, indeed, hardly place in this category such an exceptional seer as Jacob Böhme, though his case may possibly be somewhat doubtful, and he certainly penetrates much deeper than Swedenborg. Our safest course, therefore, would appear to be to select a few passages from those mystics who present the matter from a more rational or philosophical point of view, rather than from that emotional content which is the more common presentation, and we may leave it to each student of Mysticism to decide from his own point of view which of the other classical mystics should be admitted to this third stage or category of the ' Way.'

Let us take first of all the attempt which is made by Plotinus to describe the nature of Union. Without a very long quotation it is not possible to do more than give a few disconnected sentences from the Ennead VI, *IX*, 9, 10, 11.

" The soul beholds the fountain of life, the fountain of intellect, the principle of being, the cause of good, and the root of soul. . . . For we are not cut off from this fountain, nor are we separated from it, though the nature of body intervening, draws us to itself. But we are animated and preserved by an infusion from thence, this principle not imparting, and afterwards withdrawing itself from us; since it always supplies us with being. . . . Here, likewise, the soul rests and becomes out of the reach of evils, running back to that place which is free from ill. . . . And this is both the beginning and end of the soul. It is the beginning, indeed, because she originates from thence; but it is the end, because *the good* is there, and because when the soul is situated there, she becomes what she was before. . . . But that *the good* is there, is indicated by the love which is connascent with the soul; conformably to which, Love is conjoined in marriage with souls, both in writings and in fables. For since the soul is different from God, but is derived from him, she necessarily loves him, and when she is there she has a celestial love; but the love which she here possesses is common and vulgar. . . . The soul also proceeding to, and having now arrived at the desired end, and participating of deity, will know that the supplier of true life is then present. . . . When this takes place therefore, the soul will both see divinity and herself, as far as it is lawful for her to see him. And she will see herself indeed illuminated, and full of intelligible light; or rather she will perceive herself to be a pure light, unburthened, agile, and becoming to be a God, or rather being a God, and then shining forth as such to the view. . . . Becoming wholly absorbed in deity, she is one, conjoining as it were centre with centre. . . . Hence this spectacle is a thing difficult to explain by words. For how can anyone narrate that as something different from himself, which when he sees he does not behold as different, but as one with himself ? . . . Since, therefore, there were not two things, but the perceiver was one with the perceived, as not being (properly speaking) vision but union ; whoever becomes one by mingling with deity, and afterwards recollects this union, will have with himself an image of it. . . . Being as it were in an ecstasy, or energising enthusiastically, he became established in quiet and solitary union, not at all deviating from his own essence. . . . When situated there, he will *see* the principle and will be conjoined with it, by a union of like to like, neglecting nothing divine which the soul is able to possess. . . . This, therefore, is the life of the Gods, and of divine and happy men, a liberation from all terrene concerns, a life unaccompanied with human pleasures, and a flight of the alone to the alone.''

It is hardly necessary to inquire here whether the union of which Plotinus speaks thus is a union with the absolute Absolute, or whether it is not rather a union with the more immediate source and goal of the human soul : that is to say with the supreme deity or Logos of Humanity. It is possible that the ineffable union which Plotinus is said to have experienced only some three or four times, may have been of a still higher order : a union with an absolute Principle transcending even that which he connotes by '' *the one*,'' or '' *the good* '' ; but the fact that he speaks in the final passage which we have quoted of this state of union as being '' the life of the Gods,'' would appear to lend colour to the conception that it has not reached the absolute Absolute ; and Thomas Taylor in his translation adds the following note to this passage :

"From this *solitary* subsistence of *the one*, the solitariness of all other divine natures is derived, and their ineffable association with themselves.   Hence Plato in the *Timæus* says, ' that the Demiurgus established heaven (i.e. the world) one, only, solitary nature, able through virtue to converse with itself, indigent of nothing external, and sufficiently known and friendly to itself.' ''

Hence the Demiurgus, or Logos, may be *the one* here referred to by Plotinus. We have already sufficiently explicated the concept of an Absolute beyond the Logos, or Logoi, or ' Gods,' to show that speculation as to whether such an Absolute is reachable in the highest state of ecstasy is futile and unprofitable. Sufficient unto the mystic is his own individual experience of union.

Let us turn from Plotinus to one or two of the Christian mystics. We may take first of all Ruysbroeck as being one of the clearest, sanest, and most philosophical of these, with the emotional element duly held in restraint.

"When love has carried us above all things, above the light, into the Divine Dark, there we are transformed by the Eternal Word Who is the image of the Father ; and as the air is penetrated by the sun, thus we receive in peace the Incomprehensible Light, enfolding us and penetrating us. What is this light, if it be not a contemplation of the Infinite and an intuition of Eternity ? We behold that which we are, and we are that which we behold, because our being, without losing anything of its own personality, is united with the Divine Truth which respects all diversity." [1]

As may be seen from the above extracts, the most philosophical of mystics cannot wholly refrain from mention of the dominant attractive power and factor in the return of the soul to its source : the great principle of *Love*, which in all cases, whether human or divine, is the *unitive* principle *par excellence* in our nature : that strange mystic principle which *burns* within us with the intensest fire of emotion we are possible of experiencing, and always compels to action for the attainment of the closest possible union with the object to which it is directed. We shall have more to say of this characteristic of Mysticism almost immediately.

We may now note in the following quotation from Tauler the use of a somewhat different imagery, and one which approaches more nearly to that language of ' negation,' which we have already noted as being alone applicable to the Absolute when we endeavour to express it in conceptual language.

"Now this Divine Abyss can be fathomed by no creatures ; it can be filled by none, and it satisfies none ; God only can fill it in His Infinity. For this abyss belongs only to the Divine Abyss, of which it is written : *Abyssus abyssum invocat.* He who is truly conscious of this ground, which shone into the powers of his soul, and lighted and inclined its lowest and highest powers to turn to their pure Source and Origin, must diligently examine himself, and remain alone, listening to the voice which cries in the wilderness of this ground. This ground is so desert and bare, that no thought has ever entered there.

[1] *De Contemplatione.* Hello, p. 145.

None of all the thoughts of man which, with the help of reason, have been devoted to meditation on the Holy Trinity (and some men have occupied themselves much with these thoughts) have ever entered this ground. For it is so close and yet so far off, and so far beyond all things, that it has neither time nor place. It is a simple and unchanging condition. A man who really and truly enters feels as though he had been here throughout eternity, and as though he were one therewith; whereas it is only for an instant, and the same glance is found and reveals itself in eternity." [1]

We may give one more quotation from a mystic of a somewhat different type. St. Teresa, speaking of her own experience, says :

" It (the soul) neither sees, hears, nor understands anything while this state lasts, which is never more than a very brief time ; it appears to the soul to be much shorter than it really is. God visits the soul in a manner which prevents its doubting, when returning to itself, that He was within it and that it dwelt in him. So firmly is it convinced of this truth that, although years may pass before this favour recurs, the soul can never forget it nor doubt the fact. . . . The soul perceives by a certitude which remains in the heart, and which God alone can give. . . . I maintain that a soul which does not feel this assurance has not been united to God entirely." [2]

There is rather a discrepancy here with Tauler, who says that one who has really been in that state " feels as though he had been here throughout eternity " ; whereas St. Teresa says that " it appears to the soul to be much shorter than it really is." We should be rather inclined to the view that St. Teresa did not go so 'high,' or so 'deep' as Tauler. We may note also in St. Teresa's phraseology that there is nothing of the more mystical 'ground,' but rather the concept of a *personal* God.

What is the practical result for the individual mystic of this final achievement ; does it unfit him for any active participation in the affairs of this world ? In many cases it has doubtless done so, and has made of him a close recluse. Broadly speaking, however, we should hardly consider that in such case there had really been *the* supreme achievement of union, for we should hold that that achievement must, in the great majority of cases at all events, result in a quality of life manifested on the outer plane in a degree of activity

[1] *The Inner Way*, Sermon on John the Baptist.   Ed. Library of Devotion, p. 98.
[2] *The Interior Castle*, Fifth Mansions, chap. i, 8.

otherwise impossible. We cannot, however, pass judgment in individual cases, and say that where the mystic is a close recluse he is *wrong* to be so. His mode of life may be not merely what is necessary for that individual at that particular stage of his evolution, but it may also be precisely what is best for the Race ; for he may possibly do more on the *inner* planes of the unitary consciousness of the Race by reason of his contemplative life than by a more visible and appreciable activity on the outer plane. No single effort is lost in the sub-consciousness of the Race.

In the case of a very large number of our classical mystics, however, we find that the supreme achievement having once been attained to, it no longer absorbs the entire concentrated efforts of the individual, but is set aside for an active life of devoted service to the Divine Will. The beatific vision may and does recur, but it is not sought for its own sake, and the supreme achievement does not make of the individual a mere passive contemplative, a recluse withdrawn from all contact with the world, but on the contrary—and this is the test—it produces a marvellous, and in a certain sense miraculous, capacity to produce ' works,' to effect results of a most extraordinary and far-reaching nature.

We have in the first place the great literary works which these mystics have produced ; though these works do not present on the whole the marvellous character to which we are now referring. It is the physical energy and material results produced by the individual who, at their inception, would be judged to be utterly unfitted for, and incapable of accomplishing them, that is the astonishing and characteristic feature of the truly *vital* mystic union. The weak physical body, and even the uninstructed and deficient intellect, becomes the vehicle of a superlative degree of energy and forcefulness and fruitfulness. The mystic who has truly touched the supreme Source of his life and consciousness, brings back and retains an inner vitality, an inner ' fire ' as a permanent acquisition. He has, as it were, opened up a channel between the lower self and the higher Self : a channel previously choked with the obstacles he has now overcome and cleared away ; he has established a real vital and substantial organic correspondence and harmony between his lower and his higher vehicles, a correspondence which is a real structural fact on the psychic, mental, and spiritual planes of his being, as well as in the physical body itself, and which now creates such a harmony and receptivity in all his bodies, that the divine Will of the Higher Self is done on earth through the physical body in a manner which could not possibly be effected without this organic connection and harmony, or when the lower self acts in its own self-will.

A classical example of this inflow of energy overcoming physical weakness and disability is that of St. Paul. Of his ' weakness ' or ' thorn in the flesh '—supposed by some to have been epilepsy—we are told by him that he " besought the Lord thrice, that it might depart from me " ; but he was told, " My grace is sufficient for thee : my power is made perfect in weakness." We are so accustomed, however, to regard Bible narratives and Bible characters as being in some manner altogether on another plane than those of other historical records, that it will seem to many that the same standard of comparison cannot be applied to St. Paul as we should apply, for example, to St. Francis d'Assisi, to St. Catherine of Sienna, to St. Teresa, to Eckhart, to Suso, or to Madame Guyon. Yet there are many points of similarity, and more especially the fact that in spite of great physical weakness and disabilities, and apparently insuperable external obstacles, they one and all engaged in missionary efforts, and effected results which, when studied in detail, are little short of miraculous. In the most unpromising soil, in the most discouraging outward circumstances, somehow or other the spiritual vitality of their life finds a receptive medium, or creates it for itself. Wherever St. Francis goes he makes Franciscans. St. Catherine of Sienna, after the most extreme mystical experiences, goes out into the world and becomes one of the greatest characters of the fourteenth century ; her boundless activities including not merely her literary work, but also tendance on the poor, the sick and the plague-striken, as well as her larger religious and political work, extending even to a reformation of the Papacy. St. Teresa, over fifty years of age, and apparently a chronic invalid, and in abject poverty, travels through Spain finding converts everywhere, and founding reformed convents of an extreme of austerity and asceticism where had previously been indifference to spiritual things and monastic abuses of the grossest kind. Eckhart is the great moulder of German Mysticism and mystical philosophy at the commencement of the fourteenth century. Suso, his disciple, practising for years the most terrible self-inflicted tortures, and then, " a mere wreck of a man to look at," is pushed out into an active life by the force of the monitions of his inner consciousness : a life from which he had a natural shrinking, and in which he suffered mentally even more deeply than he had previously suffered physically. Madame Guyon, one of the greatest of the Quietists, leads a life of the utmost activity, devotion, and self-sacrifice in the face of the greatest difficulties and the most cruel and bigoted priestly persecution.

These results, of course, may and do obtain in the case of individuals who are not by any means distinguished as being great mystics. Joan of Arc is a classical example, and we might also instance George Fox, the founder of the Quaker community, and more recently General Booth. But the point is, that from those who have made a claim to the supreme vision of union with the Absolute or God, we do obtain, and are justified in demanding, fruits or works of a corresponding nature.

(II) The second great characteristic of Mysticism is the fact that the mystic is essentially a lover.

Love, as the great unitive principle, is both the method and the goal of the mystic. At all stages and in all degrees it is pre-eminently Love, ardent, burning, overwhelming Love which is the great impelling force, determining and governing all his efforts and aspirations, his joys and his sorrows, his attainments and his failures; and in this, as in all other matters pertaining to this deepest and most mysterious of our human emotions, the more ardent the love and the more exquisite its satisfaction, the more poignant is the grief and suffering which the lover has to endure. None have ever experienced the immeasurable bliss of Love to the same degree as the mystics, and none ever have or can suffer as the mystics have suffered, as, for example, in the " dark night of the soul," when the *response* of the Infinite—which we have previously noted—to their ardent and burning desire for union which has already been to some extent satisfied, appears to cease, and they conceive that they are utterly and for ever abandoned by the object of their love. This " dark night " is principally characteristic of the Christian mystics, and is more a product of the theology and doctrine which the Christian mystic imports into his higher mystical consciousness from the region of the lower mind, than of Mysticism or the spiritual consciousness in its pure nature. Speaking of this experience, St. John of the Cross says :

" The greatest affliction of the sorrowful soul in this state is the thought that God has abandoned it, of which it has no doubt; that He has cast it away into darkness as an abominable thing. The thought that He has abandoned it is a grievous and pitiable affliction. . . . For, in truth, when the soul is in the pangs of the purgatorial contemplation, the shadow of death and the pains and torments of hell are most acutely felt, that is the sense of being without God, and chastised and abandoned in His wrath and heavy displeasure. All this and even more the soul feels now, for a fearful apprehension has come upon it that this will be with it for ever." [1]

This apprehension could not be felt where there is a true philosophical appreciation of the eternal unity of the individual and the Absolute ; it is the product of a purely theological concept of God and of sin. Nevertheless, in other forms of Mysticism the same principle holds good : in proportion as Love is the absorbing dominating passion, untempered by philosophical judgment and reason, the lover will suffer at some time or other to the degree that he enjoys. In this, as in all other matters, reason should hold the balance between the extremes—but then it is just the principal characteristic of love to throw reason to the winds. How often do we not see the folly and illusion of love ; how often do we not forgive the unreason in the lover for the sake of Love itself ?

The immediate object or ideal which the individual mystic sets up in his mind as the focus of this impassioned love, may vary very widely in its nature or form ; but whether that object be merely Nature herself—as with some of our great nature mystics and poets—or whether it be fixed on some more personal or personified object as an embodiment of the supreme Divine Love—as for example the personal Saviour of the Christian mystic—it is always some aspect of the unitive Life Principle which we term the Absolute or God which is both the object and the attractive power. Thus Krishna (the Logos) is represented as saying in the

[1] *The Obscure Night of the Soul*, Bk. II, chap. vi.

Bhagavad-Gita, " In whatever way men approach me, in that way do I assist them ; but whatever the path taken by mankind, that path is mine, O son of Pritha."[1] And again : " In whatever form a devotee desires with faith to worship, it is I alone who inspire him with constancy therein, and depending on that faith he seeks the propitiation of that God, obtaining the object of his wishes as is ordained by me alone."[2]

A whole volume might be filled with examples of the expression of this passionate love of the Infinite or God which is the one absorbing and all-embracing motive of life for those with whom the term *mystic* is most commonly associated ; and little as we may as yet have experienced this ourselves, we cannot but feel as we read and collate their testimony to the response which they obtain, that this great principle of Love lies at the Heart and Source of all being, all existence, and is, as it were, a golden key which we already possess— since, in our inner nature, we are *one* with that Heart and Source—though we have not learnt to use it—or are not even conscious of possessing it— which can open for us the gates of that Paradise of infinite and immeasurable Bliss which is our true life and being in eternity, and which lies all around and about and within us *now.* The mystic has learnt to use this key, and seeks not merely to tell us of that bliss of which he has become a partaker, but would fain instruct us also in the use of the key. Let us at least listen humbly, not scornfully or superciliously, to his message ; forgiving his extravagances, where these are only too plainly visible, for the sake of Love itself, even as we forgive the earthly lover his occasional illusions and blindnesses.

To select from the classical mystics any passages bearing upon this great characteristic would be an extremely difficult matter, since it has so many phases and such varied expressions. We shall, therefore, instead of attempting to do this, make a selection of a few passages from a very beautiful little modern book recently published by an anonymous author, who exhibits this characteristic as clearly as any of the classical mystics ; but tempers it with a rationality which the latter do not by any means at all times display. These extracts will also serve to show that this characteristic of Mysticism is by

[1] Chap. iv, 11.　　　　　　[2] Chap. vii, 21, 22.

no means a thing of the past. The work here referred to is entitled, *The Golden Fountain, or, The Soul's Love for God ; being some Thoughts and Confessions of One of His Lovers.*[1] The *formal* side of the work is Christian ; but it is notable that whereas the object of the love and devotion of the author commenced by being centred on the personal historical Jesus, it passed from thence to the Cosmic Christ, and at a further stage to the Absolute Godhead. These stages the author refers to as her " three conversions," and they correspond broadly with the three stages of the mystic 'Way' which we have already noted. Referring to these three ' conversions,' she says :

"For myself, I experienced three conversions : the first two of terrible suffering, and the third of great and marvellous joy, in which it is no exaggeration to say that for a few moments I seemed to receive God and all the freedom of the Heavens into my soul. I am not able to say exactly how long this experience lasted, for I was dead to time and place, but I should judge it to have been from fifteen to twenty minutes."[2]

After the first ' conversion ' her love continued to be centred upon the " Man Jesus " ; but after the second conversion she says : " Jesus, without my knowing how it came about, passed out from the Perfect Man into the Christ of God." There is a very close analogy between this and the experience of Jacopone da Todi.[3] Describing this ' second conversion ' she says :

"This having continued almost exactly the two years, upon Easter morning, at the close of the service, the horrible anguish came on me again as I knelt in the church. I was not able to move or to show my face for more than an hour ; and to this day I am not able to dwell upon the memory of that awful pain, for I think I should go mad if I had to enter again into so great a torture of the spirit. I endured to the utmost limit of my capacity for suffering—for this I will say of myself, I did not draw back, but went on to the bitter end. And the suffering was caused by the sight of that most terrible of all sights : the vision of myself as over against the vision of Jesus Christ, and I died a death for every fault. Whoever has felt the true wailing of the soul, such an one knows the heights of all spiritual pain. The heart and mind, or creature, suffers in depths ; but the soul in heights, and this at one and the same time, so that the pain of repentance is

---

[1] John M. Watkins. 1919. [2] P. 19.
[3] Cf. Evelyn Underhill, *Jacopone da Todi*, p. 240 *seq.*

everywhere. And the depth of the suffering of the creature is co-equal with the height of the suffering of the soul, and the joint suffering of both would seem to be of co-equal promise and merit for their after joy and glory ; so that it would seem that the more horrible our pain the quicker is our deliverance and the greater our later joys." [1]

Speaking of her ' third conversion,' she says :

" This third conversion produced a fundamental alteration of my whole outlook and grasp on life. It brought me into direct contact with God, and was the commencement of a total change of heart and mind and consciousness ; the centre of my consciousness, without any effort of my own, suddenly moving bodily from a concentration upon the visible or earthly to a loving and absorbed concentration upon, and a fixed attention to, the Invisible God—a most amazing, undreamed-of change, which remained permanent, though fluctuating through innumerable degrees of intensity before coming to a state of equilibrium. And now Christ went away from me, so that I adored Him in God. After this for some weeks I went through extraordinary spiritual experiences, the like of which had never previously so much as entered into my heart to imagine; I came to all these experiences with great innocence and ignorance, never having read any religious or psychological book, and I think now that it is perhaps easier to have it so." [2]

Speaking of the character and method of this love, she says :

" We know that the love of the heart can be beautiful and full of zeal and fervour ; but the love of the soul by comparison to it is like a furnace, and the capacities of the heart are not worthy to be named in the same breath. Yet, deplorable as is the heart of man, it is evidently desired by God, and must be given to Him before He will waken the soul. To my belief, we are quite unable to awaken our own soul, though we are able to *will* to love God with the heart, and through this we pass up to the border of the Veil of Separation, where He will *sting the soul into life* and we have perception. After which the soul will often be swept or plucked up into immeasurable glories and delights which are neither imagined nor contrived, nor even desired by her at first—for how can we desire that which we have never heard of and cannot even imagine ? And these delights are unimaginable before the soul is caught up into them, and to my experience they constantly differ. The soul knows herself to be in the hands and power of another, outside herself. She does not enter these joys of her own power or by her own will, but by permission and intention and will of a force outside herself though perceived and known inside herself. No lovers of arguments or guessing games can move the soul to listen when she has once been so handled. For to know is more than to guess." [3]

[1] Pp. 21, 22.   [2] P. 26.   [3] Pp. 39, 40, 41.

The *response* from the object of devotion to which we have previously referred is very marked in the above passage. The following passage is characteristic of much of the outpouring of many of the classical mystics.

" God, once found, is so poignantly ever-present to the soul that we must sing and whisper to Him all the day. O marvellous and exquisite God ! I am so enraptured by Thy nearness, I am so filled with love and joy, that there is no one, nothing, in heaven or earth to me save Thine Own Self, and I could die for love of Thee ! Indeed, I am in deep necessity to find Thee at each moment of the day, for so great is Thy glamour that without Thee my days are like bitter waters and a mouthful of gravel to a hungry man. How long wilt thou leave me here—set down upon the earth in this martyrdom of languishing for love of Thee ? And suddenly, when the pain can be endured no more, He embraces the soul. Then where do sorrow and waiting fly ? and what is pain ? There never were such things ! [1]

What did I ever do that He should show me such kindness ? I did nothing except this : I desired with all the force of my heart and soul and mind and body to love Him. I said, ' Oh, if I could be the warmest, tenderest lover that ever thou didst have ! Teach me to be thy burning lover.' This was my perpetual prayer." [2]

Compare this latter paragraph with what Jacob Böhme says as to his method.

" I only sought the heart of love in Jesus Christ, and when I had obtained that with great joy of my soul, then was this treasure of natural and divine knowledge opened and given unto me." [3]

The following is her description of the supreme experience of the ' third conversion,' or attainment of the unitive state.

" How can a contact with God be in any way described ? It is not seeing, but meeting and fusion with awareness. The soul retaining her own individuality and consciousness to an intense degree, but imbued with and fused into a life of incredible intensity, which passes through the soul vitalities and emotions of a life so new, so vivid, so amazing, that she knows not whether she has been embraced by love or by fire, by joy or by anguish : for so fearful is her joy that she is almost unable to endure the might of it. [4]

Of other forms of contact we have a swift, unexpected, even unsought-for attainment, which is entirely of His volition ; that sudden condescension to the soul, in which in unspeakable rapture she is caught up to her holy lover. These are the topmost heights which the creature dare recall, though to the soul they remain in memory

---

[1] P. 47.
[3] Cf. Penny: *Studies in Jacob Böhme*, p. 22.
[2] P. 118.
[4] P. 41.

as life itself. The variations of these forms of contact are infinite, for God would seem to will to be both eternal changelessness and variation in infinitude.[1]

But the most wonderful flights of the soul are made during a high adoring contemplation of God. We are in high contemplation when the heart, mind, and soul, having dropped consciousness of all earthly matters, have been brought to a full concentration upon God—God totally invisible, totally unimaged, *and yet focussed to a centre-point by the great power of love.* The soul, whilst she is able to maintain this most difficult height of contemplation, may be visited by an intensely vivid perception, inward vision, and knowledge of God's attributes or perfections, very brief; and this *as a gift*, for she is not able to will such a felicity to herself, but being given such she is instantly consumed with adoration, and *enters ecstasy.*[2]

In the highest rapture I ever was in, my soul passed into a fearful extremity of experience: she was burned with so terrible an excess of bliss that she was in great fear and anguish because of this excess. Indeed, she was so overcome by this too great realisation of the strength of God that she was in terror of both God and joy. It was three days before she recovered any peace, and more than a year before I dared recall one instant of it to mind. I am not able to think that even in Heaven the soul could endure such heights for more than a period. These heights are incomparably, unutterably beyond vision and union. They are the utmost extremity of that which can be endured by the soul, at least until she has re-risen to great altitudes of holiness in ages to come." [3]

Such is the testimony of a modern devotional mystic : the testimony to the fact and nature of *Love* as the great unitive principle, and as experienced to the utmost possibility of our present nature.

Shall we as mere cold psychologists, as mere ' rationalists,' seek to drag down these trancendental experiences of the very highest and divinest part of our nature into the region of the formal mind and consciousness, and endeavour to explain them learnedly as mental states, ' complexes,' ' auto-suggestions,' etc., etc., as if such terms could really *explain* anything of the nature of mind, let alone that which transcends mind ? Or shall we not rather recognise that on their *formal* side these experiences must necessarily be associated with mind forms, ideas, and images or symbols which form the content and even the very structure of the mind ; but that in themselves they altogether transcend mind, and are a revelation of the immeasurable, inconceivable heights and depths of our nature in its capacity for an ultimate realisation

[1] P. 91.   [2] P. 100.   [3] Pp. 137, 138.

of unity with that great LIFE by and through and in which all things and all creatures live and move and have their being, and which, in Its own Nature and Being—whether we now conceive of it as an impersonal Absolute or a personal God—is, to a degree utterly beyond all thought, beyond our most daring conceptions, beyond our highest flights of imagination, our aspirations, hopes, fears, or beliefs, a Principle of GOOD—poor feeble word—of Boundless Bliss, Love, Harmony, Freedom; in which even that which we now *call* evil is but a part of its Absolute Perfection.

These mystical experiences of union are possible because we are not merely partakers of the Absolute Perfection; we do not merely drink from the cup which is offered to our lips —though this may be a preliminary experience—but we are, in the wholeness and completeness of our nature, that Absolute Itself, and never can be aught else, whether we ascend into Heaven or descend into Hell.

These mystical experiences are possible not merely because we can and may *attain* to the heights and depths of the Universe, not merely because every power in the Universe— and there is no power that is not a *living* power—is ours to acquire and to exercise, but because in the wholeness of our nature, in the Self-in-Itself, we *are* those powers; and the meanest thing we do, as well as the loftiest, is never done in any other power.

And so we arrive at the great fundamental law of life, that whatsoever a man seeketh that shall he most surely attain, be it good or be it evil, either here or hereafter, either now or in a thousand years—which are but as one day—for to seek is to desire and to will, and to desire and to will is to exercise the omnipotent power of the One Self which, being omnipresent as well as omnipotent, is not absent from the very least; and which, being omnipotent, cannot fail to have its corresponding objective result or *realisation*, in the least as in the greatest, for even thus is produced this whole phenomenal universe wherein the Self experiences in degree and in kind.

And thus the mystic, in singleness of heart, and with great strength of desire and will, cultivating what Böhme calls " the power in the light which is God's love-fire," attains in due time that transcendental vision or union which he has placed before himself as his goal. The *form* which his attainment appears to assume may be accounted for in the region of the formal mind; hence the variety of mystical as well as of religious experience. But the principle is the same in all cases, and it is principle not form we are now endeavouring to elucidate.

Will and desire are the living creative powers of the One Self, and of every individual self. But they may be active in the phenomenal world either with or without that other balancing power for which the best term is perhaps *Wisdom*. Without this they are potent for evil; they are potent for good just in proportion as they are governed by it. And the empirical fact remains that the individual has to learn wisdom through a long and painful evolutionary experience. Let none think that the mystic is a chance product, or that a personal God favours one individual more than another. Each individual contains the Infinite, each is capable of an interior realisation of his own infinite personality in heights and depths which perhaps no mystic has as yet ever attained to, seeing that there are still limitations of mind and body. But whether it be in saint or in sinner, the great Law works: " Whatsoever a man soweth, that shall he also reap." The living powers which he evokes, his ideals, images, and imaginations, rise up within him, and, attracting their like, gather from the Cosmos those elements which build for him the vehicle of mind and body which he wears now, or shall wear at some future time. And even thus shall he stand before his fellows, and take his place in the cosmic Whole; it may be " as a vessel unto honour," it may be " as a vessel of wrath fitted (only) unto destruction "; or, as Böhme puts it: " The God in him, in Whose ground he standeth, maketh him what he can serve to be according to the utmost possibility."[1]

Yet at each moment is placed before the individual a choice; and if—having learnt wisdom—he chooses well, who shall say through what suffering and strenuous strife he may not have come to enable him thus to choose; and if he chooses ill, then through pain and suffering he shall surely come at last to the knowledge of the great Law; to the realisation of it as embodied in his own nature; whereby,

[1] *Election*, chap. ix, par. 26.

he is no longer in bondage to the Law, for the Law is now his own Will, his own Action, in all its harmonious perfection. Though acting in and with it, he yet stands as it were outside of it, untouched by its necessity, or Fate, even as the One Self, the One Life, is immanent in and through All, yet is not called ' God,' save only as being transcendent, " according to the Light wherewith He dwelleth in Himself."[1]

"*What that subtle Being is, of which this whole Universe is composed, that is the Real, that is the Soul, That art thou, O S'vetaketu.*"[2]

[1] Böhme: *Signatura Rerum*, chap. viii, par. 42.
[2] Chândogya Upanishad, vi, 14. 3.

CHAPTER IX

MYSTICISM AND OCCULTISM

"I, too, have sought to know as thou to love,
Excluding Love as thou refused'st Knowledge,
Are we not halves of one dissevered world,
Whom this strange chance unites once more ? Part ! never ;
Till thou, the Lover, know, and I, the Knower,
Love ; until both are saved."

BROWNING : *Paracelsus*.

"The crowning race
Of those that, eye to eye, shall look
On knowledge ; under whose command
Is Earth and Earth's, and in their hand
Is Nature like an open book."

TENNYSON : *In Memoriam*.

"This, therefore, is manifested by the mandate of the mysteries, which orders that they shall not be divulged to those who are uninitiated. For as that which is divine cannot be unfolded to the multitude, this mandate forbids the attempt to elucidate it to any one but him who is fortunately able to perceive it."

PLOTINUS : Enn. vi, *ix.* 11.

CHAPTER IX

MYSTICISM AND OCCULTISM

OUR subject must now assume another aspect. Rational
Mysticism needs something more than what we have now
found to be the content of Mysticism in the sense in which
that term has come to be understood at the present time.

We have exhibited Mysticism as a realisation in actual
conscious experience in our inmost spiritual nature, and in a
region transcending intellect, of our oneness or unity with
the Absolute or God ; and we have exhibited the method of
Mysticism as being pre-eminently a path of devotion, of intense
religious fervour, and of passionate love. We have exhibited
it thus because such has come to be the historical meaning and
development of the term, though it does not appear to have
been its original significance. The origin of the word may be
traced back to the Greek Mysteries and Mystery Cults, and
always implied an *initiation*. With the rise of Ecclesiastical
Christianity, however, many of the rites and terms previously
associated with the Eleusinian and other Mystery Cults were
taken over by, and were subsequently represented as originating
in, and belonging exclusively to, the new Religion.[1] Like all
the pre-Christian origins of Christianity, much of this connection of the 'new' religion with Gnôsticism and the Initiatory
Mysteries is lost in obscurity, though modern scholarship
has succeeded in tracing a few of the links, and from time to
time some ancient document is discovered which is for ' orthodoxy' more or less of a startling disclosure in its bearing upon
the commonly received notions as to the unique character
and origin of the formulated religion which has dominated
the Western World for so many centuries, and which has so
recently been tried and found wanting.

Whatever may have been the original nature and source of

[1] Cf. W. R. Inge : *Christian Mysticism*, Appendix B.

these ancient Mysteries and Mystery Cults from which our term *Mysticism* is thus derived in its association with Christian doctrine and ceremonial practice, it is clear that to-day Mysticism does not imply any *initiation* in the sense of the disclosure to a candidate of knowledge already acquired and in the possession of a Cult, or of some Heirophant, Initiate, or Adept instructed and learned in a secret knowledge which might be imparted to the candidate by such an initiation.   It is no longer connected with the great tradition of a true esoteric knowledge or Gnôsis, carefully guarded and only handed on to the most tried and approved individuals.   It is true that many of the great Christian mystics have put themselves under the guidance of a spiritual Director of the orthodox Church ; but their actual mystical experience was always independent of, and by no means resulted from, any specific knowledge or initiation imparted by these Directors, who were themselves, as a rule, anything but mystics or initiates.   To-day, therefore, we have to make a broad distinction between Mysticism and that knowledge of our deeper nature and constitution in its relation to the Cosmos in actual structural fact which may be known in the form of a *science*, and with which the term *Occultism* appears to have become more or less definitely associated at the present time.

Like the term *Mysticism*, however, *Occultism* may cover a multitude of sins both of omission as well as of commission, which those who have the clearest and most exalted view of either the one or the other must find themselves compelled to repudiate.   There are also in Occultism, as in Mysticism, many degrees of attainment and many phases of experience.

With the decay of Gnôsticism and the Mystery Cults, so far as these were known and outwardly recognised as representative of inner and secret teachings which could only be communicated to suitable candidates, there does not appear to have been any real cessation of the great fact or tradition of the existence of this esoteric knowledge or Gnôsis ; it was only that—owing to the persecution by the Christian Church, and the dark ages which resulted from the dominance of Ecclesiastical authority—the possibility of it was withdrawn from the knowledge of the world at large, and confined more strictly to secret schools and communities.   It is, therefore, extremely difficult to-day to trace any connected historical links in this tradition, or to say what are the genuine claims of the Masons, Templars, Alchemists, Rosicrucians, and other Cults to have been custodians, at one time or another, of the Ancient Wisdom and Occult Sciences; nor is it necessary in this present work that we should make any attempt to establish such a connection. We are concerned with principles rather than with historical details.

An enormous and widespread revival of the tradition took place in the latter part of the last century, through the work of a very remarkable woman, Madame H. P. Blavatsky, who, in 1875, founded the Theosophical Society, and thus inaugurated that great modern movement known as *Theosophy*, which has done so much to introduce Eastern religious philosophy to the Western World, and which claims to be a revival of the ancient Wisdom Religion, directly inspired by great Teachers or *Masters* belonging to a supreme Hierarchy of Initiates which has always existed, and which watches over and guides the efforts of individuals, and of the Race as a whole, in that gradual growth of knowledge of the self, and its relations to and connection with the Cosmos, which constitutes the great drama of the evolution of Man on this Globe.

It is a large question as to whether, without such teaching and guidance from a Hierarchy of Initiates, the Race could ever have reached unaided the great traditions in religion and philosophy which we possess to-day, and which go back to far remote ages. The popular theory of the direct inspiration by ' God '—the Absolute ?—of certain individual prophets and teachers, has to be revised when we have overpassed the anthropomorphic conceptions of ' God ' which accompany this theory; as also must the opposite extreme view that man has had *no* inspired guidance; that he has been, and is to-day, entirely cut off from Beings in the invisible world who are as much beyond him in their evolution as he is beyond his original protoplasmic cell; and that all these ancient traditions have their origin merely in a crude animism and nature-worship.

Shall we, indeed—as so many have foolishly done, thinking that our modern science represents the furthest knowledge that has ever been attained of the nature of the Cosmos—shall we deny *a priori* the possibility of the existence of such a Hierarchy of Initiates, or of such a supreme knowledge ?

Shall we deny the existence of *Intelligences* in almost infinite
grades of Cosmic Consciousness, linking up the limited consciousness of the individual on this physical plane with the
Cosmic Consciousness of the Logos—not to say the Consciousness of the Absolute or ' God ' ?   Shall we deny the existence
of Elder Brothers of the Race, who in long-past ages, or in
previous cycles of evolution, have already accomplished that
perfection or realisation of their nature, that real knowledge
of the ONE SELF which not a few to-day have now apprehended to be not merely within their reach, but also to be
the one and only key to the whole nature of the Cosmos ?
For the great mass of Humanity, the divine origin and the
latent potentialities of their nature must doubtless still
remain unrecognised so long as a future life of bliss is
associated only with something that has been done for them,
and which they will pass on to inherit at death ;   vainly
imagining that they will then have finished *for ever* with the
further evolution of Humanity in this material world.

Well—sufficient unto each must be his belief or ' faith.'
Our object is not to bring forward historical evidence for the
existence of such a Hierarchy of World Saviours, Masters,
Initiates : much less to support the claims of any particular
School or Movement to be in direct touch with these ;   but
our endeavour is to present broad principles which will
appeal to an inner intuition rather than to an outer reason.
It is of no use trying to force knowledge on those who are
unready for it.   Every individual has a line over which he
cannot at present pass ;   and if you endeavour to force him
over it, he will only turn again and rend you.   It is the line,
or *liminal*, or limitation representing the particular stage of
evolution he has reached.   Beyond that line all is not merely
unfamiliar to him, but commonly appears also to be hostile.
The pearls of truth you offer cannot be recognised as such.
Remember also that your own pearls may appear to be
very poor baubles to those who stand beyond you, to those
whose consciousness of *unity* is deeper than your own.   But
we have a strong conviction that no effort on the part of
the individual is lost ;   that as there is no short cut to
perfection, so also there is no closed door to shut out the
aspirant from the supreme knowledge ;   that according to the
measure of his faith and effort so shall it be disclosed to

him; and that when he is ready he will receive his *initiation* as a matter of right and not of favour, and whether he belong to this, that or the other secret order, or to none at all. What is implied in that initiation we shall endeavour to elucidate in our further chapters.

We have to note here, however, that to-day there are a very large number of more or less secret Societies, Schools, or Cults claiming to possess 'Occult Knowledge,' and to be more or less in direct touch with the supreme—or with *a* supreme—Hierarchy of Initiates personally unknown to the world at large; and we are obliged to give the term *Occultism* to this modern revival of the ancient Mystery Cults without being able to distinguish clearly as to which, if any, of the individual Schools have a right to the claims which they put forward. If Occultism is mainly associated in the popular conception with certain psychic or 'astral' phenomena, or with the exercise of the individual *will* in certain 'magic' practices or ceremonies: that is no reason why we should stop short at these, and deny altogether that there is a true *spiritual* Occultism, a real *divine* knowledge of the content and meaning of the Cosmos, as valid in its nature as any knowledge which inductive science may attain to in its gradual progress and legitimate effort.

Let us look at this question in the broadest possible manner. Our primary postulate is the unity of the individual with the universal, and the necessity of *self-knowledge*—and knowledge of the *Self*—as the only key to the nature of *Reality*, or the Absolute.

Now we find that the Universe is presented to our experience in the dual manner of Consciousness and Substance (Object, Form); or Being and Becoming; or Unity and Multiplicity; or Reality and Appearance; or Perfection and Process: each of the corresponding terms of these dualities being more or less equivalent. We shall then ask: Can the Self be really known if only one of the terms of this duality is known? On the one side we have Consciousness, Being, Unity, Reality, Perfection; on the other side Substance, Becoming, Multiplicity, Appearance, Process; and we may put the question in another form: What would Consciousness be without Object, or Being without Becoming, or a bare Unity without Multiplicity, or Reality without the Appearance which it subsumes, or Perfection without that which is perfected as Process ? Assuredly they would be nothing. And if the attempt be made to know the one without the other, what will be the result ? Not nothing, for no effort in any direction to know the Self, to know any part of *Reality*, can be a lost effort ; but assuredly it will be an incomplete and one-sided knowledge.

Now, taken broadly, Mysticism is the attempt to know the Self, or Reality, on the Being or Consciousness side only ; and Occultism, in so far as it is a knowledge of *Phenomena*, on whatsoever plane of Substance, is the attempt to know the Self on the Substance or Form side only : though, in so far as the method of Occultism involves the actual functioning of consciousness on supra-physical planes, it is to that extent a knowledge of the Consciousness side as well as the Substance side of Reality. It by no means follows, however, that our individual consciousness functioning on these higher planes will result in scientific knowledge of those planes, any more than our present physical consciousness makes every one a scientist on this plane.

Our main contention, then, will be, that a true knowledge of the Self or Reality must comprise *both* these efforts ; though it does not necessarily follow that both these efforts will be made simultaneously in any one particular lifetime. We shall never understand the evolution of the individual *in* the Race, and of the Race *through* the individual, until we have abandoned once for all that narrow view of the individual which gives to him only one lifetime of association with the evolutionary progress of Man on this Earth. And so in one life the individual may be a mystic, and in another an occultist ; and at a further stage, neither of these as known to the world ; and assuredly he must have had an untold and unrecorded period of evolution in ages past, before he is able to see clearly the goal he has to attain, or the powers he may wield—" The living power made free in him, that power which is HIMSELF." [1] With the great majority of the Race to-day, indeed, this ignorance still prevails ; and assuredly there are many, many ages of evolution still to come before the Race as a whole shall have attained to that ' Golden Age ' when all shall have realised to the full their God-like nature and perfection.

We shall take, then, Mysticism and Occultism as standing

[1] H. P. Blavatsky : *The Voice of the Silence.*

broadly for these two phases or aspects of the great effort to attain to self-knowledge, and knowledge of the *Self*; and in doing this we shall bring them into line with a traditional teaching of Eastern Religion and religious philosophy, that there are two main paths which may be pursued by the aspirant for supreme knowledge and wisdom : the path of Devotion, *Bhakti*, and the path of Knowledge, *Jnāna*. In the end these two paths must necessarily unite, but for the time being they may appear as separate and distinct lines of development.

The whole of what is now known as Mysticism is, taken broadly, the effort to realise the unity of the individual with the Absolute as an actual experience on the consciousness or *feeling* side of our nature. The mystic realises and ' knows ' this blissful union in the same sense that the lover ' knows ' that he loves and is beloved, and may be satisfied with that knowledge without seeking to know anything about the history or circumstances of the object of his devotion, or the psychology of his emotion. The mystics do not care a brass farthing for the structural facts of the Universe, and the classical mystics have contributed nothing whatsoever to our knowledge of those facts. Their object has been to know the Absolute as Being, not as Becoming, and they not merely ignore the Becoming side of Reality, so far as any knowledge of it is concerned, but endeavour by every means in their power to transcend and escape from it ; in some cases committing the greatest atrocities on their physical bodies—" the temple of God "—for that purpose. This is one of the great errors of Mysticism. The occultist can never fall into this error, for all his vehicles of consciousness must be carefully trained and perfected to enable him to attain to his goal.

The mystic, then, we shall and do find to be a very one-sided development of what the man may and must be in the complete perfection of his *whole* nature in its unity with the Absolute which is Becoming as well as Being, the Cosmos as well as the Undifferentiated Godhead. And the occultist we must also declare to be one-sided and incomplete, in so far as his object is merely to attain to occult knowledge of the phenomenal side of Reality, or to obtain ' occult powers ' for his own individual use and gratification. Only, we shall say that no real occultist will do this ; and the impersonal nature of the individual's efforts will be in the main the test of his claim to the title. Unfortunately, it is the lower and personal aspect of Occultism which is commonly seen and mistaken, even by otherwise well-informed writers, as being the whole content of Occultism—using that term now as standing for a real knowledge of the *Substance* aspect of Reality—as contrasted with its *Life* or *Consciousness* aspect— or the structural facts of the Universe on all its phenomenal planes. Thus we find Miss Underhill in her classical work on *Mysticism*, taking a very low view of Occultism, which she identifies with, and prefers to call ' Magic.' Whilst obviously endeavouring to be strictly fair and impartial in this matter, she falls into the error of identifying Occultism or Magic wholly with ' astral plane' phenomena, and fails to recognise at all the necessity of a knowledge of the Substance or Form side of the total content of Reality. She cannot really conceal her distaste for and prejudice against ' Magic '; more especially as contrasted with Mysticism as a method of attaining to a transcendental knowledge of the Absolute. But in doing this she has to beg the whole question as to the nature of ' Reality.' Whilst granting that there is a warrant for the claim of Occultism to comprise " an actual, positive, and realisable knowledge concerning the worlds which we denominate invisible, because they transcend the imperfect and rudimentary faculties of a partially developed humanity, and concerning the latent potentialities which constitute, by the fact of their latency—the interior man "; [1] she will not admit that Occultism is " a method of transcending the phenomenal world and attaining to the reality which is behind phenomena."

If by this she means that the Absolute as ' Reality' is non-phenomenal, is Being only, and not also Becoming : we must immediately join issue with her. In our view, a knowledge of Reality, or the Absolute, or ' God,' comprises an *activity* which we apprehend as the World-Process, *as well as* a *passivity* which we apprehend as pure Being—or Be-ness. " The true science of ultimates," Miss Underhill says, " must be a science of pure Being." [2] But—as we have already asked—what is pure Being without Becoming ? " If there ought not to be, and were not this and that—works,

[1] *Mysticism*, p. 181.   [2] *Ibid.*, p. 181.

and a world full of real things, and the like—what were God Himself, and what had He to do, and whose God would He be ? "[1] Or, as Mr. Bradley says : " Reality, set on one side and apart from Appearance, would assuredly be nothing." [2]

Again, contrasting the method of Mysticism with that of Occultism, Miss Underhill says :

" In Mysticism the will is united with the emotions in an impassioned desire to transcend the sense-world in order that the self may be joined by love to the one eternal and ultimate Object of love ; whose existence is intuitively perceived by that which we used to call the soul, but now find it easier to refer to as the ' Cosmic ' or ' transcendental ' sense. This is the poetic and religious temperament acting upon the plane of reality.   In magic, the will unites with the intellect in an impassioned desire for supersensible knowledge.   This is the intellectual, aggressive, and scientific temperament trying to extend its field of consciousness, until it includes the supersensual world : obviously the antithesis of mysticism, though often adopting its title and style." [3]

With this we may broadly agree.   Occultism *is* " the intellectual and scientific temperament trying to extend its field of consciousness " ; or, in other words, the effort to know Reality, or the structural facts and laws of the Universe, on all planes of consciousness, and not merely as a transcendental extra-phenomenal experience.   It is the " Higher Science."   And if we look at it *solely* as this effort, it will certainly appear to be the " antithesis of mysticism " ; though, even so, it must necessarily be a legitimate phase of our development—unless, indeed, we are to deny altogether any validity or utility in a scientific knowledge of the universe. In its deeper aspects, however, Occultism is much more than this, and we shall prefer to present it as the complement of Mysticism, rather than as its antithesis ; so that a Rational Mysticism will be a combination and balance of the two modes of consciousness, knowing and feeling, or thought and emotion.

We see, then, that Occultism may be defined as the effort to know Reality on the side of *Becoming*, whereas Mysticism only cares to know it on the side of *Being*.   Occultism is the effort to know Reality in its unitary substantial nature rather than in its unitary consciousness nature.   These are broad distinctions which may be admitted simply because

---

[1] *Theologia Germanica*, chap. xxxi.
[2] *Appearance and Reality*, 2nd ed., p. 132.   [3] *Mysticism*, p. 84.

they lie in our present distinctions and use of language, though it is doubtful if they obtained in the far back ages when ' Magic ' was more specially connected with a philosophical religion, and the *Magi* were the hierophants of the *divine* Mysteries.

Miss Underhill admits that :

" The starting-point of all magic and of all magical religion—the best and purest of occult activities—is, as in mysticism, man's inextinguishable conviction that there are other planes of being than those which his senses report to him ; and its proceedings represent the intellectual and individualistic results of this conviction—his craving for the hidden knowledge. It is, in the eyes of those who practise it, **a** *moyen de parvenir* : not the performance of illicit tricks, but a serious and philosophic attempt to solve the riddle of the world."[1]

So far, good. But when she will have it that Mysticism is the only way to Reality ; when she denies that Occultism is " a method of transcending the phenomenal world and attaining to the reality which is behind phenomena,"[2] because " the apparent transcending of phenomena does not necessarily entail the attainment of the Absolute " : we can only say that this applies as much, or even more, to Mysticism as to Occultism. The latter is a transcending of phenomena in order to understand it, so to speak, from above ; whilst Mysticism, on the other hand, as we have already shown, does not care one iota for the facts of the phenomenal world, but—as Miss Underhill herself says—seeks only to *be*. " The occultist," she says, " declares ' I want to know ' ; the mystic ' I want to be.' " But, granted this distinction between Mysticism and Occultism as these terms are at present understood : shall we not have to say that the one is as necessary for the development of our *whole* nature as is the other ? To deny this is practically to deny the value of any scientific knowledge whatsoever, either on this or any other plane of consciousness. If the whole end and aim of our existence should be to escape from the phenomenal into a region of " pure Being," and this cannot be done by any path of knowledge—or at least does not necessitate as part of the process what we understand by knowledge in its relation to phenomena—we had better immediately abandon all scientific and philosophic thought and activity, and concentrate our energies on pure devotional

[1] *Mysticism*, p. 180.   [2] *Ibid.*, p 181.

mysticism. This is precisely what is done by those whom we have come to regard as classical mystics ; and it is apparently the position which Miss Underhill would defend. According to her, Occultism—admittedly a legitimate effort on the part of one side of our nature—" stands for that form of transcendentalism which does abnormal things, but does not lead anywhere." [1] That is practically saying that the pursuit of knowledge into occult regions is a phantom endeavour as a part of our effort to know Reality.

We shall join issue entirely with this one-sided view. We shall say that the mystic who only wants to *be* is as equally one-sided as the occultist who only wants to *know*. We shall say that in the development of our whole nature—that development which does not take place in one incarnation merely, nor commences with any particular physical birth, but is co-existent with the whole world-process—to *know* is as necessary as to *be*. What, indeed, *is* the whole world-process but the unfolding of the *knowledge* aspect of the total content of Reality or the Absolute ? Moreover, we have something more than a suspicion that knowledge—scientific knowledge of the laws and conditions of phenomena—will be found to be as necessary for our well-being and progress on the next plane of existence, after death, as it is on this physical plane ; indeed, on any plane of existence which is phenomenal in the sense that it is objective, there must be natural laws governing the operation of phenomena, and the modifications of the Substance which constitutes the basis of those pheno- mena—the ' matter ' of that particular plane—and a problem of the relation of the subjective self to the objective phenomena, which will be as much the subject of *knowledge* as our present physical problems—perhaps even more so. We have a strong suspicion, indeed, that without such knowledge our life in a future state may be even more of an illusion in its lack of knowledge of ' Reality ' than is our present ignorance and the limitations of physical life and form. There is a remarkable consensus of evidence in this respect in the records of so-called ' spirit ' communications ; and this is confirmed by all the teachings of Occultism with respect to the nature of the ' astral plane ' from which those communications come.

It may possibly be argued that to *be* in the mystical sense

[1] *Mysticism*, p. 181.

is also to know ; that in the attainment of the mystical union we also attain to the fulness of knowledge. But we have no evidence in the records of Mysticism that such is the case in respect of the knowledge of the structural facts of the universe to which we refer as being within the province of Occultism. None of the classical mystics exhibit any knowledge whatsoever of these structural facts, with the exception of Jacob Böhme ; and it is doubtful whether he should really be classed as a mystic. It is notable that he made no attempt to reach, and apparently never did reach, that supreme mystical experience of union which is the great effort and goal of all those whom we have hitherto regarded as being mystics. He makes no attempt to *be* in Miss Underhill's sense ; neither does he make any attempt to *know* in the sense of the occultist. He does not in any way exhibit the classical ' stages ' of the mystic ' way.' He was a great seer, and a great theosophist ; but his seership was involuntary, and his theosophy appears sometimes to savour of theological dogma—as for example in his doctrine of the eternity of the future state of the individual as determined by this present life. Thus he is neither a mystic nor an occultist in the sense in which we are now using the terms, but falls into the class of natural seership which lies midway between the two. Blake and Swedenborg occupy the same position, though Böhme's vision was infinitely deeper than either of these.

It is true, as Miss Underhill herself says in several places, that the mystic realises God as being one with the active world of Becoming, as well as existing in a transcendental region of pure Being ; but this recognition at its best is only the enhanced *feeling* of oneness of the poet, the artist, or the nature mystic, in their intense sympathy and communion with Nature ; it is not a knowledge of the how and why of the process in the actual process itself. " God according to the Persons," says Ruysbroeck, " is Eternal Work, but according to the Essence and Its perpetual stillness He is Eternal Rest." [1] We have shown in Chapter V how these " Persons " are the hypostases by means of which we make the arbitrary passage from the inconceivable " Eternal Rest " of the transcendental Absolute or " Godhead " to the empirical experience of the World of Becoming ; and though it is more than probable that the true

[1] *De Septem Gradibus Amoris*, cap. **xiv.** Quoted by Miss Underhill, p. 42.

mystic vision can and does reconcile these two modes of the ONE in a manner which the intellect alone is utterly unable to compass, yet the fact remains that we have nowhere presented to us by the mystics that *knowledge* of the Cosmos which is such a necessary factor for our well-being in the actual process of Becoming, and which is a distinct and indispensable stage in the process itself.

One has only to compare the writings of the acknowledged mystics with those of such a seer as Jacob Böhme, to appreciate the difference we are here emphasising. Böhme tells us in the second of his *Epistles* how he came by his knowledge, and in what it consists. " In one quarter of an hour," he says, " I saw and knew more than if I had been many years together at an University " ; and, indeed, the student of Böhme knows well that no University could ever impart the clear knowledge of the workings of Nature which he possessed : not to speak of his transcendental vision of " the Being of all Beings, the Byss (the ground or original foundation) and Abyss (that which is without ground, or bottomless and fathomless) "—that is to say, both the Becoming and the Being aspects of the ONE. In a word, Böhme understood the true principles of physics and metaphysics, as well as those of First Cause and Causeless-Cause. In metaphysics, Hegel, among many others, has owed much to his inspiration ; in physics, Newton is reputed to have drawn upon his writings for many of his theories. Of the manner of his vision he tells us :

" I knew and saw *in myself* all the three worlds ; namely, the divine, angelical, and paradisical (world) and then the dark world ; being the original of nature to the fire. And then thirdly, the external, and visible world, being a procreation, or extern birth ; or as a substance expressed, or spoken forth, from both the internal and spiritual worlds ; and I saw, and knew the whole Being (or working essence) in the evil, and in the good ; and the mutual original, and existence of each of them ; and likewise how the pregnant mother (genetrix or fruitful bearing womb of eternity) brought forth. . . . I saw it (as in a great deep) in the internal, for I had a thorough view of the universe as in a CHAOS, wherein all things are couched and wrapt up. . . . The same was with me for the space of twelve years . . . before I could bring it forth into an external form of writing ; which afterwards fell upon me as a sudden shower, which hitteth whatsoever it lighteth upon ; just so it happened to me, whatsoever I could apprehend, and bring into the external (principle of my mind) the same I wrote down." [1]

[1] *Epistles*, ii, 8, 9, 14.

One might ask, why have we so few of these seers ? Böhme, indeed, stands alone and unrivalled in his vision. How shall we *account* for Jacob Böhme ? Was he merely an ignorant shoemaker, favoured by a personal God, by reason of his piety and devotion, with these transcendental revelations ? Had he, indeed, no spiritual heredity, no previous evolution, no struggles and conquests in past lives whereby he gained the *right* to this illumination ? Before it came he had, as he himself tells us, " Many violent assaults of the devil " ; and that : " In my earnest Christian seeking and desire I suffered many a shrewd repulse." [1] He did not seek for the knowledge. " I never desired to know anything of the Divine Mystery," he says. The mystics have strenuously desired and sought after their union ; but not so Böhme.

" I sought only after the heart of Jesus Christ . . . and I resigned myself wholly to Him (God), that I might not live to my own will, but to His ; and that He only might lead and direct me : to the end that I might be His child in His Son Jesus Christ." [2]

Have not the great Christian mystics had this same fervent devotion and resignation of the will ? Yet we do not find that they obtained what Böhme obtained. Böhme thought that others could attain to the same vision as he possessed if they only followed his own method ; but none of his most ardent admirers have been able to do so ; they have had to content themselves with interpreting him. All our sense of law, of adequate cause, and of justice, does in fact lead us to regard any ' *favour* ' which any individual may obtain in his present life, as well as his temperament, character, receptivity, etc., as being something which he himself has earned in the long past of his evolution, and in this region of *Becoming*, in which nothing is obtained without effort.

But even when we say " he himself," we must greatly qualify the statement. Who or what is the " I myself " of any one of us ? Is it the thing of name and form which is born and dies ; or is it the birthless, deathless, immortal Ego, which passes through all the great time-cycle of evolution ; or is it something beyond and transcendental even to that ? Each and all of these in their proper relation and proportion must have

---

[1] *Epistles*, ii, 6, 7.   [2] *Ibid.*, ii, 6.

combined to give Jacob Böhme, the shoemaker, his faculty and vision. And so we shall not surmise what he was "in his last incarnation." Sufficient unto the physical body is the physical cause of birth, nutrition, physical heredity, and death. Sufficient unto the psychic body are the powers it has acquired in the course of its evolution, and which it may or may not fully manifest in or through any particular physical body. Sufficient unto the spiritual body is the creative power it derives from the ONE, and the fruit it garners from the great process of Becoming; the golden wheat that grows up in the blissful fields of Aanru.

We shall conclude, therefore, that to *be* in the sense in which the mystic attains to this state, does not carry with it any knowledge or control of natural forces in the phenomenal world other than the normal man possesses. We have noted in a previous chapter the added forcefulness and energy which the mystic appears to have at his command; but that is a different thing from the power which comes from knowledge. We are firmly convinced that our true goal is the attainment of unity with the Absolute—or rather let us say with the Logos—in knowledge as well as in being or consciousness; the attainment of a divine degree of knowledge, not by abandoning the phenomenal universe of "works and a world full of real things," but by understanding and being the master of these, even as we must suppose that they are understood in the divine consciousness of the Logos, and transcended in a freedom resulting from knowledge which can work in and through them, while at the same time transcending them. "There is nothing," says Krishna in *Bhagavad-Gita*, "in the three regions of the universe which it is necessary for me to perform, nor anything possible to obtain which I have not obtained; and yet I am constantly in action. If I were not indefatigable in action, all men would presently follow my example. If I did not perform actions these creatures would perish."[1]

The mystic realises in full and blissful consciousness his identity with a deep inner principle within himself usually identified with 'God,' or the Absolute; but he only realises this sporadically and intermittently; he only realises it on the *feeling* side of his nature; and he brings back with him from

[1] Chap. iii, 22, 23, 24.

his unitive or ecstatic state no deeper knowledge of the world
in which we live.   Nay, we have seen that in many cases this
ecstatic state is only reached by inflicting the greatest atrocities
on the physical body, which is regarded as an obstacle in the
path, and not as a vehicle to be used in an appropriate manner
in the cosmos, and in that " world of real things " in which
he is called upon to play his part.   This is one of the fundamental errors of an irrational mysticism, and does not pertain
to Occultism ; for in Occultism the physical body must be something more even than whole and sound, its very substance must
undergo a regeneration and transmutation ; it must be a
perfectly trained and responsive instrument to the will of the
self which functions in and through it on the physical plane,
as that self also functions in and through other vehicles on
other planes of consciousness.

   There is nothing to prevent the occultist from being a
mystic, but there is very much to prevent the mystic from being
an occultist ; and it is seldom if ever that the latter occurs in the
sense in which we are here using the term Mysticism.   We have
seen, indeed, Miss Underhill expressly repudiating any connection between Mysticism and Occultism as she understands
the latter term.   This is hardly to be wondered at when we
find her saying that, " the occultist is willing to rest in the
' astral ' and develop his perceptions of this aspect of the world.
It is the medium in which he works. . . .   The education
of the occultist is wholly directed towards this end." [1]   Such
a statement can only be made if the term *Occultism* is confined
to the very lowest of its aspects ; and it is not true even then.
It arises mainly from Miss Underhill's use of the term ' magic '
as being synonymous with Occultism, and her somewhat
unfortunate endeavour to expound the nature of the latter
from the works of Eliphas Lévi, who certainly cannot be
regarded seriously as an occultist.   Miss Underhill would have
done better to have taken Louis Claude de Saint-Martin as
her reference ; but she appears to treat him as a mystic rather
than as an occulist.   Saint-Martin, although connected with
and instructed in certain occult schools and practices, did not
regard these as an end, or even as a true method.   " I have
never had much taste or talent for the operations," he
says ; and again : " I am very far from having any virtuality

[1] *Mysticism*, pp. 187, 185.

of this kind, for my work takes the inward direction altogether."[1]

The following quotation shows the claim which Saint-Martin made for the existence of a traditional occult knowledge into which he had been initiated.

" For such an enterprise as that which I have undertaken more than common resources are necessary. Without specifying those which I employ, it will be enough to say that they connect with the essential nature of man, that they have always been known to some among mankind from the prime beginning of things, and that they will never be withdrawn wholly from the earth while thinking beings exist thereon. Thence have I derived my evidence, and thence my conviction upon truths the search after which engrosses the entire universe. After this avowal, if I am accused of disseminating an unknown doctrine, at least I must not be suspected of being its inventor, for if it connect with the nature of man, not only am I not its inventor, but it would have been impossible for me to establish any other on a solid basis. The principles here expounded are the true key of all the allegories and all the mysterious fables of every people, the primitive source of every kind of institution, and actually the pattern of those laws which direct and govern the universe, constituting all beings. In other words, they serve as a foundation to all that exists and to all that operates, whether in man and by the hand of man, whether outside man and independently of his will. Hence, in the absence of these principles there can be no real science, and it is by reason of having forgotten these principles that the earth has been given over to errors. But although the light is intended for all eyes, it is certain that all eyes are not so constituted as to be able to behold it in its splendour. It is for this reason that the small number of men who are depositaries of the truths which I proclaim are pledged to prudence and discretion by the most formal engagements."[2]

This testimony of " the unknown philosopher," not merely to the existence of this all-embracing occult knowledge in the science of man in his connection with the universe, but also of the existence from time immemorial of the custodians of this knowledge, cannot be lightly set aside. It links up with much testimony which is personally available to-day.

The greatest exponent of Occultism of modern times was undoubtedly Madame H. P. Blavatsky. Whatever may be thought of her personality, or of the ' phenomena ' with which she was associated, she has left in her works a record of the nature of Occultism, and of some of the treasures of knowledge

[1] Cf. Waite: *Louis Claude de Saint-Martin*, p. 47.
[2] *Des Erreurs et de la Vérité*, Part I, pp. 5, 6, 7, 8, 10. Ed. 1782.

which have been garnered by it in the past, which will be more and more justified as scientific knowledge advances—and which we may leave at that. Those who had the good fortune to be acquainted with her personally, as the present author had, know how thoroughly she despised the 'astral plane,' and all the modern phenomena connected with it ; or this may be realised by anyone who takes the trouble to study her great work, *The Secret Doctrine*. For the rest, we may refer our readers to *The Voice of the Silence* for an appreciation of the true ' Path ' of the occultist ; and we would ask where, in any of the records of Mysticism can be found the sublime teaching contained in that work as to the attainment of the final knowledge, the supreme enlightenment, the utmost goal —which means the right to ineffable bliss, and a passing out of all relations with or interest in the evolution of Humanity on this earth, with its long-drawn-out struggle, evolution, and suffering. But when this final prize is reached, it is renounced for the sake of an infinite Compassion ; and the individual becomes one of the great self-sacrificing World Saviours.

Of the conqueror of self who has reached the final goal of the occultist, she writes :

" He standeth now like a white pillar to the west, upon whose face the rising Sun of thought eternal poureth forth its first most glorious waves. His mind, like a becalmed and boundless ocean, spreadeth out in shoreless space. He holdeth life and death in his strong hand.

Yea, he is mighty. The living power made free in him, that power which is HIMSELF, can raise the tabernacle of illusion high above the Gods, above great Brahm and Indra. *Now* he shall surely reach his great reward !

Shall he not use the gifts which it confers for his own rest and bliss, his well-earn'd weal and glory—he, the subduer of the Great Delusion ?

Nay, O thou candidate for Nature's hidden lore ! If one would follow in the steps of holy Tathâgata,[1] those gifts and powers are not for Self.

Now bend thy head and listen well, O Bodisattva—Compassion speaks and saith : ' Can there be bliss when all that lives must suffer ? Shalt thou be saved and hear the whole world cry ? '

If thou wouldst be Tathâgata, follow upon thy predecessor's steps, remain unselfish till the endless end.

Thou art enlightened—choose thy way."

Such was the high doctrine which this remarkable woman, " the sphinx of the nineteenth century," presented to her

[1] One of the titles of the Buddha.

pupils. If we are to take Mysticism at its best in our presentation of its real nature and goal, must we not assuredly do the same for Occultism also in any comparison which we may make between the two? Miss Underhill identifies Occultism solely with 'Magic' and 'astral plane' phenomena, and then says that, "it does not lead anywhere." If, indeed, that may perchance be the legitimate use and limitation of the term, then we must find another term for the traditional *Gupta Vidyā* or *Gnôsis*, which has the same goal in view as Mysticism, i.e. a knowledge of Reality or the Absolute, and which does reach that goal, but with the addition of a knowledge of the Becoming aspect of Reality as well as its Being aspect—a knowledge which the mystic does not seek and does not possess.

We shall deny, however, that there is any one royal road to Reality any more than that there is any one 'religion' by which alone 'salvation' is attained. Plotinus distinguishes three distinct methods of attaining to the highest sense of union : the love of *Beauty* which characterises the poet and the artist ; the love of *Truth*, which is the province of the philosopher ; and that quality of devotion to the *Good* which constitutes broadly the conception of moral purity inherent in the Divine Nature which is the ideal of the religious sense of *righteousness*. These may be considered broadly as " the three great highways conducting the soul to ' that height above the actual and the particular, where it stands in the immediate presence of the infinite, which shines out as from the depth of the soul.' " [1]

The highest sense of union, or ecstasy, however, to which any or either of these may lead, cannot be regarded as the final completion of our nature in its expansion to Self-realisation. It is only a sporadic experience, and was attained to by Plotinus only some three or four times. We shall certainly contend, therefore, that development along each and all of these lines is necessary for the full realisation of our nature in all its heights and depths.

All experience, all rationality, all knowledge of the why and wherefore, is required to complete that perfection of our nature which is implied in the attainment of a full conscious unity with the great LIFE, by which, and through which, and in which all things are brought forth into manifestation. If there is

---

[1] Cf. Max Müller: *Theosophy or Psychological Religion*, p. 433.

any choice at all between the knowledge of that LIFE as *Being*, and a knowledge of IT as *Becoming*, it is rather to the latter than to the former that we should look for all that we can classify as *knowledge*. Nay, have we not hinted, if not clearly realised, that without such a *Becoming* the Absolute could not know itself; that this *Becoming* is in fact the one and only means of the self-revelation of the ONE SELF to ITSELF; and thereby not merely the one and only means whereby the individual self attains to self-consciousness, but also the one and only means whereby it attains to its consciousness of unity with the ONE? If there is, in fact, any one method of which it may be said that "it does not lead anywhere," it is that emotional, ecstatic, erotic mysticism, continually alternating between the extremes of bliss and misery, which is so much associated with the classical devotional mystics, but which we do not find in the philosophical mystics, and which certainly is not characteristic of Occultism. Are we to repudiate altogether the existence of a genuine rational and sane Mysticism because so much which is associated with the term is the merest emotional mono-ideism and auto-suggestion—where it is not worse—a repetition on a higher plane of that craving for individual *sensation* which is the great bar to any knowledge of the ONE SELF? In Occultism, indeed, this very *sensation*, the feeling of complete and ecstatic bliss which supervenes on any exaltation of consciousness, is regarded as a positive obstacle to be overcome. It debars the individual, unless completely overcome, from the clear perception of the *happenings* of the plane on which he is functioning, and from the right analysis and understanding of the functioning of his consciousness on that plane. Shall we bring Mysticism down to the level of a bare psychology—as, indeed, has been attempted by some—because so much of it can be 'explained' as abnormal development of certain mental 'complexes'? But if we are not to do this for Mysticism, we are certainly not able to do it for Occultism as a scientific development of an extended consciousness of the phenomenal or Becoming aspect of Reality. The mere psychism and 'astral plane' phenomena which are so much in evidence to-day in connection with the term *Occultism*, stand in the same relation to true Occultism as a *spiritual* science, that the spurious hallucinations, emotional excesses, and irrational lives of many of the so-called mystics do to the sane and rational Mysticism of, for example, Plotinus or Ruysbroeck.

If the devotional mystics have in fact contributed nothing to our knowledge of the phenomenal world and the great World-Process, and little enough to any real philosophy, we need not blame them for that ; it is not their province or *métier*. They bring the testimony of the actual experience of a unitary consciousness and a supreme bliss ; and that testimony, assigned to its proper place in the sum-total of human experience and a philosophy of the Absolute, is of immense importance. But it is neither the only road to the Absolute, nor does it exhaust the requirements of our nature or the content of Life. For the rest, the mystics help for the most part to fortify certain religious concepts and methods which have their own special and practical value and application in those formulations of Religion which are so necessary for the great mass of humanity, but which must be transcended by those who wish to apprehend the pure Reality which is above and beyond all concepts, all formulæ, all doctrines and creeds, and yet is the source and inspirer of these, even as IT is the maker of all forms in the phenomenal world, though IT will not be confined or condemned of any, and to be truly known must be known as *Being*, independent of any form, *as well as* manifested and revealed in a *Becoming* which includes all and every form, all and every individual ' thing.'

> " They reckon ill who leave me out ;
>   When me they fly, I am the wings ;
>   I am the doubter and the doubt,
>   And I, the hymn the Brahmin sings."

The mystic has a certain advantage over the occultist in being able to present his experiences to the world with the danger only of being regarded as a more or less harmless visionary, or a more or less demented dreamer. The occultist cannot present his real knowledge to the world at all. The way of the mystic is comparatively safe ; the way of the occultist is fraught with great danger. Even in the region of the comparatively low phenomena of ' spiritism ' and psychical research, there are dangers which are well recognised by many modern investigators who are by no means occultists. The dangers on the higher planes are incomparably greater.

No ' astral plane ' phenomenalist or psychical researcher, much less any physical scientist, has ever yet dreamed of what is involved in the deeper aspects of Occultism and Occult Science as a knowledge of the *spiritual* laws of the Cosmos, or of our own nature.   Are not our modern explosives and poison gases already too destructive to entrust to an unregenerate humanity ? What if—as both Tesla and the late Sir Hiram Maxim have suggested—Science should suddenly stumble upon a method of igniting the atmosphere, of effecting some kind of percussion which would instantly re-combine every chemical atom of the globe and explode it into cosmic dust ?   That Science can contemplate, even theoretically, the possibility of such a happening is suggestive to those who realise that there are certain cosmic forces which, if improperly applied, would practically have this effect.

Will it be thought that we are making too large a claim for Occultism when we say that the manipulation of such forces lies within the possible range of acquirement by the individual —not to mention *psychic* forces the manipulation of which could determine the destinies of nations and races for untold ages ?   Well then, let us leave it at that.   But let us remind our readers once more, that our main thesis is the identity of the individual with the universal, with the Absolute, with the Cosmos, *now*, in the full measure and stature of his whole being and nature.   The realisation of this wholeness—which is the province of Occultism—must necessarily bring with it not merely the *acquirement* of power to manipulate every pheno- menal force in the universe, but the actual *identification* of the *Self* with the Cosmos in all its powers, forces, activity, *Life* ; for the Cosmos is the manifestation of the ONE LIFE with which the individual learns to identify himself more and more. Mighty claim, yet the oldest of traditions—Man made in the image and likeness of God : the commencement of the Old Testament, the promise and consummation of the New.

Like many other sayings and promises of the presumed historical Jesus as recorded in the New Testament, which are quietly ignored as being ' impracticable ' : those which refer to the acquirement of occult powers as the necessary result of ' belief,' have long since been utterly discredited by a faith- less Church—which, however, can always fall back upon the *literal* Word in support of its traditional dogmas.   " He that believeth on me, the works that I do shall he do also ; and greater works than these shall he do." [1] " And these signs shall follow them that believe; in my name shall they cast out devils; they shall speak with new tongues ; they shall take up serpents, and if they drink any deadly thing it shall in no wise hurt them ; they shall lay hands on the sick, and they shall recover." [2] These words would appear to be as explicit as, and far more *literal* in their meaning and intent than, many of the passages which are so commonly quoted in support of irrational dogmas, but which can at least have an alternative symbolical interpretation ; whereas the present words are direct and practical. We have to go outside of the Church to-day, however, to ' Christian Science ' and other similar efforts, to find anything approaching an attempt, however imperfect, to realise the literal nature of these sayings in the development of the Christ principle *within* the individual.

The great mystics are historically few and far between, for they are rare blossoms of the flower of humanity. The great occultists are still fewer ; the greatest never known at all to the world as occultists. But in true Occultism as in true Mysticism there are many stages and many degrees of attainment ; and as there has been much spurious Mysticism, so also there has been and is much spurious Occultism. To deal with these perversions here would be out of place. As we have endeavoured to present Mysticism on its true and genuine side, so also we must endeavour to present Occultism, and to show that in the end the one must be complementary to the other. Moreover, we are convinced that in the immediate future they must tend once more to coalesce ; for their artificial separation—or perhaps we should rather say, the failure to recognise their complementary nature—has been due principally to the influence of dogmatic Christianity, which has associated Occult Science wholly with the " Black Art " ; and even to-day mainly associates the undeniable facts of so-called spiritualistic (spiritistic) phenomena with the orthodox Devil and his legions of demons and evil spirits.

Whatever we may believe as to the genuineness or otherwise of the claim of any historical character to be either a mystic or an occultist, there are two principles which are fundamental to the fact or the admitted possibility of either. The first of

[1] John xiv, 12.　　　　　　[2] Mark xvi, 17, 18.

these principles, the identity of the individual with the Absolute in the totality of his nature, we have already sufficiently dwelt upon. The second principle is more or less a corollary of the first. It is that there is an unbroken continuity of Life, represented by various *orders* of beings—of which the individual is only an almost infinitesimal unit—from what we arbitrarily call the 'lowest,' to that which we call the 'highest'; and that there is an unbroken line of communication through all these; so that, at whatever stage the individual may be, he will always find the possibility of communicating with individuals —whether incarnate or discarnate—who represent a further stage than that which he has himself attained. Thus in *principle* we are bound to believe in Masters, Initiates, Christs, and Buddhas, in unbroken line up to the Logos Himself, whatever we may believe respecting any particular historical character, or the claims of any particular individual. To each one of us must be sufficient in this matter the evidence personally received of the particular line of communication which has been opened up for him. There is no one favoured channel, no one community or cult, which can offer *the* knowledge or *the* method. By few or many stages, few or many lives, by various routes, direct or devious, the individual comes at last to that stage which is sometimes spoken of as the *beginning* of the 'Way'; the stage at which he definitely sees his goal and bends the whole of his energies towards its attainment. And after that, he may be in one incarnation a mystic and in another an occultist, passing through many degrees and phases, but at each step realising more and more completely—if happily he have no back-slidings—his unity with that great LIFE which *is* the Cosmos, and also HIMSELF.

Each individual assuredly, *qua* individual, fulfils a function in the great unity of COSMIC MAN, even as every atom and cell and microbe fulfils a function in the unitary whole of our physical bodies. And if one is called upon to be "a vessel unto honour, and another unto dishonour: what is that unto thee, O man: who art thou that repliest against God?" against the cosmic Law of the *Whole*? And if now, perchance, anyone may consider himself to be a vessel unto honour, let him consider well that at one time in the vast Cosmic Process he was certainly a vessel unto dishonour, and may very possibly be so again; until, indeed, he has haply realised that from the standpoint of *Wholeness*—or, if you prefer so to formulate it, in the consciousness of God—there is neither honour nor dishonour, neither good nor evil. " I form the light and create darkness ; I make peace and create evil ; I am the Lord, that doeth all these things." [1]

The mystic consciousness carries us to a region where these dualities and antitheses are transcended in a manner which, for the time being, gives the completest satisfaction to the emotional nature, and even, to a certain extent, to the intellectual nature also ; but the mystic has no control over these ecstatic flights, and, being untrained in the use of his vehicles of consciousness on the higher planes, he cannot sustain his flights, nor can he observe the cosmic relations and happenings which pertain thereto. Thus St. Augustine says :

" And then at last I saw Thy invisible things understood by means of the things that are made, but I could not sustain my gaze : my weakness was dashed back, and I was relegated to my ordinary experience, bearing with me nothing but a loving remembrance, cherishing, as it were, the fragrance of those viands which I was not yet able to feed upon." [2]

Similar passages may be found in most of the records of the devotional mystics, and will be noted in the extracts which we have already given in Chapter VIII from *The Golden Fountain* as illustrating the method and content of the mystic consciousness.

In Occultism, on the other hand, the various vehicles of consciousness are definitely trained, and the aspirant gradually advances under the guidance of an Initiate who is already master of the higher vehicles or subtle bodies which exist *now* for every one of us, but in which we, for the most part, function quite unconscious of their existence. This training involves *moral* qualities which are as much in advance of ordinary religious morality as occult science is in advance of ordinary physical science ; and just as we have had to make a distinction between Religion as a quality of life, and religion as a formulated creed or moral law, so also we must make a distinction between Occultism as a *spiritual* science, and Occultism as a mere knowledge of occult phenomena. It would be better to refer to the latter as occult science, and reserve the term Occultism for the former.

---

[1] Isaiah xlv, 7. [2] *Confessions,* Book VII, chap. xvii.

We may now turn our attention to the question and the general principle of the nature of those higher vehicles of consciousness, or subtle ' bodies,' which in the ordinary individual constitute the sub-consciousness of the sub-liminal and supra-liminal regions of the wholeness of his nature, but of which he has no definite knowledge ; which in the mystic become more or less sporadically active in vision or in illumination or ecstasy, but still without definite knowledge ; and which in the occultist become more or less normal and known vehicles of his conscious activity, under the direct control of his trained and purified will.

CHAPTER X

MAN AND HIS BODIES

" Rise after rise bow the phantoms behind me,
Afar down I see the huge first Nothing—the vapour from the
Nostrils of Death—I know I was even there,
I waited unseen and always, and slept while God carried me through
    the lethargic mist,
And took my time, and took no hurt from the fetid carbon.

Long was I hugged close—long and long.

Immense have been the preparations for me,
Faithful and friendly arms that have helped me.

Cycles ferried my cradle, rowing and rowing like cheerful boatmen,
For room to me stars kept aside in their own rings,
They sent influences to look after what was to hold me.

Before I was born out of my mother, generations guided me,
My embryo has never been torpid—nothing could overlay it.

For it the nebula cohered to an orb,
The long slow strata piled to rest it on,
Vast vegetables gave it sustenance,
Monstrous sauroids transported it in their mouths, and deposited it
    with care.

All forces have been steadily employed to complete and delight me,
Now I stand on this spot with my Soul.''

WALT WHITMAN : Leaves of Grass.

CHAPTER X

MAN AND HIS BODIES

It is tolerably evident—altogether apart from any metaphysical speculations as to the ultimate nature of Life and Consciousness, or the modes of their manifestation—that if we are to believe in any conscious entities or beings whatsoever in the Universe, whether of a cosmic or of a more limited nature, which have their existence independent of physical matter, or physical bodies ; or if we are to believe in any manner in our own conscious survival of bodily death : such individual survival, or such entities or beings, must have some substantial vehicle or *body* in or through which Life and Consciousness subsist, function, or manifest objectively.

It is also fairly evident that in our own case such a body or vehicle cannot spring into existence as the result of the death of the physical body ; it must exist now as, in some sense, the energising principle or *soul* of that body ; and, in fact, the ' death ' of the body must be due simply to the withdrawal of this *soul*, or *subtle body*, or, as it is more commonly termed, *spirit*, when the body is no longer able, by reason of injury or otherwise, to function as its vehicle. These three terms— body, soul, and spirit—are, however, commonly and even philosophically used in such a variety of ways that it will be necessary here to define more precisely the sense in which they are employed in this work, and more particularly in our present chapter.

The term *body* stands for any outwardly manifested or *objective* vehicle of Life and Consciousness, *on whatever plane of perception such a body may exist.* It is the outer garment of the soul and spirit, whether it be a physical body, or an ' astral body,' or a ' spiritual body.' When St. Paul says, " If there is a natural body, there is also a spiritual body ": we are inclined to say, *naturally*. Any *objective* ' spiritual ' world must certainly contain ' bodies ' and " a world full of real things and the like," as truly as our present world ; though it is also as certain that they will be totally different in their characteristics and action and interaction from that which pertains to our limited perceptions and consciousness under physical plane conditions. Broadly we may say, that the conditions of each ' higher ' plane must be characterised by greater freedom, greater permanency, and greater universality in the sense of a more unitary or cosmic consciousness.

We may note here once more—for it is the fundamental concept of our working hypothesis—that what we may call the *physical* difficulty—which lies at the root of Materialism—of believing in any objective world apart from physical matter, a world as ' real ' as that of our present senses and perceptions, is completely overcome when we have realised that what we call physical matter is only certain very limited modes of motion in a space-filling Substance. Other modes of motion we appreciate as light, sound, electricity, etc., but in a last analysis it is Consciousness, and Consciousness alone, which assigns to these modes their respective values, calling some of them ' matter ' and others ' force,' some ' red ' and others ' blue.' It is, therefore, quite easy to appreciate that since what we refer to as other *planes* of Substance are simply other modes of motion, other *forms* in and of the Primordial Substance, it is just as easy for Consciousness to make an objective world and substantial bodies out of any other of these modes and forms, as it is to make up our present world of physical perceptions. All ' worlds,' we conceive, are made in Consciousness on precisely the same terms. We might even look at the matter physically so far as space is concerned, for when we have realised the vast interspaces between the physical atoms, and got rid of the idea that *size* has anything to do with consciousness, we see at once that any number of objective worlds may interpenetrate our actual physical material world, and even be much more ' real ' in just the same physical sense that the Ether is millions of times ' denser ' than physical matter ; and also because " matter is composed mainly of holes," and the actual space occupied by the atoms in, say, a cubic centimetre, is infinitesimal compared with the interspaces. The difficulty, of course, must remain for that class of intelligence which needs a material concept even for God himself; indeed, we might trace the grossly material conceptions of the early Christians respecting the Second Coming of Christ, and the establishment of His Kingdom almost immediately on this Earth, and the necessity in consequence that we should have physical bodies, and must therefore assume these again out of the grave—and from this the doctrine of the resurrection of the body—to this same common difficulty of conceiving of any world as being objective or *real* other than the material world of our present perceptions. Even nowadays we are commonly asked, *Where* is this objective ' spirit ' world ? : as if it could not be *here*, even in terms of our physical concepts of matter. The term *body*, then, stands for the *objectivity* of a thing on any plane of consciousness.

The term *soul* as commonly employed refers to the incorporeal nature of man, and therefore directly implies the *present* existence of a *substantial* vehicle in which the individual characteristics of self-consciousness, reason, will, emotion, etc., inhere. In this sense it is more or less commonly identified with the term *spirit*, but this latter term will only be used here as the final or ' highest ' term of any particular manifestation : as the innermost principle, which must always be *subjective*. It is the *spirit* which *manifests* in or through soul and body. Soul on its own plane is substantial and objective, though it is not commonly so conceived, since it is subjective relatively to body. We have already seen in Chapter II that Ether is the soul of physical matter. It is *substantial*, " millions of times " more substantial than physical matter ; yet we cannot—as yet—appreciate it by any physical tests, but only surmise its existence by its effects in the physical world. It therefore stands precisely in the same relation to physical matter that our own soul does to our present body ; it is the energising principle ; but this relationship will be understood better as we proceed, when it will be seen that all three terms, body, soul, spirit, are relative, and that what is at present *soul* will, after death, become *body*—and yet there will still be a *soul*.

When we say that spirit is the *final* term, we do not mean the Absolute, or ' pure Being,' or God as the ' Godhead ' : for these are not a *term*, are not the end or summation of a series, but are the *Wholeness* of ALL, and are, therefore, outside and beyond all relations, classifications, or definitions. The word 'Spirit' is never used, either in philosophy or in theology, as a synonym for the Absolute. Spirit is simply the final term of *Manifestation*, of that aspect of the Absolute which we view as Becoming. We can only, therefore, say that "God is (a) Spirit" in the case of the hypostasised 'Persons' of the Divine Trinity; and—as we have already seen in Chapter V—it is only by means of this hypostasis that we are able to speak of a 'spiritual *plane*,' for that plane is the plane of the Logos, which it is legitimate to consider as having a relation to the 'lower' planes of the Cosmos, and as being the highest term in Manifestation. "All things were made through him; and without him was not anything made that hath been made."

Let us clearly understand that by Manifestation is to be understood that schematised plan of the Universe which we are obliged to formulate within our empirical consciousness of time and space: that is to say anything of which we are compelled to affirm that "in the beginning," and subsequently, something took place. We must never forget that any such scheme, however 'inspired,' is always within the limitations of the formal mind, and as such it must be merely a working hypothesis. It will be indigent of truth precisely to the extent that our empirical perceptions and conceptual notions of time and space are indigent and defective. The universe can never be 'explained' otherwise than in terms of MAN—until, indeed, Man realises, and thus 'becomes' what he is now, in the Wholeness of his nature, GOD.

But manifestation is a relative term. The Absolute ever-concealed Godhead is manifested in the Divine Trinity; the Divine Trinity is manifested in the Logos, who is the synthesis of the Trinity; this, however, being generally expressed in theology by saying that the 'Father' is manifested in the 'Son.' The Logos in his turn is manifested in, or as, Cosmic Man on the lower planes of the Cosmos; whilst Cosmic Man is again manifested in individual man.[1]

If now we wish to inquire more particularly as to the nature and relations of those cosmic vehicles of Consciousness which belong to the real or Cosmic Man, and their

[1] See Diagram, *infra* p. 337.

operation and function in the individual man, or temporary personality: we have three sources of information, (a) the more or less openly taught doctrines of the Occult Schools, (b) the teaching of such seers as Böhme or Swedenborg, and (c) ancient tradition and Scripture. We shall find correspondences in all of these which we may collate and re-present in our own manner, so as to exhibit in a concise form the principles both of Mysticism and of Occultism which form the main thesis of this present work.

(a) As regards the teachings of the Occult Schools, since these vary in many respects in the methods of their formulation according to whether they are based upon the Eastern Yoga or Vedânta philosophy, or the Western Hermetic, Rosicrucian, or Kabalistic systems : it would be entirely out of place here to attempt to give any details. We might summarise the teachings by saying that they all agree in this, that Man is the *measure* of the Universe ; individual man being the microcosm of the Macrocosm. The fundamental principle of all knowledge is therefore correspondence and analogy : " as above so below"; whilst the fundamental method is " man know thyself." No man can know God in any greater measure than he knows himself, and he rises through such self-knowledge to the apprehension of a unitary supreme knowledge or Wisdom which, so long as he imagines himself to be a separate self, he ascribes to a separate ' God.' The primary object of all Occultism, therefore, is self-knowledge, that is to say, knowledge and control of all and every vehicle in or through which the *Self* functions on every plane of the Cosmos. We have already sufficiently distinguished this from Mysticism in our previous chapter.

We might note here, that so far as the *soul* of our present physical body is concerned, what was previously taught only in the Occult Schools is now becoming matter for ' orthodox ' scientific investigation ; we are beginning to know something about it practically and empirically through psychical research, whilst psychology in general, and psycho-analysis in particular, is investigating in a more or less empirical manner the content and working of that *soul* considered as *mind*. We should prefer, however, in this connection, to take mind to be, *relatively*, the subjective *self* of the incarnate individual, standing one remove further back than *soul* : this latter being rather the psychic or 'astral' principle. Mind, therefore, in this relation, is the *subject* or Ego. We must not forget, however, that the formal mind of the incarnated Ego, though largely determined as to its thought-forms, or 'complexes,' by reason of its action and interaction with the outer material world, nevertheless can, and in most cases does, receive also from 'within' in the form of intuition, or 'spiritual' inspiration. This assumes in general the character of religious instinct: and, in passing through the formal mind, becomes materialised as creed, dogma, or 'belief.'

(*b*) In Swedenborg and Böhme we have some definite teachings which are more or less concise and self-contained. In Böhme especially, we have a comprehensive vision of the Absolute, both as Being and as Becoming, which is unique and unapproached in the literature of any age; though it needs a good deal of study before the uncouth language can be sufficiently mastered to appreciate the untold wealth of spiritual knowledge contained in his writings. Making all due allowances for the theological form of much of it, we find it to be in accord with the very best traditions of Occultism, and easily harmonised therewith.

We may note with both Swedenborg and Böhme a most fundamental recognition of a primary tripartite division or operation of *Principles* in the Manifested Universe or Cosmos. With Swedenborg this is what he calls the "three discrete degrees"; with Böhme they are what he calls "The Three Principles of the Divine Essence," having their correspondence in "The Threefold Life of Man": these Principles being expounded at length in two of his works which are thus entitled. Speaking of his knowledge and writings in general, Böhme says in his Second Epistle (par. 15):

"My book hath only three leaves, the same are the three principles of eternity, wherein I can find all whatsoever Moses and the prophets, Christ and his apostles have taught and spoken; I can find therein the foundation of the world and all mysteries; yet not I, but the spirit of God, doth it according to the measure, as He pleaseth."

In his Fifth Epistle (pars. 40, 41) he says:

"Man is the true similitude or image of God, as the precious man Moses testifieth; not only an earthly image (for the sake whereof God would not have become man, and put forth, unite, and espouse his heart and spirit [in deepest love] after the fall into it), but he is originally out of the Being of all beings, out of all the three worlds, viz. out of the innermost nature world, which is also the most outward, and is called the dark world, whence the principle of the fiery nature taketh its rise, as is declared *at large* in my book of *The Threefold Life*. And secondly, he is out of the light, or angelical world, out of the true Being of God; and then thirdly, he is out of this external world of the sun, stars, and elements, an entire image of God, out of the Being (*Wesen*) of all beings."

Further, in his Sixth Epistle (par. 41) he identifies Man's *spiritual* body with the Logos in the following words:

"With his spiritual body he is the true essential word of the divine property (*Göttlicher Eigenschaft*), in which God speaketh and begetteth His word, and there the divine science doth distribute, import, impress, form, and beget itself to an image of God."

His language here is clear and intelligible, and comes into line with all that we know of in occult tradition. Were it not that his vision was entirely involuntary, and attributed by him solely to "the spirit of God" working as it pleased within him, we should have to classify him as an occultist. We can hardly refrain, indeed, from speculating that in previous lives he must have acquired the knowledge and reached a high degree of initiation. No mere piety or devotion will give it: else why do none of the classical mystics display it?

No clearer statement of the fundamental principle of Occultism, that all knowledge lies in self-knowledge, could be given than is found in the following paragraph from the Ninth Epistle (par. 3).

"For the book in which all mysteries lie is man himself; he himself is the book of the Being (*Wesen*) of all beings; seeing he is the likeness (or similitude) of God; the great *Arcanum* lieth *in* him, the revealing of it belongeth only unto God's spirit."[1]

When we turn to Swedenborg we find that his doctrine is practically the same. Cosmic Man contains within himself the whole Manifested Universe, and is God's self-expression. The terminology, however, is somewhat different. The Universe he designates "The Grand Man"; and perhaps we might say that with him God is rather the Divine Man than Man the Divine God. Swedenborg's doctrine of discrete degrees is briefly as follows. Every act implies three factors: (*a*) the

[1] Is there any real difference between this and the Vedânta doctrine, "Verily he who has seen, heard, comprehended, and known the Self, by him is this entire universe known"?

act itself, constituting the external event; (*b*) a psychological process as the *immediate* cause of the act, and (*c*) a motive or purpose as the *originating* cause of the act.   In his own terminology these are, effect, cause and end, and they also correspond with organism, function, and faculty.   Cosmically we might represent these as Material World, Cosmic Mind (or Man), and God—the latter being principally identified with Love as the originating cause.   Or we might analyse them into the three principles of man as, (*a*) Body or Form (action, phenomenon), (*b*) Mind or Ideation (or perhaps Imagination), and (*c*) Emotion (or perhaps Will).

With Swedenborg also, as with Böhme, and occult teachings in general, each of the three primary principles is further divisible into a similar triplicity; and we might, indeed, find further tripartite sub-divisions, each in its turn being a *limitation* of the more cosmic aspect.   We shall illustrate this more in detail a little later on.

We may note a similar triple classification made use of by Fabre d'Olivette in his work on the *Hermeneutic Interpretation of the Origin of the Social State of Man and of the Destiny of the Adamic Race*, which is practically a synthesis of all the ancient traditions and historical records: made by a man of marvellous learning and scholarship.   Fabre d'Olivette entitles his three principles, respectively, Providence, Man (Cosmic), and Destiny; and his work is an effort to interpret history in terms of these principles.

(*c*) We may now turn to Greek philosophy, which contains so much of the Gnôstic, Eleusinian and other Mystery Traditions.[1]

The threefold division to which we have referred appears in this tradition in a somewhat different form.   We have in the first instance *soul* as the highest and purely immaterial principle: that which we are accustomed to call Spirit.   We have in the second place a subtle body of a *substantial* nature as the vehicle of the soul; and in the third place we have the *physical* body. The principal teaching centres round the nature and fate of the subtle body after death, when it becomes the 'spirit' (*pneûma*), the 'image' (*eidôlon*), or the 'shade' (*skia*).   There is a dis-

---

[1] The information here given is largely summarised from G. R. S. Mead's *The Doctrine of the Subtle Body in Western Tradition*, London, J. M. Watkins. 1919.   This work should be read by every student of our present subject,

tinct recognition that all the inner or subtle bodies are of the same substance, and that their various appearances simply manifest, and correspond with, the qualities of the immortal ' soul ' : being readily moulded in this respect by the ' imagination ' of the soul. This concept as to the power and function of the imagination is clearly set forth in the following quotation from Synesius.[1]

"For this (power of imagination) is the (one) sense of (all differentiated) senses, seeing that the spirit (*pneûma*), whereby the imagination is brought into play, is the most general sensory and the first body of the soul. It has its seat in the innermost place, and dominates the living creature, as it were from a citadel. For round it nature has built up the whole economy of the head."

This ' imagination,' according to these teachings, can even materialise a physically visible body for the discarnate individual, either of its own will if that be sufficiently powerful, or by the help of ' daimons.' (Spiritists please note.)

It is further recognised that the ' spirit-body ' has two distinct aspects—a higher in which it becomes the ' Radiant Augoeides ' or Body of Light, and a lower in which it partakes of, or is moulded by, our animal-human nature, or animal soul. In a certain sense these two aspects may exist simultaneously as being more or less in the nature of two distinct bodies. Thus Philoponus says :

"There is, moreover, beyond this (spirituous body) another kind of body, that is for ever attached to (the soul), of a celestial nature and for this reason everlasting, which they call radiant (*augoeidés*) or starlike (*astroeidés*)."[2]

We shall now endeavour to synthesise these various teachings, so as to present them as being more or less in harmony with the principles we are endeavouring to elucidate in this work. For that purpose we shall find that we shall obtain very considerable aid from a geometrical diagram, which will indicate not merely the individual principles in their cosmic aspects, but also their relational values when considered in a more limited manner. The diagram which is here given has been partly suggested by a somewhat similar one given by Fabre d'Olivette in his work already referred to. The geometrical symbols used are to be met with in many different

[1] Cf. Mead, p. 93.   [2] Loc. cit., p. 88.

systems in all ages, back to the remotest antiquity.   They are :
the point, the circle, the diameter, the cross, the triangle, and
the interlaced triangles (Solomon's Seal).   This geometrical
symbolism will be found to be expounded at considerable
length in H. P. Blavatsky's voluminous work *The Secret
Doctrine.*

Let us construct our diagram first of all as representing
the process of creation or emanation.

(*a*) " In the beginning God created the heaven and the
earth."   Apart altogether from the misleading translation
of this passage, we find that any account of the process of
creation or manifestation in Time [1] must necessarily commence
with a " In the beginning " ; and if we ask, What was there
before the beginning ? who shall give any answer ?   In the
language of the ancient *Veda*, so beautifully rendered by
Colebrooke :

> "Nor Aught nor Nought existed ; yon bright sky
> Was not, nor heaven's broad roof outstretched above.
> The only One breathed breathless by Itself,
> Other than It there nothing since has been."

Now we may represent this " beginning " by a circle.
Before we draw the circle, the " only One," the Unmanifested,

the Causeless-Cause, the Absolute, the Godhead, is represented
by the blank plane of the paper on which we construct our
diagram ; and when we have drawn our circle it is still so represented ; for, " Other than It there nothing since has been."
For the *intellect*, however, IT is now both transcendent and
immanent, or Being and Becoming—a fundamental duality
represented diagramatically by the outside and the inside
of the circle, but still the *Ground* of the inside as well as of the
outside.   Böhme—in language which cannot here be said to
be obscure or uncouth—states this fundamental concept in
the following terms :

" God (what He is in Himself) is neither nature nor creature, neither
this nor that, neither high nor deep ; He is the Abyss, and the Byss
of all beings (*der Ungrund und Grund aller Wesen*), the eternal One ;

---

[1] The moment we speak of anything as taking place in *Time*, we
have come down into the region of formal mind and—illusion.

where there is no ground or place (*Grund noch Stätte*) ; He is to the creature in its strength (or capacity) *a nothing, and yet is through all things*. Nature is *His something* wherewith He makes Himself visible, sensible, and perceivable, both according to eternity and time. All things are arisen through the divine imagination, and do yet stand in such a birth, station, or government."[1]

The circle, then, represents the field or ground of Manifestation ; all that can be known of the ever-concealed Absolute is contained within its boundary, and has *relational* aspects. It stands for the first abstract concept of the manifested universe that is to be, and therefore it is the first abstract concept of *Substance* as distinguished from *Principle*, or of *Matter* as distinguished from *Spirit*. It is the stage referred to in *Genesis* as " without form and void." There is still " Darkness upon the face of the deep "—the " waters " (of space). The content of the circle, the " World Egg," is as yet undifferentiated.

(*b*) The first stage or ' day ' in the *Genesis* narrative is the creation of *Light* in contrast with the previous *Darkness* ; and this first creation of Light is quite distinct from the creation of the light-giving bodies, the Sun and the Moon (verses 14, 15, 16). It might be considered, therefore, as a variant of the primal duality already referred to as Principle and Substance ; the content of the circle being the Light which manifests the Darkness of the ever-concealed Causeless-Cause outside or beyond the circle. We may, however, likewise consider it as the commencement of differentiation in the hitherto abstract undifferentiated Substance contained within the limits of the circle ; and, as such, it may be regarded as the appear-

ance of a nucleus, or germ-cell : symbolised by a point within the circle.

(*c*) The second ' day ' of creation is said to be the separa-

tion of the "waters" (primordial space-filling Substance) into a

[1] *Sixth Epistle*, pars. 76, 77, 78.

duality of ' above ' and ' below,' and is appropriately symbolised by a horizontal diameter. In Biology we have the primitive germinal cell separating into two, four, eight, sixteen, etc., similar cells in what is known as the *morula* stage.[1]

(*d*) The next addition to our symbolical diagram is the vertical diameter, which, in combination with the horizontal diameter, forms the well-known symbol of the Cross within the Circle. It is the highest aspect of the profoundly mystical

symbol of the Cross. The Cross without the circle represents a much lower aspect, and—apart from its use as a Christian symbol—it has been largely associated with Phallic worship. Contained within the circle it represents the Divine Man, the Logos, Cosmic Man " crucified in space." The combination of the cross and the circle is also largely used in the symbolism of astronomy, and may be traced to very ancient sources. With the coming into existence of this divine or cosmic *Man* we have the completion of the first or divine Triad or Trinity of Father-Mother-Son, or Principle-Substance-Form, whilst the third ' Person ' of this Trinity not merely manifests— as containing within his own essential nature—the higher incognisable ' Godhead,' but also is the synthesis of all the ' lower ' stages or aspects of Manifestation : the remainder of the six ' days ' of creation. This synthesis is, however, as yet simply the abstract *Idea* of the Cosmos that is to be.

(*e*) We shall now find it necessary to represent this primordial abstract Triad or *divine* Trinity—by whatever name the three ' Persons ' of it may be called—by a separate symbol, that of the triangle. But in so far as any such divine Trinity must be considered in a relational aspect to the lower planes of

manifestation, those lower planes must be viewed as, in their turn, manifesting the divine Triad, just as this latter manifests the Absolute. This duality of an upper and a lower Triad

---

[1] Cf. *Scientific Idealism*, p. 262.

or Trinity—which thus repeats the primordial duality (each triangle being taken as a unit) with which we have already dealt—is symbolised by the interlaced triangles : the lower being as it were a mirror reflection of the upper, and thus shown inverted. The two together give us the number six, and the six taken with the point in the centre as representing the Absolute, or the synthesis of the six, give us the number seven : the ever-recurring number in ancient cosmogenesis and symbolisms.

In some systems, as for example in the Kabalah, these seven are considered to be seven great primordial creative Potencies or Beings, coming into existence subsequently to the first or divine Triad, which is placed still higher. The seven, together with this higher Triad, make up the ' perfect ' number ten. To symbolise this we should have to represent the divine Triad by another triangle *outside* the circle, as being more abstract

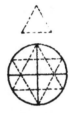

even than the first Triad we have already dealt with. It may be represented by a small triangle above the circle.

It may be noted here that if we wish to visualise our diagram as a sphere instead of a plane surface, we should have to conceive another axis passing through the centre point at right angles to the plane of the paper. This will give us the necessary three ' dimensions ' of space required for a solid. The monad becomes a duad, the duad a triad, and the triad a tetrad, " the three fall into four." Another method of enumerating the *four* is to take any individual triad and reckon all above it as unity. Thus if we take the divine Triad as *three*, and the Absolute or ONE beyond it as *unity*, we have the " Divine Tetraktys " of Pythagoras.[1]

Although the divine Triad or Trinity is *relatively* a manifestation, it is too abstract for us to speak of it rightly as belonging to the *manifested* Cosmos as extended in time and space. It is synthesised in the Logos, but the Logos—" what He is in Himself," as Böhme would say—is beyond time

---

[1] Cf. *supra*, p. 130.

and space. He is Böhme's second Principle of the " Three Principles of the Divine Essence": the Principle of *Light*. The first Principle, the Godhead, Böhme calls *Fire*: as also we find in several ancient philosophical systems, as well as in the Old Testament. The *Light*—which we saw to be associated in the first place with the dawn of manifestation— is now transferred to, and associated with, the Logos, who becomes the " Light of the World"; and in the individual, " the light which lighteth every man coming into the world" —the indwelling Christ principle. Only in the outermost and most materialised form of the doctrine is this 'light' the reputed personal historical Jesus.

This completes our widest and most abstract view of Manifestation as symbolised by our diagram; and in order to carry it to a further differentiation, so as to be applicable in a number of details in respect of both cosmic and individual man, we may fill it in as per the accompanying completed drawing.

We shall first of all represent the primordial Triad—which in reality fills the whole space of the circle, and is represented by the large dotted triangle—by three separate interpenetrative circles; and these will now stand for *Cosmic* Spirit, Soul, and Body: or the Principle, Substance, and Form of the actual Universe in their first or abstract aspects. Each of these will in its turn have three aspects, and these we shall represent by a separate triangle—represented in dark lines— within each circle. The upper or divine Triad now stands related to the two lower ones as Spirit to Soul and Body.

Considering the formation of Soul and Body as successive stages in the World-Process symbolised by the whole of the diagram, we may say that in the first instance the upper or 'divine' Triad is reflected downwards into time and space; and this reflection is represented by the large inverted dotted triangle. This is the aspect when viewed from 'above'; but when viewed from 'below' we have to make this reflected Triad our actual substantial world: it becomes the present 'reality' of the objective world, and will therefore, in the first instance, be represented by the second thick-lined triangle; whilst the first or higher Triad now appears to be subjective, and becomes the inverted interlaced dotted triangle of this second Triad. In the world of *appearance*, the Reality has always an inverted aspect. It is in this second Triad that we may conceive of substantial *Form* as being really 'born'; and with *Form* are also born the first or highest aspects of time and space, which, however, will here have nothing like the limited character which we associate with these in our present physical consciousness. We may say broadly that all Forms will, on this plane, be interpenetrative: any 'thing' can exist any 'where'; any 'event' is a *now*, and does not belong to either past or future.

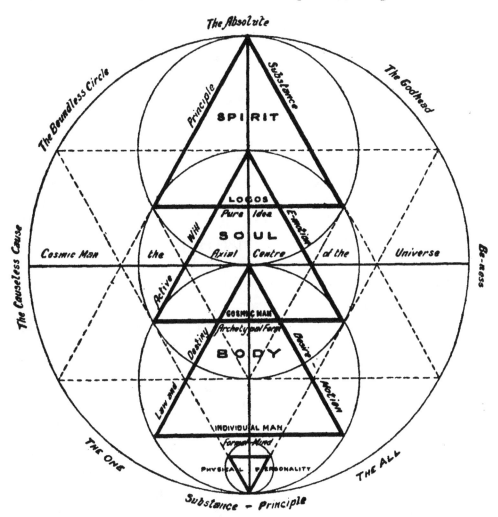

The second Triad, or *Soul*, is reflected downwards in its turn into *Body*. As with the higher Triad, it is represented first of all by an inverted triangle; but when Body becomes the substantial or 'real' objective world, it must be symbolised by the third thick-lined triangle; the higher Triad now being subjective, and represented by the interlaced dotted and inverted triangle.

Finally, we may place at the bottom of our diagram a small inverted thick-lined triangle to represent the temporal physical personality, the relation of which to the higher Triads will be explained presently.

We may now note the values and correspondences of the various Principles of the three Triads, as represented by the three sides of the triangles in each respectively. The highest Triad we have already seen to be divisible into Principle, Substance, and Form ; the *Form*, however, in this case being simply abstract *Idea*. In the second Triad the principles which are passive and abstract—relatively—in the first Triad, become active and concrete or objective. Many different terms might be given for the correspondences between the first and the second Triads, but we have here selected those which appear to express in the simplest manner the concepts we are endeavouring to elucidate. We shall say, then, that what we have called *Principle* in the upper Triad becomes active *Will* at the next remove ; what we have called *Substance* becomes *E-motion* ; and what we have called pure *Idea* becomes *Archetypal Form* ; this latter, as we have noted above, being a multiplicity of interpenetrative forms : a first remove as it were from pure formless Idea.

It may not be quite clear how Substance becomes Emotion, or E-motion. E-motion, however, is a *moving out*, and in that sense may be taken as the equivalent of the substantial basis or root cause of motion. The highest emotion is Love ; and many mystics have conceived that possibly the *substantial* nature of God may be conceived to be Love rather than anything else. Without pressing this point, however, we find it necessary to introduce Emotion as one of the trinity of principles belonging to our second Triad : the other two being, Will and Thought. We then come into line with the usual analysis of the *psyche* or *soul* into the three elements of intellect, feeling, and will. We may say more generally in reference to this Triad, that the combination of Will and Emotion—overshadowed by the higher *Idea* of the Logos—results in the production of Archetypal Thought-Forms in the Cosmic Mind ; that is to say in Cosmic Man, who is represented by this second Triad. The divine Logos—represented by the base line of the first Triad—has here definitely become Cosmic Man—represented by the base line of the second Triad.

At the next remove or descent into Matter we shall have the same correspondences, but with still more restricted and limited characteristics. The second Triad becomes subjective relatively to the third Triad; it is to the third Triad what the first is to the second. It may be noted that the base line of each higher Triad corresponds with the apex of the Triad below; and from the point of view of the consciousness special to each Triad, this apex is the ONE, the Absolute. Nothing can be known beyond it so long as consciousness is limited to the sphere enclosing that Triad; but the influence of the higher Triad is felt as an overshadowing power, if the faculties of the mind be turned inwards.

In the third Triad we have the active *Will* of the second Triad becoming *Law and Destiny*; we have *Emotion* becoming *Desire*; and we have *Archetypal Form* becoming *Formal Mind*; whilst *Cosmic Man* now becomes *Individual Man*.

We shall not yet conceive of this Individual Man, however, as being the present physical personality; for this latter is a much lower manifestation than the real individual Ego. Not merely is it limited and restricted by the conditions of the physical plane, in a manner which we must conceive to be quite foreign to the real Ego on its own plane—that of the third Triad—but it has the merest ephemeral life in the cosmic history and development of that Ego. It is represented, therefore, by the small inverted triangle at the base of the diagram. Nevertheless, even as an atom contains and reflects the *Whole*, so this ephemeral personality is seen to occupy the very apex of the inverted macrocosmic Triad.

Individual Man, or the individual *Ego*—represented by the third Triad—may be said to be a *monad*; and Cosmic Man —represented by the second Triad—may be said to be collectively a host of such *monads*; even as our physical body is a host of monads or microcosmic lives. The host of monads constituting the *body* of Cosmic Man may possibly be thought of as having some conceptual resemblance to the monads of Leibnitz.

Looking at the diagram as a whole, we see that whilst the three Triads represent *macrocosmically* the Body, Soul, and Spirit of the Cosmos: *microcosmically* or relatively, each has its own body, soul, and spirit; but always overshadowed by a ' higher '; so that even the divine Trinity is overshadowed

by the Absolute or ' Godhead ' beyond it. We may note that
Cosmic Man is the centre of the whole. His sphere lies in the
centre ; he has above him the Logos ; within him the Archetypal
World ; and below him the individual manifestations of the
material objective universe—which are his own creations.

We are now in a position to consider Manifestation as a
process rather more in detail, proceeding from above downwards. We have already dealt sufficiently in Chapter V
with the necessity for the concept of the first Triad or
divine Trinity, and we may now ask : How does pure *Idea*
become *Archetypal Form*, and subsequently Formal Mind
and physical material form ?

We are not altogether without the means of apprehending
how an objective world of form can arise out of pure subjective
idea, for we possess and exercise the same power in our dream
consciousness. In dreams we *dramatise* the subjective content
of the mind into all kinds of fantastic objective experiences—
fantastic in the judgment of the more formal waking consciousness, but not to the dream consciousness itself. The *ideas*
existing in the mind are in fact non-spatial and non-temporal ;
they are compenetrative, and any two or more may be taken
quite apart from what we appreciate as their more ' natural '
relationship and sequence in our normal waking consciousness,
and juxtaposed to make the dream drama : having the apparent
extension in time and space which we associate with our normal
consciousness of ' events.' When we awake we say that our
dreams were not ' real,' that the objects we saw had no true
existence : though veridical dreams, and dreams predictive
of ' real ' events, are by no means uncommon. Still, even in
the ordinary uncontrolled dream, things are objectively *real*
enough, and at all events the *ideas* really exist in the mind.
It is not difficult in almost every case to trace a dream to some
definite idea subjectively present in the mind ; and it is curious
how very slight the idea may be to produce a very solid dream.
Thus the fact of having seen a number of catkins lying on the
ground, and having carefully avoided treading on one, thinking
that it was a caterpillar, dramatised itself the next night
in the present writer's consciousness as a number of caterpillars in a bath which he wished to take, but could not
because he could not clear it of caterpillars. The idea of *bath*
was, of course, brought in from another experience. But dreams

can also be an orderly and rational drama, as in the case of R. L. Stevenson's novels, or Anna Kingsford's *Dreams and Dream Stories*. It is at least a not incomprehensible proposition that—given the Logos as representing the divine *Idea* of the Cosmos in all its potentiality in the Divine Mind or Consciousness—the manifested or objective Cosmos will become the *dramatisation* of those *Ideas* in various ways on various planes of Consciousness, and in various individual beings of a more or less limited nature who are capable of repeating the original process. "The original of all things," says Böhme, "lieth in the Idea, in an eternal imaging."[1] It is, indeed, extremely useful and stimulating to consider *events* as such a dramatisation. In themselves they have only an arbitrary or empirical 'reality' in consciousness, and they need not necessarily follow the sequence of our waking consciousness, nor have the time factor which we there ascribe to them; yet they reveal or manifest—could we but read them aright—eternal *Ideas* of Truth, Beauty, and Goodness, or that Absolute Reality in which all Ideas, all possible Universes, already exist, and are compenetrative, and can be combined or dramatised in an infinite variety of *manifested* Universes. What value, indeed, have manifested Universes at all, except as a revelation of these Eternal Ideas, which are the only fundamental *Reality* we can conceive of as having eternal Duration?

When these Eternal Ideas in the mind of the Logos take objective form and shape, we have not merely the birth of time and space, but also the birth of *Substance*; for we have to consider them empirically as substantial forms, whether on the 'spiritual' or on any lower plane. We may say that they come into existence in the first instance as an act of ideation on the part of the Logos, such act having that 'creative' power whereby to *think* a thing is to bring it immediately into objective existence. This is precisely analogous to what we do in our dreams; but in dream we have ordinarily no power to fix or control these objectivisations, or to relate them with what we are pleased to call in our waking state of consciousness the 'real' world. But is this 'real' world truly more real, more permanent, than the dream world, or is it not merely that it has a different *time factor* and a communal validity? It is our common experience that our 'real'

[1] *Theosophic Questions*, 12, par. 4.

world is not really permanent from moment to moment, that it is a perpetual flux and becoming; and, indeed, we have mathematical physics taking such absolute abstractions or *unrealities* as point-instants, or point-events of no dimensions, and which do not correspond with anything in our experience, as the factors of its symbolism of the 'real' physical world. What, indeed, has *rate* of change to do with the question at all? The apparently extended events of a lifetime can in dream consciousness take place in a 'time' which in waking consciousness is represented by a fraction of a second. In the consciousness of a drowning man the same thing is experienced. In mystical consciousness it is even more pronounced. From the notebook of a modern mystic I take the following extract, written from personal experience:

"In the Sphere (of Cosmic Consciousness) past, present, and future are rolled into one, and so are Consciousness and Substance. In the Sphere you act in order to know; and also the reverse occurs; anything that you hold in consciousness or think about, happens; consciousness and happenings are inseparable. And so the Gods have arranged that it is only possible to get much contact with the Sphere when you have learned to keep still in body, soul, and mind. You must never want anything nor think about anything there, for if you do it is very liable to happen, and you find on returning to normal consciousness that all that you have been casually thinking about has happened: which is most inconvenient; or it may be that you have got exactly what you have been wishing for: which can be equally inconvenient, for a whole Æon of time has elapsed between desiring and getting; (that is to say, $1\frac{1}{2}$ minutes may have gone by) and the thing of your choice no longer fits the occasion. To the mystic state of consciousness $1\frac{1}{2}$ minutes is equal to a whole manvantara of time; so it is a great hindrance to come back after $1\frac{1}{2}$ minutes and find yourself surrounded by and bound to the primitive wishes of your previous life all materialised. As soon as people begin to get prompt answers to their thoughts as well as their prayers, it is time for them to give up both thinking and praying. For the mystic the only prayer to pray is, 'Thy will be done.' He sacrifices himself entirely to the highest he can conceive, and only prays to be a tool in that guiding hand. In states of ecstasy he experiences union with his God; in normal life he knows himself to be a chosen servant of that God. He watches the mystery at work around, and as he watches learns."

How and in what manner the *creative* power of the Will can bring ideas or 'thought' into a 'real' happening on the physical plane, is one of the deepest secrets of Occultism.

It is beginning to be studied in its lowest form, or its next remove from physical matter, in some of the ' materialisation ' and other physical phenomena of psychical research and so-called spiritualism. We are not without evidence in the records of Occultism that this objectivisation of the content of the individual mind in a more or less permanent manner is the normal condition of the life of the discarnate 'soul'; whilst the modern records of communications from the ' other side ' are crammed with this same fact. It is in this manner, indeed, that individuals create for themselves their own heavens and their own hells—and many ' places ' which are neither the one nor the other—and will share these with others whose mental content is sufficiently similar to establish a ' telepathic ' rapport. How much of the common ' reality ' of our present plane of physical perceptions is due to such a rapport, is by no means as yet fully realised ; but we must consider it to be a fundamental principle, that on *any* plane of objective consciousness there is no difference in the principle which operates in the giving of objective validity to the subjective content of the individual self or Ego. We must remember also that our common test of ' reality ' is simply that we share with others a communal consciousness of the thing or event. We only call our dreams ' unreal ' because they are not thus shared with others.

To return to our diagram, we shall say that what we have called Principle, Substance, and Idea, in the higher abstract Triad, become active Will, Emotion, and Thought in the next Triad ; this *Thought* being Cosmic Mind in which *Idea* becomes objectivised as *Archetypal Form*. It is here that all species in the Mineral, Vegetable, Animal, and Human kingdoms are elaborated, and are subsequently *dramatised* as the ' lower ' planes of objectivity, which, when thus dramatised, assume an apparent *reality* of their own. In certain mystical states of consciousness in which *cosmic* happenings are realised, this can be clearly understood. Even in saying that this drama takes place in Cosmic Mind, or the Mind of Cosmic Man, we are already making a concession to the formal mind which separates and individualises. The whole ' process ' takes place within the higher sphere of the Logos ; nay, we must even go higher still and say that it is all an aspect of the ONE, that aspect of REALITY which we call *Becoming*. The representation of it as

' higher ' and ' lower ' is the necessity of the individual formal mind—at the very bottom of our diagram—but even in this formal mind we recognise the same principle at work in the production of objectivity ; and we may, indeed, say that it is because we can recognise it there that we postulate it as the principle operative on the ' higher ' planes, confirmed as this is by the direct experiences of mystical consciousness.   In the lower mind of the individual man this principle gives rise to the ' categories ' of time, space, causation, etc., with which we are so familiar, and which give to our life on the physical plane the character of Law and Destiny.   The *Forms* here are not created ; they are re-arrangements of existing material—or what *appears* to us to be material—but then, even on the ' highest ' plane, what can we have but re-arrangements of existing *formless* (to us) *Ideas* ?   We speak of ' creative art,' but the material form which serves as the expression of that art is merely a skilful combination of existing materials ; whilst even the *idea* must be derived from the higher sphere of Cosmic Mind.   In the scheme we are here presenting it is Cosmic Mind, or Cosmic Man, who ' creates ' archetypal form by bringing *idea* into objectivity—unless, indeed, we may be said to ' create ' our dreams, which, however, we can be said to do only in a secondary sense, since the *forms* are already in the mind.   In a similar manner we may be said to ' create ' our objective world after death ; but in reality this must be considered to be merely a re-arrangement of material, of forms already existing in the individual mind, and possibly shared with a larger collective or group-mind.   Occultism has for its main object the freeing of the individual from the illusions of these relative values of the objective worlds, on whatever plane they may be encountered.   The mystic who only cares to *feel* cannot thus free himself ; indeed, he is all the more likely to fall under the influence of the illusion, and more particularly in the idea that he has reached the Absolute when he is in reality only at the apex of one of the lower Triads.   Like a climber on a mountain who sees in front of him a peak which he takes to be the summit, but when that is reached he sees another and a further height : so, also, the absolute Absolute is not reached in this great World-Process by anything that the *individual* may hold in his field of vision.   It will not be reached at all until individuality, even that of Cosmic Man,

is altogether transcended—and yet remains ! Each Triad
has an apex, a *point* which when reached *may* be transcended,
and which is then seen to open out into the fuller life of the
Triad immediately above it. It is this *point* that is too often
taken for the Absolute. " I saw God in a point," says St.
Teresa, and many mystics have had the same experience in
various ways. The genuine occultist is just as liable to make
the same mistake as the genuine mystic as to the nature
of the plane which he has reached. As for the untrained
psychic or *soi-disant* mystic, he is, when under the influence
of strong religious emotion, as likely as not to take a third-
rate elemental, masquerading in a thought-form, for a vision
of Jesus Christ.[1]

Passing from the second to the third Triad, it is here that
the *formal mind* is born, though we shall not assign to consciousness operating entirely within this sphere the extreme limitations of time, space, and causation which we experience on
the lower physical plane, represented diagrammatically by
the lower inverted triangle. The base line of this latter may
be considered to correspond with the base line of the Triad
above, and it is here that the metaphysician exercises what he
is pleased to call the " method of pure thought." He tries in
vain to pass from this region of necessity and law to the higher
region of freedom, which, however, he intuitively feels must
exist, and which by his very effort he tacitly admits.

Passing to the sphere of the lower inverted triangle of
physical personality, we may note that the inversion symbolises
a very real fact of our present consciousness. The reality
of things on this physical plane does appear to us to be precisely the opposite of that which these things are in the higher
consciousness, or in their true spiritual nature. Take our consciousness of space for example. Outwardly it appears to

[1] This has been fully recognised by many of the Christian mystics. Thus
St. Teresa says : " I know by experience that there are souls which, either
because they possess vivid imaginations or active minds, or for some other
reason of which I am ignorant, are so absorbed in their own ideas as to feel
certain they see whatever their fancy imagines " (*Interior Castle*, Sixth
Mansion, ix, 6). Also : " When anyone can contemplate this sight of our
Lord for a long time, I do not believe it is a vision, but rather some over-
mastering idea which causes the imagination to fancy it sees something "
(*Ibid.*, ix, 5). Madame Guyon also distrusts objective visions, which, she
says, can be simulated by the Devil, but that " that which is unconnected
with all forms, images, species, and above visible things, the Devil cannot
enter." (*Vie*, Pt. I, chap. ix.)

expand to infinity; inwardly it appears to contract to the infinitely small; and matter appears to be infinitely divisible. And so the sides of our diagrammatic triangle are seen to be continued upwards and outwards by the dotted lines of the sides of the large macrocosmic triangle, whilst the inverted point or apex represents the opposite of infinity, the mathematical zero-point, or the infinitely divisible atom. In mystical consciousness it is just the reverse; the ALL is contained in the point, in the " tip of an Autumn spikelet "; and is that " divine spark " which can be found in the infinitely small just as readily as in the infinitely great.

We have already remarked on the deceptive nature of physical matter. It is not physical matter which is the 'real' *substantial* thing, but the invisible and, to us, insubstantial Ether. 'Time' also, as we know it, is an inversion of Reality.

It is on the base line of the lower personal Triad, considered as a reflection of the base line of the Triad above, that the battle of the metaphysicians is fought over the question of the independent reality of the objective material world *per se*; that is to say its existence apart from the mind of the subjective perceiver (*per-se*-ver). The position taken in this work has already been clearly indicated as that of Idealism. We conceive it to be the function of what we call *Mind* to objectivise *Idea*. The real existence of objects is in the mind—cosmic or individual. The Self, the perceiver, who is beyond the mind, sees them *in* the mind, and nowhere else. It sees them there as *form*, having an apparently independent validity in time and space, which are the *modes* of his perception—a *how*, not a *what*. The independent validity which we assign to objects on this physical plane is due to the fact that we are firmly convinced that these external objects exist independently of our *individual* consciousness; the external world goes on whether we are alive or dead. In this conviction we are right; simply because the external world of *Nature* exists in the Cosmic Mind; is only reflected in the individual mind; and can only be re-arranged therein, not created. Yet even so, there is still a certain amount of individual *colouring* contributed by the individual mind to the most ordinary objective thing on this plane of perception. No two persons see the same thing exactly alike, but the common perception is sufficiently alike to give a collective *reality* to this physical world. The individual derives his consciousness from the larger consciousness of Cosmic Man, and it is this Cosmic Man, not the individual, who 'creates' that objective world which is the same, yet not the same, for each individual man.

It will be seen to be characteristic of the scheme and diagram we are here employing to illustrate our conceptual ideas of the World-Process of Becoming, that it is apparently—speaking in these terms—a very long way from our present individual or personal consciousness to the Absolute, or even to what may more truly be called the spiritual plane. We have to consider that in terms of the formal mind the existence of an objective universe or world necessitates three things : (*a*) *Spirit*, the subject or self, the perceiver and actor ; (*b*) *Soul*, the substance of the form ; a dual principle, in one sense passive, and in another active ; and (*c*) *Body*, the form itself, the object, or 'matter.' But these three terms have only a relational value when we differentiate the individual from the universal or cosmic. For each Triad there is a Spirit, Soul, and Body, whilst the apex of each constitutes a perspective vanishing-point, entirely of a relative nature, at which we place a relative Absolute. That the true *spiritual* world lies immediately on the other side of the grave is one of the grossest errors of the common material intellect : only one remove, in fact, from the still grosser error of the resurrection of the physical body.

In our previous Chapter on the " Characteristics of Mysticism " we have noted the three progressive stages of the mystic consciousness, very inadequately classified as Purification, Illumination, and Ecstasy ; and we might say, in referring these to our diagram, that they represent the progressive expansion of consciousness into the third, second, and first of our Triads, respectively. We might note that this takes place as it were along the vertical axis of our diagram : a line which I have previously referred to as the direct line of connection with the Absolute, and as contrasted with the horizontal axis which is simply a line of extension leading nowhere, i.e. our normal extension of things in time-space. It is along this vertical line that consciousness rises in mystical states, assuming the characteristics of each plane in turn. Driven by ardent desire for union with his Source, the mystic presses up, heedless of the conditions of the plane through which he passes, even as a mountain climber, eager only to reach the summit, pauses not to study the ground over which he passes, or the landscape which expands to his vision. But by very reason of this precipitate flight the mystic is unable to remain on the heights; his untrained bodies or vehicles of consciousness cannot accommodate themselves to the rarefied atmosphere of these upper regions. "In the highest rapture I ever was in," says the author of *The Golden Fountain*, " my soul passed into a fearful extremity of experience: she was burned with so terrible an excess of bliss, that she was in great fear and anguish because of this excess. . . . It was more than a year before I dared recall one instant of it to mind."[1] The occultist progresses less rapidly, and learns to remain on, and observe the condition of, each plane in turn as he rises. But the mystic and the occultist are only pioneering in a region which all humanity and every individual must traverse in due course, and must be content to follow with slower footsteps along the track already indicated to them by the pioneers. Happy they, indeed, who can recognise that their well-being depends upon their following this road. So many, so very many, spend life after life wandering in side-tracks which lead nowhere; and in pain and sorrow they presently seek to return, at least to the point where they originally left the upward path.

It may be of interest to note here that Swedenborg distinguishes his " discrete degrees " and " continuous degrees " as being in the one case an " altitude " or height—corresponding to the vertical diameter in our diagram—and in the other case a " latitude " or breadth—corresponding to the horizontal diameter. Thus he says:

"All things which exist in the spiritual world and in the natural world, in general and in particular, co-exist at the same time out of discrete degrees and out of continuous degrees, or out of degrees of altitude and out of degrees of latitude. That dimension which consists of discrete degrees is called altitude or height, and that which

---

[1] *Vide supra*, p. 289. Professor Royce—with some show of reason—says that : " The mystic ignores the sum of the series. He cares only for the final term itself, viewed as the last limit which the other terms approach"; and he points out that, " as a fact, however, it is not only the goal but the whole series of stages on the way to this goal that is the Reality " (*The World and the Individual*, First Series, p. 191). It is in fact the recognition of this *Wholeness* which, in our contention, constitutes Rational Mysticism.

consists of continuous degrees is called latitude or breadth; their position relatively to the sight of the eye does not alter the denomination. Without a knowledge of these degrees nothing can be known of the distinction between the three heavens; or of the distinction between the love and wisdom of the angels there; or of the distinction between the heat and light in which they are; or of the distinction between the atmospheres which environ and contain. . . . Causes do not produce effects by continuity, but by discreteness; for the cause is one thing, and the effect is another. The distinction between the two is as between prior and posterior, or as between the thing that forms and the thing that is formed. . . . There are three heavens, and these distinct by degrees of altitude . . . each heaven, however, is divided in itself, not by degrees of altitude, but by degrees of latitude. Wisdom thus decreases all the way to ignorance, as light decreases to shade. This takes place by continuity. It is the same with men. . . . There are also in man, as in heaven, continuous degrees or degrees of latitude."[1]

We have already noted that Swedenborg designates his three discrete degrees as *effect, cause,* and *end*; and we may now note how he applies these to the conditions and qualities of the inhabitants—called by him indiscriminately *angels*—of his three heavens—corresponding to the three Triads of our diagram.

"In the spiritual world there are three heavens arranged according to the degrees of altitude. In the highest heaven the angels excel in all perfection the angels of the middle heaven; and in the middle heaven the angels excel in all perfection the angels of the lowest heaven. The degrees of perfections are such, that the angels of the lowest heaven cannot ascend to the first threshold of the perfections of the angels of the middle heaven, nor these to the first threshold of the perfections of the angels of the highest heaven. . . . These distinctions may be comprehended in some measure by this consideration, that the thoughts of the angels of the highest or third heaven are thoughts of *ends*, and the thoughts of the angels of the middle or second heaven are thoughts of *causes*; and the thoughts of the angels of the lowest or first heaven are thoughts of *effects*. It is to be observed that it is one thing to think *from* ends, and another to think *of* ends: also that it is one thing to think *from* causes, and another to think *of* causes; and again it is one thing to think *from* effects, and another to think *of* effects. The angels of the lower heavens think *of* causes and *of* ends, but the angels of the higher heavens *from* causes and *from* ends; and to think *from* these is the mark of the higher wisdom, but to think *of* these is the mark of the lower wisdom. To think from ends is the way of wisdom, to think from causes is the way of intelligence, and to think from effects is the way of science."[2]

[1] *Angelic Wisdom*, Part III, pars. 185, 186.
[2] Loc. cit., par. 202.

Swedenborg is not much in vogue to-day, though his teachings come so near to those of modern Spiritualism that there may possibly be a revival of his doctrine. The quotation we have given above is perhaps one of the most philosophical in all his writings. It will readily be seen that our diagrammatic Triads may equally stand for the three planes of Wisdom, Intelligence, and Science, as for any of the other designations we have given to them in borrowing terms from other systems.

Something must now be said as to the nature and function of *Will*, and its transformations on the various planes of Consciousness.

The term *Will*—like so many other terms which are commonly employed as if we knew all about them—has a great variety of meanings, both in ordinary use and in metaphysics ; and in the latter more especially we find, when we endeavour to ascertain therefrom the nature of Will, that there is a hopeless disagreement. With Schopenhauer, Will is a blind irrational Desire for sentient life, lying at the Root of the manifested Universe, which is essentially evil in its nature. As such it is the main characteristic of the ultimate and absolute *Subject*. The view which we shall take here is the more common one that Will is one of the three necessary factors in any *psychic* activity ; the other two being Thought and Emotion. Nevertheless, we may borrow from Schopenhauer the concept of the *dynamic* nature of the Will ; and if we confine the term to this aspect of the Subject or Self, it will help us to a very considerable extent to clear away the confusion of ideas which commonly surrounds this question, more especially in connection with the misleading term Free-will.

We shall define Will, then—in its lower aspect—as the dynamic energy of Thought. It is that mysterious ' force ' by means of which Thought impresses itself upon Matter, and produces Form. We have already seen that in its highest aspect it is—in combination with E-motion—the producer of Archetypal Form. In its lowest aspect it is the power of translating a thought—or a psychic activity which need not necessarily be conscious—into a physical action ; it is the power by which mind acts upon and moves the matter of our physical bodies ; whilst Cosmic

Will, the Will of the Logos, acts upon and causes forms to arise in Primordial Substance.

In our highest Triad we do not recognise Will as a separate principle, because we have not as yet got *Thought*, but only pure *Idea*. Thought has form, pure Idea is formless. Thought is active, pure Idea is passive—or rather we should say that Thought is the active aspect of pure Idea. As soon as this active aspect appears—in our second Triad—Will appears, and Feeling or Emotion also appears—that is to say, they are *conceptually* differentiated. We cannot really separate Thought, Will, and Emotion; and we might say with equal truth that Will is the dynamic energy of Emotion or Desire as that it is the dynamic energy of Thought. We might perhaps in a certain sense say that " behind Will stands Desire "—or Emotion on the higher plane—and we may say, further, that Thought *directs* Will. Here again, however, it is difficult— on the lower plane—to distinguish between thought and desire: the latter being so often the ruling principle over- riding reason. On the higher plane, however—where we must consider that supreme Divine Wisdom exercises its sway— we must conceive that Will is wholly directed by that supreme Wisdom (*Sophia*); and it is in this sense that we commonly speak of the Divine Will. Von Hartmann endeavoured to modify the stark a-logical Subject-Will of Schopenhauer by introducing a more or less logical *Idea* as a guiding principle, and thus to a certain extent mediating the systems of Hegel and Schopenhauer; but this effort does not appear to have met with any success as a permanent contribution to Ontology.

It is necessary that we should here distinguish between Will as an impersonal dynamic force, and the same term as commonly used to denote a personal wish, intention or purpose; for it is here that so much confusion arises in connection with so-called free-will. The proper sense in which this latter term should be used is simply *freedom of choice* between two or more alternatives. This choice is made *before* the Will is exercised to bring about, on the *physical* plane, the event or action decided upon. The most confirmed theoretical fatalist always *acts* from moment to moment as if he had this freedom of choice— as he actually has. That his choice will be determined by *motives*—i.e. thought and desire—does not militate against his freedom of choice *within limits*. He is limited by the laws of the plane on which he is acting, by his own individual powers, and by Destiny. As regards the first of these limitations—or what we commonly term natural law—there is no question as to our inability to act contrary to this. Even when we 'break' some law of nature, we only do so within the limits of some other natural law. As regards the limitations of our own individual powers, these are largely of our own making and choice. A man becomes, let us say, a drunkard. In his sober moments he may earnestly desire and resolve to break with his vice, but again and again he falls a victim to it. What would be the use of making any effort to reform him if we believed that he was absolutely fated to be a drunkard; that he had not at each moment a choice of ways? We commonly say that his will is weak; but it is only weak in that particular direction: just in the same sense that a particular muscle may be too weak to sustain a certain strain. In other directions his will may be strong: as witness the noble self-sacrifice exemplified in the story of Sydney Carton.[1] In the case of the drunkard who cannot break with his habit, however much he may desire to do so, the dynamic energy of the will in its action upon the physical body is not strong enough to overcome the dynamic energy of the psychic 'complex' which he has set up in that particular form. "A man's foes shall be they of his own household." In so far, indeed, as the *desire* to break with a vice is strong, the will may even be said, in a conventional sense, to be strong also; but it is not strong enough to overcome the combined demands of the cells of the physical body which have been habituated to the drink. Of course where there is no desire to break with the vice, the malady goes much deeper.

Behind our choice at each moment doubtless lies *motive*: the interaction of thought and desire; nor can we have any doubt but that these also are largely conditioned by causes operative on a plane beyond our normal cognisance. We may leave it to the metaphysicians, however, to wrangle as to the amount of freedom or otherwise which obtains in this respect; and we may grant to them that, in the ultimate, everything in the phenomenal world, the world of Manifestation, is conditioned and determined by a supreme Will. In doing this we shall not in any way be negating the teaching that on each

[1] Charles Dickens: *Tale of Two Cities.*

and every plane, and with each and every individual, there is freedom of choice within the limits of the laws on any particular plane. There is freedom to re-arrange, but not freedom to create; though, *relatively*, we may call it a ' creation.'

Our object being simply to present the subject in the form of a working hypothesis, it will be seen that an absolute doctrine of determinism would be fatal to any working hypothesis whatsoever—unless, indeed, fatalism can itself be called a working hypothesis. We must in fact admit what is tacitly granted in all our actions, freedom of choice and action within the limits of Law and Destiny.

But what do we mean by Destiny? It will be said that to admit Destiny at all is fatalism. In the view we are here taking, however, such is not the case. Destiny is simply the limitation imposed by an already exercised freedom of choice, or what is commonly called free-will. It is the restriction which is imposed as we descend from the absolute Freedom of the ONE to the limitations and inertia of matter on the physical plane. The free-will of the higher plane is the Law and Destiny imposed on the lower plane. Within the limits of any particular plane, however, we make our own destiny from moment to moment—or at least we may say this of the conditioning of our action on our present plane of consciousness, and apply it *mutatis mutandis* to all planes of manifestation—remembering that all such planes are *limitations*. If I choose to go down one road rather than another, I shall meet with a different set of events. Those events may or may not be part of a destiny determined by higher powers ; that is to say one can conceive of a higher controlling power which *might* determine which road I should take, but ordinarily would be quite indifferent to it. One's own higher self, for example—the individual man of the third Triad—who must be considered to have a consciousness of ' events ' which immeasurably transcends the limited view of the lower personal self—may be conceived to influence the lower self on occasions, so that one set of events rather than another shall ' happen ' to that lower personality—that is to say, shall come up in the surface consciousness of the time and space sequence.

To widen our concept: we can conceive of a certain Destiny for Humanity as a whole which will not in any way be altered by the actions of individuals within the limits of the Laws which govern that Destiny. Individual man can modify the course of Nature on the Earth in many minor ways, but he cannot alter the course of Nature as a whole: that is to say, those *cosmic* happenings which are determined by a higher power, or by higher powers.

Let us take a physical illustration. Conceive a closed cylinder containing a gas under pressure, and an operator who desires to keep the pressure constant. In order to do so he must keep the temperature constant, and in doing this he impresses his *will* upon the molecules of the gas in the form of a *law* which is simply this, that the *mean free path* and *velocity* of the molecules shall remain constant. The individual molecules may have greatly varying velocities, and all kinds of paths or directions of movement, but it is a matter of utter indifference to the operator—who is on another *plane* of action, a cosmic plane relatively to the contents of the cylinder —what may be the individual movements of the molecules. We may conceive of each individual molecule being perfectly free to choose any path it likes, and to jostle and love or hate its neighbours to its heart's content: it cannot thereby alter one jot of the cosmic will and purpose of the operator. Should we introduce Maxwell's " sorting demons," however, the case would be different. Clerk Maxwell imagined that if the cylinder were divided into two compartments by means of a partition with one or more trap-doors in it—each door being under the control of a demon—then it would be possible for the demon to open the door as soon as a high velocity molecule approached, let the molecule through, and then close the door again. In this manner one division of the cylinder would gradually be filled with higher velocity molecules than the other, and thus the pressure in the one compartment would be raised, and in the other it would be lowered. In such case, any outside operator would have to interfere with the work of the demons in order to keep the pressure constant in each compartment.

The common conception that ' God,' the Absolute, personally effects this interference with our physical actions, cannot be held for one moment when we have really grasped the principles on which action takes place from plane to plane. Such a concept is merely a survival of the crude idea that the *spiritual* world is the whole content of the invisible universe, and lies immediately beyond physical matter. It is beginning to dawn upon the modern mind, however, that though the ' spirit ' world lies just beyond physical plane consciousness— or as some would say ' beyond the grave '—that world is by no means the *spiritual* world.

What, then, do we really mean by the Divine Will, or the Will of God ? We mean simply the ultimate Law and Destiny impressed upon the manifested Universe or Cosmos *as a whole* through that highest divine Potency which we call the Logos. But since not merely is the Universe as a whole the manifestation of Life and Consciousness—differentiated conceptually as Thought, Will, and Emotion—but also each and every individual part is such a manifestation, from the highest divine Potency, Creator, or God, down to the smallest divisible particle. Each individual within its own sphere and limitations exercises precisely the same powers which we attribute to Life and Consciousness *per se*: that is to say to the *Self-in-Itself*, stripped of all limitations and conditionings—the absolute Reality. We can only think, will, and feel because we *are* the One Life and Consciousness ; and if what we at present call ' we ' can only do these within limitations, still, *within those limitations* we do them precisely on the same terms, so to speak, as the Absolute itself: that is to say with the spontaneity or freedom which belongs to these things or powers in themselves. " Each Ens (Entity) of the forth-breathed Word hath a free will again to breathe forth out of its own Ens a likeness according to itself." [1]

In a certain sense, therefore, the Divine Will operates in every part or individual, just as much as in the Whole viewed as it were from a higher plane ; and we can not merely never act contrary to it—in just the same sense that we can never act contrary to natural law—but we can never act at all except in the very quality and power of it. In what sense, then, can we pray, " Thy will be done on earth as it is in heaven "; or in what sense can we speak of making our will one with the Will of God ? We can only do this in a very relative sense, and in connection with a *moral* law. Not merely does our relative freedom of will or choice depend upon our acting from motives determined from the higher or more inner planes of our being—our *whole being* comprising the whole

---

[1] Böhme: *Mysterium Magnum*, xxii, 24.

Cosmos—but in proportion as we thus act from the spiritual part of our nature, our will may be said to conform with the Will of God, that is to say the Cosmic Will, in so far as this Will previously appeared to be something separate and superior to ourselves; whereas we have now identified ourselves with that from which we had previously imagined ourselves to be separated by reason of our consciousness and desires being turned outwards instead of inwards. To that outgoing, however, there is a limit set; it is the limitation of physical matter, or the physical plane of consciousness. "Thus far shalt thou go and no farther." Moreover, all paths, all roads, lead ultimately to that final consummation which is and was the Divine Will "from the beginning." The individual may choose a path through a relative heaven or a relative hell, but contrary to the divine Will in its absoluteness he never has acted, and never can act. "Other than IT there nothing since has been." On the stage of life the individual may now play the king, and anon the fool—not that kings are never fools—it is his own choice; or who knows that perchance he must play every part, that of the king as well as the fool, that of the sinner as well as the saint, before he is fitted to be a God—and because of a higher choice, not at present recognised as his own.

We might note here in connection with our diagram, that the Triads represent the three keys which may be used in the interpretation of the New Testament Scriptures. We have first of all, as the lowest Triad, the outer historical key which attaches to the reputed historical individual man Jesus of Nazareth. It is the key which consists of "the narrative of the doctrine," and which goes no further. It is the only key acknowledged by the Church. Take away the historical validity of the Gospels, and what becomes of 'Christianity' so called? But it is a key which has long since become rusted and has stuck in the lock. Fortunately, so many who have given up the use of it have been able to discover the use and value of the second key.

The second key—represented by our second Triad—is that of the indwelling Christ Principle: "Christ in You." It is only found in the Gospels by implication, but it is explicit in the Epistles of Paul. For those who possess this key it would not matter if to-morrow the whole of the Gospel narratives were discovered to have no historical validity whatsoever. It is not too much to say that in modern thought—notwithstanding the official blessings given to the romance *When it was Dark*—the centre of gravity of Christianity outside of the Church is being transferred to this higher plane, the plane of the Cosmic Christ, who is also Cosmic Man, " crucified in space."

The third key is still higher, or deeper, or more inner. " I know a man in Christ," says St. Paul, " such a one caught up even to the third heaven . . . and heard unspeakable words which it is not lawful for a man to utter." This third key is the hidden mystery of the Logos, beyond even the Cosmic Christ-Man. We are introduced to it in the opening verses of St. John's Gospel; and the whole of that Gospel, symbolically interpreted, adumbrates this mystery. Glancing at our diagram we see this as the highest or first Triad.

We have already noted in the extracts which we have given in Chapter VIII from *The Golden Fountain*, that this modern mystic found her spiritual consciousness centred in the first instance on the " Man Jesus "; that after her second 'conversion' it was transferred to the " Christ *of* God "; and subsequently, after her third ' conversion,' to the " Christ *in* God." We have thus a remarkable confirmation in actual experience of the principles which we have here been endeavouring to elucidate.

It is exceedingly interesting to note the correspondence between the three aspects or ' Bodies ' of the Divine Manifestation as found in the Christian Scriptures, and the teaching of the Mahāyāna School of Buddhism with reference to the three Bodies of the Buddha. This doctrine of the *Trikāya* represents that the highest aspect of the Buddha—or of the Buddhas, since it is the goal of every individual to become a Buddha—called the *Dharmakāya*, or essence-body—corresponding with Brahman in the Vedânta system—is timeless and unconditioned: the impersonal ground, as it were, of Buddhahood. Not merely so, but it is the ground of unity of all sentient beings. It is in fact what we have here been calling the Logos. The second Body is the heavenly *manifestation* of the Dharmakāya, and is termed the *Sambhogakāya*, or Body of Bliss. It is a stage or plane lower than the Dharmakāya, which has, so to speak, now descended to the first region of Form. It is in fact in every respect what we have represented by our second Triad.

The third Body—represented by our third Triad—is that of the *Nirmānakāya*, or the 'Body of Transformation,' emanated or projected from the Sambhogakāya. The Nirmānakāya is an *Avatār* or incarnation of the Deity, in precisely the same sense that Jesus is such in the Christian doctrine; and it is curious to note that some Buddhist sects have a doctrine of the illusive appearance of the earthly Buddha which is absolutely similar to the Christian 'heresy' known as Docetism.[1]

I am unwilling to end the present chapter on a note of scepticism, but it is at least necessary to add a word of warning lest any of the presentations here made should appear in the light of dogmatic statements. We are firmly convinced that no method of formulation or systematising of any principle that has ever been given to the world in any Scripture, tradition, or teaching, can be other than a presentation in terms of the formal conceptual mind; and that when it is said that the *truth* of the matter *is* so and so, it must always be understood under this reservation: that the statement is in each and every case limited not merely by the 'categories' of the mind, but also by further special limitations imposed upon these. It is only by the widest possible knowledge and freedom from prejudice that we can get rid to any extent of these special limitations. The moment we give in our adherence to any particular system as being authoritatively *the* truth, we subject ourselves to these special limitations, and shut ourselves out from a wider knowledge and a clearer light. This is not saying that the light we have obtained, or that we find in that system, may not be, for the time being, quite sufficient for us; it may, indeed, be all that our capacity or receptivity can deal with, and we should only condemn it when it is placed in the way of progress as a stumbling-block for others.

We must put the question, then, as to whether any of these Triads or Trinities which have so much resemblance to one another, and which we find to be doctrinally and dogmatically taught in various forms in various religions, have any validity at all in *Reality*: that is to say outside of the formal conceptual mind? Have we not, indeed, clearly seen that in whatsoever

[1] Cf. *Buddha and the Gospel of Buddhism*, by Ananda Coomaraswamy, D.Sc.

form the doctrine of the Trinity may be presented, whether ancient or modern, philosophical or theological, it is an *intellectual* construct, a necessity of the formal mind, and that as such it belongs to the region of Appearance not of Reality? It is not sufficient that any doctrine of the Trinity has been ' revealed '; revelation is only as is the capacity of the recipient. Nor is it sufficient that certain mystics have ' seen ' the Trinity, and have understood it in mystic vision in a more or less transcendental manner. Those who have done so have been those who had a prior familiarity with their own special form of the doctrine. Those who do not hold the doctrine in any form, do not thus apprehend the Absolute; as, for example, the Buddhist or the Sufi. The fact is significant, that every mystic must not merely formulate his vision in terms of the religion of which he is a devotee, but that the vision itself takes on that form.

Who shall say, then, whether, as mind evolves and we come to realise things in a wider and deeper aspect—our very consciousness of time and space undergoing a corresponding change—our present normal necessity for a threefold classification may not change into a fourfold one, or into something which is neither threefold nor fourfold? A line viewed end on, may appear to be a point; a superficies seen edgeways, appears to be a line; a solid may seem to be a superficies, and a four-dimensional figure a solid—and perhaps that is precisely what our ' solids ' are. Already we are beginning philosophically and mathematically to consolidate our hitherto sharply defined concepts of time and space into a single four-dimensional concept of space-time;[1] whilst the doctrine of Relativity still further accentuates the difference between the necessities of conceptual and perceptual methods of representation. Euclid's axioms of conceptual abstract space are not invalidated by Einstein's equations for the location of perceptual objects in space-time. Einstein's equations will need further revision as further physical discoveries are made, whereas Euclid's propositions for three-dimensional space will stand for all time, and would not be invalidated even if our consciousness expanded to a perception of four dimensions of objects in space.

[1] Cf. *Proceedings of the Aristotelian Society*, vol. xxi, Art. " Space-Time," by S. Alexander.

The philosophical doctrine of Relativity has long since recognised that all must be relative outside of the Absolute : that is to say, so long as there is that which thinks itself to be an individual subject, everything will be relative to that subject : with a more or less common perception shared with other similar subjects.

Our freedom from illusion, our knowledge of *Truth*, depends entirely upon our ability to recognise this relativity; to put things in their proper place in relation to the Whole— or, as Swedenborg says, to think *from* ends and not *of* ends— and, above all, to become the disinterested spectator of the great World Drama in all its phases and successive scenes, even while, at the same time, we recognise ourselves as the author and the actor: the Absolute *as well as* the individual.

CHAPTER XI

THE GREAT LAW

"Glory about thee, without thee; and thou fulfillest thy doom
Making Him broken gleams, and a stifled splendour and gloom.

Speak to Him thou for He hears, and Spirit with Spirit can meet—
Closer is He than breathing, and nearer than hands and feet.

God is law, say the wise; O Soul, and let us rejoice,
For if He thunder by law the thunder is yet his voice.

Law is God, say some: no God at all, says the fool;
For all we have power to see is a straight staff bent in a pool;

And the ear of man cannot hear, and the eye of man cannot see;
But if we could see and hear, this Vision—were it not He?"
                    TENNYSON : *The Higher Pantheism.*

"What has ever happened, what happens, and whatever shall or
may happen, the vital laws enclose all: they are sufficient for any
case and for all cases—none to be hurried or retarded—any miracle
of affairs or persons inadmissible in the vast clear scheme where every
motion, and every spear of grass, and the frames and spirits of men
and women, and all that concerns them, are unspeakably perfect
miracles, all referring to all, and each distinct and in its place."
                    WALT WHITMAN : Preface to *Leaves of Grass.*

CHAPTER XI

THE GREAT LAW

THE various lines of thought which we have endeavoured to present in our previous chapters would now appear to converge or solidify into a few fundamental principles, which are easily grasped without any reference to the technicalities of a meta-sophistical dialectic: "that grey web of reason," as H. Fielding calls philosophy. Here, however, as we have previously pointed out, we rather think that he has mistaken metaphysics for philosophy. "It is all a dull, weary barrenness," he says, "with none of the light of hope there. Hope and beauty and happiness are strangers to that twilight country." [1]

With this we heartily agree, having once upon a time ourselves endeavoured to find a satisfactory solution of the great problem of life in that "twilight country."

But when we have once clearly understood the necessary limitations of the intellect, and the legitimate province and use of the mind, in the same manner that we have understood the necessary limitations and the proper use and function of the physical body and senses; and when we have caught at least some partial glimpse of the region of freedom which transcends these limitations: we are no longer bankrupt of hope; and beauty and happiness come and dwell with us and shed their radiance over the twilight country of the 'rational' mind.

In our present, and in our concluding chapter, then, we shall endeavour to gather together the various strands of thought which pass through our previous chapters, so as to present them in a more or less summarised manner, while at the same time pointing out to a certain extent their practical application to our everyday life and consciousness. We must endeavour to present them in the first place so as to be applicable to

[1] *The Hearts of Men*, 3rd ed., p. 279.

empirical facts, to that region of experience in which we commonly live and move, the essential characteristic of which is *Law*, and a seemingly fatalistic sequence of cause and effect. This is one aspect of our dual consciousness. The other aspect is that region of *Spirit* which always overshadows all our thinking, however empirical it may be ; which is partially revealed in our *moral* nature considered as an effort to obey an inner monition more or less opposed to the individualistic interests of the outer self ; but which is only fully realised in a *mystical* consciousness which can, at times, wholly detach itself from the empirical, and soar unimpeded to the transcendental region of the *Ideal*; that region where freedom and beauty and love reign supreme, because therein all things are known and seen in the wholeness of an eternal perfection. This latter aspect of our life and consciousness we shall endeavour to dwell upon somewhat more fully in our final chapter.

In the first place, then, what we should now have clearly recognised is, that each plane of our nature has its own laws, and that we can never explain the ' higher ' in terms of the ' lower,' though we may be able to refer the lower to the higher as cause thereof. The laws of mind are no more applicable to the region of Spirit than the laws of the physical body —chemistry and mechanics—are applicable to mind. The higher is only *conditioned* by the lower as working in or through it ; the lower is a *limited* manifestation of the higher. Spirit, Mind, Body : each of these stands in its own province and is governed by its own specific laws on its own plane ; yet these planes interpenetrate, and each and all act and interact together in the constitution of that harmonious Whole which is Reality. The ' higher '—in the sense of being more universal or cosmic—is never limited and conditioned by the laws of the lower, as if it were forced and constrained into that limitation as a departure from its own province and freedom. The lower is only a particular mode of its activity, and as such it is necessarily a limitation and a relativity, that is to say a *thing*, but never a ' thing-in-itself ' ; for if so, it would be cut off from and have no dependence upon the higher cause. It is only thus limited and apparently isolated or individualised as the result of a limitation of consciousness ; as the result of the Self, as it were, *thinking* Itself into a limitation and a separation, and, for the time being, acting in each limitation, in each *thing*, as if it were a separate self.

Thus the One Self, whole and undivided, is behind or within every individual thing ; but it is only, as it were, paying attention to that thing in a limited sphere of action. We have precisely the same principle operating in the distinction between our *liminal* and our *sub-liminal* consciousness or self. The normal self, the liminal or surface consciousness, only pays attention to a limited order of things in the total content of the psychic self ; and even the liminal self, that which we normally and conventionally speak of as the ' I,' abstracts itself continually by paying attention to some special thought or line of action, to the utter neglect and forgetfulness of all others. But the others continue to exist ; they are not absorbed in the momentary interest of the ' I '; the total psychic self is still as total as it was before the abstraction took place. The ' I ' abstracts itself, and yet the totality remains—truly an enigma for the intellect. When the abstraction is over, the ' I,' the self, can fall back upon a wider perception and field of action ; and, in abnormal states, upon a deeper Self at present known in psychology as the subconscious. But we see no reason why we should limit the subconscious—or rather the supra-conscious—of psychology by any definite line which cannot be overpassed so as to include a wider and still wider cosmic whole. We cannot, in fact, in that Continuum which we conceive to constitute Reality, draw any line of definite separation, save only as an *appearance* ; whilst in certain exalted mystical experiences we have the actual fact of this deeper realisation of the cosmic nature of the Self. The whole of our earth life or incarnation may be regarded as being in the nature of this abstraction by the deeper cosmic Self, which at death falls back again upon the wider interests of a higher plane, where it continually abides, and which it has never really left. In the language of modern psychology we might say that the individual man is a " dissociated complex " in the larger content of the real Ego ; whilst the Ego in its turn is a " dissociated complex " in the still larger personality of Cosmic Man—the Logos. As something is added to the content of the individual subconscious when we abstract ourselves by exclusive attention to some particular thing or line of action—that is to say by what we garner as the result of that attention—so also something is added to the content of the deeper self as the result of that abstraction which we call earth life.

We may note from the above that the practical method by which the deeper consciousness attained in the mystical experience is reached, is precisely what our principle indicates ; it is the letting go of the limitation, first of all of the physical senses, and then of the formal mind ; and in this manner, abandoning the individual and the particular, the individual self falls back upon the Cosmic Self, and realises that that which formerly appeared to be of another nature and order, is no other than its own nature and true Self.

When we pass from the limitations of the lower self to the deeper Cosmic Self, and from that again to the Absolute, or the One Life, we recognise that all the 'lower'—Nature, Object, Manifestation, the World-Process—is the *activity* of the One Self-existent Reality. If the 'Reality' were purely passive, there could be no world at all. Not merely so, but it appears to be necessary to postulate that the One Self as pure Subject could not even know of Its own existence as Subject. Thus there would not merely be no world, there would be no Self, no 'Reality.' Strictly speaking we cannot attribute either passivity or activity to the Absolute ; but if we attribute the one we must also attribute the other.

In one sense the activity of the Self may be taken as a 'creative' activity : as a will and a choice ; in another, and perhaps a deeper sense, we may say that it is not merely the very *nature* of the Self to be in ceaseless action ; it is not merely a spontaneity ; it is not merely that Subject must express Itself as Object in order to know of its own existence ; but we conceive that no slightest activity, no stirring or e-motion can take place in the Subject or Self without this objective result ; the activity *is* the object, and the object *is* the activity. Thus, from the point of view of the individual, we see in the object, in the thing, in the action, not merely *how* the Self acts, but in the same limited degree we see *what* the Self is ; we know and apprehend Its content. We commonly recognise what the individual is, in character etc., by what he does ; and there does not appear to be any reason to apply any other principle to the larger Self of the Cosmos. Have we not seen, indeed, that the one *is* the other? Thus Mr. Bradley tells us:

"We can find no province of the world so low but the Absolute inhabits it. Nowhere is there even a single fact so fragmentary and so poor that to the universe it does not matter. There is truth in every idea, however false; there is reality in every existence, however slight; and, where we can point to reality or truth, there is the one undivided life of the Absolute."[1]

Philosophers and poets and, above all, mystics, have been telling us this over and over again in a hundred ways and forms; yet how feeble is our recognition of the underlying fact that the experience of the individual, however fragmentary or seemingly poor it may be, is *to that extent* the experience of the Absolute Self. The ' I ' who experience, however much I may limit myself in thought, however much I may ignorantly think of myself as an individual and separate self, am never other than the One Self. And it is only because of this fact that Mysticism is possible, for its very essence is the realisation of the unity of the individual with the universal, the loss of the illusion of separateness, the identity of subject and object, of ' creature ' and ' God '—yet with no loss of *personality*. In this experience the mystic simply realises to a greater or lesser degree—in some cases to a degree which appears to be a final Absolute—what he *is*—and always has been. To the individual it of course appears as an attainment of something he was not previously—and so it is *qua* individual; but we may realise that the great quest assumes quite a different aspect when we have apprehended intellectually, or as a deep *faith*, that we are already one with the Absolute, and that our quest is not for something which we do not possess, but is simply a self-realisation.

The supreme experience of the mystic consciousness, however, can, under present conditions, only be an occasional experience; but the application of the truth for which it stands must profoundly modify our whole outlook upon the problem of life, and our whole attitude towards the world in general, and the part we are called upon to play in the great drama of the World-Process. It is, in fact, the one basic truth and the real foundation of all Religion and religions, however much these may differ in their outward forms, and in a more or less

[1] *Appearance and Reality*, 2nd ed., p. 487.

clear apprehension of their real *raison d'être*. Moreover, we are profoundly convinced that this deeper and all-inclusive *faith*, which the unity of the mystic consciousness justifies, can be intellectually or rationally attained, even without any very deep mystical experiences; it can be acquired when we have realised the *laws* of our nature, and have abandoned all arbitrary systems of authoritative dogma. It can be held when we have learnt to distinguish between physical, mental, and spiritual laws in their operation and application within their own special province; when we have ceased to endeavour to explain the Absolute and the Cosmic in terms of the individual and the particular. We shall accept all empirical facts, and relegate them to their proper sphere. The mystical consciousness as an empirical fact cannot be explained in terms either of matter or of mind; indeed, consciousness itself, whether mystical or otherwise, is incapable of being thus explained. But consciousness, awareness, feeling, emotion, are much more intimate, are much more the *self*, than any form of matter, than any body we may possess; and a close analysis shows us also that they are much more the *self* than any form of mind or conceptual thought.

But whilst accepting the empirical fact of a mystical consciousness transcending mind, it does not follow that we shall accept this, that, or the other mystical *doctrine* as a representation of any final or ultimate Truth. We can, in fact, only accept the testimony of the mystics where there is unanimity and agreement in broad outline and principle. We shall not accept any theological mysticism or mystical theology which professes to expound the nature of God or the Absolute; for we have clearly recognised that the moment we begin to say of this Unitary Reality that It *is* so and so, we have already descended into the region of mind and relativity. We may certainly accept that It *is* so and so in a relative sense, for It *is* all that ever can be experienced in consciousness; but in relation to anything which can be thus known and defined, we shall always have to seek for the limiting *Law*; we are in the region of action and Law.

We conceive, then, of Reality—the uncaused Self-existent Whole—as an absolute *Continuum*, which, from the very fact of Its unitary nature, is the privation of Relativity and, therefore, beyond all definition ; for definition implies something other than the thing defined, something other than the terms in which it is defined. To reach the Absolute in thought, thought must become absolute : that is to say, it must stultify itself and cease to be thought. But it does not follow from this that the Absolute is a *privation*. On the contrary, we have to conceive of It as being so much the fulness of all things that in It all possible universes are already ' given ' ; not in any manner either static or kinetic, such as we commonly associate with those terms in physics, but in a *potential* manner. The term *potential* is in reality only a name for something which exists in a mode or order other than that of our normal perception or conceptual thought. We may say simply that what exists in the Absolute does not exist as *form* ; or we may say that it is only as form that we can conceive of it as *ex*-isting,[1] and that in Itself it rather *per*-sists, or *sub*-sists.

Every game of chess which it is possible to play *per*-sists potentially ; and it is conceivable that even in our individual subconsciousness—to go no deeper—all games may per-sist in such a manner that it would be possible for any individual to bring forward as it were, to bring to the surface of the normal consciousness, to make to *ex*-ist, any one of the innumerable possible games in a manner analogous to that in which we bring to the surface a ' memory.' But if we ask where or how the memory exists—or persists—or what the memory is when we are not making use of it, or when we have ' forgotten ' it—seeing that there is no slightest experience which is ever really forgotten, and which cannot be reclaimed from the subconscious under abnormal conditions —the question has no answer to which we can attach any ' rational ' meaning. We can only say that it persisted, or subsisted, as a part of the content of the self ; but how, where ? If, with the materialist, we refuse to go any further than the brain, we have to show how or in what manner memory can inhere in dead mechanical particles which are in a state of constant flux and change and elimination from the system. If we go beyond the brain, what further form of substance known to science shall we fall back upon ; what further body or vehicle of the self ? " Memory," Bergson

[1] Latin, *ex*, out, and *sisto*, to stand.

tells us, " is just the intersection of mind and matter." [1] But this does not help us with the question, where and how? Memory, however, is of the past, but creation is of the future ; and yet we may affirm that nothing was ever created which was not already *potential*, which did not already sub-sist— from all Eternity, and in all Eternity.

We shall say, then, that all possible universes *persist* eternally in *Reality*, just as all possible games of chess *persist* already, are already ' given ' in the nature of that which is capable of ex-hibiting them. The *activity* of the Potentiality —that is to say of the Absolute—which we term *Life*, consists in the *realisation* of this potentiality in the manner which we term *consciousness* : that is to say in subjective and objective states of feeling and perception ; and such consciousness is necessarily a limitation, something less than the Whole, that is to say, a *Form*, something which *ex*-ists. It is the content of the Self, yet now appears as a not-self. Conscious-ness and Form, or limitation—or more generally, the objective world—thus arise together. How or by what process these ' games,' these dramas, these art productions which we call Universes, arise in the One Consciousness or Self, we are unable to determine. Perhaps the Self Itself does not know. We do not even know how we can translate our own will into the common action of the movement of a limb. If we could know this we should probably know the greater fact—if indeed it be a greater fact.

But as there is no doubt about the empirical fact of the limitation and the form, so also there is no doubt about the fact of an expansion of consciousness by which the normal limitations of our physical consciousness and self are overpassed and transcended. Putting these two facts together we have the clearest possible conception of the nature of the individual self, of the present empirical ' I.' For some reason—which some day I shall doubtless clearly realise—*I* who am the *Whole* have limited myself along a definite line of action by *ignoring* all except that which immediately concerns the object I have in view, the particular ' creation ' which I wish to realise. When that is worked out, I shall fall back upon a larger and deeper ' I '—not necessarily the Absolute. But though I have thus limited myself, I do not cease to exist as the larger deeper

[1] *Matter and Memory*, p. xii.

Self, nor can I define or limit that Self short of the Absolute: though it may be ages and æons before that is reached. I am like the artist selecting particular colours and materials for a special picture. All existing colours and all existing materials are at my disposal—they are myself. The potentiality of all possible forms, of all possible universes, lies in my own essential nature; but I limit myself to those which I require for a special 'creation.' The absolute consciousness of the Whole would be unconsciousness of any *thing*; it would be the absence of any objective universe, the absence of perception, if not of con-ception. Conception—or ideation—we may regard as the limitation whereby a perception results. It is the *mental* act whereby something is taken out of the Wholeness of the *Continuum* and set before the Self for the time being as the centre of its interest and action. At certain privileged times—provided I have reached a certain stage of evolution—I can fall back upon the *Continuum*, upon my deeper Cosmic Self; and, abandoning the limited mental form, know myself in utter freedom and union of subject and object. But we may conceive that the act of individualising a particular *thing* out of the potentiality of the *Continuum*—no matter whether that thing be a universe, or a particular game of chess, or the very commonest physical object—is, in the first instance, not merely a *mental* action, the isolation of an *idea* : it is the bringing into existence of the mind itself. The action *is* the mind, and the mind *is* the action. As soon as it has taken place it becomes necessitous and fatalistic ; the action is 'given' from beginning to end ; that is to say it has now come 'down' from a potentiality into an actuality which is 'determined' in the mind as certainly and as clearly as a chair or a table is 'determined' as soon as it comes into actual ex-istence. It has entered the region of law and necessity, or rather it makes this region by its very existence: it *is* the 'region' ; the limitations which determine it are the *nature* of the thing, whether it be a universe, a single world, or a single atom in or of that world.

Let us follow up our chess analogy. The expert chess player can isolate in his mind some particular game, and see it, as it were, as a whole, from beginning to end, not as a succession of moves ; or shall we say that the succession takes place so rapidly in his mind that the intervals of ' time ' between the moves are not realised. In this latter case we should have almost absolute time. Absolute time, or absolute simultaneity of all the moves, would be no ' time ' at all. We need not split hairs, however, as to whether in a consciousness in which time does not appear to enter, there is *really* an infinitely minute interval between a succession of events, or whether they are absolutely simultaneous ; the empirical fact is the same in each case, though, strictly speaking, where there is an *event* there must be *time*, however rapid. But in any case we have here a multiplicity in a unity. The game of chess as a whole is a unity, the various pieces and moves are a multiplicity. Now let us further suppose that the unitary consciousness which can see the game as a whole— we might call it the *Logos* of that particular game—can, by a similar process by which the particular game was individualised out of the still larger Whole, constituted of the potentiality of all possible games, cause each individual piece on the chessboard to have an individual consciousness limited to its own particular functions and moves, but with no knowledge of the game as a whole : that is to say, with no knowledge of the *future*, which the Logos *does* know. The Logos would, as it were, endow each individual piece with a portion of his own consciousness; or, to put the matter the other way round, each individual in the multiplicity would, *qua* individual, think of himself as something separate and distinct from the unitary consciousness which contains and *is* the multiplicity. This the individual piece would do just to the extent that he is paying attention only to his own particular environment and functions or moves in the game.

Carrying the analogy a little further, we can see that, although the game as a whole is *determined*, the individual actions of the pieces on their own particular squares are (supposing the pieces to be alive and intelligent) by no means so. Each piece can do pretty well what he likes on his own square, and—so long as he does not endeavour to move out of his square of his own individual will—the player, the Logos, may be quite indifferent to his actions. But the piece is really restricted to his own square by the ' laws of nature,' that is to say the laws of the game. He finds, however, that apart from his own free will he is sometimes moved from one square to another. He finds also that in a certain unaccountable manner, for which there is no apparent reason, some of his fellow pieces get moved off the board altogether, and he loses sight of them. He comes to regard his own removal or 'death' as an inevitable event which must take place sooner or later ; but, not knowing the game, he has no means of determining when it will occur. The Logos knows, because we have presupposed that a particular game is being played, and from this fact the particular time when any piece 'dies' is fatally determined. Being unable to communicate with pieces which have thus been removed—though some of his fellows assert that they have been able to, and can do so—he comes to regard the game as something which, after his removal, will interest him no more ; whilst some even imagine that their removal means their utter extinction. We might conceive, however, that— the pieces being endowed with intelligence and with a faculty called memory—some of them presently begin to ask what it all means ; and, by making observations of their moves and of so much of the game in general as they are able to observe and remember of past events, they presently begin to formulate certain *laws* of the game, and even to appreciate the fact that there must be some kind of a method and purpose underlying it. They may even pass from the mere empirical facts of the specific events, which we call moves, to an analysis of their own consciousness, and ask what is the relation of that consciousness to the game as a whole. In some mysterious manner the moves which have been made in the past by the individual inhere in his consciousness as *memory* ; although they are 'past' they are also 'present' in memory : they do not ex-ist, but they per-sist. The individual may even find at times that by abstracting himself from his immediate environment, by losing sight of the other individual pieces around him, and of his own apparent individuality, he may attain to a sort of unitary consciousness which gives him a much deeper insight into the game than he can ordinarily achieve. He may in fact, fall back in varying degrees upon the unitary consciousness from which he derives his individual consciousness ; and at such moments he may experience not merely the sense and knowledge of the unity of the whole, but also enter into an appreciation of the æsthetic sense of beauty, fitness, harmony, delight in the game, which we may suppose to be present in the unitary consciousness of the Logos.

We must not, however, press the analogy too far. If we go any further we should have to conceive that the pieces only arrive at this stage of intelligence by a process of evolution: in fact we should have to consider the ' creation ' of the pieces, and of the board as the field of their activities, as being a part of the ' game.'

We have noted in our previous chapters the effort of physical science to transcend its own proper sphere, and to invade the province of metaphysics in an effort to *explain* not merely our psychical states, but even Life and Consciousness itself in terms of physical law. We have noted also the modern revolt against this on the part of the pure empirical physicist, who would even exclude the Ether from the region of his rigid mathematical analysis of ' Matter ' as being simply that which is actually appreciable to the physical senses, and which can be numbered, measured, and weighed. The very latest form of this empiricism—which we must welcome as a restriction of physics to its own proper sphere—is to be found in the Einstein theory of Relativity. Pure metaphysical or Euclidean space is here entirely abandoned, and ' space ' means simply certain geometrical properties determined by the presence of matter. Thus Einstein says :

" We can draw conclusions about the geometrical structure of the universe only if we base our considerations on the state of matter as being something that is known." [1]

Under these conditions it is found that it is not physically true that two parallel straight lines, if prolonged, will never meet. Matter—i.e. the physical universe of matter, or at least *our* universe—has no such straight lines. In other words, *space* geometrically conditioned from the data of the physical senses in their appreciation of matter, appears to be curved, and is finite, not infinite. It is the same with ' time.' It has altogether a different meaning from that conceptual time with which metaphysic deals, when we treat it merely as that which we actually *observe* in the motions of material bodies and in the phenomenon of light. Thus

[1] *Relativity, the Special and the General Theory*, trans. R. W. Lawson, D.Sc., p. 113.

simultaneity does not mean the simultaneous happening of two or more events in an abstract time, as if, for example, a clock a thousand or a million miles away were registering the same *absolute* time as a clock situated with any particular observer. Simultaneity in the physical sense is simply the simultaneous happening of two or more events *for the observer*, and at his own particular point. There is, in fact, in this theory no such thing as an absolute time. Every moving body has a *relative* time, which will differ from that of another moving body, and is dependent upon the relative velocities of the bodies. Some very curious results follow from this treatment of time and space. For example, a rigid rod moving in the direction of its length, when observed from another body conventionally considered to be at rest, is apparently shorter in proportion to its velocity than what it must be considered to be physically ; and if it moved with the velocity of light it would, for the particular observer and special point of observation, have no length at all.[1] Now, does anyone believe that this is *reality* ? The actual bar cannot really be half a dozen different lengths at one and the same time to suit different observers moving at different velocities. Although we cannot know what the absolute length of the bar is—since we have no absolute standard of length with which to compare it—we are still compelled to conceive that it *has* an absolute and invariable length independent of *our* motion relatively to it. We have here, in fact, pure appearance, not reality ; and nothing in the empiricism of the theory can stultify our sense of an abstract time or space. The theory is perfectly justifiable as physics, and for that very reason it cannot invade the region of metaphysics—as some have appeared to think that it can. Some very hasty and misleading deductions, indeed, seem to have been already put forward as resulting from this misunderstood empiricism. It has no bearing whatsoever on the philosophical issue as between idealism and realism, or as between absolutism and pluralism.

We have postulated as a nearer approach to some conception of Reality, that on a ' higher ' plane of consciousness the appreciation of a distant event—in other words the *trans-*

[1] *Relatively, the Special and the General Theory*, trans. R. W. Lawson, D.Sc., p. 35.

mission—will take place with a rapidity as much in excess of the velocity of light as the latter is in excess of the physical motions of material bodies ; whilst on the plane of the Absolute—which is no *plane*—the ' transmission ' is instantaneous. In the absolute *Continuum* we conceive that the potentiality of every *event* subsists and persists as an interpenetrative, congruent, eternal, ever-present NOW. But the moment we step out of this we must necessarily have Relativity, and an apparent *transmission* ; and the further we ' descend '—that is to say, the further we depart from unity into differentiation and individualisation—the more time and space become appreciable values, having longer and longer intervals and greater and greater separative values. Inverting the process, we pass from the physical to the psychic, and from the psychic to the spiritual, at each remove throwing off the artificial and conventional limitations of time and space which go to condition in consciousness the particular activities of each special plane.

In metaphysics as distinguished from philosophy, we have noted the same tendency as in science to explain in terms of mental faculty what lies beyond and is outside of the powers and functions of the Mind. The metaphysician as distinguished from the philosopher endeavours to interpret the higher in terms of the lower, because he has seen no further than mind ; he has found nothing deeper in his own nature wherewith to interpret the universe than his ' rational ' faculty as conditioned by the ' categories.' In the case of the physicist who has seen no further than matter, and therefore endeavours to explain even his own life and consciousness in terms of matter : we speak of him as a *materialist* ; but in the case of the metaphysician, who will admit of nothing beyond the ' rationality ' of the mind, we have no equivalent word—perhaps because the corresponding limitation has not yet been clearly recognised. If we call him a ' rationalist,' we find the term commonly associated with materialism. We have seen also that there is a higher rationality which may be associated more properly with philosophy, and above all with a philosophical mysticism, in its recognition of the rationality of our whole nature as having its root in Spirit : in a Reality of which both matter and mind are limitations and appearances.

Now we have found it necessary, in order to *relate* Appearance and Reality, to postulate an absolute *Substance* which is essentially a *Continuum*; an undivided Self-existent *Principle* which is Infinite in the literal sense of the term, as being not-finite: that is to say, as not being capable of appreciation or definition in any terms of our empirical consciousness, however much these terms may be abstracted. We have further postulated that *Forms* arise in this Substance; these Forms being the presentations by the Self to Itself, in an objective manner, of the content of Its own Self-existent Being, or Be-ness. We conceive, further, that each form is endowed in its own special and limited manner with the same attribute of the One Self which enabled that Self to ' create ' the form. The *subjectivity* of the form is the subjectivity of the One Self—it is as deep and unfathomable and infinite—but the *objectivity* of the form—that is to say the form *qua* form—is necessarily limited and conditioned. In so far, however, as the form associates ' itself ' only with the objectivity, its subjectivity—that is to say its *apparent* selfness, that which it *thinks* itself to be—is thereby limited also.

Although for practical and empirical purposes we commonly associate ourselves wholly with our physical bodies, yet we never really do so; we never really and wholly think of ourselves as confined to the actions and functions of our physical self. The materialist may profess to do so, but only by ignoring certain facts of his consciousness. The deeper subjective self always lies behind our surface consciousness, and refuses to be suppressed; there is always something *more* in our consciousness than is given in matter. We may state this in another manner by saying, that whilst the *form* can never be other in reality than the One Substance—that is to say the absolute SELF—in its life and consciousness *qua* form— that is to say in its individual *action* as form—there is a limitation and a restriction which is measured by, or corresponds to, the *objectivity* of the form in its relative action and interaction with other forms.

Here, then, we appear to gain a very clear apprehension and understanding of ourselves as being both free and limited. We are free subjectively: that is to say in Spirit, and in proportion as we approach the Absolute; we are bound and conditioned objectively: that is to say in matter and form, and in proportion as we recede from the Absolute. And if we also appear to be bound and limited subjectively, it is only because, and in proportion as, we identify ourselves with matter and form instead of with Spirit.

Here we claim to have reached a perfectly rational Mysticism—one in which we can take every empirical fact of our life and consciousness, every natural law to which we appear to be subject, for exactly what it is, and yet *live* our real conscious spiritual life far above the level of these empirical facts. Much more than that : by thus transferring our centre of consciousness from the periphery to the real centre, we enter into a realisation of the æsthetic value of the whole ; the process is no longer for us a dull barren mechanical thing ; it becomes endowed not merely with a meaning and a purpose, but also with a beauty surpassing all thought or expression otherwise than just precisely as it *is* expressed in what we call Nature and the Laws of Nature : in the great art production of the World-Process itself. We enter into the Great Freedom —not a freedom *from* the Law, but a freedom *in* the Law. We enter into *peace*, the peace in which our strife is ended because there is no longer any question of ' our ' will against the One Will. We are unified with that Will, and in that union we enter into the infinite peace of the harmonious Whole.

We may note now, that most of the modern movements of religious thought of a *quasi*-mystical nature, such as Theosophy, Christian Science, New Thought, or the ' New Mysticism ' in general, have at root this concept of the transcendental nature of the Self, and the possibility, by certain methods more or less clearly recognised and individually advocated, of transcending the normal limitations of personality. It is recognised that the self should be the master, not the slave of circumstances ; it is recognised that bodily states and outward events can be largely controlled and influenced by thought and will ; but at the same time we are obliged to say of many of these movements, that the fundamental principles are largely presented in an empirical and irrational manner which, though they may catch the popular fancy, cannot really be regarded as a solid contribution to a philosophical mysticism. Not merely is this so, but in many cases the real spiritual element is entirely lacking ; they are purely individualistic; the 'I, me, and mine' is sadly prominent; and the material money-element barely concealed.

When we turn from these to the more purely empirical science of modern psychology, we find a distinct movement in the direction of a recognition of our fundamental principle of the illimitable nature of the Self. In the fact of the *subconscious* we have the first step out of the purely physiological psychology of the past century; and in such philosophical efforts as that of Bergson we have a further step in the endeavour to link up the new psychology with metaphysical modes of thought. Over and over again Bergson insists that our normal life and consciousness is a limited thing, cut out of or differentiated from a larger Whole for a special purpose. Life transcends thought. It is thought which produces the limitation.

" The intellectual tendencies innate to-day, which life must have created in the course of its evolution, are not at all meant to supply us with an explanation of life : they have something else to do.[1]

In explaining life by intellect, it limits too much the meaning of life : intellect, such at least as we find it in ourselves, has been fashioned by evolution during the course of progress ; it is cut out of something larger, or, rather, it is only the projection, necessarily on a plane, of a reality that possesses both relief and depth.[2]

Intellectuality and materiality have been constituted, in detail, by reciprocal adaptation. Both are derived from a wider and higher form of existence.[3]

Intellect has detached itself from a vastly wider reality, but there has never been a clean cut between the two ; all around conceptual thought there remains an indistinct fringe which recalls its origin. And further we compared the intellect to a solid nucleus formed by means of condensation. This nucleus does not differ radically from the fluid surrounding it. It can only be re-absorbed in it because it is made of the same substance."[4]

Precisely. The *Substance*, that which sub-stands, is the One Self, eternal, immutable ; and mind equally with body is a limitation, a differentiation, a form : always capable of being re-absorbed in that from which it springs. We regard this re-absorption as the destruction of *form*—since neither matter nor mind is ever other than the One Substance. Objectively it is the disappearance of matter; or of the particular material body in which the self is for the time being

[1] *Creative Evolution*, p. 22.   [2] *Ibid.*, p. 55.
[3] *Ibid.*, p. 197.   [4] *Ibid.*, p. 203.

acting and functioning ; subjectively it is the expansion of consciousness by reason of the letting go of its particular attention to the limited form : that is to say, it is the abandonment of the individual self in a greater or lesser degree.

In so far as modern psychology approaches the problem of mind from the side of its action and reaction with physical matter, Bergson is undoubtedly right in saying that " Intellectuality and materiality have been constituted, in detail, by reciprocal adaptation." That is the aspect of mind when viewed from below, and it may be said to apply broadly to mind considered as intellect. But when viewed from above, from the point of view of evolution, or the World-Process, as an out-breathing and an in-breathing of the ONE : we find in mind much more than a reciprocal adaptation, for there must be a Cosmic Plane of Mind long preceding the evolution of physical matter, and having at least one intermediate plane, that of the Ether, between itself and that matter. Here we trace the same principle in the relation of the planes to each other that we trace in the relation of the whole process to the ONE. Each ' lower ' plane is derived from the higher and more cosmic plane by a process of limitation ; it draws its life and energy from the higher plane, and is not merely capable of being re-absorbed therein, but must inevitably be so in the course of the cycle of devolution which we usually term *evolution*.

Applying this principle of re-absorption to our efforts to know *life* as it is in itself, Bergson rightly insists over and over again that we must abandon intellect for what he calls *intuition* ; we must relax the " tension," which is the attachment to the individual and the particular, and we must, as it were, " detend " by falling back upon the *wholeness* of our life. This process is precisely that of Mysticism, and, as we have tried to indicate, it cannot stop anywhere short of the Absolute. Bergson, however, does not as yet appear to have identified it with Mysticism in any of the classical forms or phases of the latter.

In *Matter and Memory* he develops this thesis still further.

" If living beings are, within the universe, just ' centres of indetermination,' and if the degree of this indetermination is measured by the number and rank of their functions, we can conceive that their mere presence is equivalent to the suppression of all those parts of objects in which their functions find no interest. They allow to pass through them, so to speak, those external influences which are indifferent to them; the others isolated, become 'perceptions' by their very isolation.[1]

What you have to explain, then, is not how perception arises, but how it is limited, since it should be the image of the whole, and is, in fact, reduced to the image of that which interests you.[2]

Why insist, in spite of appearances, that I should go from my conscious self to my body, then from my body to other bodies, whereas in fact I place myself at once in the material world in general, and then gradually cut out within it the centre of action which I shall come to call my body and to distinguish from all others?[3]

One general conclusion follows from the first three chapters of this book: it is that the body, always turned towards action, has for its essential function to limit, with a view to action, the life of the spirit."[4]

If this is the new metaphysic, it must quickly come into line with all that is best in Mysticism. How vastly illuminating in every direction, in physics, in psychology, in religion, in mysticism, is this easily grasped principle that individual *things*, whether material particles or individual selves, are limitations of the One Substance, Substance-Principle, or SELF, for the purpose of *action*—not a dry, dead, mechanical action, a mere clashing of unconscious atoms, as the materialist would have us believe, but the spontaneous action of a LIFE, immeasurably and inconceivably joyous, blissful, harmonious, free.

In and behind each individual is the *whole* of that LIFE; it is one and indivisible; It is Continuity, Unity, Passivity as *Being*; It is Multiplicity, Relativity, Activity as *Becoming*. It is immanent in all things, for the 'thing' is never other than IT; yet to the thing *as thing*, to the individual as 'creature,' It is supremely transcendent—and must ever be so as long as the individual remains individual. Who shall say, however, to what heights we may not rise in our individuality, in power, knowledge, bliss, and yet see and know the Absolute no nearer—nor any further off—than we see and know it at present. Nay, it may even be conceived that to see and know it completely would be the dreamless, functionless slumber of complete oblivion, the suspension of all thought, of all consciousness?

---

[1] *Matter and Memory*, p. 28.   [2] *Ibid.*, p. 34.
[3] *Ibid.*, p. 44.   [4] *Ibid.*, p. 233.

To speculate whether—as in the view of Eastern philosophy—after incalculable æons the whole universe goes into this dreamless *Pralaya*, would not appear to serve any practical purpose. It is only carrying out to a *logical* conclusion the principle of correspondence and analogy which holds good in our empirical knowledge of the cycles of involution and devolution, or integration and disintegration, which we judge to be of universal application ; that is to say it is one of those cases—analogous to what we find in the generalisations of science—in which we carry to the universal the operation of principles found to hold good within the limited range of our empirical experience. Whether this is justifiable or not is an open question. It might be interesting, however, to note here that in one of the most recent ' revelations ' from the ' other side '—one, indeed, which has created a much wider interest than any of the other very numerous works of this class which have more or less recently appeared—the following statement is made, by the communicating ' spirit ':

" We are sometimes asked how many spheres there be. Well, having explained what we have above, I do not apprehend that we shall be asked that question by you. Did you ask it, we, who are only of the tenth of these zones, would perforce have to answer, We do not know, and much doubt whether our answer to you would differ were you to put that question a million million of æons hence, and we having progressed all the while." [1]

How much this differs from the orthodox presentations of ' heaven ' will be readily appreciated, but it falls into line with all that we have said above.

Seeing, then, that we thus, as individuals, live and move and have our being in this region of *Law*; that we are most certainly limited and conditioned in order that we may fulfil a definite function in the Cosmos, and the purpose of a higher Will, which, when reunited with it, we shall presently discover to have been no other than our own Will: it would clearly appear that any violent effort to renounce our present duty, to refuse those actions which immediately present themselves to us as those which we were *intended* to do ; or, further, any rebellion against our particular lot or ' fate,' would be the very greatest unwisdom. It is quite true that there is

[1] *Spirit Messages, The Life beyond the Vale*, Rev. G. Vale Owen, vol. i, p. 176.

a difficulty here, in so far as it is often by no means clear—indeed, it is often extremely difficult to determine—what it is we are intended to do, what line of action we *ought* to take. We may find ourselves for the time being in circumstances which are anything but congenial, or which do not give anything like the full scope for the work which we feel we are fitted to do, and which might rightly be regarded as ' higher ' than that into which we appear to be forced. Under such circumstances, are we to accept the circumstances as being the higher Will, and make no effort to free ourselves from them ? By no means. Who ever said that the individual should never aim at anything higher ? The whole of evolution is precisely that aim. But it is our *attitude* towards the lower as well as towards the higher which counts. If we are in rebellion against the lower, and shirk our duty in due fulfilment thereof, we may possibly succeed for the time in throwing it off. But we have left something undone ; something we shall certainly have to go back to. The only road to the higher is the present thing well and faithfully done. It is as if in building a house we were to neglect or scamp some of the lower work ; the whole building must suffer ; some time or other the work would have to be done over again. Our progress, or evolution, *is* such an actual building ; the building of a *temple* ; the building of bodies ; and, more particularly, of *a* Body " eternal in the heavens " ; [1] a Cosmic Body, imperishable and untouched when worlds and systems disintegrate.

Further, we recognise that the lower is just as much our own will and action as the higher. Setting aside the deeper principle that the whole Law is at root our own Will, we must recognise that any circumstances arising from our own freedom of choice must necessarily be the result of that choice. If we have chosen wrongly, the law will set us right ; but what room is there for rebellion or complaint ? When the cause which placed us in any particular set of circumstances is exhausted, or the purpose fulfilled by duty well and rightly done, the operation of the natural law will itself move us on to the higher task. I affirm there is nothing in the whole universe that can happen to me that is not the result of what *I* have willed and chosen. Even when I appear to suffer

[1] II Cor. v, i.

injustice or injury at the hands of another : if I look deep enough I find it to be not merely absolute justice, not merely my own sins returning upon my own head, but the very *best* that could have happened to me to pass me forward to a higher knowledge and power. Does a man desire to cut my throat, or to rob my purse ?—I affirm it is impossible for him to do so unless I have at some time or other by my own will and act conferred upon him the power. I may be, and probably am, sorry that I conferred that power. I do not remember to have conferred it. I would rather not have my throat cut, or my purse robbed ; but that is no reason why I should blame some one else for the misdeed. But, it will be asked, what of the man who does the cutting and the robbing ; is this not a justification of his act ? By no means. The choice is his also to do or not to do. Have we not read : " The Son of man goeth, even as it is written of him ; but woe unto that man through whom the Son of man is betrayed ! " A dark saying, perhaps, yet pregnant with the deepest issues of the individual will and choice.

That it should sometimes be extremely difficult to determine what it is we are intended to do, would appear to be inevitable where there is freedom of choice within very wide limits ; freedom to go out into further individuality and separation, as well as to take the return road to unity and harmony ; freedom to go the way to hell as well as to heaven. Moreover, the very essence of the process would appear to be the development of self-reliance ; the evolution of a centre of consciousness and action which shall not be shaken or disintegrated under any circumstances, either individual or cosmic ; to permit, in fact, that the man should become the God. We see this process operating in the mass to-day in the almost universal tendency towards Democracy. The Race as a whole is coming to its adolescence. The youth must now begin to think and act for himself, to become a law unto himself. The parental authority is over ; the autocratic rule of the King and the Priest is drawing to a close. But Democracy will make many faulty attempts, will have many failures and setbacks before it can achieve its destiny, before it can enter the further stage and exhibit the more rational wisdom of a mature manhood. We are learning a bitter lesson just now ; we are paying a heavy price for the experience we are gaining. It is true that just as the youth might have saved himself many errors, and perhaps much suffering, by listening to the advice of his parents and elders, so also humanity has much store of wisdom and many wise men to guide its efforts, would it but take heed of these. But the fact is that nothing is ever learnt by mere precept. Experience is the only teacher. Precept is invaluable, because it can appeal to, and bring to the surface, innate knowledge gained in previous lives, which might otherwise remain untouched in the depths of the subconscious; or it can touch those spiritual instincts in our nature which we should rather assign to a supra-consciousness. We all know what a powerful effect can be produced at times, even in the most seemingly obdurate character, by what we call 'an appeal to the better nature.' That is simply an appeal to an already existing sub-consciousness, which then comes to the fore, as it were, comes into action in the surface consciousness which we normally associate with the 'I.' It is *remembered*, not as a specific event, but in the form of an intuition; it makes its appeal as something which the individual already *knows*. This appeal to the inner experience is the true function of e-ducation [1] as distinguished from in-struction.[2] But at root there is only one teacher—experience. No child or man can be *taught* by precept, but he may be *educated* thus. No 'teaching,' even of what is commonly thus called—the alphabet, for example—is ever anything else but experience; it is never a precept but always a percept. But *education* is quite a different matter; it can be effected by precept as well as by percept; the soul, the inner man, can be *reminded* of its origin and experience—even as Plato taught. It is—or at least should be—the drawing out of all that the individual is capable of becoming or doing in virtue of that vast store of past experience which lies in the depths of the subconscious, and which, as we have already seen, goes back, even physically, to the very first dawn of conscious life on this globe.

"Rise after rise bow the phantoms behind me,
   Immense have been the preparations for me,
   All forces have been steadily employed to complete and delight me,
   Now I stand on this spot with my soul."

    [1] Latin *e*, out, and *duco*, to lead.
    [2] Latin *in*, in, and *struo*, to pile up, to set in order.

Who can doubt, when looking at what we already know of the history and evolution of Humanity, that it is just this power of learning by experience which constitutes that evolution? Who can doubt that this process is analogous in the race as in the individual? Nay, is it not the evolution of the individual that makes the evolution of the race, and the evolution of the race that makes the individual. This is, in fact, the very strongest argument for the doctrine of reincarnation, whatever the *modus operandi* of that principle may be? Nothing but experience will teach either the individual or the race; nothing but experience—action, the actual doing of the thing—can carry either the one or the other from one stage to the next in the great World-Process. And for the *education* of the Race, do we not see that at certain periods great teachers arise, who endeavour by precept and example to appeal to the deep experience of the soul, to the 'better self' within? They do not teach dogmas or creeds, or even doctrines, these great souls—unless, indeed, the inherent divine nature of man which one and all have taught may be called a 'doctrine.' The doctrines and the creeds, the formulated beliefs, follow afterwards, and are imposed upon the original precepts by a method of perversion and obscuration arising in the inability of mankind in general to accept a pure spiritual truth, free from the elements of conceptual thought on the one hand, and the self-seeking of the individual on the other.

And to-day, when dogmas and creeds are in the melting-pot, as well as much else which has served humanity for better or for worse in the past, but can no longer do so because of a wider knowledge and the perception of a deeper truth: would it not be well if our teachers and preachers were to get back to the pure *precepts* of the Christ and the Buddha, and throw clean overboard, in their exoteric and literal interpretations—*and let the world know that they have done it*—the pagan myths, and metaphysical creeds, and damnatory clauses which they miscall 'Christianity,' and of which they have not the wit to recognise the original *spiritual* sense? Some have already done this, but the world rather more than suspects that very many of our official representatives of 'Christianity' have abandoned in their own private judgment these irrational elements, but have not pluck enough to say so openly. Thus the late George Tyrrell says : " It cannot be denied that the desire of Modernists to hold to the Church at all costs (in which they are right) acts as a bias on their perfect candour, and makes them far too ingenious." [1] Would it not be better if religion were represented once for all as a *quality of life,* and let the creeds be what they may so long as they achieve this ? We do not say that creed—even the old orthodox Christian creed—is of no value. Creed and doctrine there must be ; and there must be varieties of these corresponding to the knowledge and advancement of the individual ; but they are secondary, not primary ; they are merely the reasons which men endeavour to find for the faith which is already in them, for the fruit of their past experience, for what is in the heart, not in the head. What may appear to be perfectly rational at a certain period of history and the diffusion of knowledge, or at a certain stage of the evolution of the individual, may, and indeed must, be quite inadequate when a further knowledge and experience is achieved. Countless millions have lived and died without the Christian creed, and countless millions will continue to do so ; yet our modern Scribes and Pharisees still seek to bind men's consciences, and compass sea and land to make one proselyte. They have not the wit enough to see that millions whose faith is formulated in other creeds are nearer to the kingdom of heaven than they are. Nay, is it not written in their own Scriptures that the publicans and harlots will go into the kingdom of heaven before they themselves?

If religion is to become a real living power in our modern Democracy—a real social, political, international power, even to the ending of War—it must touch the hearts of men irrespective of creed. What is at the root of all the trouble in Ireland but religious intolerance and priestcraft ? We are profoundly convinced in the first place that nothing but real religion as a quality of life can save Democracy ; and in the second place, that the appeal of all teachers and preachers should be to a recognisable *law,* a *natural* law of man's moral and spiritual nature. The great mass of our population in our so-called ' Christian ' countries have no religion at all, because religion has always been presented to them as a matter of belief. They do not believe the Christian creed as

[1] *George Tyrrell's Letters,* p. 62.

it has been presented to them—it is too irrational. What have they to put in place of it ? We might answer that there is very much if they would only look for it, but comparatively few have the time or the inclination to do so ; and the masses remain untouched. Perhaps what is required for these more than anything else is something which they can assimilate with their own experience *now*, not something which may or may not have happened several thousand years ago to some ancient patriarchs supposed to have been specially privileged and favoured by ' God.' " What's Hecuba to him, or he to Hecuba." Put any ancient name you like in the place of Hecuba : what interest has it for us *now*, unless we can interpret it into some recognisable law or principle applicable to our own experience. If men are to be saved they must be saved *now* ; made whole and clean and sane *now*—their future salvation will then look after itself.

The fact is that the authority of a dogma unsupported by any appeal to reason as embodied in recognisable natural law, any *ex cathedra* statement, has no longer any general validity in this democratic age when men think for themselves to a very large extent, and do not look upon either kings or priests as specially privileged vicegerents of God. We may see, indeed, in the change from autocracy to democracy the key to much that is otherwise obscure and tangled in the web of human destiny. The real king of a future sane and enlightened democracy will claim no kingdom either by heredity or by conquest ; he will rule because he is a supremely wise man, and is recognised as such. The real priest will be the man so free from all taint of worldliness, self-seeking, or self-assertiveness, or the sordid necessity of living in a palace, or of keeping a wife and family on a mere pittance, that he will be able to exhibit in his own person, in his own life, in his own inspired words, the reality of his knowledge of the deeper mysteries of our spiritual nature, so that he can point out the way to those whose duty still holds them to lower levels. King and priest will be as democratic as mechanic or peasant. There will be no aristocracy in the present sense of the term; no aristocracy of birth or of wealth which will give a man a spurious and unmerited power over his fellows. Inequalities of capacity, skill, knowledge, attainment, wisdom, genius, there always must be: and an aristocracy in the true sense that the best must rule ; but along with this there will be no *class* antagonisms ; where all work is alike regarded as honourable, as a duty to the community, the most lowly or unskilled will be seen to occupy their proper place in the whole, as well as the highest and most responsible.

We say that it is towards this Democracy that humanity is moving ; but it is still far ahead—perhaps countless ages. It cannot be achieved without many failures and much bitter experience. Old institutions, more particularly old vested interests, die hard ; whilst humanity itself, as a whole, has by no means reached that stage of spiritual evolution wherein alone this millennial state of society can be accomplished. We have only to look at the vast depravity of Humanity which the Great War has disclosed, to realise how long it must take the individuals and the Race to be purged therefrom. Therefore we say once more, the real road to Democracy does not lie in either revolution or legislation; it lies in Religion *as a quality of life*. That the rule of an ignorant, licentious, and godless democracy would be infinitely worse than that of a monarchy checked by parliamentary representation—or even without such a check—has been amply demonstrated of late in the affairs of Russia. We must regard the present upheavals as part of the price which humanity has to pay for its experience: for the great change which must sooner or later be accomplished. " Think ye that these Galileans were sinners above all the Galileans, because they have suffered these things ? I tell you, Nay: but, except ye repent, ye shall all in like manner perish." [1]

If, then, the inevitable change which takes place in the youth as he approaches to manhood is now finding its exemplification in Humanity as a whole; and if that change is to be accomplished with honour and dignity and purity, and not in a wild abandonment of all restraint, and in riotous living: what we need above all things is a clear knowledge of the natural laws which are operating to effect the change, and which we as individuals must make use of and obey if we would not make mistakes for which we individually, as well as humanity as a whole, will have to pay in bitter experience. But those

[1] Luke xiii, 2.

who teach and instruct us must be those who have a real knowledge of the laws of our moral and spiritual nature: laws which can be recognised as a natural extension of the laws of nature as experienced by us in this present material world, so that it can be seen that there is no arbitrary separation between 'natural' and 'spiritual,' but that together they form one harmonious Whole. No religion which makes of itself the great exception, or which stultifies any part of human experience or knowledge, can have any chance of surviving the present change from the autocracy and authority of king and priest to the freedom of thought and action which is now demanded.

We may see this principle in operation in the enormous interest which now centres round the phenomena of so-called Spiritualism. The survival of bodily death, and the possibility of communicating with invisible personalities, is about to be established as universally recognised scientific facts. Many prominent experimenters, thinkers, and writers, in science, literature, and religion, can now be cited as unhesitatingly declaring their conviction of these facts. They are facts which can be demonstrated *here and now*, and as such are precisely those which appeal to the popular understanding as against historical events or miracles supposed to have taken place uniquely and once for all many centuries ago. The Church may continue to ignore the present facts, or to declare them all to be the work of 'demons'; but in doing so it is only alienating still further the interest and belief of the community in general in its antiquated dogmas. Scientific evidence will always in the long run supplant dogmatic authority; whilst scientific scepticism is also a healthy check on the natural tendency to credulity and superstition which still obtains in all matters connected with the unseen world.

To return to the nature of the rule of action for the individual. We admit that the choice is not always easy, the way not always apparent, even where we would willingly do the divine will could we but see and know it clearly. But this very difficulty arises mainly from our habitual attention to outward and individual things with their conflicting interests, rather than to an inward knowledge and experience which would come to our aid in proportion as we cultivated the habit of referring to it. This reference, with the ordinary religionist, takes the form of prayer for guidance; and it is simply a natural law that such prayers should be answered, no matter what 'God' they may be addressed to. The 'God' is, for most people, a necessary focus of attention, so to speak. Of course the God must be believed in : that is the essence of the matter. But the full-grown spiritual man—the man whose will is already at one with the Divine Will, and who has realised his own divine nature—does not ask any *personal* God for this guidance, any more than the full-grown physical man continually goes to his physical father for instructions. But even without this measure of attainment, shall I present petitions to Jehovah or to Brahmâ, to Vishnu or to Shiva, to Osiris, to Isis, or to the Virgin Mary? Shall I *worship* any of these? Are not all these the *personified* presentations of one and the same spiritual fact; is not the devotee of one just as near to that fact as the devotee of the other? I will worship none of them in their *exoteric* presentations. I will worship each and all in what they represent in the eternal nature of man in his relation to the Universe. The underlying fact is the consciousness of a relation between my own spiritual nature, and the universe as an expression of a supreme Spirit. We have seen how this must necessarily appear as a duality in the intellect; and for the common understanding 'God' must always be a person *other* than the universe and the 'creature.' We are, therefore, very, very far from condemning any form of sincere devotion and worship. Reliance upon a heavenly Father, or worship of a Virgin Mother, is the *natural* refuge and expression of those who stand at a certain stage of evolution. A universal *form* of religion is impossible for this very reason. The aim of missionary effort should be to raise to a higher level *through the already accepted form*; but this, of course, cannot be done by any religion arrogating to itself an exclusive truth.

Speaking now, however, of the full-grown spiritual man, or at least of those who have " put away childish things," we would say that such a one is in the position of the full-grown physical man who has now become a law unto himself. He has realised, to some extent at all events, the God *within*, and that the very purpose and condition of his evolution is that he should rely upon *that*, identify himself with it, find therein his illimitable strength and freedom.

That we can accomplish nothing spiritually—or even materially—without this appeal to a spiritual principle, is the one fact which emerges more and more fully as we progress in the knowledge and experience of life in all its phases. To expect spiritual results without that invocation of spiritual forces—which invocation is *in itself* the setting in motion and exercise of our own spiritual powers, the transference of our centre of consciousness and action from the material to the spiritual—would be as irrational as to expect physical or mental results without the exercise of the corresponding powers which we ourselves possess.

We are very far from saying that there are no personal spiritual helpers, no agents of the Great Law, on other planes of existence ; but their very power to help is largely conditioned by the effort of the individual himself. Below the plane of the Logos, in the *manifested* universe, all action is governed by Law ; and the individual can no more be helped from a higher plane apart from natural law—in the widest sense of the term—than he can help himself on this plane without such knowledge. For the *practical* means of doing any action, whether on this or any other plane, a knowledge of natural law is essential. We may, no doubt, live and have a very tolerable existence without much of this knowledge, and by availing ourselves of conditions brought about by others who have such knowledge. All members of the community benefit more or less directly by our scientific knowledge, only acquired by the devotion and labour of a few. Place any number of ordinary people on an isolated island, and, given the means of feeding and clothing themselves, they might lead a very tolerable existence. But they could not do what we in our larger communities and with our scientific knowledge are able to do ; and it would probably take them a very long time indeed to attain to our present scientific achievements.

Any who think that the same principle will not hold good in the ' next world,' will, we are afraid, find themselves sadly disillusioned when they get there—concerning which principle there is a very considerable unanimity in the ' communications ' from the ' other side,' of which we now hear so much. It is the special province of the occultist to learn the laws of the higher planes *now*; and though he is not yet accredited to or recognised by the world at large—and, indeed, does not expect to be so under present conditions—we may at least detect as one of the modern movements of thought, and as an approach to occult teachings, a complete breakdown of the old ideas as to the nature of that region of conscious existence, the 'other world,' which lies immediately beyond the portals of death. There is a departure on the one hand from the superstitious fear engendered and fostered by priestcraft, and on the other hand a realisation that the 'hither-hereafter' lies very near indeed to our present world, and is in very close touch with it. It would appear to be inevitable, indeed, that as psychical research becomes more and more an acknowledged science, the purely religious idea which has for so long a time attached to the passage from this world to another state of existence should lose more and more its hold upon the imagination. There is nothing more religious than any other fact of our nature in the mere fact of the survival of bodily death; nor can we commend the 'spiritualism' which makes a 'religion' out of the mere fact of the possibility of communicating with those who have 'passed over.' That possibility either is or is not a scientific fact which must be linked up with the general sum of our knowledge; and—as has been pointed out by many writers on the subject who are themselves fully convinced of the fact—the mere fact itself does not give any warrant for the further and deeper belief in the *immortality* of the soul.

Why, indeed, should the next stage of our existence, the next phase of our individual life, be considered to be any more *supernatural*, or 'spiritual,' or sacred, or religious, or to be more a thing of awe, or wonder, or fear, than our present state? Is not dying quite as common and 'natural' an event as being born? Is it not profoundly true that " death is too common an event to be an evil "? We might very well think, indeed, with some of the old philosophers, that there is more cause to rejoice when a man dies than when he is born.

We may say with profound conviction, that if there is one thing more certain than another about the conditions of existence on any plane of *objective* 'reality,' whether here or hereafter, it is that there will be *laws* which govern the objective world special to such plane ; and that the measure of our power for action on any of the planes will be our knowledge of those laws.

On our present physical plane of action we are conditioned by the mechanical and dynamical laws of matter. There is every reason to believe that on higher planes, matter—the objective complement of consciousness—is much more plastic, much more responsive to the direct action of thought and will than on this plane. Nevertheless, we cannot too often insist, that whether the objective ' thing ' be a harp of gold, or any other object which is seen, and handled, and in some manner fashioned ; not merely is it *objective* on precisely the same terms that our present world is objective, but there will be, in the first place, Cosmic Laws governing the objectivity of the plane in general : and, in the second place, specific laws which determine the nature of the ' thing ' on its own plane, and which must be utilised for specific actions, and for further knowledge and progress.

In the great Law of *action* to which the whole manifested universe is subject, we see at root the power of the living Subject to express Itself as co-relative Object ; and we see correspondingly that each object mirrors as it were the particular portion of the Subject which it stands to represent. We thus see an infinite variety and complexity of forms, yet the same law operating in each and all. Thus, as Böhme states this principle :

"Every thing's centre as a piece of the outspoken Word re-outspeaketh itself, and compriseth or frameth itself into separability or distinguishability (*Schiedlichkeit*) after the kind and manner of the Divine speaking.[1]

Each Ens (entity) of the forth-breathed Word hath a free will again to breathe forth out of its own Ens a likeness according to itself.[2]

The centre of the mind is come out of Eternity, out of God's omnipotence ; it can bring itself into what it will and whither it will."[3]

Thus *natural law* is the law of the living Will, on whatsoever plane it may operate ; and in each further ' outspeaking ' there is a further limitation, not merely of the form, but also of the *will*. This limitation exists just in

[1] *On the Knowledge of All Things*, par. 12. See also *Epistles*, vi, 12–14.
[2] *Mysterium Magnum*, chap. xxii, par. 24.
[3] *True Resignation*, chap. iii, par. 20. Bath ed.

proportion as the individual subject or consciousness is identified with the form, and is unable to rise above it : in the first instance in conceptual thought, but finally in actual consciousness.

But that which is outspoken is never really detached from that which outspeaks ; and thus we obtain multiplicity within unity : ever expanding from the particular to the universal, from the individual to the cosmic ; an infinite number of selves—or shall we say *monads* ?—within the One Self.

What is the real significance of all this? Is it not simply that the apparently individual self never in reality can or does transcend its *Self* in any action or experience, either in perception or in apperception? Is it not that the Self is all-sufficient in Itself ; that it not merely need not, but *never can* go outside of Itself for any experience, any knowledge, any 'revelation'? From the individual standpoint a very great deal must necessarily *appear* to come from the outside, and to be the not-self. To the individual, wholly wedded to a sense of individuality and separateness, everything but his own body will appear to be a not-self. But even such a one is unconsciously a mystic. There is an immediately *felt* unity which he calls ' I,' and which is the unity of an infinite multiplicity which he calls his body: the unity of an infinite multiplicity of physical atoms, even if nothing more. He is unable to relate conceptually this feeling of unity with the fact of multiplicity. The *felt* experience which he calls ' I ' is of a mystical nature. Thus A. E. Taylor, in his *Elements of Metaphysics* (p. 413), says :

"In holding that all genuine individuality, finite or infinite, involves a type of immediate felt unity which transcends reduction to the relational categories of thought and will, we may fairly be said to have reached a conclusion which, in a sense, is mystical."

When this principle of the unity of the Self has been clearly grasped, and has become the ruling power in a man's life, he may be said to have reached his spiritual manhood ; he stands at last spiritually adolescent ; he enters into his heritage in the universe ; he attains the freedom of the universe ; he has at-oned his will with the Great Law ; he faces the future with neither desire nor fear ; he knows that there is no law to injure him outside of himself ; all things have become lawful for him, though all things may not be expedient, and he will be careful lest his freedom should be a stumbling-block to others.

But he has still much to learn of natural law, both on the physical plane and on the higher planes of action. Within the great Cosmos he sees before him an ever-widening field of action, and he will play his part therein, whatever it may be. But he does not now play his part as one who blindly and despairingly gropes in the dark. He is already rich in experience; he knows the law of cause and effect; he knows how to sow, and how to wait patiently for the harvest; he knows that he cannot sow tares and reap wheat. He knows that no slightest thing can happen to him save of his own will and choice—if he do but go deep enough to find these. He knows that there is no royal road to 'heaven.' He knows that he may have much to suffer and endure for past sins; perhaps even more to suffer and endure out of the Great Heart of Love with which he now finds himself more and more at-oned, and which may lead him in the end—the endless end—to the great self-sacrifice of the World-Saviours; the *continual* sacrifice of the Christ, unknown and unrecognised as underlying the whole great World Drama, since Man is—Man.

Whilst, therefore, the individual thus stands firm in the knowledge of his spiritual centre, of his infinite freedom, of his illimitable nature and life: he recognises at the same time the empirical fact of an individual existence subject to limitation and law; and he recognises that to ignore the distinction between the lower and the higher Self, between the ONE and the individual, between the 'creature' and 'God,' would no more be a rational Mysticism than to ignore the distinction between matter and Substance because there is only one Substance, would be rational physics—or, for that matter, rational metaphysics. Rational Mysticism is that Mysticism which recognises *both* facts simultaneously, in a manner not explicable by the formal mind, but nevertheless in a manner which not merely gives the utmost satisfaction to that deeper rationality of our whole nature to which we have so often referred, but also the power to participate in the phenomenal world, in the infinite activities of the Self as *Becoming*, and yet at the same time stand outside of action as unmoved

Being; as non-attached to action; as the witness and the spectator of the great World-Drama, as well as the actor and the act.

Here and there—even in our present semi-evolved world—are born a few who, out of the infinite struggle of the past, have at last acquired the necessary power of will and desire to press forward to the utmost heights of attainment which the human consciousness has been capable of glimpsing, or which has been presented by those who had already passed to those supreme heights. Let none think that the mystic or the occultist is a chance product, or that a personal God favours one individual more than another. Each individual contains the infinite, each is capable of a realisation of his own infinite life in heights and depths which perhaps no mystic has as yet touched, seeing that while in the flesh there are still limitations of mind and body.

And so, whether it be for saint or for sinner, the Great Law works: the great Living Power of which each partakes in degree and kind, whereby the idea, the imagination, the thought, takes form, and substance, and shape; and gathers from the Cosmos the elements to which it is akin; and builds, now, or at some future time, the *body* wherein the individual may be either a slave or a master.

In ignorance of the Law there is darkness and evil, but to know the Law and to obey is the perfect freedom, nor can we indicate any single law of which we could say that it would be better abolished or modified.

It is written that he who seeks shall most assuredly find. It cannot be otherwise, for he himself is the embodiment of the creative law; he is both the seeker and the thing sought; " the centre of the mind is come out of Eternity, out of God's omnipotence; it can bring itself into what it will and whither it will." [1] But in one direction lies separation and bondage, in the other direction unity and freedom. And the one law which determines whether the one or the other shall result is the moral law; the law that the individual self shall not seek to possess *for itself*. We see the action of this law plainly written in the evil and suffering which prevails in the world; and who can doubt that if the counter principle of Love were to pervade and prevail in every human heart, the evil and sorrow and pain of the world would vanish as a nightmare?

[1] Jacob Böhme: *True Resignation*, iii, 20

CHAPTER XII

THE GREAT FREEDOM

"Then he arose—radiant, rejoicing, strong—
    Beneath the Tree, and lifting high his voice
    Spake this, in hearing of all Times and Worlds :—

> *Anékajátisangsârang*
> *Sandháwissang anibhisang*
> *Gahakárakangawesanto*
> *Dukkhájátipunappunang.*

> *Gahakárakadithósi ;*
> *Punagehang nakáhasi ;*
> *Sabhátephasukhábhaggá,*
> *Gahakútangwisang khitang ;*
> *Wisangkháragatang chittang ;*
> *Janhánangkhayamajhagá.*

    MANY A HOUSE OF LIFE
HATH HELD ME—SEEKING EVER HIM WHO WROUGHT
THESE PRISONS OF THE SENSES, SORROW-FRAUGHT ;
    SORE WAS MY CEASELESS STRIFE !

    BUT NOW,
THOU BUILDER OF THIS TABERNACLE—THOU !
I KNOW THEE ! NEVER SHALT THOU BUILD AGAIN
    THESE WALLS OF PAIN,
NOR RAISE THE ROOF-TREE OF DECEITS, NOR LAY
    FRESH RAFTERS ON THE CLAY ;
BROKEN THY HOUSE IS, AND THE RIDGE-POLE SPLIT !
    DELUSION FASHIONED IT !
SAFE PASS I THENCE—DELIVERANCE TO OBTAIN."
                                        The Light of Asia.

CHAPTER XII

THE GREAT FREEDOM

FREEDOM! Freedom at last!—the Freedom of the upper airs; the Freedom of the Spirit that "bloweth where it listeth."

Have we not sought for it long and earnestly—ages and ages long—scarce knowing what it was we sought; "hearing the sound thereof, but not knowing whence it cometh and whither it goeth"?

Does not Humanity still seek it: in toil and strife, in pain and suffering, in sorrow and grief, in darkness and silence; darkness, where we had strained our sight to see; darkness—or only phantom lights. Silence, where we had strained our ears to hear; silence—or only mocking voices.

Freedom! The Freedom of the Universe; the freedom of the perfect Law; the freedom of the perfect Love; the freedom of the Self which knows *itself* to be the perfect Law and the perfect Love; which knows the Universe to be its own infinite Will, its own unutterable Bliss; which knows now, at long last, that what it sought had always been closer and nearer than any external thing; that it was its own self-realisation; the silent eternal depth of its own Being.

Freedom from Matter, from the body of desire—cycle after cycle of strife for the conquest of Matter; body after body built and rejected—prison-houses of pain, not Temples fit for the dwelling of a God.

In the darkness of the underworld I have been as a seed-germ hidden in the soil—and, hidden in the heart of the germ, a spark of the ONE LIFE. Pushing my roots and fibres deeper and deeper into matter; but at the same time instinctively thrusting a stem upwards to the light and freedom of the upper world.

26

Light, Freedom, Knowledge; air to breathe, room to expand—infinite room. At last I thrust my head above the soil; I see the light; I glory in the sunshine; it is as wine in my veins. I breathe the upper airs; I exult in my freedom—freedom to expand illimitably; freedom to re-become the Infinite Flame.

The Freedom of Knowledge. Knowledge of my whole nature; of the meaning and fruition of the past; of the infinite content of the future; of the centre where past and future meet in an eternal NOW.

I have still my roots in matter; but I know now why they are there. I no longer regard them as encumbrances, as cause of pain and sorrow. I no longer identify myself with them—or with the soil—as the content of my being. I am matter, but I am also Spirit—and the two are one. I draw nourishment from the soil; by the alchemy of my nature I transmute the lower into the higher: into leaf and flower and fruit; into a thousand beauties and ten thousand joys.

The Freedom of Truth. The Truth of all things—and all things contained in the infinite Truth. Freedom to accept all things—good and evil; light and darkness; freedom and bondage; bliss and pain; spirit and matter. The recognition of a perfect Whole—the recognition of identity with the Whole.

Freedom also from the limitations of mind; from the effort to explain the unexplainable; no longer the necessity to do so, for I *am* the unexplainable—and if I had explained myself I should cease to exist.

I have built many bodies—endeavouring to explain—and tried many ways, and followed many teachers who have cried ' lo here! ' and ' lo there! ' the final truth! Now I know these for what they are; now I appraise them at their true value; now I know that the Truth is that the Great Law is everywhere—and above all that I embody in my Self the Great Law.

I have sought the Truth in many lands, and in many ages; I have worshipped in strange Temples long since in ruins, or buried in the sands of the desert, or covered by the rolling ocean—their name and existence utterly forgotten. Strange rites have I seen and assisted at; propitiations and sacrifices to strange Gods—not strange then—even to Gods supposed to delight in blood and human sacrifices; Gods cruel as the priests who ministered to them, and by whom they were invented, in ignorance, misconception, or self-interest.

> " ' What would you have of us ?
> Human life ?
> Were it our nearest,
> Were it our dearest,
> (Answer, O answer)
> We give you his life.'
>
> And the priest was happy,
> ' O, Father Odin,
> We give you a life.
> Which was his nearest ?
> Who was his dearest ?
> The Gods have answered ;
> We give them the wife ! ' " [1]

To-day, as in the dim past, the multitude strive for freedom and light : scarce knowing what it is they look for. And to-day, as in the past, the multitude bow down to strange Gods, to priest-made Gods—but mostly to the great God Mammon.

Great world-teachers have proclaimed the truth, and pointed out the way to the freedom of the Spirit; but their teaching has been debased and their light obscured by man-made doctrine, by the formulas of the blind leaders of the blind.

As in the past, so to-day : sufficient unto each man is the measure of his capacity to see and to hear—and none can be taught beyond that capacity. To-day, as in the past, the multitude require a sign ; there is speech of a ' second coming '—the first not yet understood. They look as of old for an outward sign : not knowing that it can never be seen *without* until it has been seen *within*. Thrones are falling, and the authority of the priest is waning ; but it cannot wholly cease until each man has learnt to be a priest and a king in his own right : in the kingdom of his own spirit— which is the kingdom of all.

[1] Tennyson: *The Victim.*

Freedom ! Is not that at root the deepest felt necessity of our nature ; is it not instinctively felt to be our birthright ? In the world of men and the action of communities and nations, what magic word is there like unto Freedom ? Political freedom, religious freedom : for these heroes and communities and nations have suffered, and died—recently, and all through the ages.

Individual freedom ; freedom of the Will ; freedom to go to the Devil if one likes—the Devil being just as much a part of the *Self* as the God. Will not a man knowingly go to the Devil in order to assert a mistaken freedom ? Tell a child that he must or must not, and ten to one he will not or he will, as the case may be. To be a slave, to be under compulsion of another—what worse fate can you impose upon a man ? The timid man is turned into a hero if he have but a fighting chance for his freedom ; and martyrs have died by thousands for the freedom of their conscience —in all and every religion.

And yet—strange perversity of human nature—we remain slaves to our own bodies, to our appetites, to our passions. Also our so-called Civilisation continues to impose slavery, in fact if not in name, on thousands and millions. There are necessary restrictions for the individual which must be submitted to for the sake of the community, but only in the cracked brain of the anarchist do these appear to savour of slavery. The free man willingly obeys the laws of his country when they are just—and often when they are unjust ; until he can constitutionally remedy them. The man who earns an honest and legitimate wage does not feel himself to be a slave—but the sweated worker does.

And the laws of Nature ?—do we feel ourselves to be slaves to these, or do we resent them because we are compelled to obey them ? By no means. The materialist and the pessimist may, because these see no ' rationality,' no beauty, no purpose within or behind these laws. But even such, recognising the laws of nature as being impersonal and inevitable, have not the same resentment as when compulsion attaches to a person, or a system, or a government. The intuition of freedom lies so deep in our nature that we will not be compelled even by a God—as witness Shelley's version of the myth of Prometheus.

" To suffer woes which Hope thinks infinite ;
　　To forgive wrongs darker than death or night ;
　　　To defy Power, which seems omnipotent ;
　　To love, and bear, to hope till Hope creates
　　From its own wreck the thing it contemplates ;
　　　Neither to change, nor flatter, nor repent ;
　　This, like thy glory, Titan, is to be
　　Good, great and joyous, beautiful and free ;
　　This is alone Life, Joy, Empire, and Victory."

The religionist commonly takes a half-and-half view of natural law, and dissociates it from spiritual law. The laws of nature are the will of his God ; he may fear and hope to escape from them at death ; but still he does not resent them.

But the man who is spiritually free neither fears nor resents ; and it is of this spiritual freedom we would now write. Above all, the mystic-occultist, the Magus, the Master, the man who really *knows*, stands in a freedom unrealised, undreamed of by the great majority of men—even denied by our academical and professional teachers and preachers.

We are no longer subject to a natural law when we know how to control and use it ; it then becomes subject to us— and there is no natural law that we may not control ; that is not our own illimitable nature. If I can lift my hand, it is but the pledge that some day I shall be able to lift a world. The progress of *physical* science is the record of the gradual subjugation of the mechanical forces of Nature by man. But there is also a *psychical* science, only just beginning to be understood by a few in its possibilities of the control of the body and mind. And beyond that again there is a *spiritual* science, the powers and possibilities of which in the control of Cosmic Forces are as unlimited as the First Cause Itself—for it is the identity of the *Self* with that First Cause.

It is to this Spiritual Science, this knowledge and conquest of Natural Law on all the planes of our existence, this Spiritual Freedom, that a Rational Mysticism should lead us ; it is the goal and consummation of our effort : the " far-off divine event " which the Race as a whole must achieve in due course ; which the individual may attain to here and now, because he is free to step out in advance of the race. As the race must attain to it in and through matter, so must the individual attain, here and now. Let none think that they will attain after death if they have not attained here and now. The physical world is a part of the wholeness of our nature ; we must conquer it now—or leave the conquest to be done in a further incarnation. Something is, and can, and must be accomplished on this physical plane which cannot be accomplished on any other, however much ' higher ' that ' other ' may be—but thousands of years do not suffice to accomplish it. A part of you may go on : even to the highest—and here again is the double mystery of the individual and the universal—but another part has been left behind, incomplete, undeveloped: a seed-cause of your future incarnations. Nay, we have seen that all of humanity, whether passed on or left behind is—*oneself*.

There is nothing you shall ask me concerning myself which I will not both affirm and deny. How will you define or limit my *Self* ? I have had no past incarnations, and shall have no future ones. As individual, my present ' I ' is unique and solitary ; as universal, all past lives were my incarnations ; I will take any you like to name, and assert that it was mine. The future holds for me a further illimitable number.

> " I am owner of the sphere,
> Of the seven stars and the solar year,
> Of Cæsar's hand, and Plato's brain,
> Of Lord Christ's heart, and Shakespeare's strain."

I am both individual and universal ; I am both bond and free ; I am both matter and spirit ; the one necessitous, limited, conditioned—as I myself have willed—the other illimitably free, inexpressibly blissful, eternally Self-existent. Shall I glory in the one more than in the other ; is not the part as perfect in its part and function as is the Whole in its Wholeness ?

Limitation is not necessarily imperfection. But if I speak as part, as individual, I must speak as that which appears as yet to be by no means perfect ; as that which has still to attain ; as that before which stretches an illimitable future of progress and action. If I speak not thus, how shall any understand ? Deep in my own heart I reserve the supreme secret of my own nature. " My secret to myself." It may be spoken of, but is incommunicable ; none can hear it outside of his own soul; and not until he has heard it there can he hear it anywhere—and everywhere.

"Not as though I had already attained, either were already perfect."[1]   What, then, is the path and the method? It may be summed up in one sentence: *the rational use of the natural laws of our whole being.*

Within the region of Law—the region of action, achievement, attainment—there is nothing accomplished without knowledge of the law, and obedience to the law. Freedom *from* the law, transcendence of any particular law, is only attained by knowledge and use *of* the law. Every fact of nature, of the great World-Process, of our own individual experience, points to this fundamental principle. There is no short cut to any final goal. There is no final goal at all. The joy of life is in action; the supreme bliss of boundless Love is in the outgoing of spontaneous creation. This is not to say that there are no intermediate stages of inaction, of rest, of unconscious sleep—perhaps ages and ages long. But these are not final, however long they may last. Every day we are glad for a time to sink into unconscious sleep; it is a law of our present nature that we need that sleep; but it is not our *life*; we only rejoice in it in so far as it renews and strengthens us for further waking activities. Perhaps some day (Day of Brahmâ) it may be found to be a law of our Cosmic Nature that we need to sink into the unconsciousness of the Absolute; but we shall not remain there; old Universes will pass away, but we shall awake to the activities of new ones.

The rational use of natural law, on each and every plane of our existence—co-extensive with the Universe. No one doubts that in order to produce physical effects we must comply with physical laws and conditions; why, then, should we think that it can be otherwise in regions of life, consciousness, action, transcending the physical, but continuous therewith? We do not say that it is necessary for every one to be a scientist, for we may utilise the law empirically, through the knowledge of the scientist, without exactly knowing the why and wherefore of the process we employ. The artist may experience the joy of his creative work without knowing precisely the chemistry of the colours he employs;

[1] Phil. iii, 12.

but without science the colours would not have been available for him. Our knowledge and conquest of physical nature is still very deficient. We cannot consider that it is complete so long as we are unable to achieve for ourselves a perfect physical body, a perfect vehicle for the Self on the physical plane, a body not merely immune from disease, but one which is a perfect instrument for the higher Self to do what it will on the physical plane. And in this fact we shall find the first condition of our further progress. The Self *must* conquer physical matter—for what other purpose are we *in* matter at all ? This conquest takes on a dual aspect : it has to be accomplished both outside and within the individual. Externally the conquest is the progress of science, the knowledge of natural law ; within it is the conquest of the lower self in its attachment to the things of physical sense life. Closely associated with the body is the animal soul, the subtle psychic body of *desire* for physical sensation ; a mighty force only to be overcome in the strength of the higher spiritual nature. Here the individual has still to wage a perpetual war against what St. Paul calls, " a different law in my members warring against the law of my mind " (or *will*—the spiritual law of the " inward man ").[1] Here we shall have many a fall, many a lapse, many a period in which we have wearily to repair the past mistakes—and even thus is the history of the individual and of humanity written.

But the natural law of all this is sun-clear. It is no arbitrary law, much less is it a dogma. It is simply the course of evolution. The physical must evolve in the first place before the spiritual can operate in or through it ; and the things of sense thus become an acquired habit of the past evolution, not easily to be abandoned. If we continue to fix our desires and energies on the things of this world, *for their own sake* ; if we continue to turn the mind outwards instead of inwards ; if we neglect our higher and deeper nature ; if we do not place that *first*, and make all else subservient to it ; if we deliberately quench the spirit—we can only expect to reap that which we sow. Our harvest will be ashes and dead-sea fruit, simply because—as history shows—none of these things endure ; and when they have

----

[1] Rom. vii. 22.

passed from us we are bankrupt and poor indeed. There are no riches, no possessions, but those of the soul—of what the soul *is* in its own quality.

First and foremost, then, in the achievement of our freedom, we must place the conquest of our own lower nature in its tendency to go out into physical life and sensation ; and this can, naturally, only be done in proportion as we transfer our centre of interest, of will and thought and desire, from the lower to the higher ; it can only be done in the strength and power of the higher : for how should the lower which does not want to do it, stultify itself ? The first step is to realise as the deepest conviction of our soul that the higher does exist: not merely as a power to conquer the lower, but also as the only permanent *reality* of the self, the only source and supplier of anything that is of value in life : of the good, the true, and the beautiful.

But this conquest of the lower is not, as so many suppose, the neglect, vilification or destruction of the body in its physical senses and functions. We have to *conquer* matter, not to ignore or abandon it. The body should be the facile, adaptable, easily controlled instrument of the self; and as such it should be as perfect as possible. It is the outer court of the temple of the God within ; shall it be less perfect, less clean, less dedicated to its proper use and function than other portions of the structure ? The conquest of matter must mean in the end that all physical laws are subservient to us ; it must mean that we can form and make, and preserve or destroy our physical vehicle at will, and for the purpose of the higher Self alone. At present we do not even know how fully to preserve our bodies immune from disease ; and where we have learnt something of the laws of health, we commonly neglect or deliberately disobey them. Coming down into incarnation we do not appear as yet to have learnt how to choose our parents wisely and well ; much less have we learnt—as we shall do later on—to do without parents altogether. This will doubtless seem fantastic to most ; but if we are all to become Christs, shall we do less than the Christ is reputed to have done ? " The Jews said unto him, What sign showest thou unto us ? Jesus answered and said unto them, Destroy this temple, and in three days I will raise it up."[1]

[1] John ii, 18, 19.

If we were to make the most of our present physical body, if we were to make it the perfect instrument it should be : we should find it capable of doing much which we at present consider to be impossible ; and we should find that it became responsive to finer forces in nature to which we are for the most part at present blind and deaf. Here again we are not without exemplars, but their testimony is either disbelieved, or else commonly regarded as of little or no scientific value. Yet they are indications of natural faculties which must sooner or later become our common heritage by evolution, whilst other and still more cosmic faculties will appear as further possibilities—there is no limit.

We must, however, strongly emphasise the fact that these higher developments and subtler senses and powers are worse than useless unless accompanied by a moral and spiritual quality of life. If sought for merely for personal gratification and selfish ends, they are proportionately more potent for evil than mere physical powers and possessions. There is nothing either good or bad in itself, but only as it is either the servant or the master of the soul—that is to say either as the individual is unattached and undesirous, or otherwise. When we are unattached, undesirous of possessions or powers for their own sake, we may possess all things, and have all powers without evil. When a diamond is no more to us *as a possession* than a pebble on the beach, we should be fitted to possess all the diamond mines in the world—and not until then. Paradoxically also, the less we desire to possess the more we really possess ; the more the world and all that is in it becomes to us a treasure house of untold riches which none can take from us. Thus Thomas Trahern writes :

"Your enjoyment of the world is never right till you so esteem it that everything in it is more your treasure than a King's exchequer full of Gold and Silver. And that exchequer yours also in its place and service. . . . I remember the time when the dust of the streets were as pleasing as Gold to my infant eyes, and now they are more precious to the eye of reason."[1]

Very much that is good and wholesome is being taught at the present time as to the control of mind, and the influence of thought upon the body. Very much of this, on the other

[1] *Centuries of Meditation,* i, 25.

hand, is anything but good and wholesome from a spiritual point of view, for it has nothing of real spirituality in it, and is tainted with personal desires and material interests. In the control of the lower by the higher, the mind is naturally the intermediary ; right thought must precede right action ; it is the mind, indeed, which is the real battle ground between the higher and the lower. The lower physical animal nature claims the mind on the one hand, fills it with thought-images derived from the physical sensuous life, and endeavours to use it for its own ends. There is no subtle tempting devil in the case at all ; it is simply the natural law of our physical evolution through the animal kingdom. It is what *we* are here for—that we may experience it, and finally conquer it. It is only as we reach a certain stage of evolution that we are conscious of a higher *we* which demands that we should conquer the lower nature. Then begins the struggle and the battle ; and it is in what we call the mind or soul that the battle is waged. The soul stands between spirit and matter, between time and eternity. We may represent the struggle in the language of conventional religion as being a conflict between God and the Devil for the possession of the soul ; but at root there is neither personal God nor personal Devil in the case—there is only the One Life and the One Law of the manifestation of that Life. If the higher is to conquer, the mind must be turned and oriented to it, must be dominated by it, and be filled with it when not occupied with the practical affairs of the outer world. We *live* in the spirit, but *act* in matter, or the ' world.'

There are innumerable ways in which this spiritual quality of life can be cultivated : beginning with the most familiar one of prayer, or of the worship of some ideal historical religious character—Christ, Krishna, Buddha : it matters not who, for the *natural law* which produces the desired effect is the same in each and every case in which there is a genuine belief and devotion. It is the turning of the mind—the *habit* of turning—to the spiritual *ideal* which is the important thing in the first instance ; the wider and clearer light which can dispense with forms and personalities will follow later. In the first instance, however, the particular ideal will be considered by the devotee to be unique ; to be the one and only means of his salvation ; and, indeed, it is in the fact of that implicit and exclusive belief that the efficacy of the means resides. When that belief becomes weak, or expands into something else, there are other means available—for the mystic and the occultist. But unfortunately the exclusive religious ideal, though eminently fitted for the great majority of the race at their present stage of evolution, has its evil as well as its good aspect. The psychology and history of religion shows us very clearly wherein lies its strength, but also wherein lies its weakness. Individual and exclusive belief, or devotion to a particular historical character, is largely associated with superstition, credulity, priestcraft, dogmatism, and intolerance. To achieve a real spiritual freedom we must be in bondage to no creed, no dogma, no special form of religion. All creeds, all observances, all religions are mine; but I will not be in bondage to any. Each has its rightful place and function in the evolution of the individual and the race; but I will admit no special favour of God for any of them. They have their day, and they pass away in proportion as knowledge and truth grow from more to more.

Freedom to follow one's own religion, to observe its special rites and ceremonies—even to the blessing of battleships and guns by bishops; while Angels weep and the Devil looks on and laughs—is much, very much. Men have fought and have died as martyrs for such freedom—in many religions; for it is the principle of freedom, the fixity of the soul on what it believes to be *true*, not the quality of the special religion which inspires to this degree. But freedom *from* all or any particular religion is still more—provided we have Religion itself. To see the one underlying truth in all; to see religion in the wholeness of Humanity, not in a specially favoured race, or a chosen few; to see it as a natural law of one's own nature in the indissoluble oneness of that nature with the Universe: therein lies freedom indeed; a freedom long sought, long prayed for by many whose very doubts and difficulties were represented to them in the ignorance of their youth as being a deadly sin.

I will condemn no man for observing the Sabbath—according to the commandment of Moses, or any other legislator his conscience may approve of. But I will condemn him if he seeks to bind others to his own particular observances. Let him show me the *natural law* of his observance, and I will willingly follow him ; but I will not do so for any arbitrary law of his own or anyone else's ' God.' There are natural times and seasons for work and for rest, for fasting and for festival. These are determined mostly by astronomical events, by the positions of the Sun, Moon, and Planets, and are interpreted in their higher aspects by Astrology. There is hardly a single religious festival or observance in the world which is not astronomical and astrological in its origin ; but their connection with the *spiritual* laws of our nature in the correspondence of these with physical law has been forgotten, or deliberately ignored and suppressed by dogmatic religion : the arbitrary *fiat* of a tribal God, or the authority of a book having been substituted.

Get back to Natural Law—there is freedom not bondage in the observance of that Law. The natural law of our physical well-being is much the same for each and every individual in a particular environment : it may be tropical, it may be arctic, or anything in between. But the natural law of our *action* on the physical plane, the use which the individual shall make of his physical body and powers is not the same for each and all ; it depends entirely upon the stage of evolution which has been reached by the individual, and the next advance which he is entitled to make. When the man abandons the animal stage, and begins to recognise a higher *moral* law, the physical must become subordinate to that law. At a further stage a still higher *spiritual* law is recognised, and what might be perfectly legitimate and moral for the lower man becomes undesirable in view of a further achievement which is now in view.

The 'religion' which teaches that Matter is a mistake, that it is the result of something which has gone wrong with the divine plan, that we have got to put up with it for one life-time as best we may, and then get rid of it for ever and ever : such ' religious' teaching can only be regarded as a survival of some of the most primitive ideas of mankind, and has been one of its greatest curses. LIFE, the ONE LIFE, expresses Itself in countless millions of physical worlds and universes. Shall we suppose that the laws which govern this little speck of a globe are unique and exceptional ; that they differ in any way from the *spiritual* Law by which universes come into existence and go out again ?

Still worse is it when it is taught that the physical body is a thing inherently vile; that it must be despised, and neglected, and macerated and mutilated for the kingdom of heaven's sake. That the physical body appears as the enemy of the spiritual life, when first the spiritual is recognised as a 'higher' law, we have already seen to be simply the result of the natural law of evolution. But we do not conquer our enemy by running away from him; some day he will turn up again, some day the conflict must be renewed until we *have* conquered; and until then the law gives us body after body according to the seeds of physical desires and actions which we have sown. We cannot too often repeat, that it is only as the individual conquers and accomplishes *here and now*, that either he or the race can achieve in the future. Man can only *manifest* Spirit in proportion as he conquers Matter. The body is the steed which the Self must control and drive for its own purposes; but if you want to train a steed for your use, you do not set about it by making it a mere wreck of an animal. And if we have not learnt to control matter—not even our own physical body—how can we expect to be able to act in a cosmic body, or be trusted with those spiritual forces and powers of which Matter is the form and expression? If we have not yet learnt to create, govern, and control our present physical bodies, how can we expect to be trusted with that word of power by which worlds and systems and universes are brought into existence—or may be destroyed in an instant?

We say again, that morality and spirituality have no validity, no meaning even, apart from *embodied* life. There is no 'spiritual' world which is *objective*, which is not also 'material,' on precisely the same terms, and by the same creative law, that our present 'world' is objectivised, or in which we shall not have 'bodies' subject to laws which must be known and mastered. The real spiritual *attainment* is not a departure from objectivity and action to subjectivity and passivity, but it is the great freedom which can only be reached when the self knows itself as the one *as well as* the other. Spirituality is not a departure from the physical as if it were something to be got rid of once and for ever; but it is in the first place the conquest of the physical so that action therein is perfectly free and unrestrained; the limited physical laws of matter being capable at any moment of being over-ruled by higher cosmic laws. In the second place, it is the taking up of the physical into the larger cosmic Whole, so that the physical loses its isolated and individual aspect. Like the individual self, which is only individual by an arbitrary limitation and convention, the physical 'plane' is only a 'plane' by a similar artificiality. The convention is convenient and necessary for action, and must be retained in language, or temporarily assumed even when we have risen to the larger perception of the wholeness and oneness of the Universe in all its phases. What, indeed, *is* the Manifested Universe but this temporary assumption by the One Self of an infinity of conventionally limited selves?

Mysticism must necessarily found on the principle of unity, the unity of the higher and the lower, of Spirit and Matter, of the Self and the self. But how shall this obtain if we regard the lower as a mistake and a misfortune, as something to be debased and got rid of as quickly as possible? Traditional mysticism flies from the lower to the higher; a Rational Mysticism will recognise in the lower the proper expression of the higher in degree and kind; an expression in which no single part, no single factor, no individual unit is either unnecessary or imperfect in its proper relation and proportion to the perfect Whole. In reality there is *no* individual; the individual is the limitation of a self-determined transcendental consciousness, and Mysticism is the throwing off and rejection of the illusory limitation. When that is rightly and truly done, matter, the physical universe, the physical bodies we function in for the time being, whether on this or any other 'plane,' will be seen not to be *other* than the Supreme Self, but as Its incomparably beautiful and harmonious expression—the expression of its inexpressible delight and bliss. The spiritual is naturally mystical, simply because it transcends intellect and the lower life of action in which intellect and matter are complementary: that life which has " detached itself from a vastly wider reality," but between which there has never been " a clean cut."[1] But Spirit—as something which we arbitrarily distinguish

---

[1] Cf. *supra*, p. 379.

from Matter—does not transcend the Life of the Cosmos as a Whole; and if we must—at least conceptually—separate it from the 'lower' life of the intellect in the interaction of this with matter, we can only do so as a convention, and as a 'convenient fiction,' just as we separate cause and effect. The one is necessarily as *natural* as the other, for they are complementary aspects of the One Fact.

We have presented the conquest of the lower self as the first and foremost necessity for the achievement of the Great Freedom: the Freedom of the Universe, the Freedom of the Spirit, the Freedom in which all things are ours, " whether Paul, or Apollos, or Cephas, or the World, or life, or death, or things present, or things to come."[1]

We have represented what is surely merely a truism: that the conquest of the lower self can only be achieved in proportion as the individual turns away from the attractions and distractions of the merely animal sense life, and centres *himself* in the higher, wider, deeper life of the Spirit. We have seen that this is achieved in the first instance to a certain extent in what is commonly known as religion. The individual, through his evolutionary experience in many, many lives, begins to have a real innate instinct, an inner conviction that there *is* a higher region of his nature, a higher law than that which governs his merely animal existence. This instinct, or intuition, cannot in any sense be *given* to the individual, or imparted from outside as a mere instruction. It can be called *out* by precept or example; for the soul hearing or seeing these, will then *remember*, and the individual will fall back upon this deeper consciousness; or, in modern psychological language, it will be brought up into the *liminal*, it will become part of the normal surface consciousness. But when it thus emerges it needs a *form* which it can lay hold of, and by which it can express itself: a concrete point of attachment as it were; and the most natural thing for the individual to do, when he feels this power and attraction of the deeper self, is to lay hold of and refer it to any form of religious expression with which he may be familiar as being common to his parents, or to the community into which he

[1] 1 Cor. iii. 22. How sadly the Christian Church has missed this great doctrine of Freedom—the Rational Mysticism of the Apostle Paul—attained by the birth of the Christ *within*, not by a belief in an historical Jesus merely.

has been born. He may do this gradually, or there may be a sudden 'conversion,' a sudden uprush of the hitherto suppressed life of the spirit. The great majority get no further than this; they settle down comfortably in a certain form of religious belief and observance—and there they stick. The average individual, being unable to deal with abstract concepts, or with mystical intuitions which do not appear to have any definite *form*, requires some 'real' historical basis on which to rest his belief in a spiritual world. Christ, Krishna, or Buddha cannot be for him spiritual *principles* personified, but must be personal Saviours, exemplars, divinities, on whom he can fix his love and devotion; nor can the devotee of any one of these find any satisfaction in any of the others. This is very natural, very right, very appropriate for the individual at his particular stage of evolution; and no one should seek to destroy this 'faith,' but rather to deepen and strengthen it so that it may naturally develop into something less restricted. For those who pin their faith to any historical character, however, there will always be the historical difficulty. They have a blind faith in their particular Scriptures, and will be extremely sensitive to any historical or critical attack upon these.

Speaking of the value of the personal Jesus to the Christian, the author of *The Golden Fountain* says:

"These first few steps we take holding to the hand of Jesus. For the so-called Christian there is no other way (but he is no Christian until he has taken it). For the Buddhist, doubtless, Gautama is permitted to do the same. But for those who are baptised in Jesus Christ's name, He is their only Way."[1]

This recognition that devotion to the personal Buddha can accomplish the same result as devotion to the personal Christ, is one of the many desirable changes in the religious conscience of 'Christians' which we shall hope will obtain more and more in the immediate future. It is certainly coming to be recognised by thoughtful students of comparative religion who have freed themselves to a large extent from the deadly influence of the old theology, which necessitated that anyone who was not a 'Christian' was simply a benighted 'heathen.'

[1] P. 47.

This inner conviction and innate power of the spirit, whether feebly or strongly present, is something which is gained only by evolution, by experience in and through matter ; though the individual has commonly no recollection of the various steps of the upward road which he has ascended with the Race. The individual and the Race is animal before being human—not to go any further back—and it is nothing but experience, that is to say the fact of *living* and going from stage to stage, which can have made either the individual or the race what he or it is at any particular moment. Life is only known in proportion as we *live* ; and as we progress from matter to mind, and from mind to Spirit, we find that we have *life* more and more abundantly. The individual evolves through the experience of the Race, and the Race through the experience of the individual. We are in agreement here with Bergson. The past of the Race is whole and complete in the actual individual *self* of each ; each one adds to it by his present experience, and he could, did he but know how, call up from his deeper self to his normal consciousness, to his *memory*—and even as something more than memory, as actual vision—any and every event of his own past evolution—which is the evolution of the whole Race. As it is, this past experience is latent in the subconsciousness as *faculty* in general, or as some special faculty which may or may not come to the surface as an activity in any one particular life.

But since individuals stand at such widely different stages in the scale of evolution ; since there are individual limitations within the racial experience : it is only natural that this inner innate sense of a spiritual nature should not merely express itself in a wide diversity of forms—for the most part wholly dependent upon a precedent degree in the evolution of *mind* —but the very instinct itself must necessarily have lowly beginnings, and can only gather force and power as the individual experiences, suffers and expands. It is one and the same power, one and the same Spirit, that makes the fetish worshipper and the Christian, the Brahmin, the Buddhist, or the Moslem. Do you think your own *form* of religion is better and higher and contains more of truth than any of the others ?—it can only be so in proportion as it is *inclusive* of them, not exclusive.

Setting aside, now, religion as commonly understood, and passing beyond a certain average development of this innate instinct for the deeper things of the spiritual life as commonly expressed in religious creed and observance: we find a comparatively small number in whom this instinct or intuition is exceedingly strong; they have a rich past experience which wells up within them as a more or less irresistible power to mould and direct their thoughts and energies in this the latest phase of their evolution. And with these we find two main recognised directions in which this power may express itself. It may be manifested in a supra-intellectual direction, in a more or less intuitional or mystical philosophy, in the search for those deeper laws of the cosmos which pertains to what we have termed Occultism; or it may express itself in an ultra-devotional manner, in a religious mysticism of the classical order, in which the ruling principle and motive is that deep sense of the blissful attraction and unity of the Spirit which we term *Love*.

To suppose that either of these strongly marked tendencies could be manifested in any individual haphazard, that they could be other than the fruit of much effort in the past, and must have had the same feeble beginnings, the same gradual evolution as every other faculty or power of thought and action which men collectively or individually possesses: is simply to abandon natural law for either the arbitrary will of a personal God, or the sheerest chaos and chance. Nor shall we grant, either to the mystic or the occultist *as such*, any finality in what we may perceive them to have already attained. We shall not do so for two reasons. In the first place we are quite incapable of appreciating what *final* means, even when we use the word conventionally and as meaning finality in the sense of the evolution pertaining to our present humanity. Such a *final* achievement is that which is commonly ascribed to Gautama Buddha; but who knows what that achievement really involved, or what the life of the Buddha is now? What a man really becomes when he has achieved his final conquest *in this world*, when he is no longer subject by reason of his *Karma* to the stream of human evolution, is necessarily and naturally hidden from our partial knowledge and feeble imagination—though we have hints of it in Eastern religious philosophy.

" He standeth now like a white pillar to the west, upon whose face the rising Sun of thought eternal poureth forth its first most glorious waves. His mind, like a becalmed and boundless ocean, spreadeth out in shoreless space. He holdeth life and death in his strong hand. Yea, He is mighty. The living power made free in him, that power which is HIMSELF, can raise the tabernacle of illusion high above the gods, above great Brahm and Indra."[1]

In the second place, we shall not grant that either the mystic or the occultist *as such* has finally achieved, because we are firmly convinced that to reach this Great Freedom the individual must be both mystic *and* occultist; must know the Law as well as experience the Love. In any particular life the tendency to the one may be more pronounced than to the other: may in fact be the dominating influence. But the individual must pass through all experiences; there is no short cut. He may make the road shorter or longer by his own efforts, for he is himself the road. By using the law wisely and well he may attain where others fail; but to do this he must know and utilise the law. Love may conquer many difficulties, surmount many obstacles, ensure safety where pitfalls and snares abound; indeed, we may say broadly that it is infinitely better to develop Love in the first instance, to follow first of all the path of Devotion rather than that of Knowledge. Without this development there is always the danger that knowledge may be turned to purely individual and selfish ends; in which case the use of super-physical law becomes Black Magic. There is a foolish freedom and a wise freedom, a lawless freedom and a law-abiding freedom. Every man is a law unto himself; he embodies in himself the universal Law; but he may be a law unto himself on the side of God or on the side of the Devil; that is to say—as Böhme would put it—as a manifestation of God's ' love-fire ' or his ' anger-fire.'

Knowledge gives power and freedom to act; and we say that it is not merely our right and our privilege to *know* in all the heights and depths of our nature, but that we are here in physical life for no other purpose—the great World-Process is the path of Knowledge; it is the self-revelation of the Self to Itself, whether we consider the Self as universal or as individual. The knowledge which we appear to acquire

[1] *The Voice of the Silence*, The Seven Portals.

from outside, from the not-self, is found in any close analysis
to be nothing but the disclosure to ourselves of our own
nature and powers; it is the expansion of the individual to
include more and more of the universal—*which is already
there*. If knowledge of all things did not already exist, how
could the things exist ? If God is not already infinite Love,
how could any mystic ever experience that Flame of Love ?—

> " Love, timeless, measureless, great !
> Flame in this heart of mine ! "

For some reason or other of which we have no knowledge
or recollection, we have limited and restricted ourselves for
a definite purpose. We have now to unlimit ourselves; to
' detend,' as Bergson calls it. Our evolution is the recovery
in what we call *knowledge* of the whole content of the Self—
the individual expands into the cosmic and the universal.
We have to *know* as well as to *be*; either of these without
the other is only one half of our nature. But whether in
any one particular life we should cultivate the one in excess
of the other, is a matter into which many factors and
circumstances enter which are special to each individual.
Speaking broadly, our effort should be to maintain an equal
balance and progression of the two; but it is probable that
this is seldom practically possible; or at all events we seldom
find it to obtain in any one individual. As already stated,
it is better in the first place to *be* than to *know*; and indeed,
as we shall now endeavour to show, there is a natural law
that we must *be* before we can *know* in any transcendental
sense : it is the natural safeguard of occult knowledge.

Some have conceived of the universe as the manifestation
of blind irrational forces—having presumably found nothing
but these within themselves. We have found it otherwise;
we have seen the possibility of an infinite progression in
knowledge; the possibility of acquiring a knowledge which
can do what it will with natural law in heights and
depths commonly assigned only to the ' Gods '—the knowledge
which the Gods exercise when they bring worlds and systems
into existence, and take them out again. Theoretically, this
knowledge is within the reach of every individual; it is the
legitimate fruit of our evolution. Practically, however, this
knowledge is held in check at every stage by a moral and

spiritual law which humanity as a whole is as yet very far from understanding or practising, although it has not merely been clearly enunciated by all the great teachers the world has ever known, but can also be distinctly recognised in our common experience as being operative in communities, nations, races, as well as in individuals. This law we must now endeavour to state and explicate as the one law, the one and only condition, under which Humanity as a whole, and the mystic and the occultist in particular, can hope to reach those transcendental heights of knowledge and perfection of Being which we have more or less clearly perceived to be our goal and our divine birthright. It is the final and supreme law under which the Great Freedom can be achieved. It appears under the form of a *law* so long only as we have not achieved; but it ceases to be a law and becomes the very nature of *Being* itself when the individual self has been finally and utterly purged of all its individual selfness.

Stated, then, in the form of a law it is this : *the individual self can never acquire anything permanently for itself.* That is the great check which operates as a *natural law* to limit the acquisition of knowledge, power, possessions, used purely for individual and selfish purposes.

We have seen that the great World-Process is an outgoing and a return ; an outgoing into differentiation, separation, individuality, and a return to unity : the return of the 'spark' to its source in the Eternal Flame. But it will be clearly recognised that such a 'return' involves at each step the renunciation of all those individualising tendencies, forces, attractions, which have operated in the outgoing half of the cycle, and which have produced the apparent separation of the *self* from the *Self*, and the apparent self-will of the former as being opposed to the 'higher' Will of the latter. So long as the individual self retains any trace of these outgoing tendencies, it is necessarily held back in exactly that degree and proportion from the achievement of the return. But this is only saying in other words that the return can only be made by a complete abandonment of all self-seeking, of the 'I, me, and mine.' The individual self must be *lost* before the Self can be found—not lost *qua* individual, but lost as being *nothing but* individual.

This is the great moral and spiritual law which operates

as a check at every stage of the return, lest acquired knowledge and power used for purely individual and selfish ends should grow to infinite proportions, and involve worlds and systems in endless suffering and ruin.

Whether or no there may be any actual truth in the great tradition of the fall of Lucifer as involving our present world in all its pain and woe, or whether it be merely an allegory : we see at least in that tradition a recognition and statement of this same great law. Satan arrogated to himself his God-derived powers, and wished to establish his own independent kingdom. In the allegory this is naturally represented as a personal conflict with a personal supreme God ; but in reality it stands for a profound principle in the very nature of the Wholeness of Being and Becoming. Sooner or later—it may be in years, it may be in æons— individual self-seeking defeats its own ends ; it comes to a limit where it must either turn back or be utterly destroyed and disintegrated.

When we are no longer in rebellion against this *law*, when we have to some extent recognised it and endeavoured to conform our life thereto : what do we find ? We find that the *law* assumes another aspect, such an aspect, indeed, that we no longer regard it as a *law*, for it now appears as the very deepest principle of our nature, it is realised as the supreme quality of life itself, the one and only revealer of the supremely GOOD. Only through this quality of life can we enter into the supreme Freedom; only this can give us the right to possess all things; only by this can we attain to the eternal Peace and the ineffable Bliss which abides for ever in that *Centre of Being* which is the inmost sanctuary of all that exists— and of our own hearts.

This mighty power which is both Law and supreme quality of Life, is LOVE. " Love," says Ruysbroeck, " is the eternal action of God."[1]

The very essence of Love is self-sacrificing renunciation —which is no renunciation but a joy.

"Glory of warrior, glory of orator, glory of song,
    Paid with a voice flying by to be lost on an endless sea—
Glory of Virtue, to fight, to struggle, to right the wrong—
    Nay, but she aim'd not at glory, no lover of glory she :
Give her the glory of going on, and still to be.

[1] *The Seven Degrees of Love*, chap. xiv.

The wages of sin is death: if the wages of Virtue be dust,
 Would she have heart to endure for the life of the worm and
  the fly?
She desires no isles of the blest, no quiet seats of the just,
 To rest in a golden grove, or to bask in a summer sky:
Give her the wages of going on, and not to die."[1]

The self-renunciation of pure love is no longer a law or a commandment. When love has taken full possession of the heart there is no longer the slightest thought of a sacrifice. Love transmutes everything which it touches—the utmost renunciation, even the utmost pain and suffering—into a pure joy, so that even the extreme of pain becomes the extreme of bliss. Some of our mystics have exhibited this strange quality of transformation in an extraordinary degree: of which we have noted one example.[2] James Hinton appears to have found in this principle the key to the great problem of human suffering which he so earnestly endeavoured to reconcile with his deep conviction of God's supreme Love. As stated by him, Love itself is incomplete and imperfect without pain.[3] But pain necessarily loses this pure quality as the complement of love when the opposite principle of self-regard is dominant. Centre your attention on the pain, and think only of it as something personal and individual to yourself, and it presents itself as an evil and a curse.

Although pure Love is no longer a *law*, although it gives the complete and final freedom from law by transmuting law into pure will, and by giving us the right to know and to possess and to *be* all things in their highest quality and perfection: it must remain a law and a commandment in its application to conduct and action for the individual, the community, and the Race still struggling towards a perfection only dimly recognised, and still to a very large extent subject to the natural law of Sin. We see its operation as a law in every department of our human life and consciousness. Whether in the family or in the community, whether in religion or in politics, the law of harmonious life and progress is the Law of Love, the law of the spontaneous sacrifice of all and every individual and selfish will and desire for the good of others. So soon as any individual wants something

---

[1] Tennyson: *Wages.*   [2] Cf. *supra*, p. 254.
[3] Cf. *The Mystery of Pain*, chap. iv.

for himself, and has no regard to the requirements of others in the attainment of the object : he has already separated and isolated himself, and his action is destructive, not constructive ; sooner or later it will defeat its own end, and will bring to him sorrow and suffering. It is the path of limitation, restriction, bondage : the very antithesis of that Great Freedom which is to be found only in the Law of Love. Love is the master key of the Universe in all its heights and depths.

"So if thou seekest fame or ease or pleasure or aught for thyself, the image of that thing which thou seekest will come and cling to thee—and thou wilt have to carry it about ;

And the images and powers which thou hast evoked will gather round and form for thee a new body—clamouring for sustenance and satisfaction ;

And if thou art not able to discard this image now, thou wilt not be able to discard that body then : but wilt have to carry it about.

Beware, then, lest it become thy grave and thy prison—instead of thy winged abode, and palace of joy." [1]

This Law which is thus applicable to the individual applies also to communities, nations, races—perhaps to whole worlds. How else shall we interpret history ? If we are to believe tradition, the world has already suffered more than one great cataclysm which utterly destroyed vast civilisations wholly given up to 'iniquity'—which at root is nothing but individual self-seeking. How else did the Roman Empire, the Spanish Empire, the German Empire fall ? The greatest Empire the world has ever known—the British Empire—now stands at the parting of the ways. Will it go the way of the others ? So certainly as individualistic aims and ends fail to be subordinated to the good of the whole community, and the whole community fails to subordinate itself to the progress of the Race as a whole in a real League of Nations, so surely will the British Empire disintegrate as all others have done under this law : and may possibly involve the whole world in a greater cataclysm than any it has yet known. It is not impossible to conceive of a world-cataclysm which should utterly destroy every one of our present 'civilised' nations, with all their achievements in science and art: leaving only a few individuals, and necessitating that

[1] Edward Carpenter : *Towards Democracy*—" The Secret of Time and Satan."

Humanity should re-climb once more the path of knowledge. It is possible to conceive that there might be no other means of checking the cumulative effect of that individualism which is the dominant factor in these ' civilisations ' to-day—that combined individualism which fattens and battens on vast material prosperity and the control of enormous financial interests, and which makes of our modern *commercialism* the embodiment of a ruthless selfishness.

In religion, as in politics, the same individualism obtains; and by reason of the same law is equally self-destructive. Churchman looks askance at Dissenter, and both regard with suspicion the Roman Catholic, whilst the latter treats all others as ' heretics,' and arrogates to himself the exclusive membership of the Church of Christ and the entry into the kingdom of heaven. Has the Great War changed any of that ? Not one whit. Has not religion, indeed, received a most decided set-back ? Are there any real signs that any-thing *fundamental* has been learnt by the community as the result of the War ? We fear that the answer must be in the negative. Where are now the *ideals* of a new Earth on which peace should reign, for which so many thousands fought and died ? What has become of the cry, " War to end War " ? The old bad principles of our social, commer-cial, and industrial life continue to assert their supremacy. Extravagance, folly, waste, greed, are as rampant as ever ; immorality with all its attendant vice and disease is even more prevalent than formerly. It is all unutterably sad ; yet can we not see clearly that it is due simply to the neglect of the one and only law which can remedy it—the Spiritual Law of Love.

The Law of Love was the one and only Law enunciated by the Christ and the Buddha ; the one and only *spiritual* law which they recognised. It is the root principle with which religion and the priesthood and the Church should be concerned. Let the Church teach and preach, and above all *exemplify* that law in its own ' community of saints,' and it will very quickly convert and rule the world.

Thus we find that the Law of Love, the law of self-renunciation, is the one and only condition and safeguard of knowledge ; whether it be our material scientific knowledge, or those deeper powers which the occultist may acquire. It might be thought that our progress in material science is not governed by that law; but what has the Great War been but an object lesson in the fearful disaster and destruction which results from the acquisition of such knowledge ungoverned by the Law of Love? The War would not have assumed its enormous proportions, and have resulted in such vast destruction, but for the fearful power of our modern scientific achievements. The self-destructive effect of the neglect of this Law, and the employment of the opposite centrifugal power which lies in each individual—but to which also there is a natural check in pain and suffering—may not be immediately obvious in the history of the individual or the community; indeed we only see its cumulative effect in such disasters as the recent War—or even in still larger world cataclysms—but in the long run it is inevitable.

Freedom is an achievement; it grows in measure and degree in proportion as the individual and the race evolves; it is acquired step by step, as is every other faculty, power, and quality of life. In the lower stages of our evolution we experience necessity; nay, we experience it now to such a degree that some can regard freedom of action even in the commonest matters of choice in our daily actions as an absolute chimera. But neither absolute necessity nor absolute freedom can obtain outside of the Absolute: that is to say, in anything that is *individual*, whether it be an atom or a God. In the World-Process, freedom, like all other things, is exhibited in degrees and stages. Man has proportionately more freedom than the animals; and we see in front of us possibilities of freedom which dwarf our present powers to insignificance. Should we climb to the highest heights of Cosmic Being, achieve the freedom of the Gods, and take our place in the supreme Hierarchy of divine Creators—as one day we assuredly shall do—there will still be for us the necessity of a higher Law and Will which, even then, will be *beyond* us, though identified with us. The Will in its own nature, and when it acts, is free; but it only acts within limitations in any manifestated Universe or World-Process. To assert that the individual—whether individual man or individual God—is absolutely free, is as erroneous as to assert that he is absolutely necessitous. And so we would guard here against the misinterpretation and misrepresentation of this doctrine of the freedom of the Spirit. Freedom must necessarily have its dangers and abuses in common with every other power to which Man attains, and which he has to achieve by experience; and freedom is only too prone in our present human nature to degenerate into licence. But here again the supreme law of Love is both the law which checks and the principle which endows. Freedom, like knowledge, is safeguarded by the law of Love. Let the freedom be merely an individual and a selfish thing, and sooner or later it will be discovered that it has of itself forged fresh chains to bind the individual in a region of necessity. Only in utter self-sacrificing Love can the supreme degree of Freedom be achieved; a Freedom which makes even necessity free.

We must confine ourselves here, however, to the more immediate question of the individual as mystic and occultist, in his endeavour to press forward in advance of the Race to those transcendental heights which have opened out to his vision, but which are not yet even seen afar off by the great majority of his fellows.

For such there is a rule of life and conduct, and a renunciation to be made, which does not apply to the masses.

> " Four higher roadways be. Only those feet
>   May tread them which have done with earthly things.
> *Right Purity, Right Thought, Right Loneliness,*
>   *Right Rapture.* Spread no wings
>
> For sunward flight, thou soul with unplumed vans !
>   Sweet is the lower air, and safe and known
> The homely levels; only strong ones leave
>   The nest each makes his own.
>
> Dear is the love, I know, of Wife and Child;
>   Pleasant the friends and pastimes of your years;
> Fruitful of good Life's gentle charities;
>   Firm-set, though false, its fears.
>
> Live—ye who must—such lives as these.
>   Make golden stair-ways of your weaknesses; rise
> By daily sojourn with those phantasies
>   To lovelier verities.
>
> So shall ye pass to clearer heights and find
>   Easier ascents and lighter loads of sins,
> And larger will to burst the bonds of sense,
>   Entering the Path."[1]

[1] *The Light of Asia,* Book **VIII.**

In the enunciation of this Law we can recognise no incongruity between the teachings of the Christ and the Buddha. If the one taught in a form appropriate to an anthropomorphic Monotheism, and the other in a form applicable to a philosophical Mysticism : what of that ? Are we still in bondage to forms ? The fundamental teaching of each is, that only by and through the great Law of Love can the perfect Freedom be attained.

There are supposed to be many 'hard sayings' in the Gospels—even as they stand. There would appear to have been many much 'harder' which were withheld because the disciples, and much more so the world in general, would have been utterly unable to receive them—not being able to understand what they had already received. But there are no 'hard sayings' for those who stand ready to renounce to the uttermost.

Should we wish to write of the higher path, we should have to commence another volume. Our main object has been to exhibit the *rational* nature, that is to say the *natural law*, of the whole content of our life and consciousness, whether we take it at the lower levels of our physical evolution and progress, or whether we essay to climb to summits of knowledge and being which mystic and occultist have glimpsed, and have set before themselves as their goal : having, indeed, renounced everything which this world holds to be of value in order that they might reach the supreme achievement.

We have seen that we have historical examples of some who have thus achieved as a passing experience or ecstasy ; and at least two reputed examples of what devotees consider to be a final attainment. The Christ and the Buddha stand out pre-eminently beyond all others as the greatest teachers and exemplars. Setting aside all forms and formulas, all "precepts and doctrines of men," we can see in these two great world 'Saviours' one and the same Law exemplified, one and the same 'Way' pointed out. I see no conflict with Natural Law in any region of our experience in the reputed teachings of either the one or the other. I see in both the exhibition of the fundamental fact of *the Divine Nature of Man* ; but neither of these teachers originated the teaching of this fact. For an earlier recognition of it we may go to Greece, to Egypt, or to India ; to Scriptures written before either the Buddha or the Christ appeared—how many centuries before we cannot say.

" What that subtle Being is, of which this whole Universe is composed, That is the Real, That is the Soul, That art Thou." [1]

At present the divine spark burns dim within our hearts —or seems to us to burn dim : for we only regard it through veil upon veil of the matter in which we have involved ourselves, and the grossness of our personal desires and passions. But in that inner sanctuary of our being which can never be defiled—however much the outer courts may be given over to the money-changers—the Divine Flame of Love burns in its pure intensity, and by its very nature guards its own abode. In the scorching heat of that Eternal Flame, anything of *self* which endeavours to approach falls dead and utterly disintegrated. And so only the pure in heart can approach that sanctuary ; only those who have learnt to *be* the Flame can enter therein ; or pass freely in and out in that perfection of knowledge which gives to them the Freedom of the Universe in all its heights and depths— Messengers of the Divine, and Redeemers of the Human.

We have gone out from our Divine Source, and we return thereto—that is the World Process : the history of MAN. That is also the beginning and the end of Religion.

We have gone out from our Divine Source in consciousness only ; in *fact* we have never departed therefrom—for how can anything really be separate from the all-inclusive ONE ? Therefore is our return accomplished by freeing ourselves from the false sense of separation.

Whatever we may appear to be in outward relation and proportion to other individual lives, or to other things, in this Great Universe which is the *manifestation* of the Infinite ONE : we, and they, and all things, are life of the ONE LIFE, and substance of the ONE SUBSTANCE.

The mystic is one who has realised this in a degree which for the ordinary man is unreachable, and even unintelligible. And now and again in ecstatic consciousness, in the depths of his own nature, the mystic enters into union and unison with that all-pervading LIFE, and realises in a superlative

[1] *Chândogya Upanishad*, vi, 14, 3

degree the Glory, the Beauty, the Harmony, and the Love, which are its very Essence, Substance, and Being.

Thus the supreme FACT of our life and consciousness is, that in any final analysis the *individual life* and the ONE LIFE are one and identical.

"THAT ART THOU."

EPILOGUE

SPIRIT

Out of the birthless and deathless world,
  Timeless and spaceless,
Out of the womb of the Infinite,
Into the world of beginning and end,
Into the regions of time and space,
  I who am Spirit, not flesh,
  I who am born not, nor die,
  I who dwell in Eternity,
Own to no parentage,
Own no beginning nor end,
  Came, yet came not, coming,
  Here and such as you see.

All that you see of me here is but seeming;
  Moving and changing
I change not nor move,
In the motionless depths of my Being.
  Spirit, full-filling all fulness,
  Ineffable bliss of ineffable Love,
Thinking the thoughts that no thought can attain,
Loving the Love that no life can express,
I, limitless, limit myself, appear but remain,
  Ever and ever forth-giving myself,
  Inexhaustible, fathomless, endless;
And the thoughts that I think,
Are the warp and the woof of the garment I wear,
  And the Love
Is the beat of my passionate Heart,
The incomprehensible secret of ALL.